AUTOCOURSE
CART
OFFICIAL CHAMP CAR YEARBOOK

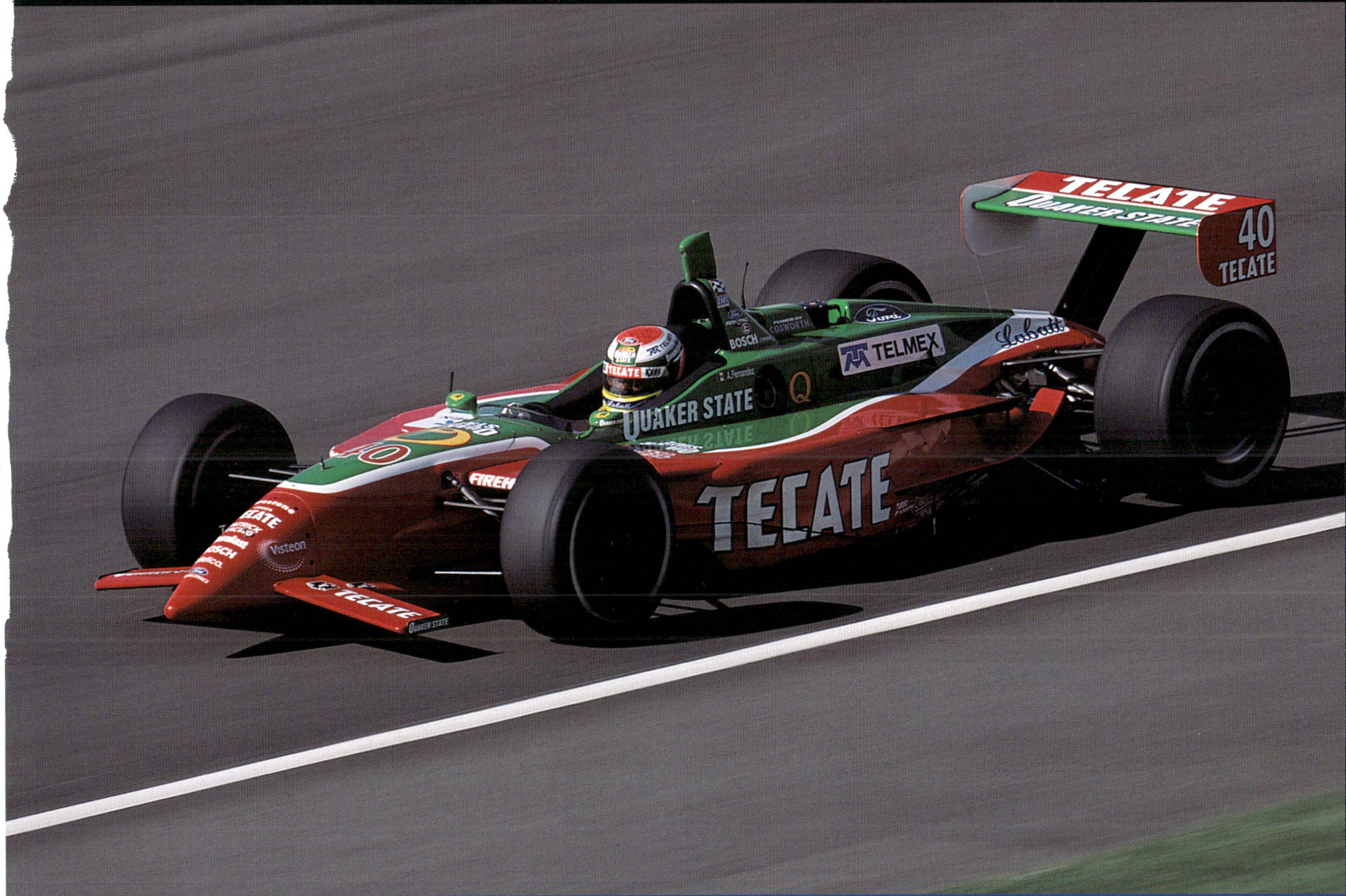

2000-2001

HAZLETON PUBLISHING

THE ROCKINGHAM 500
HOME FROM HOME

Rockingham Motor Speedway is proud to become a host for the FedEx Champ Car World Series from September 2001. We are ready to give a warm welcome to the teams and the fans at Britain's new motorsports stadium for the new millennium.

Set in the historic heart of England, Britain's only superspeedway is the perfect location to showcase the art and the engineering of Champ Car, whilst the surrounding areas provide extensive and varied activities for corporate guests and supporters alike.

We look forward to welcoming you.

UK Enquiries:
Tickets 08700 134044
Corporate 0845 305 0900

International Enquiries:
hospitality@compass-group.co.uk
www.rockingham.co.uk

22 September 2001

contents

FOREWORD *by Gil de Ferran*	5
EDITOR'S INTRODUCTION	8
TURNAROUND'S FAIR PLAY *David Phillips profiles 2000 CART FedEx Series champion Gil de Ferran*	14
TOP TEN DRIVERS	25
OVERNIGHT SENSATION *David Phillips reflects on an impressive rookie season for Kenny Bräck*	36
TAKING STOCK *Eric Mauk looks back on a year of changes at the top at CART*	38
THE 2001 FEDEX CHAMPIONSHIP SERIES SCHEDULE	40
TEAM-BY-TEAM REVIEW	41
TRIBUTES *Jeremy Shaw remembers those who lost their lives in 2000*	68
FACTS & FIGURES	69
FEDEX CHAMPIONSHIP SERIES *A race by race analysis*	71
DAYTON INDY LIGHTS CHAMPIONSHIP REVIEW	192
TOYOTA ATLANTIC CHAMPIONSHIP REVIEW	198

publisher
RICHARD POULTER

editor
JEREMY SHAW

art editor
STEVE SMALL

production manager
STEVEN PALMER

managing editor
ROBERT YARHAM

text editor
IAN PENBERTHY

business development manager
SIMON SANDERSON

sales promotion
ANNALISA ZANELLA

marketing and new media manager
NICK POULTER

race car illustrations
PAUL LAGUETTE

photography
ALLSPORT USA

AUTOCOURSE CART OFFICIAL CHAMP CAR YEARBOOK 2000-2001
is published by
Hazleton Publishing Ltd.,
3 Richmond Hill, Richmond, Surrey
TW10 6RE, England.

Color reproduction by
Barrett Berkeley Ltd., London, England.

Printed in England by
Butler and Tanner Ltd., Frome.

© Hazleton Publishing Ltd. 2000.
No part of this publication may be reproduced, stored in a retrieval system or transmitted, in any form or by any means, electronic, mechanical, photocopying, recording or otherwise, without prior permission in writing from Hazleton Publishing Ltd.

ISBN: 1-874557-99-3

Dust-jacket photograph:
2000 CART FedEx Series champion
Gil de Ferran
Title page photograph:
Adrian Fernandez
Photographs by Robert Laberge/Allsport USA

U.S. advertising representative
Barry Pigot
2421 N. Center Street
PMB 128
Hickory, North Carolina 28601
Telephone and fax: (828) 322 1645

acknowledgments

The Editor and publishers wish to thank the following for their assistance in compiling the *Autocourse CART Official Champ Car Yearbook 2000–2001*: Bobby Rahal, Andrew Craig; Merrill Cain, Cheryl Chamberlin, Cathie Lyon, Tara Martorana, T.E. McHale, Ron Richards, Rena Shanaman, Steve Shunck, Nate Siebens, Mark Tate, Tonya Trasatti, Mike Zizzo; Nancy Altenburg, Tom Blattler, Lisa Boggs, Susan Bradshaw, Francois Cartier, Scott Denby, Laz Denes, Kevin Diamond, Ben & Belinda Edwards, Steve Fusek, Kika Garcia-Concheso, Deanna Griffith, Jana Griffiths, Alison Hill, Tom Hollett, Paul Laguette, France Larrivee, Kathi Lauterbach, Dan Layton, Dan Luginbuhl, Brent Maurer, Eric Mauk, Woody McMillin, Chris Mears, "Crusher" Murray, Steve Nickless, Max d'Orsonnes, Paul Pfanner, David Phillips, Steve Potter, John Procida, Sid Priddle, Andrew Punzal, Patty Reid, Mark Robinson, Adam Saal, Alex Sabine, Susan Schroeder, Ken Severson, Lisa Sommers, Greg Spotts, Rosa Elena Torres, Brian Wagner, Melissa Watson, Katie Welch, Carol Wilkins; and Tamy Valkosky.

This book is dedicated to the entire Champ Car community, and to the memory of Tony and Shirley Bettenhausen.

photography

The photographs published in the *Autocourse CART Official Champ Car Yearbook 2000–2001* have been contributed by:
Allsport USA: Robert Laberge/Jon Ferrey/Jamie Squire/Al Bello/Darrell Ingham/Craig Jones/Andy Lyons/Donald Miralle; Honda Performance Development; Ford Motor Company; Mercedes-Benz USA; Toyota Racing Development; John Morris/M-Pix.

DISTRIBUTORS

UNITED KINGDOM
Haynes Publishing plc
Sparkford
Near Yeovil
Somerset BA22 7JJ
Telephone: 01963 442030
Fax: 01963 440001

NORTH AMERICA
Motorbooks International
P.O. Box 1
729 Prospect Ave., Osceola
Wisconsin 54020, USA
Telephone: (1) 715 294 3345
Fax: (1) 715 294 4448

REST OF THE WORLD
Menoshire Ltd
Unit 13, Wadsworth Road
Perivale
Middlesex UB6 7LQ
Telephone: 020 8566 7344
Fax: 020 8991 2439

www.autocourse.com

We Run With The Best

The Official Sponsors of the CART FedEx Championship Series

Visit CART.com

foreword
by Gil de Ferran • 2000 CART FedEx Series champion

When I was growing up in Brazil, there was a book in my home. The book was about the same size as the one you hold in your hands now, and it used to be located at the bottom right-hand corner of a shelf that my dad made out of three varnished planks of wood and some different-looking red brick. Despite its rustic appearance, it looked quite nice, with a mixture of books (including an encyclopedia that I won in a drawing competition) and ornaments.

The book was where it was because it stuck out and my mother didn't want anybody tripping on it. She didn't need to worry much, since the book was out of its place most afternoons; eventually it ended up living in my room anyway. Unfortunately for me, it was in a language that I did not know how to read. But after staring at it so often for extended periods each time, I could swear to you that not only could I understand everything, but I could also smell, hear and feel the cars and people I was looking at.

The book was a copy of the 1974 AUTOCOURSE. It reviewed the season in Europe and America, and the main feature of the book was my great countryman, now twice world champion, Emerson Fittipaldi, driving a car painted very similarly to mine! The book is still in my father's house.

Thank you all, particularly you Roger.

Enjoy.

Above: De Ferran was presented with The Vanderbilt Cup by his boyhood idol Emerson Fittipaldi.
Photograph: Robert Laberge/Allsport USA

© 2000 American Honda Motor Co., Inc.

IT'S ABOUT SPEED.
IT'S ABOUT TEAMWORK.
IT'S ABOUT INNOVATION.

**Oh, who are we kidding?
It's about winning.**

While it's true that technology we develop from racing might end up in the Honda you drive, we'd be less than honest if we didn't admit that, for us anyway, the real thrill is winning. It's what motivates our team of engineers to take what they learn from racing and apply it to our production engines. Sure, it's a challenge to continually try to build a better engine, even after we've won, but it's something we take pride in. It's also a big reason why we keep on, well, winning.

POWERED by HONDA

A WINNING FORMULA

by Jeremy Shaw

EDITOR'S INTRODUCTION

Left: Adrian Fernandez has attained superstar status in his native Mexico.
Darrell Ingham/Allsport USA

Above: Bruce Wood *(left)*, CART Program Director for Cosworth, accepts the Manufacturer's Trophy from Hal Whiteford, CART's President of Racing.
Robert Laberge/Allsport USA

Right: Juan Montoya spearheaded the newly ultra-competitive Toyota assault.
Darrell Ingham/Allsport USA

EDITOR'S INTRODUCTION

Left: Gil de Ferran emerged victorious from a sensational season that produced a new CART record 11 different winners.
Jon Ferrey/Allsport USA

Bottom: Roger Penske and Gil de Ferran hoist aloft the historic Vanderbilt Cup.
Robert Laberge/Allsport USA

EXTRAORDINARY. There's really no other way to describe the 2000 CART FedEx Championship Series season. With 18 races in the books and two remaining, no fewer than nine drivers still held at least a mathematical chance of winning the title, and with it both a $1 million bonus and the prestigious and historic Vanderbilt Cup, newly replacing the PPG Cup as the ultimate prize for the CART champion. *Nine* drivers. Think about that for a moment. Many of the leading auto racing championships might struggle to come up with nine potential winners at the *beginning* of a season, let alone have that many in contention virtually down to the wire.

Given the unusual circumstances, and, most particularly, the fact that no driver was able to assert his superiority as the season unfolded, some critics suggested that the Y2K FedEx Series was the one nobody wanted to win. In reality, of course, the opposite was true. It's been said many times before, but the quality of the competition in Champ Car racing just continues to improve. It did so again in 2000. The caliber and pedigree of the contestants were top-notch, and virtually all of the 31 drivers who competed during the season came away with some notable accomplishment or another. For example, the 20-race season produced a new CART record of 11 different winners, including a streak of seven races at the beginning of the year that saw as many different visitors to Victory Lane. A total of 16 drivers, representing nine teams, earned a podium finish, while no fewer than 24 drivers led at least one lap. Remarkable statistics.

Appropriately, the outcome of the championship remained undecided until the closing moments of a dramatic season finale at California Speedway. Five drivers had traveled to Fontana with a chance of securing the top honors. Three of them – Roberto Moreno, Paul Tracy and top rookie Kenny Bräck – were knocked out of contention before half-distance; the remaining two, Gil de Ferran and Adrian Fernandez, fought it out to the bitter end. Whoever emerged victorious would have thoroughly deserved the accolades. Each was seeking his first CART crown. Both would have made great stories, too, representing two of the most famous organizations in the business.

On the one hand, de Ferran, from Brazil, was looking to complete a magnificent transformation for Roger Penske's Marlboro-backed team, which had gone winless in the previous four seasons and undergone a thorough overhaul following the 1999 season. Mexico's Fernandez, on the other hand, driving for another of CART's founding fathers, U.E. "Pat" Patrick, was seeking to become the first Hispanic driver to claim the honors.

Only six cars were running at the finish of the rain-interrupted Marlboro 500 Presented by Toyota (curiously, one of no less than five races subjected to weather delays during the season), but they included de Ferran and Fernandez. Ultimately, de Ferran survived the carnage aboard Penske's Marlboro Honda/Reynard to finish third and secure the championship spoils by a 10-point margin. Penske's record-extending 10th National Championship, his eighth in the CART era, was assured. But it was a close-run thing. Honda had amassed a magnificent record of reliability in recent years, yielding three CART Manufacturer's Championships in four years, yet de Ferran was the only Honda representative still around at the checkered flag, all of the other HR-O V8s having succumbed to one problem or another. No one had anticipated the mechanical frailty, yet it was most likely a function of the escalating rivalry between the various engine giants than anything else.

In the end, Honda was forced to cede the coveted Manufacturer's crown to Ford-Cosworth, which secured its first title since 1995 with the brand-new, ground-breaking, ultra-compact XF design. There were more than a few hiccups along the way, including a batch of oiling system difficulties that accounted for three Ford front-runners in the first race at Homestead. Longtime Ford representative Michael Andretti attracted more than his share of mechanical ills as the season progressed, effectively costing him a chance of winning a long overdue second CART crown, but the Ford was consistently competitive and a worthy winner.

Honda, as ever, proved its effectiveness, but the real story in 2000 concerned the emergence of Toyota as a serious threat for honors. Costa Mesa, California-based Toyota Racing Development achieved a major coup when it coaxed Target/Chip Ganassi Racing away from the Honda fold

The Vanderbilt Cup – A glorious re-creation

EVER since PPG Industries signed on as the series' title sponsor in 1980, just one year after the formation of the Championship Auto Racing Teams (CART) organization, the ultimate ambition of every Champ Car driver was to win the PPG Cup. For the 2000 season, however, following PPG's withdrawal from the sport, a new trophy was sought. That goal was achieved at the end of July, when CART interim President and CEO Bobby Rahal announced that a re-creation of one of the most prized trophies in American auto racing history, The Vanderbilt Cup, would be presented to future FedEx Series champions.

The Vanderbilt Cup was conceived by auto racing pioneer and railroad magnate William K. Vanderbilt Jr., who, driving a 90-horsepower Mercedes, established a record of 92.2 mph for the flying mile at Ormond Beach, Florida, in 1900. Four years later, the inaugural Vanderbilt Cup road race was held in Nassau County, New York. George Heath was the first winner, while legendary names such as Ralph DePalma, Dario Resta and Ralph Mulford were among those to claim the spoils during the next 12 years. After a lengthy hiatus, The Vanderbilt Cup races were revived briefly in 1936. Famed Europeans Tazio Nuvolari and Bernd Rosemeyer added to the trophy's legacy before the outbreak of World War II led to another lengthy furlough.

Almost six decades later, in 1996, when CART ran the inaugural U.S. 500 at Michigan International Speedway, the Vanderbilt family gave permission for a replica of the famous silver Cup to be made, as was the original (which now resides in the Smithsonian Museum), by renowned jewelers Tiffany & Co. Jimmy Vasser's name was etched onto the new Cup as the first winner, joined in subsequent years by Alex Zanardi, Greg Moore and Tony Kanaan prior to the trophy's latest return to prominence.

EDITOR'S INTRODUCTION

Right: Juan Montoya proved himself a master of the ovals, claiming five of his seven poles on the left-turn-only tracks.
Jamie Squire/Allsport USA

after winning its record-setting fourth consecutive championship in 1999. Nevertheless, when the announcement was made in the press center at Fontana prior to the 1999 season finale, TRD General Manager Lee White caused some mirth as he proclaimed that "our new RV8E engine is going to be a nuclear-tipped, armor-piercing missile, and in 2000 we absolutely intend to kick the door in." After four years of largely fruitless toil, it seemed rather a bold statement. History will relate that White knew of what he was talking. The RV8E was an extremely potent piece of equipment.

A variety of niggling problems kept Toyota out of Victory Lane until the sixth race at Milwaukee, but it could quite easily have won every race until that point. Its final tally of five wins fell someway short of providing an accurate barometer of Toyota's competitiveness. More representative was its total of laps led, 1023 out of 2830 (36.15 percent), placing Toyota ahead of both Ford and Honda.

Mercedes-Benz, by stark contrast, suffered a dismal season, and ultimately pulled the plug on its Champ Car activities, citing a desire to focus its energies on Formula 1. It was sad to see the German luxury car maker withdraw after providing a wealth of promotional activities and inestimable prestige during its six-year involvement.

There were myriad other changes to the fabric of Champ Car racing as the 2000 racing unfolded. Tragically, stalwart driver-turned-team owner Tony Bettenhausen was killed along with his wife Shirley and close friends Russ Roberts and Larry Rangel when their light plane crashed in rural Kentucky one cold morning in February. Their loss was keenly felt within the tight-knit CART community. Bettenhausen was among the most well-liked, straightforward and respected personalities in the entire paddock, and it was heartening to know that his legacy was being perpetuated by his own team members, who rallied around the family, led by elder brother Merle Bettenhausen, and ensured that the Bettenhausen Motorsports organization would continue.

In similar vein, it was appropriate that the memory of another fallen friend, Greg Moore, should be honored at the CART Awards Banquet when rising Brazilian star Helio Castroneves was presented with the Greg Moore Legacy Award. The honor was bestowed on Castroneves (who, ironically, took over Moore's ride at Marlboro Team Penske following the Canadian star's untimely death in the 1999 season finale at California Speedway) in appreciation of his dynamic personality and his talent behind the wheel – the same traits that made Moore such a popular figure among fans, drivers and media alike.

Performance Chart

Driver	Wins	Poles	Fastest laps	Most laps led
Juan Montoya	3	7	6	5
Helio Castroneves	3	3	3	4
Paul Tracy	3	1	1	0
Gil de Ferran	2	5	2	3
Michael Andretti	2	0	2	1
Adrian Fernandez	2	0	1	1
Roberto Moreno	1	1	0	1
Jimmy Vasser	1	0	1	0
Cristiano da Matta	1	0	0	1
Max Papis	1	0	0	0
Christian Fittipaldi	1	0	0	0
Alex Tagliani	0	1	1	2
Dario Franchitti	0	2	1	1
Kenny Bräck	0	0	1	1
Patrick Carpentier	0	0	1	0

The 2000 season was notable also for the changes that took place within the CART organization. Chairman, president and chief executive officer Andrew Craig, who had guided CART through its public share offering in 1999, came under increasing pressure from other board members in the early part of the year, culminating in his resignation in June. He was succeeded on an interim basis by three-time champion driver-turned-team owner and accomplished businessman Bobby Rahal, who, following a protracted search for a permanent replacement, later handed over the reins to experienced sports and entertainment industry executive Joseph Heitzler.

During Rahal's jurisdiction, several opportunities originally formulated by Craig came to fruition, including news that CART's 2001 schedule would be expanded to a record 22 races. The CART board of directors decreed that the Homestead-Miami Speedway and Gateway International Raceway ovals were no longer appropriate venues, and instead added events at the high-banked Texas Motor Speedway oval, an exciting new temporary street circuit in Monterrey, Mexico, and two purpose-built ovals in Europe – the EuroSpeedway at Lausitz, Germany, and Rockingham Motor Speedway near Corby, England. CART's first-ever foray to Europe was keenly anticipated, while confirmation of Adrian Fernandez's abilities during the season ensured that tickets were selling briskly in Mexico.

CART's growth wasn't confined to its venues, either. The FedEx Series drew an average of 25 cars to every race in 2000, down from 28 one year earlier, and even though, sadly, the Della Penna and PPI teams seemed unlikely to return in 2001 as this book went to press, several new entries were set to bolster the field to at least 29 cars. Mo Nunn Racing, indeed, confirmed its intention of fielding an extra car for returning 1997/'98 champion Alex Zanardi; Forsythe Championship Racing was slated to return in partnership with famed German team Zakspeed (fielding cars for Bryan Herta and one other driver to be named); the newly formed Fernandez Racing (headed by Adrian Fernandez and former Target/Chip Ganassi Racing Managing Director Tom Anderson) would join the fray with a two-car entry for Fernandez and Japan's Shinji Nakano; and another start-up operation, Sigma Autosport, already had started testing with Brazilian rookie Max Wilson.

The signs, therefore, were extremely positive as the CART FedEx Championship Series spread its wings into the new millennium.

Jeremy Shaw
Rancho Santa Margarita, California
December 2000

Driven to perform

THE entire CART community was abuzz in early February at the Spring Training open test following news that actor Sylvester Stallone would soon be commencing work on a brand-new movie based around the CART FedEx Championship Series. Now, granted, Stallone had hardly set theaters alight with his most recent projects, but he remained a hugely popular box-office draw – and an influential figure in Hollywood – through the success, in particular, of his "Rocky" series of films, which dramatically heightened public awareness of boxing.

Finnish-born Renny Harlin, a long-time race fan who worked with Stallone on the 1993 action picture "Cliffhanger" was selected as director/producer. In addition to Stallone, Burt Reynolds ("Smokey and the Bandit"), Kip Pardue ("Remember the Titans") and supermodel Estella Warren provided the main acting talent, while Champ Car stars, including Michael Andretti, Juan Montoya and Dario Franchitti (who, appropriately, announced his engagement to real-life film star Ashley Judd during the summer) were invited to play cameo roles as filming took place at several FedEx Series events during the season.

"We're blending fact and fantasy," declared Stallone *(right)*, who plays the part of an aging racer lured back to competition after a serious injury. "This will be very authentic – an interactive experience for the millions who love racing."

Auto racing fans in the United States already were fully aware of the ramifications of such a movie. "Days of Thunder" might not have been a critically acclaimed success, particularly among racing aficionados, but there is little doubt that it exposed NASCAR Winston Cup racing to a broad new audience. Stallone's "Driven" due for general release in April, 2001, was expected to do the same for CART. No wonder the sponsors, in particular, were so excited.

THE EUROPEAN PREMIERE!

Gentlemen start your engines!

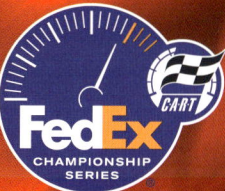

GERMAN 500

SEPT. 2001, 13th – 15th

Champ-Car-Ticket-Hotline
+49 (0)1805 - 88 01 88
(0.24 DM/min.)

Online orders
WWW.EINTRITTSKARTE.DE

FIREHAWK® CHOICE OF CART CHAMPIONS 1996-2000

The lessons we learn on race day are in the tires you count on every day.

With a record 51 wins at the Indy 500®, Firestone knows Indy racing like no other tire company. And if we can develop the kind of quick acceleration, grip and stability required for **CART** racing tires, just imagine how well our line of Firehawk street performance tires will perform for you. Firehawk performance tires are speed rated from S to Z and specially engineered for crisp handling and legendary performance. And now you have a choice of Firehawk street tires made with either **UNI-T®** or **UNI-T AQ™** technologies. **UNI-T**, the **U**ltimate **N**etwork of **I**ntelligent **T**ire **T**echnology, is designed to deliver outstanding wet performance, especially wet stopping, while still providing excellent dry performance. And **UNI-T AQ** Ultimate Tire Technology adds the power of **EPO™** (**E**xtended **P**erformance **O**ptimization) with Dual-Layer Tread.™ So even as its tread wears down, its wet performance stays up for outstanding wet braking. See your local Firestone retailer and check out the complete line today.

Firehawk SZ50 EP with UNI-T AQ
Z-Speed Rated
Ultra-High Performance Street Tire

Firehawk SH30 with UNI-T
H-Speed Rated
High Performance Street Tire

Firehawk SS20 with UNI-T
S & T-Speed Rated
Performance Street Tire

Firehawk
Indy® Racing Slick

BORN AT INDY.
PERFORMS EVERYWHERE.™

America's Tire Since 1900
1-800-807-9555
www.firestonetire.com

Indianapolis 500,® Indy 500® and Indy® are registered trademarks of the Indianapolis Motor Speedway.

FIRESTONE TIRES:
TOO GOOD?

When the 2000 racing season began, it marked the first time since 1994 that all Champ cars would run on the same tire. Although the Firestone Racing program didn't seek to be the sole tire supplier in CART, it undertook the new role with a commitment to provide all drivers with the highest quality racing tires ever used in a competition.

Perhaps the most obvious result of every car running on Firestone Firehawk racing radials was a record number of 11 different winners. Unlike the past five seasons, where it was obvious the Firestone-equipped drivers had a definite advantage, in 2000 the field was much more level. Some drivers said that made their jobs significantly more challenging.

"In the past I could sometimes count on the other guy's tires going off," said **MICHAEL ANDRETTI**, who has now completed two seasons on Firestone tires. "But not this year. Everybody has 'em; that makes race strategy more important than ever."

Race strategy was indeed affected, and several drivers took advantage of the legendary consistency and durability of their Firestone tires to win an event. More than one Champ car driver in 2000 opted for fuel-only pit stops, saving precious seconds because their tires were still race-worthy. **PAUL TRACY**, who won three events, credited the lasting performance of his Firehawks for his win at Long Beach.

"We were able to run two stints on a set of Firestone tires in the race," Tracy said. "They lasted unbelievably well; they were perfect all day."

In race after race, the Firestone tires provided drivers with the sure-footed performance required in a world where speed rules. The most dramatic example occurred in late October when **GIL DE FERRAN** set a new world record of 241.428 mph at California Speedway. De Ferran, in his first season on Firestone tires, had his best year in CART, winning five poles and three races on his way to the 2000 CART drivers' championship. One of those, the win at Nazareth, gave team owner Roger Penske his 100th Champ car victory.

"Throughout 2000, we heard two remarks quite frequently," said Bridgestone/Firestone Motorsports Director Al Speyer. "The drivers who had been on our tires in past seasons said 'same great tires;' the drivers who were using our tires for the first time said 'wow.' Anytime you can get a 'wow' from one of these guys, you know you've done very, very well."

Speyer said being the sole tire supplier provided new challenges and opportunities for Firestone Racing.

"When we found ourselves without a competing tire company, we knew there was no room to relax. No other racing series in the world competes on as many different kinds of tracks, in such different weather and temperature conditions. We may have the only tire on the track, but it has to perform in some of the fastest, most challenging motorsports environments you can find. When you couple that with the logistics of supplying tires to all teams for all races, practices and testing sessions, it's an awesome task. Fortunately the men and women of Bridgestone/Firestone are dedicated to their work, and that showed all season long."

The last 5 consecutive CART champions have won on Firestone tires.

GIL DE FERRAN

MICHAEL ANDRETTI

PAUL TRACY

GIL DE FERRAN

Firestone — America's Tire Since 1900

GIL DE FERRAN & TEAM PENSKE PROFILE

TURNAROUND'S FAIR

Photographs: Jamie Squire/Allsport USA

Left: A pensive Gil de Ferran prepares himself mentally before climbing aboard his Marlboro Honda/Reynard in Toronto.
Robert Laberge/Allsport USA

Bottom left: The new champion catches up with some personal business *(far left)* during a hectic post-Fontana media tour that included an appearance on the Late Show with David Letterman *(right).*

Bottom right: A conservative but nerve-wracking run to third place in the season finale secured the FedEx Series crown.
Jon Ferrey/Allsport USA

WHEN the world's fastest driver took the most important checkered flag of his career at a snail's pace at California Speedway, it capped one of the most remarkable turnarounds in CART history. Thanks to the 11th caution period of the rain-delayed, attrition-filled Marlboro 500 Presented by Toyota, Gil de Ferran was traveling some 200 mph slower than when he set a new world record in qualifying at 241.426 mph.

But speed was the last thing on de Ferran's mind when he crossed the finish line. What mattered were the 14 championship points that went with his third-place finish. Not only did they give de Ferran his first CART title, but they also secured an unprecedented eighth CART championship for team owner Roger Penske.

As any Champ Car fan can attest, there were times in recent years when it seemed that Marlboro Team Penske might never win another race, let alone another title. In May of '97, Paul Tracy scored the team's 99th Champ Car win, and it appeared to be just a matter of time before the team reached the century mark. But '97 turned to '98, which turned to '99, and the wins quit coming.

There's no simple explanation for the drought. Certainly the team was hamstrung by the increasingly uncompetitive products supplied by Mercedes-Benz and Goodyear; certainly a driver line-up headed by Al Unser Jr. failed to produce; certainly going it alone with the promising, but complex, Penske PC27 chassis exacerbated the situation.

Roger Penske pulled out all the stops to get back on top in 2000, revamping his technical package, driver line-up and management structure. But while Honda engines, Firestone tires and Reynard chassis afforded the team a level playing field, ultimately, it was the people who made the difference.

Nobody made a bigger difference than de Ferran. In his sixth CART season, the 32-year-old Brazilian had won races for Jim Hall and Derrick Walker, but had not driven for a team with the resources to mount a championship challenge.

Although Marlboro Penske Racing was just such a team, it was a team at perhaps the lowest ebb in its glorious history. For in addition to its winless streak, Penske had lost two drivers in '99 when Gonzalo Rodriguez was killed at Laguna Seca and Greg Moore, slated to be de Ferran's teammate, died in his final race with Player's/Forsythe Racing.

Yet de Ferran discovered a team looking forward rather than in its rearview mirrors.

"I did not find a negative team or a worn-down team," he recalls. "Quite the contrary. The attitude was like, 'It's a new beginning.' They were all hungry to get started; all raring to get going because, obviously, they had been through difficult times and it was just a 'can't wait to begin' sort of thing."

De Ferran was not the only new guy in town. In young Helio Castroneves, he had a teammate whose irrepressible spirit was matched by his brilliant talent. The pair quickly formed an effective working partnership, one that developed into a close personal relationship as the season progressed.

"Throughout the year we had a great time together and I have to say today, the 31st of October, that I have to consider him my friend," said de Ferran the morning after clinching the CART title.

"He's a very different character from me, but he's a very fun guy to be around and I enjoy his company a lot. As far as being a driver is concerned, he is a very good race-car driver. Don't get fooled by his mask. Underneath that kind of easygoing, cheerful sort of lad, he's a very determined and very serious guy."

The two complement one another well, on and off the track. In contrast to Castroneves' infectious in-your-face enthusiasm, de Ferran is an understated – but no less fun-loving – character.

"You've got to enjoy what you do and have a good time doing it," he says. "You spend 80 percent of your time tackling your job and you must have a good time; you've gotta have a good time, otherwise you're gonna spend 80 percent of your time miserable, so you just become a miserable bastard. But I'm a happy fellow."

De Ferran and Castroneves found themselves working for a fellow named Tim Cindric, who had been lured from Team Rahal by Roger Penske to assume the role of president of Marlboro Team Penske. Thus to Cindric fell the formidable task of putting all the various new pieces together in the hope of returning Marlboro Team Penske to its accustomed place among CART's elite teams.

PLAY

by David Phillips

GIL DE FERRAN & TEAM PENSKE PROFILE

Below: A potent blend of pace, patience and consistency paid dividends for de Ferran.
Robert Laberge/Allsport USA

He proved equal to the challenge.

"He's only a young guy and he's in a position of tremendous responsibility that requires tremendous maturity because he's leading a team of over 100 people," says de Ferran. "It's a daunting task for anyone, especially somebody in his early 30s. But I'll tell you, Tim is a very confident fellow. He's a great leader in my view. He's got fantastic personal skills.

"He's done a lot of good things this year but, if I was to pick one out, it's that he put everybody in the same bandwagon, everybody in the same line pulling in the same direction."

That was quickly evident. De Ferran confirmed the promise of a productive winter testing program by planting his Marlboro Honda/Reynard on pole for the season opener at Homestead.

"I certainly had a lot of confidence in the work that we'd been doing...but it was like foreplay, I guess," he says. "When the curtain's finally open is when you must perform. When we did that, especially in Homestead, it was very reassuring."

But ultimate success proved elusive. Handcuffed by conservative fuel strategy at Homestead and Long Beach, de Ferran was sidelined by a broken exhaust header in Rio and soldiered on to come home a distant ninth in Japan. Appropriately, the breakthrough came at the Nazareth race, only a short drive from Penske's race shop in Reading, Pennsylvania.

"It was a very special day," said de Ferran. "It was one of those days when everything went right for us. I have won races before and Roger has many victories. But to win that race together was almost indescribable."

Castroneves earned a win of his own at Detroit, while de Ferran underlined Penske's growing confidence with another win at Portland. Although that would be his last win of the year, de Ferran continued to score points with regularity and headed to Australia looking to clinch the title. A ferocious duel with Juan Montoya for pole underlined his philosophy of continuing to drive in "attack" mode, a philosophy that sounded great until he was eliminated by a first-corner shunt.

Yet de Ferran refused to allow himself to be discouraged.

"I was very disappointed but, from my eyes, there was nothing I could have done different to avoid the incident," he says. "Driving back to the pits, I was already turning the page in my mind and thinking, 'Even if I go into Fontana in second place in the championship, we're still in a good position.'"

Ultimately, de Ferran went to Fontana with a narrow points lead over Adrian Fernandez and promptly took his fifth pole of the season in record-setting style. Despite having the fastest car in the world, however, he ran a strategic race for the better part of two days thanks to a dose of precipitation, California-style. The rain turned a nail-biter of a race into a Chinese water-torture test, one made all the more tense by a string of incidents that threatened to derail de Ferran's title hopes.

The realization that he had fulfilled a lifelong ambition of winning a major international championship proved overwhelming. After the race, de Ferran crept into the pits and sat in his car, helmeted head in hands, overcome with emotion, before emerging to accept the accolades from the crowd of well-wishers.

"I tried to keep my emotions in control very, very strongly today," he said. "I dreamed all my life of winning a title like this...you keep pursuing things and then you cross the line and you try so hard to keep everything out of the way, and then everything floods."

It was left to the architect of the turnaround to put Marlboro Team Penske's 2000 season into perspective. Typically, Roger Penske proved up to the task.

"The championship is one thing," said Penske. "But the way this team has turned itself around with the adversity and the tragedy last year with Greg [Moore] and Gonzalo Rodriguez, it just shows that the whole team was up to the task. This is not my win, this is not Gil's win; this is a team win."

Now comes the hard part: going for CART title #9 in 2001. But with people like de Ferran, Castroneves, Cindric and, of course, Penske at their disposal, smart bets will be on Marlboro Team Penske. Again. At last.

TEAM KOOL GREEN
FIGHTS THE HARD FIGHT

SEASON 2000 WITH TEAM KOOL GREEN

Team KOOL Green drivers Paul Tracy and Dario Franchitti battled for honours throughout one of the most open CART seasons ever.

IT is the mark of true champions to persevere in the face of adversity. Every effort must overcome obstacles en route to the ultimate goal, but only the very best do so with the same determination and focus put forth during the best of times. And then come away stronger for the effort. Everyone at Team KOOL Green would agree they faced some adversity during the 2000 season.

Following a stellar 1999 season that saw Dario Franchitti and Paul Tracy combine for five wins, including three dominating 1-2 victories, and finishes of second and third respectively in the championship standings, the TKG driving duo were poised to make another serious run at the drivers' title.

While a lot of teams made driver, chassis and/or engine changes, TKG was set to run the same drivers with the same engine/chassis package (Honda-Reynard) for a third-consecutive year. And it bolstered its already strong technical package with a comprehensive wind-tunnel program overseen by Tino Belli, the team's talented aerodynamicist. The work in the wind tunnel was combined with an extensive track-testing program headed-up by team managers Tony Cotman (Tracy) and Kyle Moyer (Franchitti), and conducted by a top-flight staff of engineers led by Scott Graves.

Franchitti had taken some much-needed time off following the 1999 season, while Tracy handled the bulk of the initial off-season testing and development of the team's new 2000 Honda-Reynards. The plan was for Tracy to do the majority of the track testing leading up to CART's Spring Training test days in early February, then have Franchitti take over the brunt of the task leading up to the season opener in March.

However, on February 10th, in the closing moments of the two-day Spring Training test, Franchitti's car suffered a mechanical failure in the right rear suspension and he hit the Homestead Speedway wall, causing several injuries including a broken pelvis.

As a result, when the team returned to Homestead for the season opener on March 26 — just six weeks later — Tracy was in high gear while Dario was just happy to be starting the race. Franchitti, who had embarked on a rigorous rehabilitation program, overcame the obvious pain for a respectable 11th-place finish.

Tracy put on one of his now legendary charges through the field to move from 17th on the grid to the lead, eventually finishing third. Tracy's dramatic run earned the Budweiser Hard Charger Award for making the biggest improvement from start to finish. "We had the chance to win this thing," Tracy said afterward. "But I'm really happy to get third when we had a 10th-place car."

Franchitti said he didn't suffer any substantial pain but admitted "It was a pretty long day out there. I felt fine, except for a small bump when they dropped the car off the airjacks and it bottomed out pretty hard. I leaned heavily on the area of my injury and I felt it."

In front of more than 100,000 people in Long Beach, Tracy continued what became his trademark for the 2000 season, as he tenaciously fought his way from another 17th-place starting position to win the 16th race of his career and take the lead in the championship. It was the first time since going into the Molson Indy Toronto in 1997 that Tracy had led the drivers' standings.

Tracy went on to score his third-consecutive podium with a third-place finish in Brazil, and with a sixth-place finish in Japan two weeks later, he built himself a 14-point lead in the championship.

Franchitti was still feeling the effects of his injury and lack of off-season seat testing time. Following a DNF at Long Beach and an 11th in Brazil, he appeared poised to turn his season around in Japan. Taking a page from team-mate Tracy, he qualified 17th then proceeded to work his way through the field for a solid second-place finish, his first podium of the year.

After a string of races that saw Tracy score only 11 points in six events, he returned to form with another brilliant drive through the field, this time in front of his hometown fans at the Molson Indy Toronto. Starting 12th, Tracy carved his way through the field for a rewarding third-place finish. He followed it up a week later with the pole – and a new track record – at Michigan Speedway, then a run to seventh in the 500-mile race.

Franchitti also had a good run at Michigan, as he started fourth and finished third —his best qualifying and race result ever on a superspeedway.

Road America looked promising for Franchitti when he scored his first pole of the year, but a mechanical failure ended his day and it was Tracy who claimed the win with another brilliant come-from-the-back charge

"When I was coming up the hill

SEASON 2000 WITH TEAM KOOL GREEN

Paul Tracy *(right)* took three victories, and remained a title contender right to the last round of the gruelling 20-race series.

Dario Franchitti *(bottom)* overcame a serious injury in pre-season testing to bounce back to his best form by mid-season. The Scottish driver will be looking forward to better luck in 2001.

to take the green flag, the car just died," recalls Paul. "I radioed the team and they told me to reset the electronics and that did the trick. After that I just put my head down, got into the 'zone' and drove."

Two weeks later it was all TKG on the streets of Vancouver, as Franchitti earned his second-consecutive pole, with team-mate Tracy starting alongside. Franchitti led easily for much of the race, before Tracy's pit crew got him out ahead of Dario on the final stop. Tracy went on to lead the TKG duo home to their fourth 1-2 finish in the last two seasons and become the first back-to-back winner of the season in CART.

Franchitti's second-place finish in Vancouver, combined with his third-place result the next week at Laguna Seca, moved him up to eighth place in the standings with four races to go.

The results were hard to come by for Tracy towards the end of the season, but 11th at Laguna Seca and a strong fourth-place finish in Houston kept him in the championship hunt.

Though his title hopes remained alive until the season finale at California Speedway, a mechanical failure early in the 500-mile race ended Tracy's day and championship dreams. He finished the season with three wins (tied for most in series), one pole and fifth place in the driver standings.

Franchitti also suffered an early mechanical problem in the season finale, capping what he termed a "character-building" season. Franchitti's 2000 season, highlighted by two poles and four podiums, netted him 13th place in the drivers' championship.

SEASON 2000 WITH TEAM KOOL GREEN

TIME OUT

ONE might be inclined to assume that after the rigors and intensity of a day of competition on the race track, professional race drivers would be looking for more sedate ways to spend their spare time.

Not a chance. When Paul Tracy isn't driving the Team KOOL Green Champ car, you're apt to find him on the open road, at the controls of one of his custom-built Harley-Davidson motorcycles that are his pride and joy or working on and racing one of his Paul Tracy Karts. Or, depending on the season, he might be making waves in his powerboat, taming the moguls on a ski slope, or joining friends in tackling mountain-bike trails.

Among Paul's custom-built motorcycles is a recent addition from the famed technicians at Ron Simms Bay Area Custom Cycles in Oakland, California. The bike has been described as "one man-sized hunk of American iron," with a massive frame and huge 131 ci engine that give the bike a commanding presence on the roadway. When Paul isn't cruisin' with his magnificent machines, he might be found at motorcycle events such as Bike Week at Daytona Beach or the annual Harley rally in Sturgis, South Dakota, indulging in his passion.

"When you drive race cars for a living you tend to look at street vehicles for their visual appeal," Tracy said. His current "head turner" is one of the new Honda S2000 sports cars. "It's a little two-seat convertible that I can run around town in doing errands and still have some fun. It's a new model so there aren't a lot of them on the road and people are always trying to figure out what it is. They're quite impressed when they realize it's a Honda. It's not your typical Honda."

Tracy can't drive his Team KOOL Green Honda-Reynard on the highways, and he's limited to the amount of people and packages he can carry in his Honda S2000 convertible, so even he has a practical car. "When I need a bigger car for taking friends out to dinner or whatever, I've got an Acura RL. It's a nice four-door sedan that can carry up to six people in comfort."

When Tracy needs to carry an even bigger load he takes his Chevrolet Crew Cab Dually out of the garage. "I own and sponsor a kart racing team and I use the Dually to tow a trailer with karts and equipment to the track. I also use it to tow my boat to the lake."

Franchitti's life away from racing is more sedate — but not much. His personal vehicles include a Ferrari 355 Spyder, Ferrari F40, Acura RL and Ducati 916 Senna motorcycle.

"As much as I enjoy racing, I try to keep a balance in my life by having some interests away from the track," Franchitti said. "Of course, I spend a lot of time training in the gym, but I also like to mix in some fun stuff like soccer and water skiing."

Besides his intense physical regimen, Franchitti's time away from the track also includes working on his golf game, riding his mountain bike and hanging out with friends.

But it's racing that is his passion and his profession, and he intends to be on form in 2001.

"This is the second year in a row that Team KOOL Green went to the last race at Fontana with a chance to win the championship, and I think that's a credit to the entire organization,' Franchitti said.

"From a personal standpoint, the 2000 season was a big contrast to last year, when we were in the hunt right to the end. It's been frustrating, but I've also learned a lot about myself. I have no doubt that I'm going to come back strong next season."

Of course, team-mate Tracy shares his optimism.

"We had a very good season, but we just fell a little short of our goal of winning the championship in both 1999 and 2000," Tracy said. "Everyone at Team KOOL Green knows we're capable of taking it all, so we've set that as our goal again for 2001 — and this time we don't intend to be denied. Our strategy is simple: work hard in the off-season, take the season one race at a time, try to score maximum points at each event, and don't let up until the championship is ours."

With such a strong team pulling together in a bid to achieve that elusive championship, there's little doubt that at the end of the 2001 season the green and white Team KOOL Green cars will continue to be among the leaders in the ultra-competitive FedEx CART Championship Series.

TEAM KOOL GREEN

12 SECONDS OF TEAMWORK CAN WIN

It's been called the "the most dangerous 12 seconds in sports".
It has become consistently the most frenetic "break" in motorsports action.

Four wheels must be changed, a tank must be filled with 35 gallons of fuel and wings may need adjustments. More and more, as cars are designed and manufactured with equal skill and the drivers are among the finest tuned athletes existing, time in the pit can determine the eventual race winner.

Here are some things you need to know about pit stops:

- Stops are scheduled on the minimum consumption rate of 1.85 mile per gallon from a 35-gallon tank

- A 200-mile race will require two, sometimes three stops

- A 500-mile race will require at least 5 stops

- Only six crew members can go "over the wall"

- Two crewmen re-fuel the car… The fueler attaches the three-inch diameter main fuel hose so the 35-gallon on-board fuel cell can be filled by gravity flow, taking 10 seconds. The vent man connects both the fuel vent hose and the air jack hose, which raises the car off the ground.

- Four members then change the tires (which weigh about 35 lbs each) in about 6 seconds and then make any wing changes requested by the driver

- The entire stop for a full load of methanol can be done in 10 to 12 seconds

TIME LINE DURING A FULL FUEL LOAD

Minus one lap: Signal to driver for next pit stop and crew moves into position

Driver enters pit lane : Maximum Speed of 50 mph

PIT BOX

-30 seconds:	Six crewmen are over the wall and are ready
0.0 seconds:	Car stops in pit box
0.5 seconds:	Fuel and vent hoses are connected and the car is raised
1.0 seconds:	Air guns are in place on all four wheel nuts
2.0 seconds:	Wheels are off the car
3.5 seconds:	Driver resets his fuel meter
5.0 seconds:	New tires are on
6.0 seconds:	Car drops
6.5 seconds:	Crewmen on the front tires may do a wing adjustment
10.0-12.0 seconds:	The car is fully serviced and driver takes off

THE RACE

RACING INTANGIBLES

Illustrations & desktop editing:
© Alain Boisjoly 2000

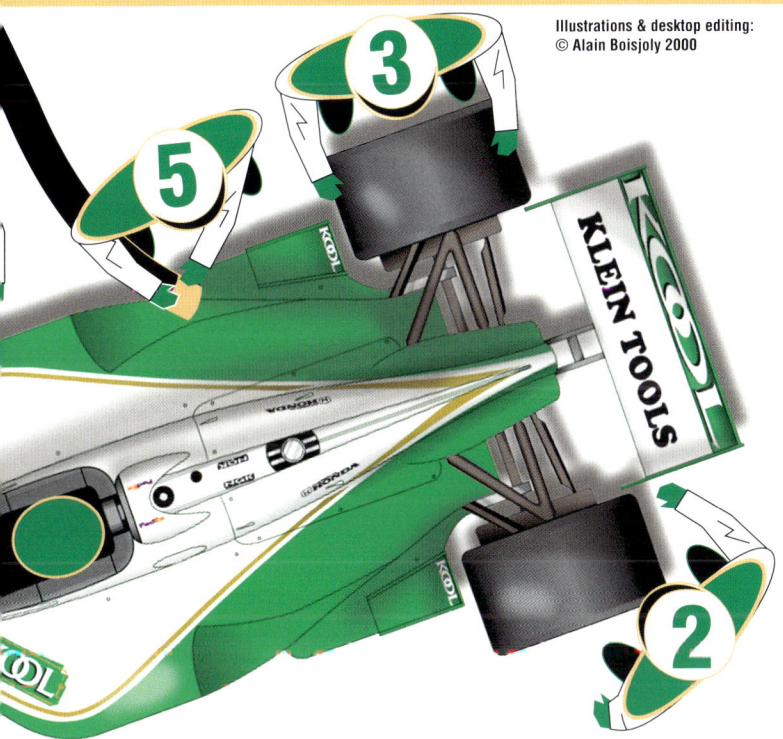

WHO DOES WHAT DURING A PIT STOP!

#26 Paul Tracy's pit crew

1 – Outside Front: Tony Cotman
2 – Outside Rear: Chuck Miller
3 – Inside Rear: Steve Price
4 – Inside Front: Leonard Gauci
5 – Fueler: Eric Haverson
6 – Vent/Jack: Jeff Stafford

Pit Strategy: Barry Green
Engineer: Tony Cicale
Pit-to-car Radio: Barry Green

#27 Dario Franchitti's pit crew

1 – Outside Front: Kyle Moyer
2 – Outside Rear: John Cummiskey
3 – Inside Rear: Kris Badger
4 – Inside Front: Alex Herring
5 – Fueler: Keith Badger
6 – Vent/Jack: Jack Christiansen

Pit Strategy: Scott Graves
Engineer: Tino Belli / Steve Challis
Pit-to-car Radio: Kim Green

MUCH of the success of Team KOOL Green can be attributed to the quality of the individual team members, and particularly the job they do on pit stops during the races.

For the second year in a row, the crew of Paul Tracy's #26 Team KOOL Green Honda-Reynard, led by crew chief Tony Cotman, won the prestigious $50,000 Craftsman Pit Crew Challenge. The team kept their unbeaten streak alive by defeating four other crews that had earned the right to compete in a final pit stop competition at the last race of the season.

"Pit stops are a huge element of race strategy and I know that the guys on this team take great pride in being able to help Paul in a race. And I think the drivers respect us and appreciate what we do for the team," said Cotman.

"We sure do," Tracy agrees. "The difference between a great pit stop and an average one might be just a second or less but that can translate into several spots on the track.

"On the other hand, poor pit stops can prevent a driver from winning a race. Dario and I, as drivers, have to have complete trust and confidence in our pit crews. It's like football or baseball, you can have the greatest quarterback or pitcher in the game, but if you don't have the team members to catch the ball or hit it, you won't win consistently."

Franchitti concurs. "Pit stops are so critical to our overall success that we have a special pit stop pad set up in the race shop where the guys can practice. They take it very seriously and it shows."

But even the best team in the business is only part of the mix for success.

Tracy and Franchitti know it's crucial to follow a personalized fitness routine to be competitive in the CART FedEx Championship Series, and physicians will back them up. Studies show that race drivers regularly sustain heart rates of about 175 beats per minute during a race. This kind of stamina and strength places them in the high-performance athlete category, along with marathon runners.

"Driving a race car is the toughest thing I can think of," Franchitti said. "I've biked in the mountains for four to five hours and it doesn't even come close to the physical exertion from driving."

Considering drivers face more G-force loads in one lap than astronauts do during the launch of the space shuttle, it's little wonder they need to be in top physical condition. Add in cockpit temperatures that can soar over 130°F during a two-hour race, and drivers must deal with mental fatigue as well as physical, so it's little wonder that Franchitti has sometimes lost almost 10 pounds during a race.

Tracy and Franchitti don't slow down when they get out of the car. While both drivers spend time in the gym doing both cardiovascular and strength training, they prefer to get their exercise by faster means. Tracy snowboards, plays volleyball, and bikes (dirt and mountain) in the hills surrounding his Las Vegas home. Franchitti goes running, skiing, mountain biking and gets in the odd game of soccer with pals like Max Papis at the track.

WHAT'S YOUR PLEASURE?...

Specifics	2000 Civic Coupe Si	2000 Team KOOL Green Honda/Reynard
Sticker Price	$17,545.00 (msrp)	$600,000.00 (approx.)
Engine	DOHC, 16-Valve, In-Line 4, VTEC™, Aluminum-Alloy	Turbocharged, Aluminum Alloy Block V-8
0 – 60 mph in…	7.4 seconds	2.2 seconds
Horsepower @ rpm	160 @ 7600	800 @ 14,000
Gas Mileage	31 miles per gallon	1.85 miles per gallon
Fuel Capacity (gal.)	11.9	35
Standard Transmission	Manual	6 Speed Sequential
Curb Weight (Manual, lbs.)	2612	1550
Length (in.)	175.1	199
Width (in.)	67.1	78.5
Height (in.)	54.1	36
Alloy Wheels	15" Alloy Wheels	15" BBS Forged Magnesium
Tires	All Season 195/55R15	Firestone Firehawk slicks
Warranty	36 mos. / 36000 miles	You break it, you buy it!!!
5-Year Maintenance/ Repair Costs	$3,239	Unlimited….
Trunk Space (Manufacturer, cu. ft.)	11.9	Trunk? That's where the engine goes!
Seating	5	1…at a time
Special Features	**2000 Civic Coupe Si**	**2000 Team KOOL Green Honda/Reynard**
Airbags	Standard	Nope. Cushioned padding does the trick.
Air Conditioning	Standard	Driver flips their visor up to cool down
Tachometer	Standard	Standard
Power Windows	Standard	No roof, no windows.
Power Locks	Standard	Just try to steal it!
Tilt Steering	Standard	Removable steering wheel
Front Bucket Seat(s)	Standard	Contoured to driver's body
AM/FM / CD Player	AM/FM Stereo with CD Player and 6 speakers and clock	Two-way radio
Beverage Holder	Standard	On-board water bottle
Pit Stop	3 - 4 hours	Less than 15 seconds

2000 Civic Coupe Si: A scorching 160-horsepower, all-aluminum dual overhead camshaft and 1.6 liter VTEC™ engine.
Five-speed transmission, 4-wheel double wishbone suspension, HV shock absorbers, front and rear stabilizer bars,
P195/55/R15 tires on 15-in alloy wheel and 4-wheel disc brakes.

TEAM KOOL GREEN

2000 FEDEX CHAMPIONSHIP SERIES

TOP TEN DRIVERS

In accordance with the *AUTOCOURSE* tradition, Editor Jeremy Shaw offers his personal ranking of the best of the best in the 2000 CART FedEx Championship Series, taking into account their individual performances, their level of experience and the resources at their disposal.

Top Ten portraits by Jamie Squire/Allsport USA

top ten

gil de ferran

ROGER Penske made an astute choice by selecting Gil de Ferran to lead his team out of the wilderness. The understated, highly intelligent and cosmopolitan de Ferran (who was born in France, raised in Brazil and now resides happily in Florida with his English wife, Angela) had paid his dues during four years in Champ Cars and was more than ready to reap the rewards. Increasingly, his efforts with Walker Racing had been hamstrung by ineffective Goodyear tires, yet de Ferran never once doubted his own ability. He *knew* a switch to Marlboro Team Penske would afford him the opportunity to challenge for the championship, and never lost sight of his goal.

De Ferran did not waste his time in seeking ultimate speed during winter testing. Instead he concentrated on building a rapport with his team and understanding the nuances of his car. He was well accustomed to the Honda/Reynard package from his days with Jim Hall and Derrick Walker, of course, but had never driven on Firestone tires prior to his first test with Penske. It was a new experience, too, for the team. They learned quickly together and, despite characteristically conservative predictions prior to the first race, promptly snared the pole first time out at Homestead...and second time out at Long Beach. On each occasion, de Ferran lost the opportunity of winning because he chose to push hard rather than concentrate on saving fuel. Typically, he took the sixth- and seventh-place finishes in his stride, preferring to dwell on the positives: He had two poles to his credit and had scored valuable points.

De Ferran went on to claim a 100th Champ Car win for Penske at Nazareth, added another victory at Portland and quietly accumulated points without ever appearing to be a dominant force. He remained calm following an accident while in position to clinch the title in Australia, and finally tied up the spoils with a workmanlike effort at Fontana. Mission accomplished.

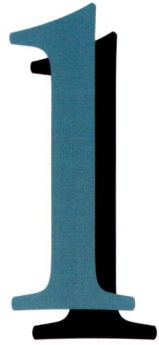

Date of birth: November 11, 1967
Residence: Fort Lauderdale, Florida
Team: Marlboro Team Penske
Equipment: Honda/Reynard/Firestone
CART starts in 2000: 20
FedEx Series ranking: 1st
Wins: 2; **Poles:** 5; **Points:** 168

top ten

JUAN Pablo Montoya is a rare talent. The Colombian faced an uphill struggle when he began the defense of his magnificent 1999 championship with unproven equipment, but, even at the relatively tender age of 25, he never flinched in the face of adversity. Not surprisingly, given his performances during a sensational rookie campaign, Montoya was always fast. He earned a series-high seven poles, leaving his Champ Car record at an astonishing 35 percent strike rate, and accumulated the season's best qualifying average (albeit by a slim margin, 4.1 to 4.25, over de Ferran). He led 11 different races (more than anyone else) for a total of 820 laps (more than twice as many as his nearest rival) – or 29 percent of the overall total.

Clearly, Montoya was Toyota's "secret weapon" in its quest for competitiveness, and it was appropriate that he should claim the company's first victory. The sad part was that he, and Toyota, had to wait so long – until Round Six at Milwaukee. Previously, he had leapt into the lead in the Homestead opener before succumbing to an engine problem. He failed to finish at Long Beach (engine again) and Rio, where he ran in second until halted by a gear selection problem. Even more heartbreaking was the disappointment in Japan, where, on Honda's home ground, Montoya humiliated the opposition before falling victim to a bizarre pit-lane miscue.

He failed to finish 12 races in all, mostly due to mechanical ailments, which was atypical for Target/Chip Ganassi Racing. Even then, he wasn't eliminated from the title reckoning until the 19th race, at Surfers Paradise, where he qualified on pole only to be punted into the wall by Gil de Ferran at the first corner. Again his patience had been sorely tested, yet Montoya continued to display a professional demeanor. He also scored the most spectacular victory of the year, beating Michael Andretti at Michigan Speedway by a scant 0.040 second. Sensational!

juan montoya

Date of birth: September 20, 1975

Residence: Miami, Florida

Team: Target/Chip Ganassi Racing

Equipment: Toyota/Lola/Firestone

CART starts in 2000: 20

FedEx Series ranking: 9th

Wins: 3; Poles: 7; Points: 126

top ten

AFTER blitzing the field in preseason testing (with the notable exception of Spring Training), Michael Andretti was among the firm favorites to win the 2000 CART FedEx Series Championship. He, like Newman/Haas teammate Christian Fittipaldi, had been thoroughly impressed with the new Ford Cosworth XF engine and was delighted, too, with the feel of his new Lola chassis following a switch from the effective, but complex, Swift.

Andretti drove like a true champion all year long, only for his title aspirations to be undone by a litany of disasters at each end of the season.

In the first race at Homestead, after qualifying sixth, Andretti leapt to second and was running well when his car succumbed to an oil leak. A cracked exhaust cost him a potential victory at Long Beach, while in Rio, eventually, he was disqualified from ninth place following a miscue in the pit lane that left crewman Todd Tice with a broken leg. Three races then, and no points. But Andretti bounced back with a well-judged victory in Japan, then worked his way into the lead of the point standings following seven top-six finishes from the next eight races. He struggled to eighth at Mid-Ohio, but still was looking good for the championship. Then the wheels fell off – or, at least, everything else did. He was parked by a broken CV joint at Road America, ran out of fuel at Vancouver, then suffered his greatest heartbreak at Gateway, where he qualified 15th, blasted to the front and was in complete command when his engine failed. Andretti was knocked out at Surfers Paradise by yet more engine woes, and at Fontana he was an innocent victim when he lifted off to avoid a smokescreen emitted by Tony Kanaan's blown engine...and promptly was rear-ended by Oriol Servia. The incident summed up a season in which precious little went his way.

michael andretti

Date of birth: October 5, 1962
Residence: Nazareth, Pennsylvania
Team: Newman/Haas Racing
Equipment: Ford/Lola/Firestone
CART starts in 2000: 20
FedEx Series ranking: 8th
Wins: 2; **Poles:** 0; **Points:** 127

top ten

helio castroneves

IN common with several other contenders during a truly extraordinary Y2K campaign, Helio Castroneves deserved far better than seventh in the final point standings. The young Brazilian had put himself on the map during the 1999 season, only to be left in the lurch when Carl Hogan abruptly and reluctantly closed down his team after the final race. He was granted a reprieve with Marlboro Team Penske in tragic circumstances, following the death of Greg Moore, and displayed his gratitude in the best possible way. Castroneves proved to be a real team player, whose bubbly personality made him an instant hit within the Penske organization. He gelled immediately with fellow countryman Gil de Ferran. The pair possessed entirely different personalities, but had a healthy mutual respect and, together, pushed each other to new heights.

Castroneves was consistently fast and consistently unfortunate, such that he failed to finish eight of the 20 races. He drove to a strong second at Long Beach, but that was to prove his only point-scoring place during the first six races. Among the litany of woes was a spectacular engine failure at Homestead and a broken gearbox in Rio. He, like de Ferran, struggled to find any form in Japan, then crashed at Nazareth when he bit off more than he could chew at a restart.

The long-awaited breakthrough victory came in Detroit, where he drove an exquisite race, tempering his natural speed with patience. Castroneves went on to score dominant victories at Mid-Ohio and Laguna Seca, earning a tie with Juan Montoya and Paul Tracy for most wins during the season. He also claimed the third-best qualifying average (5.65), which was bettered only by Montoya and de Ferran, and led more laps (372) than anyone except the Colombian. He was, in short, a regular contender who seems set for a long and illustrious career at this level.

Date of birth: May 10, 1975
Residence: Miami, Florida
Team: Marlboro Team Penske
Equipment: Honda/Reynard/Firestone
CART starts in 2000: 20
FedEx Series ranking: 7th
Wins: 3; Poles: 3; Points: 129

top ten

AFTER something of a breakthrough season in 1999, much was expected of Paul Tracy. By and large, he did not disappoint. Sure, there were a few examples of the old "red mist," notably at Surfers Paradise, where he was involved in a couple of scrapes in the closing stages, but they were few and far between. For most of the time, Tracy was a bona fide championship contender – arguably for the first time in his career.

The only problem was qualifying. The Canadian simply couldn't get it together often enough when the grid positions were being established. His overall qualifying average was a mediocre 10.05, ninth best on the field and an average of three positions worse than teammate Dario Franchitti. That said, Tracy posted a series of remarkable drives to make up the deficit.

Take Homestead, for example, where he struggled throughout practice and qualifying, then bolted through the field to finish third. Next time out, at Long Beach, he started 17th again, and won! He finished sixth after starting a dismal 20th at Twin Ring Motegi, and rose to grab a place on the podium in his native Toronto after qualifying 12th. But the best was yet to come. At Road America, Tracy's Honda/Reynard was stricken by an electrical glitch at the start. He dropped to the back of the field while resetting the onboard computer before mounting a sensational comeback that brought his second victory of the season. Two weeks later in Vancouver, Tracy enjoyed a somewhat easier afternoon, running second until Franchitti stalled his engine during his final routine pit stop. The pragmatic Canadian needed no second bidding as he romped to his third win of the year, vaulting him to second in the points table, only six behind Andretti. But that was as close as he would get. An uncompetitive outing at Laguna Seca, a gearbox failure at Gateway, the accident at Surfers Paradise and a comprehensive engine failure at Fontana left him a disappointed fifth at the close.

paul tracy

Date of birth: December 17, 1968
Residence: Las Vegas, Nevada
Team: Team KOOL Green
Equipment: Honda/Reynard/Firestone
CART starts in 2000: 20
FedEx Series ranking: 5th
Wins: 3; Poles: 1; Points: 134

top ten

ADRIAN Fernandez's performance in 2000 was particularly meritorious for the manner in which he bounced back into contention after failing to score points in the first two races. He qualified third for the season opener at Homestead and led for a while before his Ford Cosworth XF engine succumbed to an O-ring failure. Then he started fourth at Long Beach, only to be sidelined by an engine meltdown that sent him heavily into the wall. However, Fernandez refused to be flustered by the mechanical problems and, after qualifying a dismal 16th in Brazil, he rebounded in magnificent style by guiding Pat Patrick's Ford/Reynard to Victory Lane.

That triumph in Rio highlighted Fernandez's never-say-die attitude – and his only weakness: qualifying. All too often he left himself with too much to do on race day. Nevertheless, he repeated the recipe in Australia, where he started far down the field, 17th, but gradually worked his way into contention with the assistance of accomplished race engineer/strategist John Ward.

Fernandez might not be the fastest driver on the circuit, but he has proved himself to be among the best at taking advantage of opportunities that present themselves. The intelligent, articulate and personable Mexican has become renowned as one of the most incisive overtakers in the business and as a driver who always obtains excellent fuel economy.

Aside from those first two DNFs, Fernandez finished among the points in all but one of the remaining 18 races. The exception was in Detroit, where his engine's wastegate inlet ingested a helmet visor tear-off strip that he had discarded during a pit stop. If he wasn't in contention to win, "Mr. Reliable" realized the importance of finishing and picking up as many championship points as possible. The result was a well-deserved, career-best second in the points table.

adrian fernandez

Date of birth: April 20, 1965
Residence: Paradise Valley, Arizona
Team: Patrick Racing
Equipment: Ford/Reynard/Firestone
CART starts in 2000: 20
FedEx Series ranking: 2nd
Wins: 2; Poles: 0; Points: 158

top ten

ROBERTO Moreno has always said, "Just give me a competitive car and I'll show you what I can do." Well, in 2000, at age 41, after earning the sobriquet "Super Sub" in 1999, finally he was given that opportunity by car owner U.E. "Pat" Patrick. For only the third time since making his Champ Car debut 15 years earlier, Moreno was set to contest a full season.

The Brazilian struggled sometimes in qualifying, especially during the first half of the year when he started among the top ten only once, but his racecraft, his wealth of experience – and the accumulated wisdom of pit strategists Jim McGee and Pat Patrick himself – enabled Moreno to move forward on just about every occasion. He set the ball in motion by finishing a strong second at Homestead, and put himself in contention to win at Long Beach before his gearbox began acting up. He secured a podium finish at Motegi and looked set to do so again at Nazareth before being hindered by a slow puncture in the closing stages. Moreno was faced with a tough decision: either make a pit stop to change the tire and lose all hope of a good finish, or try to nurse the car home. He chose the latter and paid the penalty when Mauricio Gugelmin had a run on him, causing him to stray off line and hit the wall.

He erred more seriously at Laguna Seca and Surfers Paradise, which, ultimately, perhaps cost him a chance of winning the championship. By the same token, he was hobbled by gearbox woes again in Toronto, and seemed set for victory in Portland until a miscue during his final pit stop. Moreno had to make do with second on that occasion, but rebounded at Cleveland, where he secured his first-ever pole, then romped to a popular first-ever victory. By remaining in the title hunt until the final race, Moreno repaid in full the faith shown in him by Patrick Racing.

roberto moreno

Date of birth: February 11, 1959

Residence: Weston, Florida

Team: Patrick Racing

Equipment: Ford/Reynard/Firestone

CART starts in 2000: 20

FedEx Series ranking: 3rd

Wins: 1; Poles: 1; Points: 147

top ten

FOURTH in the points table represented the fruit of a fine rookie season for Kenny Bräck. The amiable Swede had spent the three previous years making left turns only in the Indy Racing League, and had acquired a wealth of knowledge under the tutelage, especially, of A.J. Foyt. He had won the 1998 IRL Championship and the 1999 Indianapolis 500. Those results – and the knowledge that Bräck had won the Barber Saab Pro Series (in 1993) and finished a close second in the European Formula 3000 Championship ('96) – brought him to the attention of three-time CART champion Bobby Rahal, who signed him to replace Bryan Herta.

Bräck impressed the team immediately with his dedication, his feedback and his speed. He earned more credibility by moving to an apartment close to the team's base in Hilliard, Ohio. Along with teammate Max Papis, Bräck was among the pace-setters at Spring Training and, after qualifying fifth for his CART debut, soon moved into the lead before joining fellow Ford contenders Michael Andretti and Adrian Fernandez on the sidelines due to an oil system problem. Papis, who had qualified 13th, went on to win the race, but it was one of the few occasions on which he was able to steal a march on his teammate. In fact, Bräck out-qualified Papis in 15 of the 20 races, gaining the sixth-best overall qualifying average (8.4), and earned nine top-five finishes (to Papis' three) to equal the series' best mark achieved by new champion Gil de Ferran.

Bräck led a total of 151 laps during the season, fifth best, and even though all but ten of those were on ovals, he proved to be equally adept on the road courses, finishing second at Cleveland and Surfers Paradise, and third at Mid-Ohio. He never managed to win a race, but might have done so on several occasions, notably at Motegi, if he hadn't stalled in the pits.

kenny bräck

8

Date of birth: March 21, 1966
Residence: Dublin, Ohio
Team: Team Rahal
Equipment: Ford/Reynard/Firestone
CART starts in 2000: 20
FedEx Series ranking: 4th
Wins: 0; Poles: 0; Points: 135

top ten

IT'S tough to know what to make of Christian Fittipaldi's Y2K campaign. In many ways, the Brazilian outshone his teammate Michael Andretti. He proved faster in qualifying seven times in the first eight races, whereupon Andretti redressed the balance somewhat in the latter half of the season. In the grid-position ranking, Fittipaldi ended up fifth, with an average placing of 7.3, to Andretti's seventh (8.7). He also displayed the same kind of aggression that allowed him to develop into a bona fide contender in 1999 – except that sometimes he appeared to overstep the mark. Certainly he was involved in more than his fair share of scrapes, and earned the wrath of Kenny Bräck for causing the Swede to crash heavily during a hectic Michigan 500 scramble.

At the same time, Fittipaldi seemed like a magnet for misfortune. He was knocked out of two races (Long Beach and Road America) by cracked exhaust headers; punted from behind in the pit lane at Toronto; and clobbered by Jimmy Vasser at Surfers Paradise. Also he lost potential top finishes at Motegi, Nazareth, Milwaukee and Laguna Seca through pit-stop miscues or strategic errors of one sort or another.

He kept his nose clean at Fontana, though, where he ran consistently and reliably to score a victory in the final race of the season. It was a deserved success. For, as in his previous three seasons, Fittipaldi had to fight back from injury – caused by a heavy crash in practice at Chicago, where briefly he was knocked unconscious and, therefore, barred from taking part in the race.

Renowned as one of the fittest drivers in the field, Fittipaldi has won only twice in his 95 Champ Car starts, but, importantly, the career road-racer now has an oval triumph to his name. The Fontana frolic will have worked wonders for his confidence.

christian fittipaldi

9

Date of birth: January 18, 1971
Residence: Key Biscayne, Florida
Team: Newman/Haas Racing
Equipment: Ford/Lola/Firestone
CART starts in 2000: 19
FedEx Series ranking: 12th
Wins: 1; Poles: 1; Points: 121

top ten

jimmy vasser

THE 1996 CART champion would most certainly have earned a higher ranking than tenth in my mind (and sixth in the overall championship) but for a lengthy sequence of races in which he was virtually invisible. Jimmy Vasser's ninth CART season started out in style, though, as he equaled or improved Toyota's best-ever finish in the Champ Car ranks in each of the first three races. The Nevada-resident Californian claimed fourth at Homestead, third at Long Beach (where he eclipsed teammate Juan Montoya) and second in Brazil. He qualified on the second row also in Japan, where he ran comfortably with Montoya until his engine failed.

But then he faded from view. In the next 11 races, Vasser qualified only twice among the top ten. By contrast, Montoya failed only once to make the top ten during that same time frame. True, Vasser used his wealth of experience to good effect by recording eight top-ten finishes, but only rarely was he competitive. Things began to turn around at Road America, where, after qualifying 16th, he recovered to take fifth, albeit largely as a result of high attrition. He added a sixth, an eighth and a seventh in the next three races, before earning an excellent victory, the ninth of his career, in Houston. Finally, the spark had returned. He rounded out the season as it had begun – on a high note – by adding a strong third at Surfers Paradise, then leading briefly at Fontana before being grounded by a gearbox malady.

So, what went wrong in the interim? Well, Vasser certainly didn't get any breaks, and more than once the chosen race strategy simply didn't work in his favor. But for the most part, he simply didn't get a handle on the car, and, given the strength of the competition, no one could overcome such a handicap. Nevertheless, Vasser still has what it takes to win at this level.

10

Date of birth: November 20, 1965
Residence: Las Vegas, Nevada
Team: Target/Chip Ganassi Racing
Equipment: Toyota/Lola/Firestone
CART starts in 2000: 20
FedEx Series ranking: 6th
Wins: 1; **Poles:** 0; **Points:** 131

KENNY BRÄCK PROFILE

Overnight Sensation

KENNY BRÄCK PROFILE

Inset: Kenny Bräck clinched Rookie of the Year honors with two races to run.
Robert Laberge/Allsport USA

Left: The Swede's Shell Ford/Reynard was a consistent contender.
Donald Miralle/Allsport USA

by David Phillips

NINETEEN races into the 2000 FedEx Championship Series, Kenny Bräck stood a chance of joining Nigel Mansell and Juan Pablo Montoya as the only rookies to win the CART championship. He'd already wrapped-up Rookie of the Year honors in Houston and, as the halfway point of the 20th and final race of the season came and went, his bid to claim the FedEx title was looking good. Needing to win the race, lead the most laps and rely on rivals Gil de Ferran and Adrian Fernandez failing to finish, Bräck was doing his part. Not only was he leading, but also he had led the most laps, despite the best efforts of Helio Castroneves, Michael Andretti and Montoya.

Although he would go on to claim the coveted point for leading the most laps, it was Bräck who was sidelined by debilitating mechanical problems, while de Ferran came home third ahead of the fifth-placed Fernandez to clinch the first CART FedEx title of the 21st century.

Disappointed to be sure, Bräck chose to accentuate the positive aspects of his final race as a CART rookie.

"That's the way it goes," he said. "Our strategy was very good today and everything was falling into place. We had to lead the most laps and we had a strong car today. Right now it is very disappointing though. We were going so well, but we also knew it is a long race. The points championship was pretty much out of our control today. We really wanted to win the race this time and we were heading in the right direction for that to happen."

Still, to come within one race of matching the feats of Mansell, a former Formula 1 World Champion, and Montoya, widely believed to be a future World Champion, can hardly be considered a disappointment for Bräck. And that point for leading the most laps? It enabled him to pip Paul Tracy – number two on the win list of active CART drivers – to fourth place in the season standings.

Not bad for a guy who had never seen most of the tracks in the 2000 FedEx Championship and who had raced on just four of them – and that when he won the '93 Barber Saab Pro Series title. In the intervening years, Bräck earned the moniker "well-traveled" the hard way. From '94 to '96, he raced in the FIA International Formula 3000 Championship, scoring four wins and coming within a gnat's eyelash of winning the '96 title. He also worked as a test driver for the Arrows Formula 1 team before moving back to the United States to compete in the Indy Racing League. It was a move that, ultimately, led him to A.J. Foyt Racing and produced an IRL championship in '98, followed by a dramatic victory in the '99 Indianapolis 500.

By mid-'99, Bräck was talking with another Indy 500 winner – Bobby Rahal – about driving for Team Rahal in the 2000 CART FedEx Championship. When the deal was announced, Bräck adopted a statesman-like stance in response to politically-charged questions about the rival series.

"I fulfilled most of my goals in the IRL," he said. "I won the championship in 1998 and finished runner-up in 1999, and won the Indianapolis 500 in 1999. I learned a lot from A.J. [Foyt], who is a master on the ovals, about how to drive them, and I think that I am ready for a new challenge. When this opportunity with Bobby [Rahal] came up and it became a reality, I really didn't have to think twice about it. Going from a race-winning outfit in the IRL to a race-winning outfit in CART, it couldn't be a better situation. I also wanted to get back into road racing, which is my background. I spent 16 years racing on road tracks and that is also a factor that influenced the decision. I was looking for a new challenge."

With only one street circuit race on the spring schedule, however, Bräck would have to wait before hitting the road circuits on a regular basis. In the meantime, he made his presence known on the "oval-intensive" portion of the schedule, qualifying fifth and leading the season opener at Homestead before he was sidelined by a broken oil seal. A couple of weeks later he rebounded from a heavy crash in practice to qualify sixth at Nazareth before the snows came.

He led again and finished fifth at the Rio "roval," then scored his first podium finish with a third place at the rescheduled Nazareth race. That was followed by a fourth place at the venerable Milwaukee Mile.

So far, his only road-racing start had ended with a crash at Long Beach. That would prove to be an anomaly, however, for he quickly established himself as a championship contender once the series tackled its midseason diet of permanent road courses and street circuits. Bräck consistently finished in the top five, highlighted by a second place at Cleveland and third at Road America. Another runner-up finish in Australia set the stage for the climactic Fontana race.

"I adapted very well to the road courses," he said. "We actually fared better on the road courses [than] the ovals, which I think may be a surprise to a lot of people. However, I didn't feel it that way when we started this program because I felt during winter testing that I got right back into road racing with the help of Team Rahal's technical knowledge about how to set the car up."

Of course, for a driver born and bred to the road courses of Europe, Bräck's performances at Cleveland, Road America and Surfers Paradise should have come as no surprise. Besides, having a three-time CART champion in your pit is sure to short-cut the learning curve.

"Bobby has been a tremendous help," explained Bräck. "He knows a lot about CART racing and that is a very nice thing to have in the team owner. I mean, I ask him about different courses we go to and try to find out what he knows, and that is a big help, especially in the first year when you have never seen some of the courses before."

While Rahal and the team surely contributed to Bräck's success, they are quick to credit the amiable, but intensely focused, Swede for regularly putting the Shell Ford/Reynard at the sharp end of the grid and in the battle for the podium.

"It's easy to say, but I don't think he has any weaknesses," said Don Halliday, Bräck's race engineer. "And he's a tough son of a bitch. Nazareth was a good example of that. He whacked his head on Friday [when he crashed during practice] and the next day he was fastest overall in practice, despite being in the 'slow' group, then he qualified sixth.

"He's tough. He's very intense; very technical – likes to be technical. He understands a lot of what's going on. And he doesn't take any prisoners."

Rookie of the Year, fourth in the FedEx Championship, four podium finishes and ten top-six finishes. As Bräck notes, about the only thing missing from his initial season of Champ Car racing was a victory. Rest assured, he plans to redress that situation as quickly as possible in 2001.

"All in all, it was a fantastic season considering the competition level in this series," he said. "To be able to be a consistent challenger for the podium and top fives in your first year, I am very, very satisfied with that. We accomplished most of our goals, although we wanted to win a race. We had our chances and on several occasions we were close. I am really confident for next year."

37

TAKING STOCK

by Eric Mauk

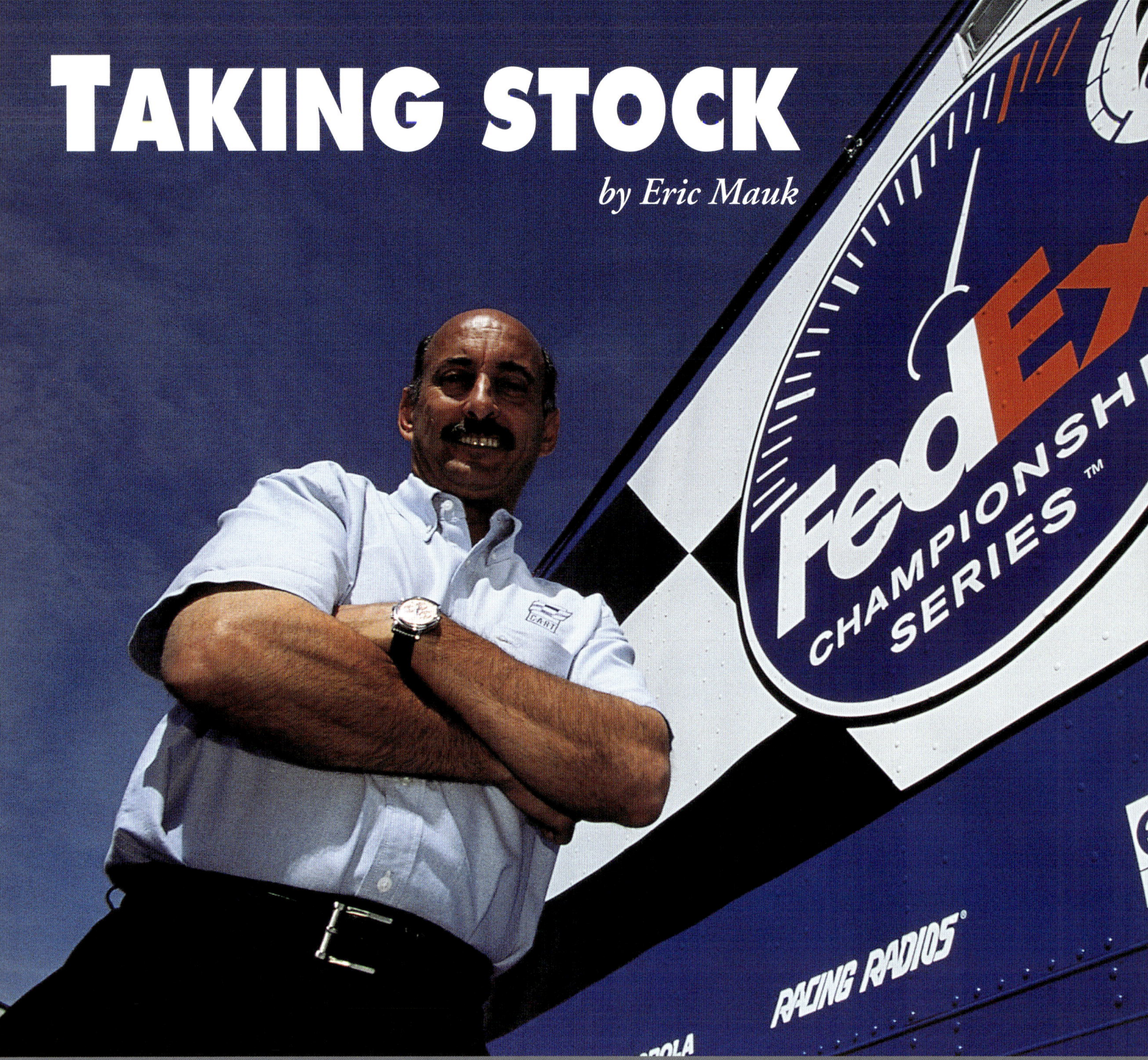

A CHANGE AT THE TOP

CHAMPIONSHIP Auto Racing Teams, Inc., sanctioning body of the CART FedEx Championship Series, underwent a series of upheavals as the 2000 season progressed, triggered when its chairman, president and chief executive officer Andrew Craig resigned from his position on a summer day in Michigan.

Craig had run the show out of the Troy, Michigan, offices since 1994 and had been responsible for many of the positive changes seen in CART – including the wealth brought to the owners and the series from the public offering of stock on the New York Stock Exchange – but he relinquished his post during the Belle Isle race weekend, rather than see his contract through to the end of the year 2000.

He was immediately replaced as CEO on an interim basis by Bobby Rahal, and as chairman of the board by veteran company chief executive James Hardymon. The duo quickly took steps to address some of the factors that they saw as needing attention, such as the 2001 schedule; but to dismiss Craig without noting the accomplishments of his reign would be a grave oversight.

The 51-year-old Brit came on board just as Indianapolis Motor Speedway President Tony George was preparing to launch the Indy Racing League. The project nearly exploded on the launch pad and Craig initiated negotiations to resolve the schism but, on his own admission, Craig's lack of experience with the nuances of North American open-wheel racing so early in his CART career kept him from taking advantage of George's unsteady position. He nearly got the two sides together again in 1999 and it appeared a resolution was imminent before George abruptly withdrew from the reconciliation talks.

Craig's move to make CART a publicly-traded company raised the value of a Champ Car franchise from $120,000 at his hiring to nearly $9 million at the end of the 2000 season, allowing several teams to meet the higher costs of competition. He also began spending series revenue in marketing and marketing research, expanded the public relations department and completely reorganised the competitions side of the business. The addition of the logistics division made it possible to add overseas events in Brazil and Japan, and paved the way for the subsequent expansion to England and Germany.

During Craig's tenure CART also normalized its previously hostile relationship with the FIA, the governing body of world motorsports, and took ownership of the Indy Lights and Toyota Atlantic series, initiating a vested interest in the two championships that would provide many of its future drivers. CART also fine-tuned the franchise system to the effect that teams had to run full-time in order to maintain their financial benefits. The ploy spurred some of the part-time teams that littered the grid in the early '90s to invest more energy into the series. Craig also cleared the schedule to allow teams to participate in the Indianapolis 500 for the first time since 1995, giving Chip Ganassi and Juan Montoya the means to win their first Borg-Warner trophy in May, beating the best the IRL had to offer in the Memorial Day classic.

Not every initiative was a success, however. The failure of the Hawaiian Super Prix, originally scheduled for the end of the '99 season, undermined the credibility of both Craig and CART as the high-profile, high-dollar event crashed to Earth without ever really coming close to reality. Sagging

Main photograph: Bobby Rahal took over at the helm after Andrew Craig resigned in June.
Robert Laberge/Allsport USA

Left: Joe Heitzler was named as CART's newest president in early December.
Allsport USA

Below left: Jim Hardymon steadied the ship and remained as chairman of the board.
Donald Miralle/Allsport USA

television ratings and disappointing attendances at some oval track venues all were key factors that hastened Craig's departure.

The Rahal regime took much of its first month in renewing relationships with sponsors and promoters, as well as building what would become a 22-race schedule for 2001. The three-time series champion also started making overtures toward decreasing horsepower in the engines – with the intent of minimizing the escalation in speed and cost – and eventually persuaded the manufacturers to decrease the turbocharger boost pressure incrementally until 2003 when a new engine formula would be introduced.

Rahal also set about working on the all-important television package, which had been blamed for much of the public's perceived apathy toward the series, hoping to negotiate a contract that would have more races shown live with more ancillary programming added. His experience as a racer allowed him to make more team-friendly moves with the full support of the other owners, including a reduction in costly testing and the (controversial) elimination of Spring Training. All the while, Rahal reminded people at every opportunity that his seat at the head of CART's table was only on an interim basis. Even as he was making moves like replacing Friday provisional qualifying with extended practice sessions in 2001, he was preparing to make his exit as a Jaguar-green pasture beckoned.

In September, Rahal announced that he was taking a job overseeing the Jaguar Racing Formula 1 program, etching his interim title in stone and setting the wheels in motion for a search for a new man to lead the FedEx Championship Series into the 21st Century. Rahal stayed on until the end of the season and remained active in steering the series, but headed across the pond soon after the Fontana finale, leaving the rest of the owners to find a successor to his throne.

Chairman of the board Hardymon took the point in the selection process, and eventually, on December 4, long-time sports and entertainment business executive Joseph F. Heitzler was named as the new president and chief executive officer.

Heitzler, 56, who campaigned an MGB successfully in SCCA amateur competition in the late 1960s, had spent the intervening 20 years establishing an enviable reputation in the business community. After a four-year stint as senior vice president of marketing for CBS Sports, he served as president and CEO of Forum Sports Entertainment, which was responsible for broadcasting National Basketball Association Los Angeles Lakers and National Hockey League Kings games. Heitzler joined CART from a position as president and chief operating officer of National Mobile Television Productions, Inc., which provided mobile broadcasting facilities to more than 8,500 sporting and entertainment events, including auto racing, National Football League, NBA, NHL and Major League Baseball.

"The opportunity to merge a passion for open-wheel racing with my business experience fulfills a life-long dream," said Heitzler. "I will strive to have all of our key groups – from investors, team owners and drivers to sponsors, track promoters and our management staff – work as a team with the singular goal of providing an enhanced sports entertainment product to our dedicated fans. With our fans' participation, we will continue to grow and prosper among the rapidly changing and new sports entertainment mediums."

The 2001 FedEx Championship Series

March 11	Monterrey Grand Prix, Fundidora Park, Monterrey, Mexico
March 25	Rio 200, Emerson Fittipaldi Speedway at Nelson Piquet International Raceway, Rio de Janeiro, Brazil
April 8	Toyota Grand Prix of Long Beach, Long Beach, California
April 29	Texas 600, Texas Motor Speedway, Fort Worth, Texas
May 6	Bosch Spark Plug Grand Prix Presented by Toyota, Nazareth Speedway, Nazareth, Pennsylvania
May 19	Firestone Firehawk 500, Twin Ring Motegi, Motegi, Japan
June 3	Miller Lite 225, The Milwaukee Mile, West Allis, Wisconsin
June 17	Tenneco Automotive Grand Prix of Detroit, The Raceway on Belle Isle, Detroit, Michigan
June 24	Freightliner/G.I. Joe's 200 Presented by Texaco, Portland International Raceway, Portland, Oregon
July 1	The Marconi Grand Prix of Cleveland Presented by Firstar, Burke Lakefront Airport, Cleveland, Ohio
July 15	Molson Indy, Toronto, Ontario, Canada
July 22	Michigan 500 Presented by Toyota, Michigan Speedway, Brooklyn, Michigan
July 29	Target Grand Prix, Chicago Motor Speedway, Cicero, Illinois
August 12	Miller Lite 200, Mid-Ohio Sports Car Course, Lexington, Ohio
August 19	Motorola 220, Road America, Elkhart Lake, Wisconsin
September 2	Molson Indy Vancouver, Vancouver, British Columbia, Canada
September 15	German 500, EuroSpeedway, Lausitz, Germany
September 22	Rockingham 500, Rockingham Motor Speedway, Corby, England
October 7	Texaco/Havoline Grand Prix of Houston, Houston, Texas
October 14	Honda Grand Prix of Monterey Featuring the Shell 300, Laguna Seca Raceway, Monterey, California
October 28	Honda Indy 300, Surfers Paradise, Queensland, Australia
November 4	Marlboro 500 Presented by Toyota, California Speedway, Fontana, California

Subject to alteration

TEAM-BY-TEAM
review

A total of 16 different teams, employing 31 drivers, contested the 2000 CART FedEx Championship Series. In the following pages, Editor Jeremy Shaw assesses some of the strengths and weaknesses of each organization.

Race Car Illustrations by
PAUL LAGUETTE

PATRICK RACING

TEAM-BY-TEAM REVIEW

IN terms of results, veteran car owner U.E. "Pat" Patrick enjoyed one of his most successful seasons ever as drivers Adrian Fernandez and Roberto Moreno claimed three victories between them, and placed second and third respectively in the final FedEx Championship Series point standings. But in terms of outright speed, especially in qualifying, both drivers often struggled to run at a competitive pace. Indeed, Moreno earned only the tenth-best qualifying average during the 20-race season, while Fernandez languished four places farther back. It was a curious anomaly, which meant that usually both drivers were playing catch-up on race day.

Of course, that they managed to do so on such a consistent basis spoke volumes for their commitment and, more importantly, the team's strategic excellence.

"We know we can win races if we can qualify at the front," declared Fernandez, "but we continue to fight even when we don't, and we get great fuel consumption."

Time and again during the 2000 season, both Patrick drivers eked more from each 35-gallon tankful of methanol than their counterparts, and frequently that would stand them in good stead in terms of pit-stop strategy. Patrick himself continued to take enormous pride in calling the races from the pit lane, and more often than not his decisions worked in his drivers' favor.

Patrick Racing's greatest strength, indeed, was its depth of experience. General manager Jim McGee, the most successful chief mechanic/team manager in the sport's history with 89 race wins and nine national championships to his credit, has forgotten more about auto racing than most people will ever learn. Team coordinator Bob Sprow also has built up a wealth of knowledge over the years, as have veteran race engineers John Ward and Ed Nathman.

Consistency and reliability were the team's hallmarks this year. Fernandez and Moreno topped the all-important Laps Completed chart, and one or other of the two drivers finished on the podium in 11 of the 20 races.

Base: Indianapolis, Indiana
Drivers: Adrian Fernandez, Roberto Moreno
Sponsors: Visteon, Tecate, Quaker State
Engines: Ford Cosworth XF
Chassis: Reynard 2KI
Tires: Firestone
Wins: 3 (Fernandez 2, Moreno 1); **Poles:** 1 (Moreno)
FedEx Series points: 305 Fernandez 158 (2nd), Moreno 147 (3rd)

ADRIAN FERNANDEZ – TECATE/QUAKER STATE FORD COSWORTH/REYNARD 2KI

ROBERTO MORENO – VISTEON FORD COSWORTH/REYNARD 2KI

ADRIÁN FERNÁNDEZ
SUBCAMPEÓN
CART 2000

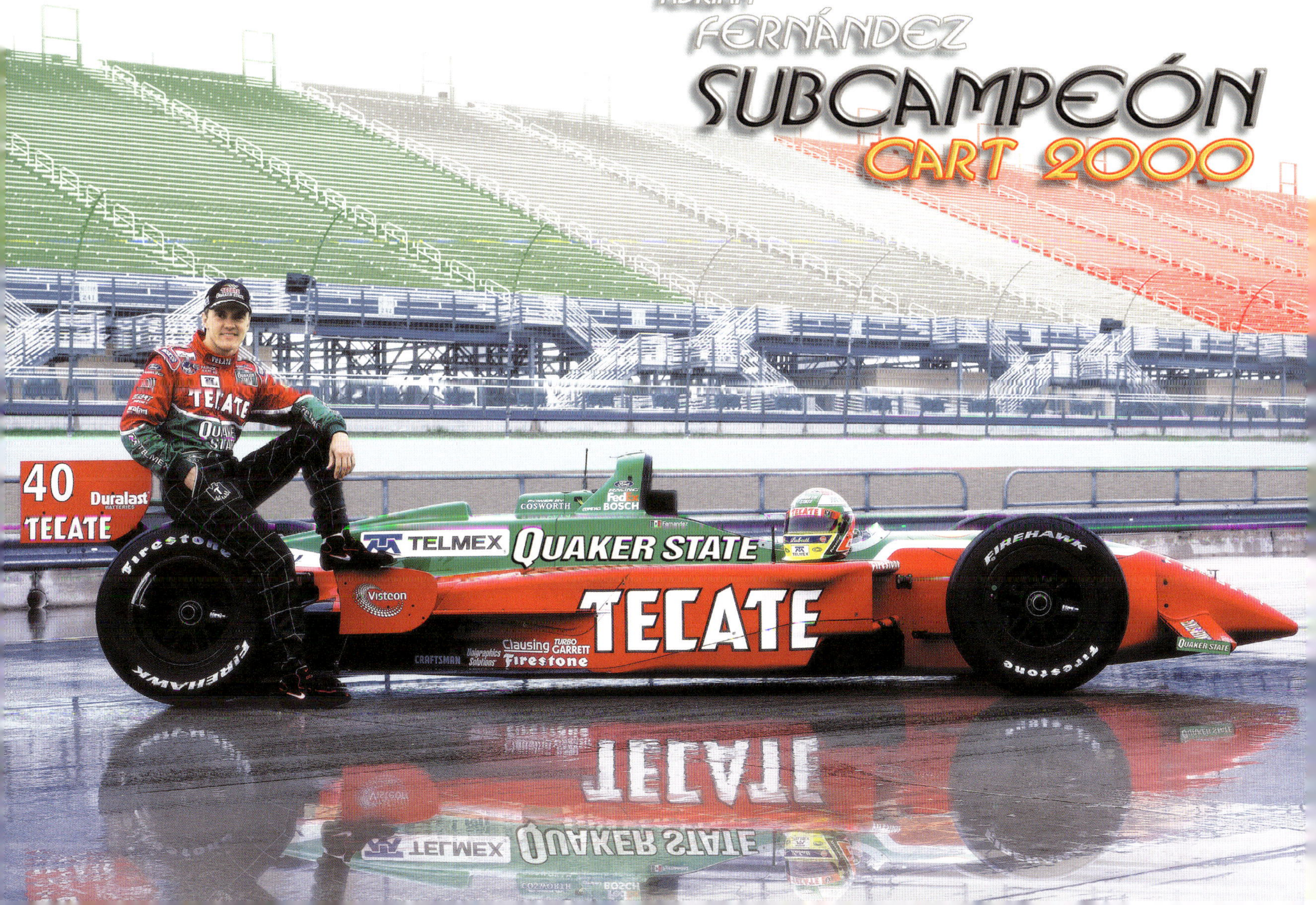

MARLBORO TEAM PENSKE

TEAM-BY-TEAM REVIEW

ROGER Penske is one of the most pragmatic characters on this planet. He is also intensely loyal. And he is not drawn to hyperbole. At the end of the season, however, a season in which his team rebounded from the depths of despair to the pinnacle of success, claiming its eighth CART Championship (and his tenth national championship), Penske took a moment to reflect on his Marlboro-backed organization's rejuvenation.

"Give this team the right tools – I think I can finally say that – and we'll get the job done," he said. "The last couple of years, it's been like hitting off the first tee with a sand-iron."

Marlboro Team Penske certainly got the job done in 2000. But it was a very different Marlboro Team Penske to the one that garnered a measly 31 points from its entire '99 campaign.

Penske effectively started with a clean sheet of paper – with new engines (Honda), chassis (Reynard), tires (Firestone) and drivers (Gil de Ferran and Helio Castroneves). He also entrusted the entire organization to Tim Cindric, formerly with Team Rahal, who became the first man to hold the title of president of Penske Racing since Mark Donohue more than a quarter of a century earlier.

The Honda/Reynard/Firestone combination was already well-proven, of course, having won four consecutive championships in the hands of Target/Chip Ganassi Racing. But Penske, typically, took full advantage of his own state-of-the-art resources at Penske Cars. Sure, the Poole, England-based entity would have preferred to continue building its own unique chassis, but Nick Goozee's team of specialists, headed by technical director Nigel Beresford and chief designer John Travis, instead threw themselves into a concerted development program aimed at maximizing the potential of their off-the-shelf Reynard 2KIs. The results were impressive. No team won more races or poles than Penske, whose cars proved to be a dominant force on both the permanent road courses and, especially, the superspeedways. The team's championship success was hard-earned and well-deserved.

Base: Reading, Pennsylvania
Drivers: Gil de Ferran, Helio Castroneves
Sponsor: Marlboro
Engines: Honda HR-O V8
Chassis: Reynard 2KI
Tires: Firestone
Wins: 5 (Castroneves 3, de Ferran 2);
Poles: 8 (de Ferran 5, Castroneves 3)
FedEx Series points: 297 de Ferran 168 (1st), Castroneves 129 (7th)

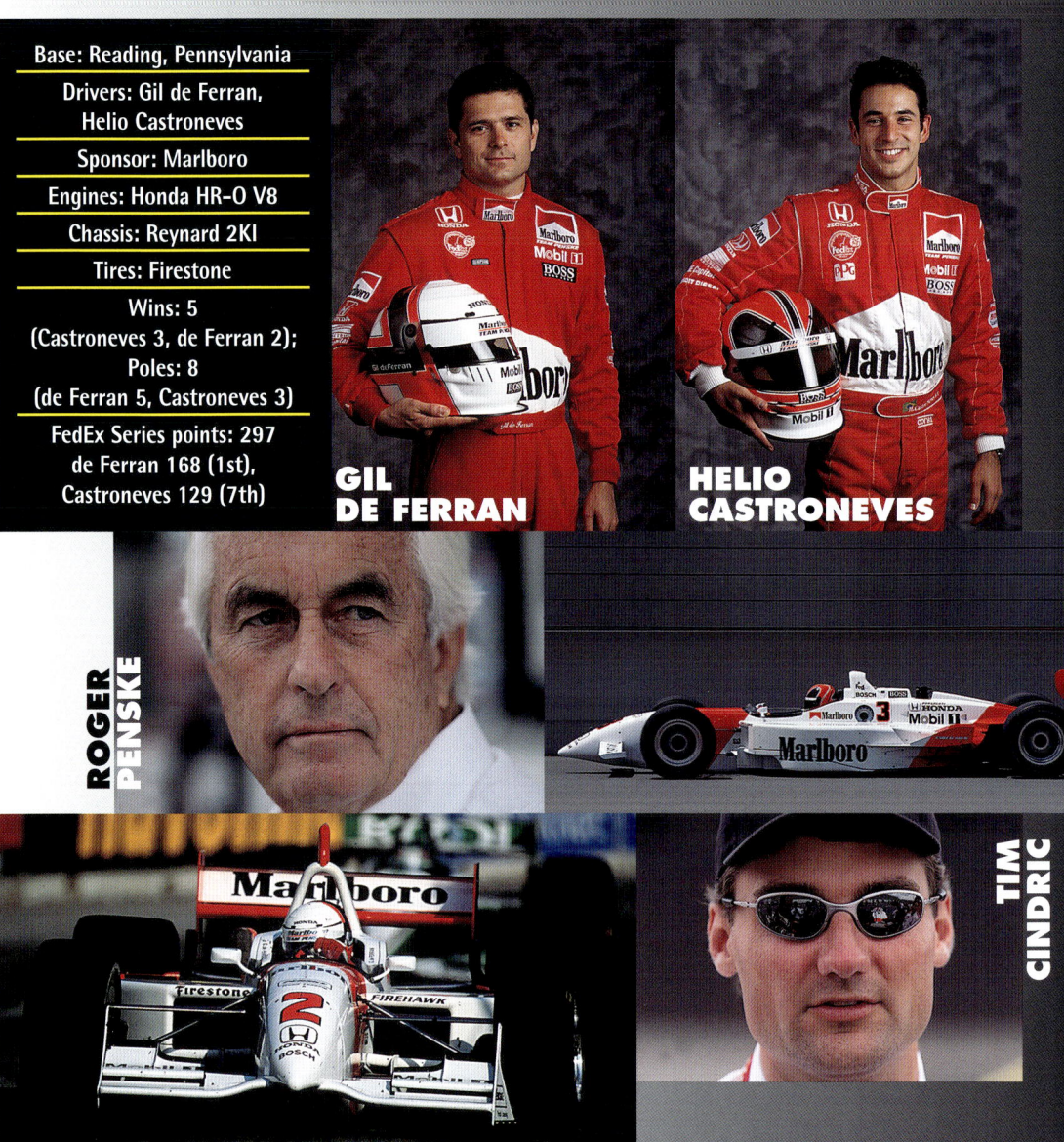

GIL DE FERRAN

HELIO CASTRONEVES

ROGER PENSKE

TIM CINDRIC

GIL DE FERRAN – MARLBORO HONDA/REYNARD 2KI

HELIO CASTRONEVES – MARLBORO HONDA/REYNARD 2KI

CROWN JEWELS

Clutch shown actual size

The F1 carbon/carbon clutch you see here represents the pinnacle of perfection in AP Racing technology.

Less than 4" in diameter, it is able to handle the energy of an F1 start and continue to perform its race function with unerring reliability. Reliability that has been a factor in the success of F1 world champions for the last 33 years.

This technology and level of service is applied to all forms of racing - including Champcars, IRL and Indy Lights - and our state of the art clutches and brakes are to be found on most entries - including the current Indy 500 Champion.

115mm 4 plate push type sintered clutch

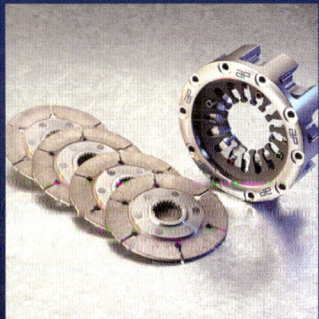
115mm 4 plate pull type sintered clutch

Six piston MMC monobloc caliper

ap Racing

The Science of Friction

AP Racing, Wheler Road, Coventry, CV3 4LB, England. Tel +44 (0)24 7663 9595 Fax +44 (0)24 7663 9559 email: sales@apracing.co.uk

website: www.apracing.com

TARGET/CHIP GANASSI RACING

TEAM-BY-TEAM REVIEW

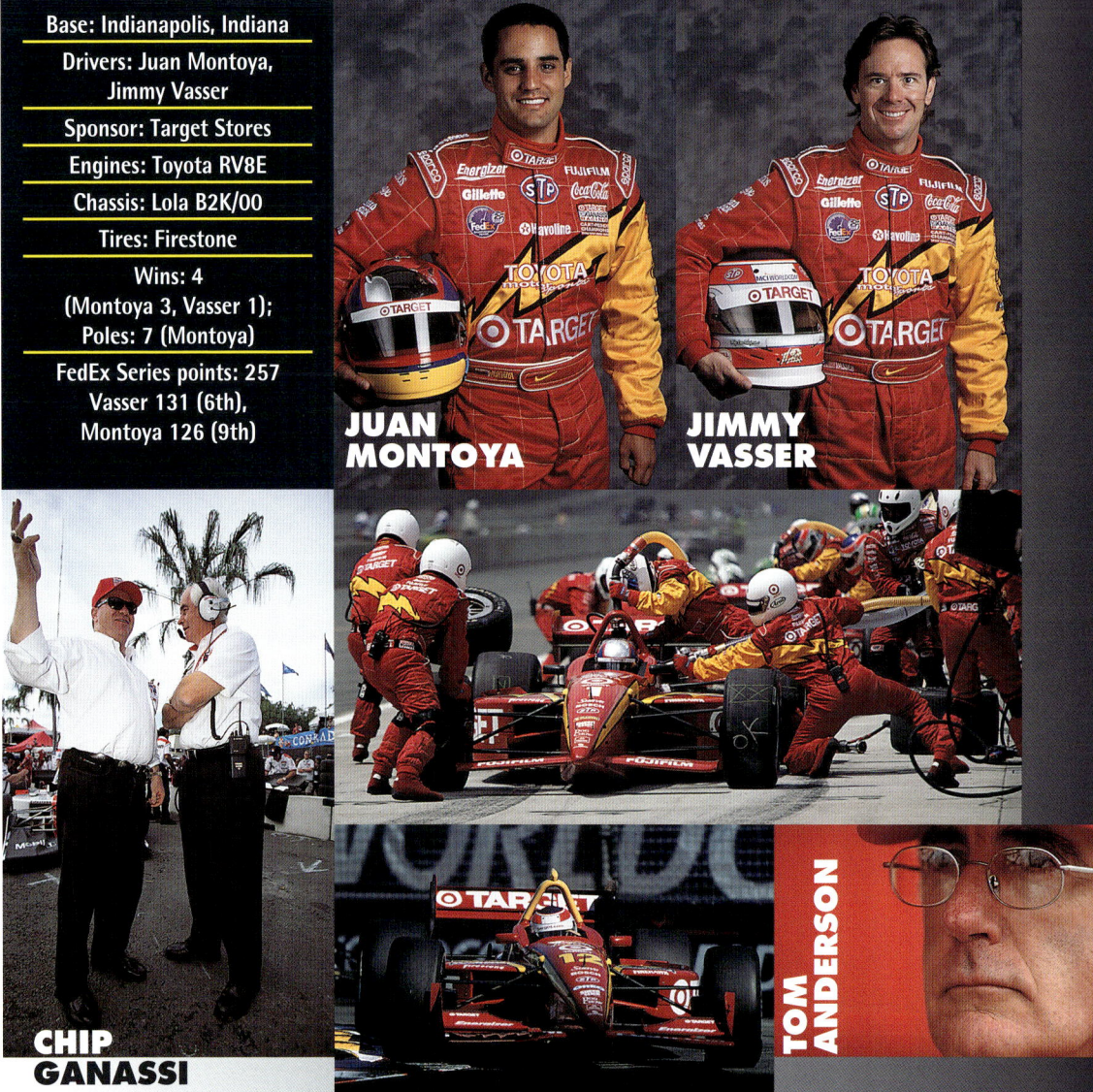

Base: Indianapolis, Indiana
Drivers: Juan Montoya, Jimmy Vasser
Sponsor: Target Stores
Engines: Toyota RV8E
Chassis: Lola B2K/00
Tires: Firestone
Wins: 4 (Montoya 3, Vasser 1);
Poles: 7 (Montoya)
FedEx Series points: 257
Vasser 131 (6th),
Montoya 126 (9th)

JUAN MONTOYA

JIMMY VASSER

CHIP GANASSI

TOM ANDERSON

SOME critics wondered what on earth Chip Ganassi was thinking at the end of the 1999 season when he turned his back on Honda, which had supplied the motive force behind a record-breaking four straight CART Championships, in favor of a new relationship with Toyota. At the time, of course, Toyota had achieved next to nothing. But when Scott Pruett snared the pole for the '99 season finale, less than 24 hours after Ganassi made his announcement, people began to pay closer attention...

"It's a hunger that I see in their attitude," declared Ganassi at the time. "[Toyota is] making a huge investment in this formula right now, and I think people that make a huge effort win."

Prescient words. It took time – and perhaps Ganassi made the learning process a little harder than necessary by switching from Reynard chassis to Lolas – but the new combo soon began to show its paces in winter testing. Defending series champion Juan Montoya and '96 champ Jimmy Vasser both expressed themselves more than happy with the new RV8E motor's horsepower and tractability, and while there were a few reliability concerns initially, these had been pretty much eradicated prior to the season opener.

The Toyota engineers must take much of the credit, but Ganassi's team hardly missed a beat either, as the organizational and motivational skills of managing director Tom Anderson continued to be crucial assets.

There is little doubt, however, that Ganassi's triumphant foray at Indianapolis blurred some of the team's focus, especially in terms of its road-course setup – much to Toyota's chagrin – and it must be said that while Montoya worked well with new race engineer Bill Pappas, the Colombian certainly grew to miss the intimacy he had enjoyed with Mo Nunn, who had left to establish his own team. Nevertheless, with even a modicum of good fortune, Ganassi might have been looking at a record-extending fifth straight championship title.

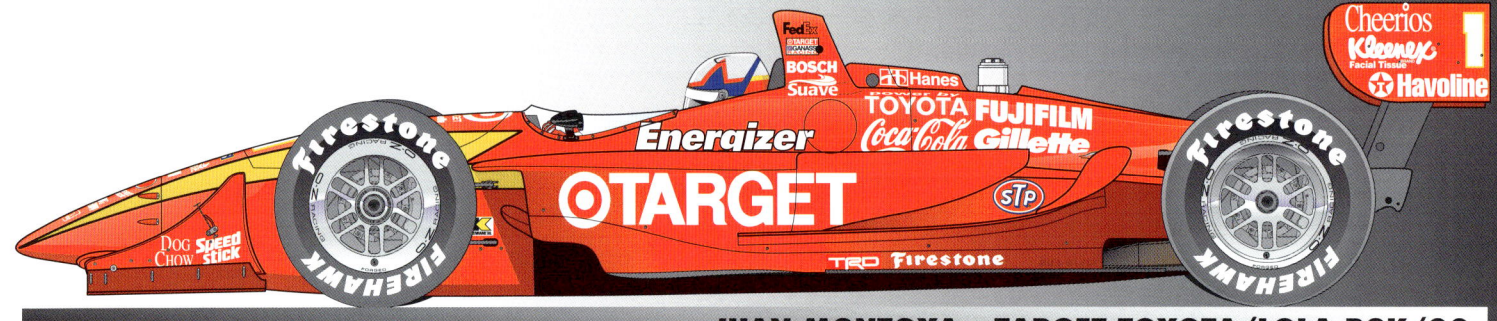

JUAN MONTOYA – TARGET TOYOTA/LOLA B2K/00

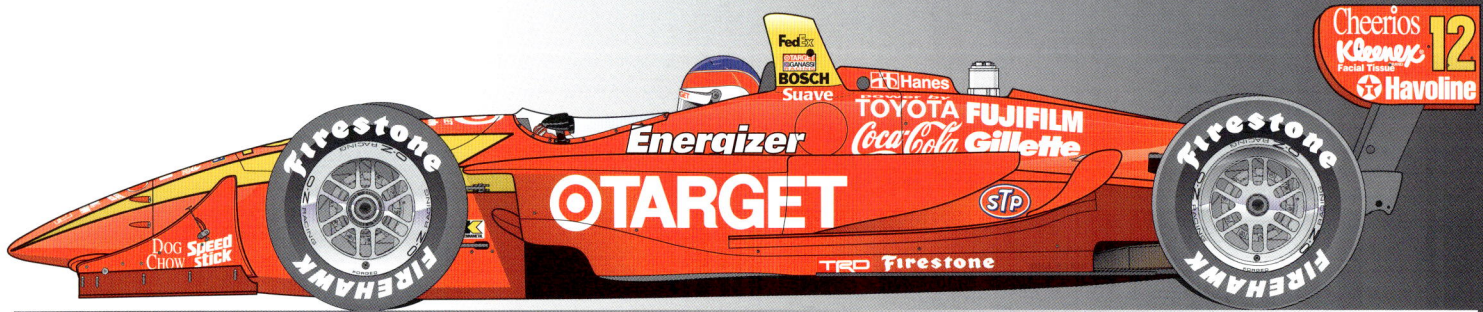

JIMMY VASSER – TARGET TOYOTA/LOLA B2K/00

Every win is for the kids.

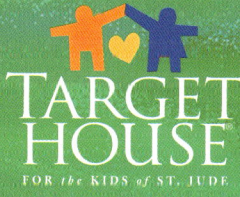

TARGET HOUSE
FOR *the* KIDS of ST. JUDE

St. Jude Children's Research Hospital
ALSAC • Danny Thomas, Founder

TARGET CHIP GANASSI RACING

©2000 Target Corporation

Our thanks to Target Chip Ganassi Racing for every little victory: $25 for every lap led; $1,000 for every pole position; and $5,000 for every race won. These generous donations go to Target House, a home away from home for kids undergoing long-term treatment for cancer and other life-threatening diseases at St. Jude Children's Research Hospital. Thanks to the team's unflagging generosity, the kids have a warm, safe place to stay. No matter how the race ends, you'll always be first in our hearts.

TEAM RAHAL

TEAM-BY-TEAM REVIEW

So near and yet so far. Such always seems to be the case with Team Rahal. When Max Papis set the pace at Spring Training, then sped to a glorious first-ever victory in the season opener at Homestead-Miami Speedway, the prospects for the season looked exceedingly good. But, as has happened so often in recent years, the reality proved to be somewhat different. Papis scored only two more top-five finishes, including a second at Detroit, and was usually outpaced by his rookie teammate Kenny Bräck.

The personable Swede soon asserted his authority on the team, thanks in no small measure to the engineering ability – and people skills – of Don Halliday, who was an excellent addition to the team after being lured from Team KOOL Green over the winter. Bräck out-qualified Papis in 15 of the 20 races and soon developed into a bona fide championship challenger. He failed to win a race, but it wasn't for a lack of effort or commitment. Papis, meanwhile, often seemed to bear the brunt of misfortune, and his composure was sorely tested during a disappointing season that had promised so much.

It's difficult to figure out what went wrong – if anything. The absence of the team's figurehead, Bobby Rahal, who was kept more than busy by his new-found commitment as interim president and CEO of CART, surely wasn't a major factor, since general manager Scott Roembke had overseen a loyal and hardworking crew at the team's base in Hilliard, Ohio, for several years. The equipment package also was well-proven, with Reynard once again securing the Constructor's Championship, and Ford Cosworth winning its first Manufacturer's Championship in five years.

But hey, Bräck remained with a shot at the championship until midway through the final race, which was an impressive achievement, and Indy Lights front-runner Casey Mears underscored his – and the team's – capabilities by turning a one-off drive in a third WorldCom-backed entry at California Speedway into a stunning fourth-place finish.

Base: Hilliard, Ohio
Drivers: Kenny Bräck, Max Papis, Casey Mears
Sponsors: Miller Lite, Shell Oil Products, WorldCom
Engines: Ford Cosworth XF
Chassis: Reynard 2KI
Tires: Firestone
Wins: 1 (Papis); **Poles:** 0
FedEx Series points: 235
Bräck 135 (4th),
Papis 88 (14th),
Mears 12 (23rd)

MAX PAPIS / KENNY BRÄCK / BOBBY RAHAL / DON HALLIDAY / CASEY MEARS

KENNY BRÄCK – SHELL FORD COSWORTH/REYNARD 2KI

MAX PAPIS – MILLER LITE FORD COSWORTH/REYNARD 2KI

TEAM KOOL GREEN

TEAM-BY-TEAM REVIEW

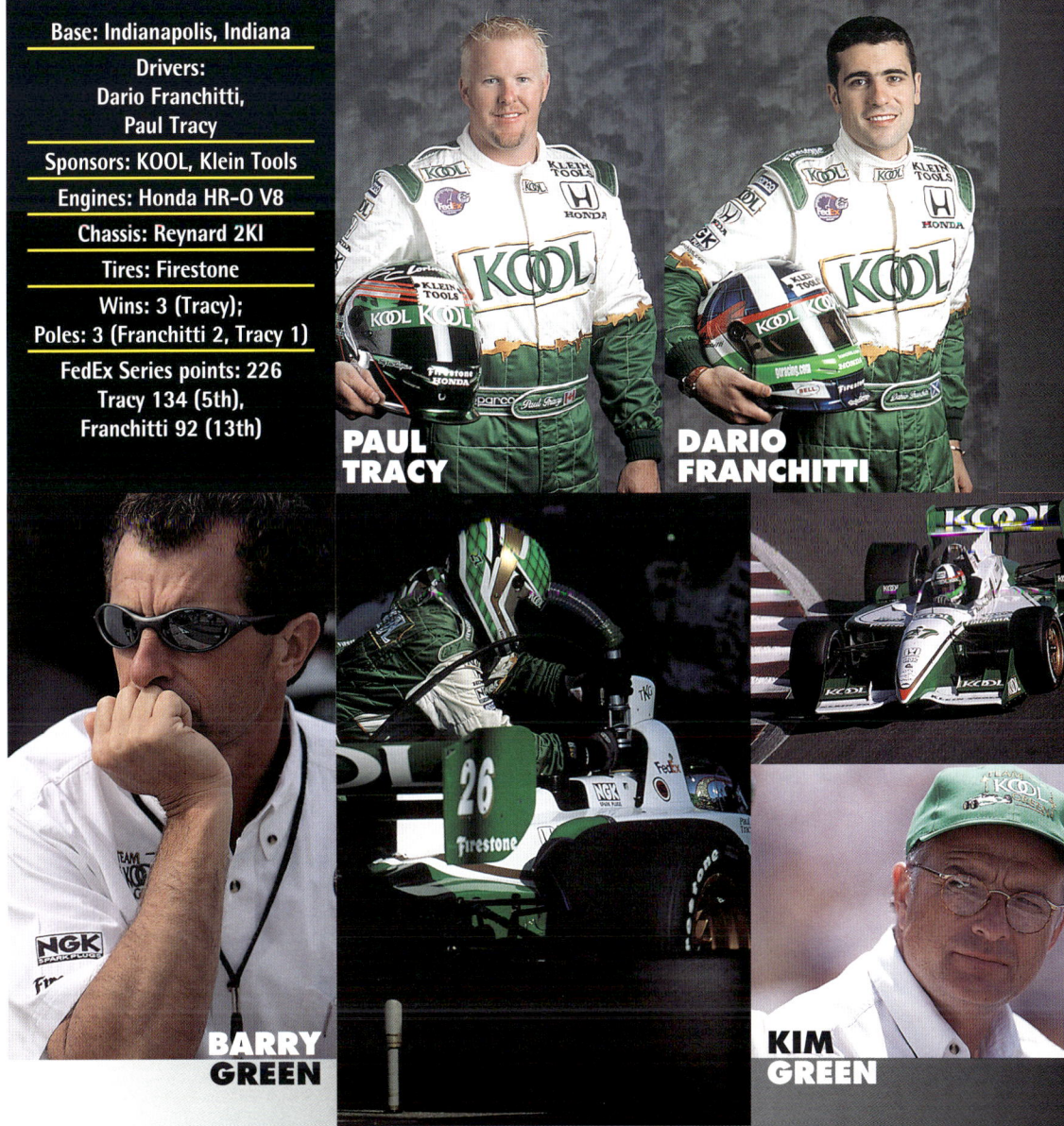

Base: Indianapolis, Indiana
Drivers: Dario Franchitti, Paul Tracy
Sponsors: KOOL, Klein Tools
Engines: Honda HR-0 V8
Chassis: Reynard 2KI
Tires: Firestone
Wins: 3 (Tracy);
Poles: 3 (Franchitti 2, Tracy 1)
FedEx Series points: 226
Tracy 134 (5th),
Franchitti 92 (13th)

PAUL TRACY
DARIO FRANCHITTI
BARRY GREEN
KIM GREEN

FOURTH and 13th in the final championship standings for Paul Tracy and Dario Franchitti, respectively, was not what anybody at Team KOOL Green had in mind at the beginning of the season. Far from it. Franchitti, in particular, was absolutely determined to go one better than in '99, when he finished equal on points with Juan Montoya, only to lose the title on a tie-breaker. Sadly, his year could not have got off to a worse start: the personable Scotsman crashed heavily at Spring Training, suffering a head injury and a broken pelvis that would keep him out of action until just prior to the first race.

Franchitti's supreme physical fitness enabled him to bounce back ahead of schedule, but the effects of the accident took rather longer to overcome. First, having missed almost all of his preseason test program, he took several races to regain his rhythm. He struggled also to come to grips with the loss – both personally and technically – of race engineer Don Halliday, who had returned to his roots in the Columbus, Ohio, area and was working instead with Team Rahal. Franchitti never enjoyed the same intimate relationship with Steve Challis.

That said, Franchitti out-qualified teammate Tracy 12 times in the final 15 races. Furthermore, in the second half of the season, only once did he start lower than the second row of the grid – a remarkable achievement given the series' extreme competitiveness. Strangely, though, his year was marked by an inordinate number of mistakes. He was also involved in first-lap skirmishes at Nazareth, Portland, Toronto, Houston and Surfers Paradise. Not all were of his making, but effectively they quashed his title aspirations.

Generally speaking, the KOOL Honda/Reynards were rarely a match for the Marlboro cars in terms of outright speed, but Tracy, curiously off the pace in qualifying (he started among the top five only six times), posted some brilliant rearguard efforts in the races and was almost always a factor to be reckoned with.

PAUL TRACY – KOOL HONDA/REYNARD 2KI

DARIO FRANCHITTI – KOOL HONDA/REYNARD 2KI

NEWMAN/HAAS RACING
TEAM-BY-TEAM REVIEW

Base:	Lincolnshire, Illinois
Drivers:	Michael Andretti, Christian Fittipaldi
Sponsors:	Big Kmart, Texaco/Havoline, Route 66
Engines:	Ford Cosworth XF
Chassis:	Lola B2K/00
Tires:	Firestone
Wins:	3 (Andretti 2, Fittipaldi 1); Poles: 0
FedEx Series points:	223 Andretti 127 (8th), Fittipaldi 96 (12th)

MICHAEL ANDRETTI **CHRISTIAN FITTIPALDI**

CARL HAAS

THE Y2K season ended on a high note for team owners Paul Newman and Carl Haas when Christian Fittipaldi secured a fine victory at California Speedway. At the same time, the euphoria was tempered by the realization that an era had passed. Michael Andretti had driven his last race for the Chicago-area organization (before embarking on a new adventure with Team Green), and thus, for the first time since its formation in 1983, with Michael's father, Mario, at the helm, the team would be going forward without an Andretti behind the wheel.

"This team feels like family," said the younger Andretti, who scored 31 of his 40 Champ Car victories with Newman/Haas Racing, but bowed out as the innocent victim in a chain-reaction crash. "It's sad to leave this way after all of the success we have had together."

The early exit capped a thoroughly disappointing end to a season in which Andretti had started out as one of the championship favorites. He lived up to expectations, too, by winning twice and leading the point standings through the summer months before the onset of an astonishing sequence of misfortunes.

Fittipaldi also encountered a litany of disappointments, which belied his growing confidence and understated ability. The vast majority of the problems were beyond the team's control. Overall, indeed, its Ford-powered Lolas were consistently competitive. Race engineers Peter Gibbons and Todd Bowland had a good handle on the cars (following Haas' decision to part company with Swift at the conclusion of the '99 campaign), and with technical director Brian Lisles they maintained a constant program of development and improvement. Team manager John "TZ" Tzouanakis, together with chief mechanics Donny Hoevel (Andretti) and Kevin Chambers (Fittipaldi), worked ceaselessly to overcome the effects of a relatively tight ship (in terms of manpower), and there is no doubt that they deserved better than eighth and 12th respectively in the final points tally.

MICHAEL ANDRETTI – BIG KMART/TEXACO HAVOLINE FORD COSWORTH/LOLA B2K/00

CHRISTIAN FITTIPALDI – BIG KMART/ROUTE 66 FORD COSWORTH/LOLA B2K/00

WE APOLOGISE FOR
THE LACK OF EXCITEMENT
IN THIS ADVERT.
WE PREFER TO SAVE
IT FOR THE TRACK.

COSWORTH *Racing*

It's in the blood

www.cosworthracing.com

PPI MOTORSPORTS

TEAM-BY-TEAM REVIEW

A TOTAL of 172 FedEx Series points represented by far the best tally for Cal Wells III in the six years since establishing his CART team in partnership with Frank Arciero. Then again, the 2000 season was the first time that his team had been on anything approaching a level playing field.

Toyota stepped up to the plate with a substantially improved RV8E motor, and Wells, having split, somewhat acrimoniously, with Arciero and regrouped under his own PPI (Precision Preparation, Inc.) banner, found his cars suddenly running at the front.

Cristiano da Matta emerged as the potential star, which wasn't at all surprising given his pedigree as a former Indy Lights champion. He had developed an excellent rapport with race engineer Iain Watt during his rookie campaign and, after some early-season problems, especially in qualifying, he became a consistent frontrunner. His – and the team's – maiden victory at Chicago was well deserved. But the Brazilian's new-found status brought unexpected scrutiny from several other potential employers. Da Matta allowed himself to be distracted by the political machinations and thus did not achieve his full capability in the latter part of the year.

Wells also had too much on his plate. He expended an enormous effort on establishing himself in the NASCAR Winston Cup arena, having snared two significant sponsorship deals with McDonald's and Tide, and alienated much of his Champ Car team by proposing a relocation to his new base in North Carolina. The result was that Wells found himself ostracized from the Toyota bandwagon, which was a great shame, since PPI really was on the verge of becoming a true powerhouse team.

One other bright spot, however, was the realization that Oriol Servia had developed into a legitimate contender. His achievement in winning the '99 Indy Lights crown was minimized by the fact that he failed to win a race, but the likeable Spaniard's tenacity and prodigious speed – highlighted by a third-place finish in Detroit – marked him as a man to watch.

Base:	Rancho Santa Margarita, California
Drivers:	Cristiano da Matta, Oriol Servia
Sponsors:	Pioneer, WorldCom, Telefonica
Engines:	Toyota RV8E
Chassis:	Reynard 2KI
Tires:	Firestone
Wins:	1 (da Matta); Poles: 0
FedEx Series points:	172 da Matta 112 (10th), Servia 60 (15th)

CRISTIANO DA MATTA
ORIOL SERVIA
CAL WELLS III
JOHN DICK
IAIN WATT

CRISTIANO DA MATTA – PIONEER/WORLDCOM TOYOTA/REYNARD 2KI

ORIOL SERVIA – TELEFONICA TOYOTA/REYNARD 2KI

bring on the traffic

No matter how fast and furious your business gets, WorldCom has the network to handle every bit of your voice, data, and Internet traffic.

In the U.S. alone, we own and operate 45,000 route miles of long distance fiber, with dedicated Internet facilities in more than 70 cities. Outside the U.S., our 60-Gbps transatlantic (joint-venture) cable system connects to our wholly owned pan-European telecommunications network—and more than 5,000 buildings throughout Europe. And then there's the WorldCom/UUNET Internet network, the world's premier IP-only backbone.

On land and under sea, the WorldCom network continues to expand worldwide—in Latin America, Asia, and the Pacific Rim—so your voice, data, and Internet traffic will have fewer detours to other networks.

Get in the fast lane with WorldCom's extensive portfolio of integrated products and services. Visit www.worldcomracing.com.

WorldCom is the official communications company of Championship Auto Racing Teams.
©2000 WORLDCOM, Inc. All rights reserved.

PLAYER'S/FORSYTHE RACING

TEAM-BY-TEAM REVIEW

THERE were no wins for Team Player's in 2000, but Jerry Forsythe's two French-Canadian drivers each came close on several occasions. Rookie Alex Tagliani, in particular, burst onto the scene in impressive style, running with the leaders at Homestead before earning a penalty for a pit-lane violation. His Champ Car debut was eerily similar to that of the late, lamented Greg Moore, who also might have won his first-ever Champ Car race – at Homestead in '96 – but for a virtually identical infraction.

Tagliani, again like Moore, also led handsomely at Rio, where he qualified on pole and was in command of the race until his inexperience caught him out at a late restart. There followed something of a midseason slump, which saw him qualify outside the top ten in six straight races, although he bounced back into the spotlight at Road America, where he grasped the lead at the start and proceeded to take control...until felled by a driveline failure. It was a cruel blow.

There were similarly mixed results for Carpentier. Far more easygoing than his extremely intense new teammate, Carpentier never gelled with Tagliani in the way that he had with Moore. In addition, as the season progressed, he felt that his support within the team had been eroded. His year wasn't helped either by a domestic accident that broke his arm and left him sidelined for three races, or a monumental crash during practice at Laguna Seca, which saw his Player's Ford/Reynard come to rest upside-down on the wrong side of the safety barriers. Nevertheless, Carpentier displayed real ability and, if not for the fact that he seemed to attract any bad luck that was going, would surely have claimed even more than his respectable tally of seven top-five finishes, highlighted by an excellent second at Gateway.

Memo Gidley also starred in three drives as substitute for Carpentier, and might have been in a position to win at Rio, but for an engine that was down on power.

Base: Indianapolis, Indiana
Drivers: Patrick Carpentier, Alexandre Tagliani, Memo Gidley
Sponsors: Player's Ltd., Indeck
Engines: Ford Cosworth XF
Chassis: Reynard 2KI
Tires: Firestone
Wins: 0; **Poles:** 1 (Tagliani)
FedEx Series points: 159
Carpentier 101 (11th),
Tagliani 53 (16th),
Gidley 5 (of 20, 20th)

PATRICK CARPENTIER — **ALEXANDRE TAGLIANI**

JERRY FORSYTHE

MEMO GIDLEY

PATRICK CARPENTIER – PLAYER'S/INDECK FORD COSWORTH/REYNARD 2KI

ALEXANDRE TAGLIANI – PLAYER'S/INDECK FORD COSWORTH/REYNARD 2KI

THE WORK

Over 650 pages and 700 colour pictures on Teams, Drivers, Cars, Key people, Mechanics, Engineers, Sponsors, Suppliers, Engine manufacturers, Media, Tracks, Officials, Addresses, Fan clubs, Web sites, E-mail...

Who they are
What they do
How to reach them

Why buy hundreds of books
when one official work answers
all your questions ?

Visit our Web site: www.whoworksin.com

Phone: +44 7000 WHO WORKS or +44 1304 214 494 - Fax: +44 1304 212 030

THE WORKS

Over 650 pages and 700 colour pictures on Teams, Drivers, Cars, Key people, Mechanics, Engineers, Sponsors, Suppliers, Engine manufacturers, Media, Tracks, Officials, Addresses, Fan clubs, Web sites, E-mail...

Who they are
What they do
How to reach them

   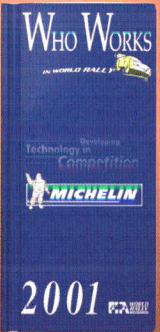

Why buy hundreds
of books when one
official work answers
all your questions ?

Visit our Web site: www.whoworksin.com

Phone: +44 7000 WHO WORKS or +44 1304 214 494 - Fax: +44 1304 212 030

PACWEST RACING GROUP

TEAM-BY-TEAM REVIEW

THERE were precious few bright moments during another desperately disappointing season for Bruce McCaw's PacWest Racing Group. The off-season winter testing program brought the promise of significant improvement from the Mercedes-Benz engines, with both Mauricio Gugelmin and Mark Blundell expressing public confidence in the latest IC108F powerplant. As it turned out, the motors were rarely a match for the Fords, Hondas and Toyotas. And even when the Mercs exhibited enough power to be competitive, they were hopelessly out-classed in terms of fuel consumption – and reliability. Against those odds, not even the combined talents of Gugelmin and Blundell were ever likely to prove enough.

Gugelmin, though, in particular, managed to rise to the occasion. Sometimes the personable Brazilian's relaxed manner tended to mask his competitive urge, but it was there all the same. Usually he was close to (or ahead of) the similarly-equipped and highly rated Tony Kanaan, and produced Mercedes' only top-five finish of the year when he claimed a brilliant second at Nazareth in May.

Poor Blundell, by contrast, never really got to grips with the car at all. He out-qualified Gugelmin only six times in 20 races, and whenever he seemed poised for an improvement, he would be struck down by unreliability or sheer bad luck. The season finale was a case in point. Blundell was hindered by an engine problem from the start and, for a change, Lady Luck seemed to be on his side when the rain set in to cause an overnight delay. Daryl Fox's crew installed a fresh motor for the restart, and Blundell soon began to work his way forward. Then, mere moments after he had drafted past Helio Castroneves to take the lead, ka-BOOM, the engine let go in the biggest possible way.

By then, Blundell already had been informed that his services would not be required in 2001. Sadly, the Englishman never had a fair chance to show that, at age 34, he still belonged at the top.

Base: Indianapolis, Indiana
Drivers: Mauricio Gugelmin, Mark Blundell
Sponsors: Nextel, Motorola
Engines: Mercedes-Benz IC108F
Chassis: Reynard 2KI
Tires: Firestone
Wins: 0;
Poles: 0
FedEx Series points: 57
Gugelmin 39 (17th),
Blundell 18 (21st)

MAURICIO GUGELMIN

MARK BLUNDELL

BRUCE McCAW

MAURICIO GUGELMIN – NEXTEL MERCEDES-BENZ/REYNARD 2KI

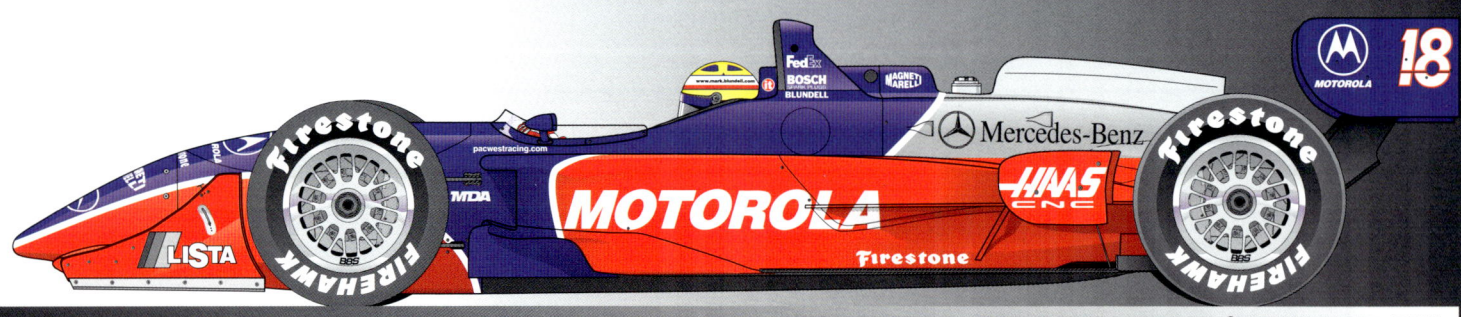

MARK BLUNDELL – MOTOROLA MERCEDES-BENZ/REYNARD 2KI

End the frustrations of calling while abroad.

Nextel Worldwide entitles the bearer to one number for use both at home and abroad. To make and receive calls without the hassle of calling cards, juggling two phones, or excessive pricing.

ONE PHONE. ONE NUMBER. WORLDWIDE.

Nextel Worldwide℠ and the *i*2000™ phone.

When you have an *i*2000 phone, you have access to the Nextel National Network — the largest guaranteed all-digital wireless network in the U.S. — and more than 70 countries around the world. With international per-minute rates comparable to international calling cards.* To end the frustrations, order this phone for $199 by calling 1-800-NEXTEL 9.

Nextel phones are manufactured by Motorola, Inc.

Nextel. How business gets done.℠   **1-800-NEXTEL 9**   nextel.com

MO NUNN RACING
TEAM-BY-TEAM REVIEW

WITH the considerable benefit of hindsight, Morris Nunn must have wondered whether he and former public relations supremo Rod Campbell had made the right decision when they elected to form their own team following the '99 season. Nunn, of course, had carved an enviable reputation as a race engineer during a successful stint with Target/Chip Ganassi Racing that yielded an unprecedented four straight CART titles with three different drivers. After every new triumph he claimed to be contemplating retirement, only to be lured back into the fold each time. But secretly, he hankered after a return to team ownership, and when he and Campbell, who had sold his hugely successful business for a tidy sum, started talking seriously – and were encouraged in the process by PacWest owner Bruce McCaw and Mercedes-Benz – they soon reached common ground.

Base:	Indianapolis, Indiana
Drivers:	Tony Kanaan, Bryan Herta
Sponsors:	Hollywood
Engines:	Mercedes-Benz IC108F
Chassis:	Reynard 2KI
Tires:	Firestone
Wins: 0;	
Poles: 0	
FedEx Series points: 28	
Kanaan 24 (19th),	
Herta 4 (of 26, 18th)	

TONY KANAAN

BRYAN HERTA

Nunn and Campbell had collaborated previously, during the former's hand-to-mouth Formula 1 venture with his own Ensign team in the 1970s. This time their efforts were rather more lavishly funded. But, unfortunately, hardly any more successful.

The Brazilian tobacco giant, Hollywood, procured the services of Tony Kanaan (who was bought out of his contract with Jerry Forsythe) for the new team, but even the ebullient South American's prodigious skills could not overcome the handicap of under-performing engines. That said, Kanaan frequently moved up to challenge the leaders, only to encounter some kind of difficulty. In the opener at Homestead, he lost a potential podium finish when he was penalized for a pit-lane infraction. In the finale at Fontana, he was scything through the order and had just taken over second place when the engine failed comprehensively. It was that kind of year.

"Well, I was trying to do what I promised to do, and that is send Mercedes off with a win," said Kanaan. "I was really excited because I had a very good car, and Mercedes has been really good to me and the team all year long, so they really deserved a good send-off."

MO NUNN

TONY KANAAN – HOLLYWOOD MERCEDES-BENZ/REYNARD 2KI

WALKER RACING

TEAM-BY-TEAM REVIEW

AFTER losing the services of Gil de Ferran, who took the opportunity of joining Marlboro Team Penske, and sponsor Valvoline, which ended its association with major-league open-wheel racing, Derrick Walker was left with a single-car effort in 2000 for Japanese rookie Shinji Nakano. The prospects looked quite good initially. Nakano, 29, a veteran of Formula 1, impressed the team with his personable nature, his feedback and his speed during early testing, and a solid eighth on his debut – his first-ever oval race – at Homestead.

Unfortunately, Nakano endured a heavy crash during his maiden test on a one-mile oval, at Milwaukee, and was hospitalized with a neck injury.

Bryan Herta stood in for Nakano at Long Beach and was on the pace immediately. The under-utilized Californian qualified and finished fifth, despite a quick spin, although a lack of time for testing – and his unfamiliarity with the team – caught up with him at Rio, where he was never on the pace. Herta traveled to Japan on standby, but could only sit back and watch as Nakano clambered stiffly back into the cockpit of the Avex Group Honda/Reynard. He qualified a respectable 11th in front of his home fans and turned some good laps in the race, but was hindered by understeer on full tanks and finished out of the points in 14th. After skipping the race at Nazareth due, once more, to a lack of testing, Nakano continued to struggle at Milwaukee, crashing heavily in the warmup, then spinning again early in the race. Basically, his confidence had been shot to pieces, and the lack of a teammate to compare notes with meant that he found it impossible to make up the lost ground. His task was made all the more difficult, of course, by the intense competition.

The only other bright moment came at Houston, where Nakano ran well in practice and made good progress in the race to equal his season-best finish, eighth.

Base:	Indianapolis, Indiana
Drivers:	Shinji Nakano, Bryan Herta
Sponsors:	Avex Group, Alpine Car Stereo
Engines:	Honda HR-0 V8
Chassis:	Reynard 2KI
Tires:	Firestone
Wins: 0;	
Poles: 0	
FedEx Series points: 22 Nakano 12 (24th), Herta 10 (of 26, 18th)	

SHINJI NAKANO

BRYAN HERTA

AL BODEY

BRYAN HERTA

SHINJI NAKANO – AVEX GROUP HONDA/REYNARD 2KI

DALE COYNE RACING

TEAM-BY-TEAM REVIEW

DALE Coyne reverted to his team's original name following the untimely death of partner Walter Payton, and once again worked busily to field a two-car team in all 20 races. Japan's Takuya Kurosawa, a veteran of Formula Nippon competition in his homeland, joined up for what was intended to be a full program, and drove sensationally well in the second race at Long Beach. He moved into the lead by virtue of a typically fine strategic call by the canny Coyne, and proceeded to maintain a good turn of speed that seemed sure to pay off with a top-five finish until he was involved in a couple of incidents.

Kurosawa, however, like countryman Nakano and fellow rookie Fontana, struggled to come to grips with the ovals and endured several hard crashes, which ultimately resulted in surgery to relieve the effects of a nagging injury. Brazilian veteran Gualter Salles took over the driving duties on an interim basis with the approval of new Korean sponsor Next Media (whose orange livery, representing its *Sports Today* newspaper, had replaced the purple of outgoing Internet provider MTCI). But after three disappointing races, Salles was replaced by Alex Barron, who, despite not having driven a Champ Car in almost a year, put the team back on the map with two spectacular drives in the final two races of the season.

Salles had driven three more races in Coyne's second Ford/Lola at the beginning of the season, only to lose his ride when Swift Engineering reached an agreement with Coyne to field a factory-tended car following the termination of its agreement with Jerry Forsythe. Tarso Marques was installed in the new Swift 011.c, but the car failed to live up to expectations and usually the young Brazilian ran at the back of the field. The lone exception was in Houston, where the Swift suddenly displayed a good turn of speed, only to break down while Marques was running legitimately in the top ten.

Base: Plainfield, Illinois
Drivers: Takuya Kurosawa, Gualter Salles, Alex Barron, Tarso Marques
Sponsors: MTCI, *Sports Today*, Panasonic, Refricentro
Engines: Ford Cosworth XF
Chassis: Lola B2K/00, Swift 011.c
Tires: Firestone
Wins: 0; **Poles:** 0
FedEx Series points: 18
Marques 11 (25th),
Barron 6 (27th),
Kurosawa 1 (29th)

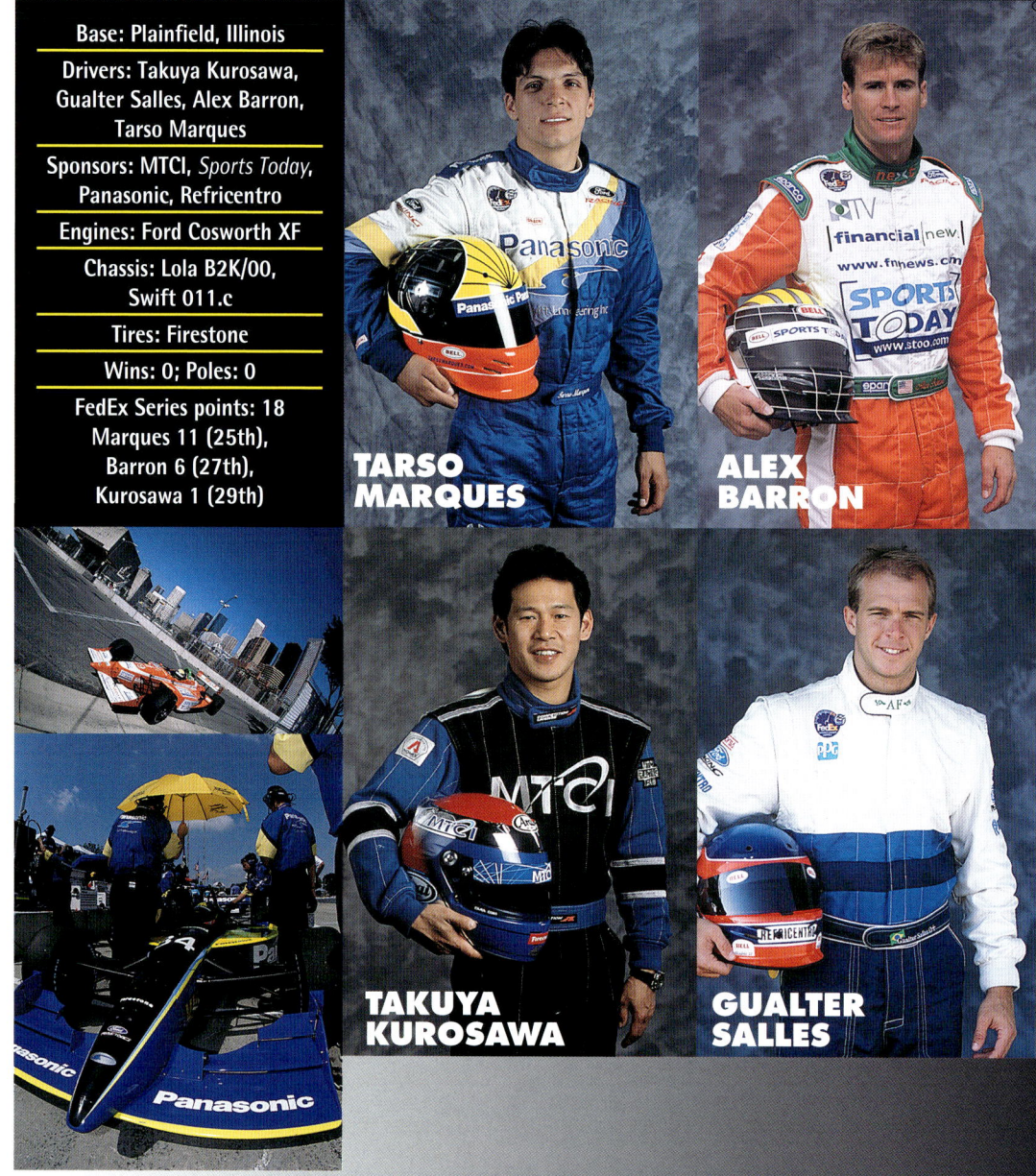

TARSO MARQUES

ALEX BARRON

TAKUYA KUROSAWA

GUALTER SALLES

TARSO MARQUES – PANASONIC FORD COSWORTH/SWIFT 011.c

TAKUYA KUROSAWA – *SPORTS TODAY* FORD COSWORTH/LOLA B2K/00

BETTENHAUSEN MOTORSPORTS
TEAM-BY-TEAM REVIEW

AFTER a dreadfully disappointing '99 season with underfunded and outclassed Japanese rookie Shigeaki Hattori, Tony Bettenhausen looked to be on the verge of turning around his team's fortunes when he signed promising Mexican Michel Jourdain Jr. and staunch supporter Herdez to long-term contracts. Then, tragically, the tight-knit group was faced with despair when Bettenhausen, his wife Shirley and long-time friends Russ Roberts and Larry Rangel were killed when their light plane crashed into a wooded Kentucky hillside on Valentine's Day.

Shaken to the core, but led by Bettenhausen's long-time right-hand men, technical director Tom Brown and team manager Joe Ward, the team held together, regrouped and embarked on the season with heavy hearts and a strengthened resolve. Later, they were joined by Keith Wiggins, the former owner of Pacific Racing, which had won just about everything there was to win in the European junior formulae before foundering in Formula 1. Wiggins had regained his feet during a spell with Lola Cars (which also was fighting for survival), but still had aspirations of fielding his own race team. He parted company with the chassis manufacturer in midseason and took over the helm of the team in partnership with Herdez, which had solidified its commitment to Bettenhausen Motorsports.

Once the team's future had been assured, Brown was able to focus more on his core strengths – making the car and driver go faster. The loyal crew, headed by chief mechanic Vince Kremer, rallied to the cause, and an eighth-place run in Detroit and seventh at Surfers Paradise, equaling his career best, were indicative of Jourdain's improvement. Appalling engine reliability proved to be an insurmountable handicap, however, and the likeable 24-year-old Mexican's progress was stymied by nine straight DNFs (did not finish) in the middle of a difficult campaign. Nevertheless, Jourdain's fifth year in the Champ Cars brought a career-best haul of 18 FedEx Series points and the promise of better times ahead.

Base:	Indianapolis, Indiana
Driver:	Michel Jourdain Jr.
Sponsor:	Herdez
Engines:	Mercedes-Benz IC108F
Chassis:	Lola B2K/00
Tires:	Firestone
Wins:	0;
Poles:	0
FedEx Series points:	18 (22nd)

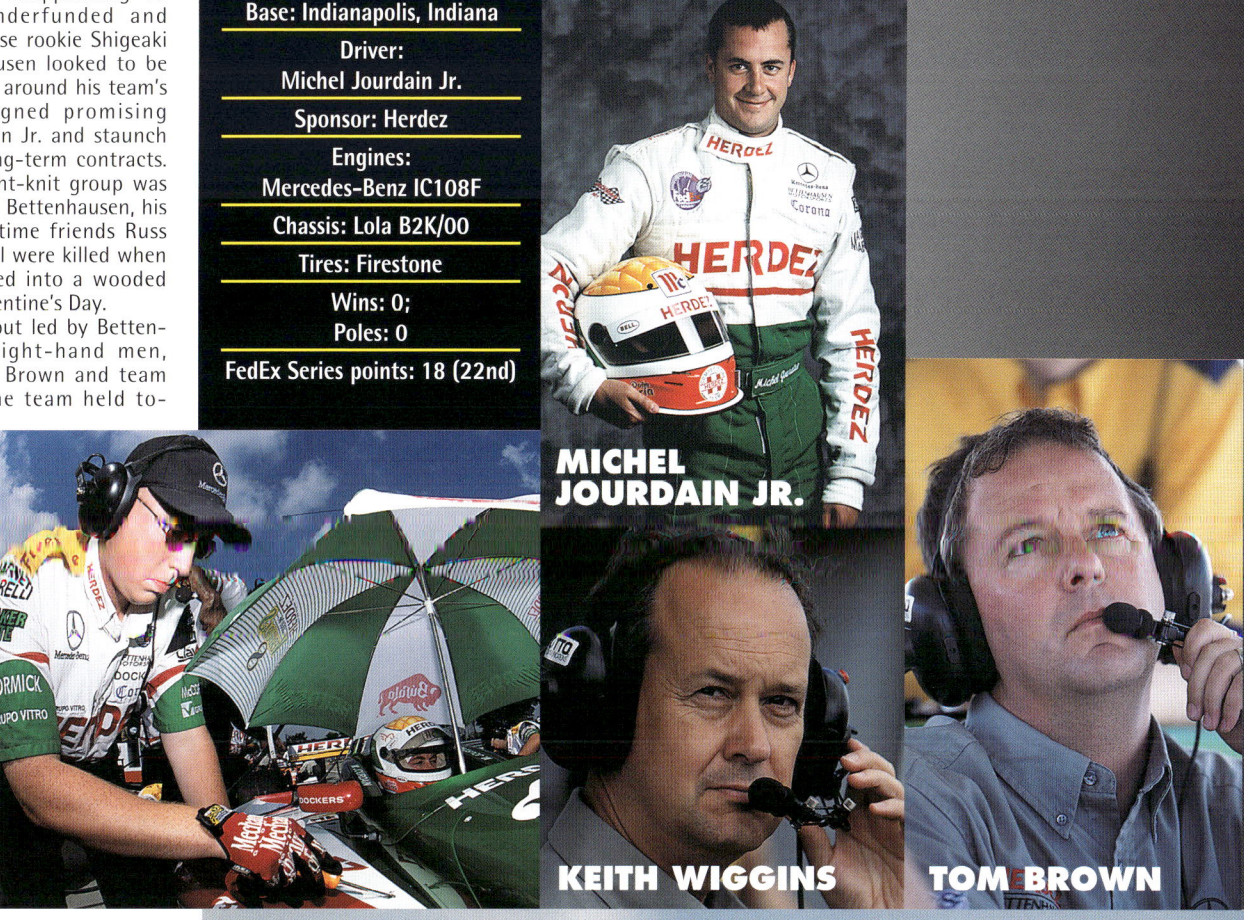

MICHEL JOURDAIN JR.

KEITH WIGGINS   **TOM BROWN**

MICHEL JOURDAIN JR. – HERDEZ MERCEDES-BENZ/ LOLA B2K/00

DELLA PENNA MOTORSPORTS

TEAM-BY-TEAM REVIEW

WHATEVER else might be said about John Della Penna, one has to give the man full credit for his never-say-die effort and his dedication to the CART cause. After struggling through the '99 season, during which he helped Toyota immeasurably with its development program, the California-based Argentinian encountered an uphill battle in raising enough sponsorship to continue at the elite level. Enter countryman Norberto Fontana, a veteran of Formula 3000, Formula Nippon (in Japan) and, briefly, Formula 1, who tested impressively during the winter at Sebring and secured a modicum of support from his homeland. Della Penna duly made a late decision to enter Fontana for the first race in place of established American Richie Hearn.

The lack of testing time and, especially, a total absence of any previous oval-track experience haunted him, however, and after a series of accidents, Fontana was replaced at midseason by Memo Gidley. The gifted Californian gelled immediately with the team and soon began to score some excellent results. He proved to be a real racer, too, notably at Michigan, where he unlapped himself on the entire field; at Road America, where he charged from 18th to a career-best sixth; and in Vancouver, where he was headed for another strong finish until the Toyota/Reynard's gearbox failed.

Indy Lights grad Jason Bright also made a fine debut in front of his home crowd at Surfers Paradise, running as high as fifth before being involved in an incident that was not of his making.

This small, hardworking team was expertly managed by Phil Howard, although Della Penna's insistence on engineering the car himself proved controversial and unpopular, which led to many internal conflicts – and the abrupt departure of original race engineer Diane Holl. An extremely tight budget also restricted progress. Nevertheless, Toyota's staunch refusal to continue its supply of engines into the 2001 season, irrespective of whether Della Penna could raise a sufficient budget, represented an uncalled-for slap in the face.

Base: Indianapolis, Indiana
Drivers: Norberto Fontana, Memo Gidley, Jason Bright
Sponsors: SonicView, DirecTV, Queensland
Engines: Toyota RV8E
Chassis: Reynard 2KI
Tires: Firestone
Wins: 0; **Poles:** 0
FedEx Series points: 17 Gidley 15 (of 20, 20th), Fontana 2 (28th)

NORBERTO FONTANA 
MEMO GIDLEY   
JASON BRIGHT

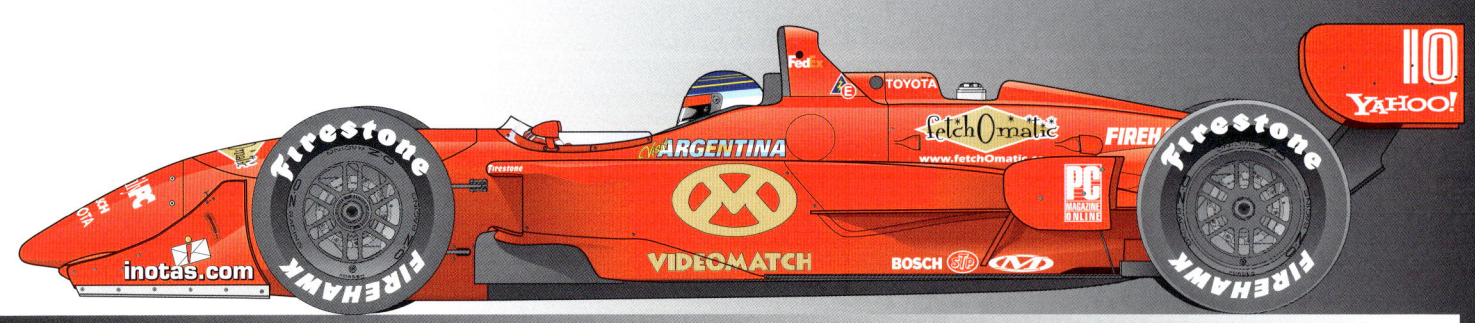

NORBERTO FONTANA – VIDEOMATCH TOYOTA/REYNARD 2KI

FORSYTHE CHAMPIONSHIP RACING

TEAM-BY-TEAM REVIEW

JERRY Forsythe originally planned to field a factory-backed Honda/Swift in all 20 races for gifted American Bryan Herta, but when the car (delivered shortly before Spring Training) proved extremely disappointing in early tests, Forsythe opted out of the first few events. Then he cited a disagreement with CART over franchise issues, whereupon Swift canceled its agreement and the team was put on ice.

Mindful of Herta's spectacular record at Laguna Seca, where he had never failed to qualify on the front row, Forsythe decided to enter a Ford/Reynard at the California road course. Using a car borrowed from the sister Player's/Forsythe team, and following only one brief test session, Herta underscored his ability by qualifying and finishing an amazing fourth, comfortably quickest of the Ford contingent. Indubitably it was one of the best single performances of the season, bringing equal credit to the Hilliard, Ohio-based team, led by general manager Tony Brunetti, team manager Steve Dickson, chief mechanic Steve Ragan and race engineer Martin Pare. Sadly, planned additional outings were canceled due to a lack of sponsorship.

Base: Hilliard, Ohio
Driver: Bryan Herta
Sponsors: Rockingham Motor Speedway, Indeck
Engines: Ford Cosworth XF
Chassis: Reynard 2KI
Tires: Firestone
Wins: 0; Poles: 0
FedEx Series points: 12
Herta 12 (of 26, 18th)

BRYAN HERTA – ROCKINGHAM MOTOR SPEEDWAY FORD/REYNARD 2KI

ARCIERO-PROJECT RACING GROUP

TEAM-BY-TEAM REVIEW

GERMAN-born Andreas Leberle was obliged to sit out the 1999 season, but he never gave up his hopes of re-entering the CART fray. Finally, less than a month before the first race, Leberle reached an agreement with veteran car owner Frank Arciero. Their new partnership was made possible through the procurement of various sponsorship deals by Brazilian Luiz Garcia Jr. Initially the small team, managed by veteran Barry Brooke, borrowed a '99 Mercedes/Reynard from Player's/Forsythe Racing, and the hastily prepared car was shaken down by Garcia just a few days before the Homestead opener.

The first of two 2000-spec Reynards was delivered in time for the third round in Rio, but Garcia was always playing catch-up due to an almost total lack of testing. The former Indy Lights contender scored points on five occasions for the tightly budgeted team, whose high point was being presented with the PPG Color & Design Award, in recognition of its spectacular Hollywood livery, at the season-ending awards banquet in Los Angeles.

Base: Zionsville, Indiana
Driver: Luiz Garcia Jr.
Sponsors: Hollywood, Embratel-21, Tang
Engines: Mercedes-Benz IC108F
Chassis: Reynard 99I/2KI
Tires: Firestone
Wins: 0; Poles: 0
FedEx Series points: 6 (28th)

LUIZ GARCIA JR. – HOLLYWOOD MERCEDES-BENZ/REYNARD 2KI

THE ENGINES

TEAM-BY-TEAM REVIEW

Ford Cosworth
Production base: Northampton, England; U.S. base: Torrance, California
Wins: 7 (Andretti 2, Fernandez 2, Moreno 1, Papis 1, Fittipaldi 1);
Poles: 2 (Moreno 1, Tagliani 1)
Laps led: 913

Photograph: Ford Motor Company

FORD Motor Company and its partner, Cosworth Racing, put a huge effort into developing an all-new, lightweight, super-compact engine for the 2000 season, and right from the word go it was clear that the motor would be the one to beat. The Ford Cosworth XF had completed over 6,000 miles of testing prior to Spring Training, whereupon Team Rahal's Max Papis and Kenny Bräck showed the fruits of all that labor by setting a torrid pace. Papis went on to win the first race at Homestead. As the season progressed, however, Ford Cosworth remained locked in a tight battle with Honda.

Ultimately, it was entirely appropriate that Christian Fittipaldi should wrap up the coveted CART Manufacturer's Championship for Ford Cosworth by winning the finale at Fontana, since he had been the first to put the engine through its paces during the fall of 1999.

"It's been a very, very challenging year," said CART program manager Bruce Wood. "People have been working 20-hour days to try and get these engines built, and it's been really difficult to support ten cars all season. When we began the season, we knew there would be days when it would be hard and days when it would be worth it, and this is one of those days that makes it worth it."

Honda
Production base: Santa Clarita, California
Wins: 8 (Tracy 3, Castroneves 3, de Ferran 2);
Poles: 11 (de Ferran 5, Castroneves 3, Franchitti 2, Tracy 1)
Laps led: 840

Photograph: Honda Performance Development

HONDA Performance Development came up just short in the Manufacturer's Championship, despite winning more poles and more races than Ford Cosworth. The latest HR-0 Turbo V8 was a further evolution of the motors that had won four consecutive driver's championships and three of the last four Manufacturer's Championships, and was no less effective. Some of the Honda drivers expressed some doubt about the new engine's competitiveness at Spring Training, but they were told "not to worry." In fact, it has become a trait that Honda does not show its full hand until it is time for the real business to begin. Sure enough, Honda was a major force, as shown by its tally of 11 poles. Only once in the final 15 races was Honda not represented on the front row of the starting grid. The HR-0, in fact, was generally reckoned to be the best engine in terms of drivability, and was always especially strong on the road and street circuits.

Ultimately, however, Honda's decision to supply only five cars (following the withdrawal of Forsythe Championship Racing) was to prove decisive. At Cleveland, in particular, all of its cars fell by the wayside, whereas Ford took a maximum score of 22 points. It was the first time in 83 races, dating back to 1995, that Honda had failed to score any points. It was never able to make up the deficit.

Toyota
Production base: Costa Mesa, California
Wins: 5 (Montoya 3, da Matta 1, Vasser 1);
Poles: 7 (Montoya)
Laps led: 1,023

Photograph: Toyota Racing Development

WOW, what a difference! After four years of Champ Car competition, all Toyota Racing Development had to show for its efforts was a best finish of fourth and a solitary pole position, gained in the final race of the 1999 season. From that seed, however, Toyota felt empowered to go for broke in 2000. Its most emphatic move came in capturing the signature of defending four-time champion team owner Chip Ganassi on a long-term contract and, clearly, he would not have made the switch from Honda for financial reasons alone. Indeed, he was convinced that Toyota would provide competitive engines for the 2000 campaign.

Turns out he was right. The updated RV8E engine, which made a promising, but unconvincing, debut midway through the '99 season in the hands of Richie Hearn, showed well in winter testing and maintained Toyota's progress when Juan Montoya secured the pole for the season opener at Homestead. The Colombian fell by the wayside after 23 laps, but teammate Jimmy Vasser went on to finish third. Later Montoya dominated the races at Motegi and Nazareth, only to be forced out by niggling problems, before finally earning Toyota's first win at Milwaukee. By season's end, he had led 820 laps – more than twice as many as his nearest rival. Toyota had arrived.

Mercedes-Benz
Production base: Brixworth, England; U.S. base: Plymouth, Michigan
Wins: 0;
Poles: 0
Laps led: 54

Photograph: Mercedes-Benz USA

IF the 1999 season was disappointing for Mercedes-Benz, its 2000 campaign was little short of disastrous. For the first time since entering the CART fray in 1995, Mercedes failed to claim either a pole or a win, and, in fact, had only one top-six finish to its credit, gained at Nazareth in May, when Mauricio Gugelmin took second.

The lack of success was frustrating and confusing, since Ilmor Engineering had produced another brand-new engine, the IC108F, to replace its diminutive predecessor, and initial signs were quite promising. Indeed Tony Kanaan led briefly during the opener at Homestead and was in contention for the victory before being penalized for a pit-lane infraction. The Brazilian also ran well at Rio, Motegi and Nazareth, where he led for 39 laps until his pit-stop strategy failed to pay off. Later Gugelmin qualified third with a developmental motor in Cleveland and Kanaan started third in Chicago. But there were no results to match.

Finally, Mercedes pulled the plug on its Champ Car program, citing the need to concentrate more of its resources on Formula 1. And hopes of leaving on a high note were scuppered when, one by one, all of the Mercedes motors failed during the dramatic season finale.

THE CHASSIS
TEAM-BY-TEAM REVIEW

REYNARD
Production base: Bicester, England;
U.S. base: Indianapolis, Indiana
Number of cars built in 2000: 51

Wins: 13
(Tracy 3, Castroneves 3,
de Ferran 2, Fernandez 2, Papis 1,
Moreno 1, da Matta 1);
Poles: 13
(de Ferran 5, Castroneves, 3
Franchitti 2, Moreno 1,
Tagliani 1, Tracy 1)

REYNARDS, as usual, dominated the field in terms of numbers during the 2000 season, with a record total of 51 new 2KI chassis being built for 12 different teams. The competition, however, was intense, with the latest Lola proving to be a match in the majority of races. Nevertheless, Reynard Motorsport cemented its sixth consecutive CART Constructor's Championship and, in fact, has never failed to win the award since it was inaugurated in 1995. Reynard has claimed 78 victories during that time (and 81 in total), compared to only 19 for its nearest rival, Lola.

The latest Reynard challenger bore a strong family resemblance to previous cars, which had evolved from Malcolm Oastler's original 94I design. Indeed, Barry Ward's team of designers clearly adopted the old adage, "If it ain't broke, don't fix it." Nevertheless, there were numerous detail changes to ensure that Reynards remained the cars to beat.

Most of the developments were incorporated as a consequence of revised aerodynamic regulations. Specifically, the width of the underbody exit at the rear of the car had been reduced, which effectively cut the amount of downforce that the cars were able to produce. Reynard responded with a package of subtle changes to the bodywork, plus a substantially revised gearbox, which assisted the underbody airflow and also served to lower the car's center of gravity. The transmission retained its transverse layout, first introduced in 1997, and employed many of the same internal components, although a series of problems were experienced as the season progressed.

As ever, most of the Reynard teams conducted their own development, independent of the factory. The majority purchased time at Reynard's Auto Research Center, a state-of-the-art facility in Indianapolis that incorporates a wind tunnel and a seven-post test rig, although Marlboro Team Penske undertook the most comprehensive development program, utilizing its own vastly experienced staff at Penske Cars in Poole, England.

LOLA
Production base: Huntingdon, England; U.S. base: Lincolnshire, Illinois
Number of cars built in 2000: 19

Wins: 7
(Montoya 3, Andretti 2, Vasser 1, Fittipaldi 1);
Poles: 7
(Montoya)

AFTER a brief hiatus with Swift Engineering, Carl Haas renewed his association with Lola Cars in time for the 2000 season. More than 30 years after Haas became Lola's first North American importer, the relationship flourished again as Lola Cars International, now owned by Martin Birrane, continued to make ground on long-time Champ Car market leader Reynard.

Only two teams employed Lolas on a full-time basis in 1999, but such was the car's promise – and so effective was the sales staff – that well over twice as many cars were built for the 2000 campaign, and, in addition to Newman/Haas Racing, no less a team than the four-time defending champion Target/Chip Ganassi organization also made the switch from Reynard. Clearly, their trust was not misplaced. The overall numeric deficiency proved crucial in the chase for the Constructor's Championship, but Lola still made significant progress, as shown by its tally of seven poles and seven wins, and the fact that its customers led a total of 1,327 laps, or 46.0 percent of the total, compared to Reynard's 53.1 percent.

Ben Bowlby remained in charge of the Champ Car design team, ably assisted in the aerodynamic department by Dr. Mark Handford, who, like Haas, had returned from a three-year sojourn with Swift. Their B2K/00 design had much in common with the previous year's car, but, as with Reynard, employed numerous subtle bodywork improvements. An all-new gearbox also was employed. Stiffer and smaller than its six-year-old predecessor, the latest transmission, which had been developed by Hogan Racing in '99, featured seven forward gears and provided a cleaner rear end to optimize the airflow generated by the new underbody regulations.

A variety of developments were introduced during the season, including, most noticeably, a couple of different nose assemblies. One, used by Newman/Haas, bore a striking resemblance to an earlier Swift design...

THE CHASSIS
TEAM-BY-TEAM REVIEW

SWIFT
Production base: San Clemente, California
Number of cars built in 2000: 4
Wins: 0;
Poles: 0

OVER the previous couple of years, Swift had appeared to be on the verge of toppling Reynard's stranglehold on the Champ Car marketplace. But how quickly things change. The American company's management contrived to alienate all their existing customers, and while the designers had planned to develop their Y2K challenger around the new Ford Cosworth XF engine, news came through in early December to the effect that Forsythe Championship Racing would be fielding the factory Swift effort – using Honda motors. Chief designer Tom Huschilt and his team hurriedly reconfigured the car to accept the larger Honda HR-0 V8, but even with an accelerated production program, the prototype 011.c wasn't ready to run until mid-January. Already it was two months behind rivals Reynard and Lola in terms of on-track development.

Initial road-course tests were encouraging, suggesting that the car provided good mechanical grip; but the first forays on an oval, which placed a premium on aerodynamic efficiency, were little short of disastrous. Bryan Herta was hopelessly off the pace during the traditional Spring Training open test at Homestead, whereupon Jerry Forsythe decreed that his team would not race the car until it was properly competitive.

Within a matter of weeks, Swift and Forsythe had parted company. Instead, Swift elected to go it alone. Honda, however, refused to supply engines, which meant yet another last-minute switch back to Ford following a hastily arranged deal with Dale Coyne Racing.

A revised car was taken to Round Four at Motegi, without having turned a wheel in testing, and it was no surprise to see the Swift at the back of the pack. Nevertheless, it finished, and in the next race, at Nazareth Speedway, survived to claim its first championship point. No expense was spared in attempting to make the car competitive, but to no avail – with one exception, at Houston, where Tarso Marques qualified 11th and ran comfortably inside the top ten before, of all things, a driveshaft broke.

THE TIRES
TEAM-BY-TEAM REVIEW

Firestone
Production base: Akron, Ohio, and Tokyo, Japan

Wins: 20
(Tracy 3, Castroneves 3, Montoya 3, de Ferran 2, Andretti 2, Fernandez 2, Papis 1, Moreno 1, da Matta 1, Vasser 1, Fittipaldi 1)

Poles: 20
(Montoya 7, de Ferran 5, Castroneves 3, Franchitti 2, Tagliani 1, Moreno 1, Tracy 1)

THERE was no real pressure on Firestone at the start of the 2000 CART FedEx Championship Series. Or was there? Arch rival Goodyear had withdrawn from major-league open-wheel competition following a disappointing few years (and the increasing domination by Firestone), which meant that Champ Car racing would begin the new millennium with a monopoly tire supply for the first time since 1994. Firestone, therefore, couldn't be beaten on the race track, but still faced plenty of pressure in being able to provide consistent, durable tires. The only way the Nashville, Tennessee-based giant was likely to make the headlines was if something went wrong.

Well, nothing did go wrong. Firestone Racing's accomplished and dedicated group of engineers could afford to be conservative in the absence of any direct competition, which meant that its tires were more durable and less prone to producing "marbles" – excess rubber that "rolls off" the tread surface and accumulates at the edge of the racing line in the corners – than in the recent past, which added considerably to the quality of the racing.

Consider the comments of Bridgestone/Firestone motorsports director Al Speyer following the dramatic season finale at California Speedway: "Once again today, tires were a very reliable component for all of the teams in a grueling 500-mile event. Max Papis actually ran about 80 laps – over 160 miles – on one set of tires. While teams had trouble with some other car components, tires weren't among them. The Firestone Firehawks performed flawlessly once again. Many teams said they were perfect."

Indeed, that became a familiar refrain as the year progressed. The drivers, too, were delighted with the service provided by Firestone, and none more so than eventual champion Gil de Ferran, who had battled against the grain with Goodyear before joining Marlboro Team Penske – also a newcomer to the Firestone fold – for the 2000 campaign.

"This was my first season with Firestone," noted the Brazilian. "I was battling against Firestone for the last five years of my CART career. I thought I knew how good they were, but when I joined the team and ran Firestones for the first time, I then understood why they were so good. To me, winning the championship with Firestone tires also made it great."

HAZLETON publishing

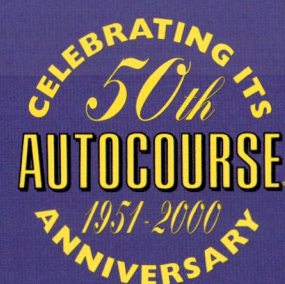
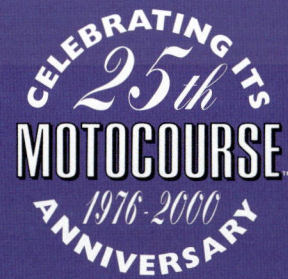

www.hazletonpublishing.com

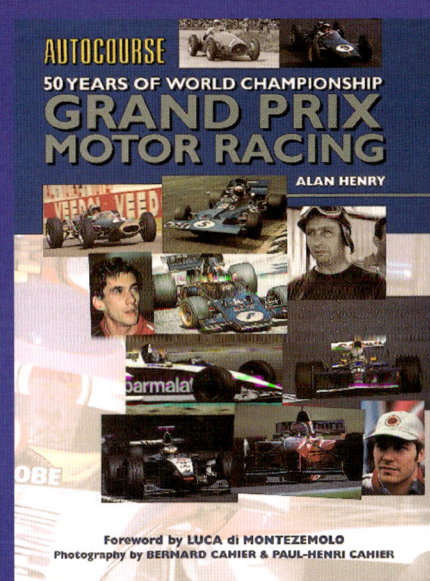
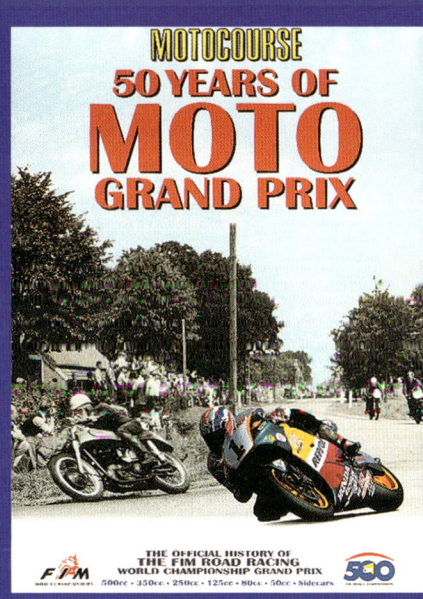
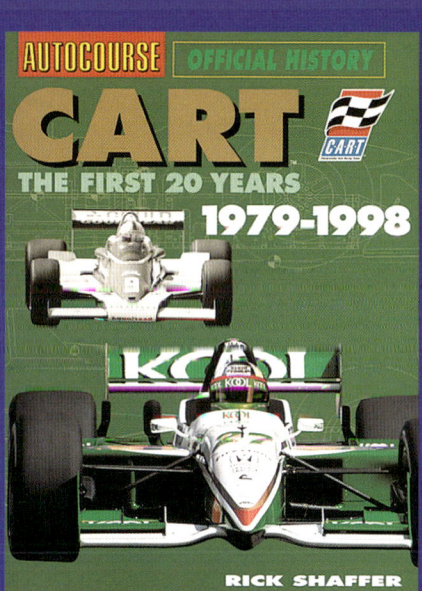

Autocourse 50 Years of World Championship Grand Prix Motor Racing
BY Alan Henry

The 1999 Formula 1 season was the 50th since the creation of the FIA Drivers' World Championship in 1950 and Grand Prix motor racing has evolved into the biggest sporting spectacular in the world. To celebrate this Golden Anniversary, Autocourse has drawn on the vast knowledge accumulated to create a book which aims to capture the flavour of each period and identify the trends and technical developments that characterised it. Comprehensive results and statistics cover five decades.

Hardback, 312 x 232mm, 336pp
Over 280 illustrations
ISBN: 1 874557 78 0   RRP: £40.00
AVAILABLE: NOW

Motocourse 50 Years of Moto Grand Prix Official History
BY Dennis Noyes

The FIM Road Racing World Championship Grand Prix (Moto Grand Prix) has, for 50 years, offered the most exciting motor sport show on earth. This book written, in most cases, by the very journalists who covered each of the periods, re-tells a half-century of Grand Prix wars, from the era when four-stroke British singles still ruled the premier 500 class, through the days of Gileras and MVs up to the present reign of the ubiquitous V4 Japanese two-strokes.

Hardback, 312 x 232mm, 208pp
Over 250 illustrations
ISBN: 1 874557 83 7   RRP: £30.00
AVAILABLE: NOW

Autocourse CART® Official History The First Twenty Years 1979–98
BY Rick Shaffer

In 1998 Championship Auto Racing Teams (CART®) successfully completed its 20th year of competition. Now in its second printing due to popular demand, CART: The First 20 Years 1979–1998 reviews the formation of the organisation and its history to date. This beautifully illustrated book examines CART's political structure, the involvement of major auto manufacturers, tyre companies and race promoters. There are also stories of famous racing families, numerous features and a year-by-year summary of the major developments in the sport.

Hardback, 312 x 232mm, 224pp.
Over 250 illustrations
ISBN: 1 874557 14 4   RRP: £25.00
AVAILABLE: NOW

AVAILABLE FROM ALL GOOD BOOK SHOPS
PLEASE VISIT OUR WEB SITE FOR DETAILS

Hazleton Publishing have produced a limited number of the *Autocourse 50 Years of World Championship Grand Prix Motor Racing*, bound in real leather with embossed lettering and signed by the author Alan Henry and chief photographers, Bernard & Paul-Henri Cahier. Each copy is presented in its own slip case.

AVAILABLE DIRECT FROM HAZLETON PUBLISHING @ £195.00 PLUS £10.00 FOR COURIER

To order your copy call Hazleton on: 44 (0) 20 8948 5151 or e-mail us at leatherbooks@hazletonpublishing.com

TRIBUTES
by Jeremy Shaw

TONY BETTENHAUSEN, 1951–2000

THE Champ Car world was truly shocked on Monday, February 14, 2000, when news filtered through of a light plane having crashed in rural Kentucky. Aboard were Tony Bettenhausen Jr., an avid private pilot, his wife Shirley and two friends and business associates, Russ Roberts and Larry Rangel. The foursome had been taking a leisurely trip back to their Indianapolis base following the previous week's Spring Training open test session at Homestead-Miami Speedway in Florida. It soon became clear that all had perished instantly.

The Bettenhausens had racing in their blood, and both grew up around the sport. Tony's father, Melvin Eugene "Tony" was a legendary name in the 1950s and early '60s, winning two National Championships before being killed while practicing at Indianapolis in 1961. Tony Jr. was the youngest of three sons, all of whom raced successfully. Older brother Merle's career was cut short by a crash at Michigan in which he lost an arm, while Gary scored four victories during a long career.

Tony Jr. followed in Gary's footsteps by racing first in stock cars, then graduating into the Champ Cars in 1979. He made a total of 103 starts, including 11 at Indianapolis, with a best finish of second at the inaugural Michigan 500 in 1981. Bettenhausen went on to finish a career-best sixth in the point standings and was named Most Improved Driver. He entered the realm of team ownership in 1986, forming the Bettenhausen & Associates team initially in partnership with stalwart supporter Jack Rodgers, neighbor Russ Breeden and longtime friend Roberts.

Bettenhausen himself retired from driving in 1993, but the team continued to flourish. Stefan Johansson and Patrick Carpentier won CART Rookie of the Year honors under Bettenhausen's guidance, in 1992 and '97, respectively. A Champ Car victory continued to prove elusive, but Carpentier came awfully close at Gateway in '97, while another rookie destined for stardom, Helio Castroneves, added another second-place finish at Milwaukee in '98.

Bettenhausen was a "people person" who enjoyed a zest for life. He was a keen golfer and friend to many. Noted journalist Robin Miller summed up "Tony B" best when he said, "He wasn't the best race car driver; he wasn't the best owner of a team or the best businessman; but he was the best person I've ever known."

SHIRLEY BETTENHAUSEN, 1952–2000

SHIRLEY Bettenhausen's father, Jim McElreath, won five Champ Car races, finished four times among the top-three point-scorers in the old USAC National Championship, and continues to race Silver Crown cars well into his 70s. Her brother, James, was killed in a sprint car accident in 1977.

She married Tony the following year and played an integral part in his career, supporting him to the hilt as a driver and assisting with the race team while raising the couple's two daughters, Bryn and Taryn. Shirley also was a staunch supporter of CARA (Championship Auto Racing Auxiliary), the organization made up primarily of driver's wives and girlfriends, which raises a substantial amount of money for charity.

In Memoriam

Russell Lee Roberts, president of Friendly Food Stores, had been friends with the Bettenhausens since the early 1970s. Born and raised in Indiana, he was among the original investors in Bettenhausen Motorsports in 1986 and was an avid hunter and fisherman, who, like Tony B, also loved the game of golf. Russ, 51, was godfather to the Bettenhausen's youngest daughter, Taryn.

Hilario "Larry" Rangel, 49, a native of San Jose Iturbide, Mexico, moved to Southern California in his teens and then on to Indianapolis, where he entered the restaurant business with brothers Raul and Octavio. He became close friends with the Bettenhausens, became a passionate golfer and auto racing fan, and regularly served up Mexican food – and bonhomie – at the team's hospitality bus.

Dick Rathmann, the older of two California-born brothers who competed regularly in the Champ Cars in the 1950s and '60s, died on February 1, aged 74, at his home in Melbourne, Florida. Rathmann, already an accomplished stock car racer, qualified on the pole at Indianapolis at a new track record of 145.974 mph in 1958, only to be involved in the first-lap wreck that claimed the life of Pat O'Connor. Brother Jim went on to win the Indianapolis 500 two years later. After their retirement from racing, the two brothers established a successful car dealership in Melbourne.

FACTS & FIGURES

Position	Driver	Car	Tires	Homestead	Long Beach	Rio de Janeiro	Motegi	Nazareth	Milwaukee	Detroit	Portland	Cleveland	Toronto	Michigan	Chicago	Mid-Ohio	Road America	Vancouver	Monterey	Gateway	Houston	Surfers Paradise	Fontana	Points total
1	Gil de Ferran (BR)	Marlboro Team Penske Marlboro Honda/Reynard 2KI	FS	6pt	7pt	17	9	1	12	9	1	14	6	18	3	2p	25	5	2	8	3pt	23	3p	168
2	Adrian Fernandez (MEX)	Patrick Racing Tecate/Quaker State Ford Cosworth/Reynard 2KI	FS	21	24	1	10	5	8	21	12	7	2	6	5	6	2	3	12	10	7	1†	5	158
3	Roberto Moreno (BR)	Patrick Racing Visteon Ford Cosworth/Reynard 2KI	FS	2	9	6	3	14	5	17	2	1pt	13	23	6	11	4	10	25	3	11	19	2	147
4	*Kenny Bräck (S)	Team Rahal Shell Ford Cosworth/Reynard 2KI	FS	18	17	10	5	3	4	24	6	2	10	22	4	5	3	9	5	11	15	2	13†	135
5	Paul Tracy (CDN)	Team KOOL Green Honda/Reynard 2KI	FS	3	1	3	6	10	15	20	18	19	3	7p	19	16	1	1	11	18	4	17	24	134
6	Jimmy Vasser (USA)	Target/Chip Ganassi Racing Toyota/Lola B2K/00	FS	4	3	2	21	7	13	7	24	8	9	21	8	21	5	6	8	7	1	3	22	131
7	Helio Castroneves (BR)	Marlboro Team Penske Marlboro Honda/Reynard 2KI	FS	25	2	24	13	16	16	1	7pt	21	16p	5†	21	1†	9	20	1p	9	5	6	9	129
8	Michael Andretti (USA)	Newman/Haas Big Kmart/Texaco Ford Cosworth/Lola B2K/00	FS	22	14	9**	1	6	2	13	4	4	1	2	2	8	18	12	14	20†	13	20	19	127
9	Juan Montoya (COL)	Target/Chip Ganassi Racing Toyota/Lola B2K/00	FS	23	19	22	7pt	4pt	1pt	18pt	17	6	24	1	12p	24	15	17	6	1p	2	24p	10	126
10	Cristiano da Matta (BR)	PPI Motorsports Pioneer/WorldCom Toyota/Reynard 2KI	FS	12	25	4	4	13	14	23	5	3	4†	17	1	17	22	7	15	4	14	4	25	112
11	Patrick Carpentier (CDN)	Forsythe Racing Player's/Indeck Ford Cosworth/Reynard 2KI	FS	5	–	–	21	3	5	10	5	7	4	14	7	20	24	9	2	19	5	14		101
12	Christian Fittipaldi (BR)	Newman/Haas Big Kmart/Route 66 Ford Cosworth/Lola B2K/00	FS	7	19	5	11	11	9	19	3	17	17	14	NS	3	14	4	10	12	6	15	1	96
13	Dario Franchitti (GB)	Team KOOL Green Honda/Reynard 2KI	FS	11	23	11	2	23	6	4	9	13	25	3	20	22	12p	2pt	3	24	25	25	23	92
14	Max Papis (I)	Team Rahal Miller Lite Ford Cosworth/Reynard 2KI	FS	1	20	16	8	22	7	2	25	18	8	9	24	4	7	8	16	6	24	16	12	88
15	*Oriol Servia (E)	PPI Motorsports Telefonica Toyota/Reynard 2KI	FS	19	6	25	24	9	19	3	8	23	11	8	15	10	10	11	17	5	9	9**	20	60
16	*Alexandre Tagliani (CDN)	Forsythe Racing Player's/Indeck Ford Cosworth/Reynard 2KI	FS	9	4	13pt	15	19	22	6	13	16	5	16	9	9	13†	18	23	14	16	22	6	53
17	Mauricio Gugelmin (BR)	PacWest Racing Nextel Mercedes/Reynard 2KI	FS	16	10	21	22	2	11	16	19	10	15	13	7	20	16	21	7	19	23	10	17	39
18	Bryan Herta (USA)	Walker Racing Avex Group Honda/Reynard 2KI	FS	–	5	20	–	–	–	–	–	–	–	–	–	–	–	–	–	–	–	–	–	26
		Mo Nunn Racing Hollywood Mercedes/Reynard 2KI	FS								16	9	18											
		Forsythe Championship Racing Ford Cosworth/Reynard 2KI	FS																	4				
19	Tony Kanaan (BR)	Mo Nunn Racing Hollywood Mercedes/Reynard 2KI	FS	10	16	18	16	8	10	NS	–	–	24	16	13	8	14	22	13	10	8	18		24
20	Memo Gidley (USA)	Forsythe Racing Player's/Indeck Ford Cosworth/Reynard 2KI	FS	–	21	8	18																	20
		Della Penna Motorsports DirecTV Toyota/Reynard 2KI	FS								10	10	12	6	16	19	22	21	–	21				
21 =	Mark Blundell (GB)	PacWest Racing Motorola Mercedes/Reynard 2KI	FS	13	8	7	19	17	17	11	20	12	22	19	23	14	11	25	13	23	20	11	15	18
21 =	Michel Jourdain Jr. (MEX)	Bettenhausen Motorsports Herdez Mercedes/Lola B2K/00	FS	14	11	15	12	18	18	8	23	22	19	15	11	15	17	23	24	16	18	7	11	18
23	*Shinji Nakano (J)	Walker Racing Avex Group Honda/Reynard 2KI	FS	8	–	–	14	–	23	15	11	15	14	20	13	19	21	19	26	15	8	21	16	12
23	*Casey Mears (USA)	Team Rahal WorldCom Ford Cosworth/Reynard 2KI	FS	–	–	–	–	–	–	–	–	–	–	–	–	–	–	–	–	–	–	4		12
25	Tarso Marques (BR)	Dale Coyne Racing Panasonic Ford Cosworth/Swift 011.c	FS	–	–	17	12	20	10	15	24	21	12	18	18	23	22	18	15	17	13	7		11
26 =	Luiz Garcia Jr. (BR)	Arciero-PRG Hollywood/Embratel-21 Mercedes/Reynard 99I	FS	17	12	12					20													6
		Arciero-PRG Hollywood/Embratel-21 Mercedes/Reynard 2KI	FS			–	23	15	21	22	14	–	12	11	17	25	24	15	20	25	22	12	NS	
26 =	Alex Barron (USA)	Dale Coyne Racing Sports Today Ford Cosworth/Lola B2K/00	FS	–	–	–	–	–	–	–	–	–	–	–	–	–	13	21	17	12	14	8		6
28	*Norberto Fontana (RA)	Della Penna Motorsports VideoMatch Toyota/Reynard 2KI	FS	15	15	23	NS	20	–	14	–	–												2
		Della Penna Motorsports DirecTV Toyota/Reynard 2KI	FS								–	21	11	20	–									
29	*Takuya Kurosawa (J)	Dale Coyne Racing MTCI Ford Cosworth/Lola B2K/00	FS	24	13	19	20	NS	NS	–														1
		Dale Coyne Racing Sports Today Ford Cosworth/Lola B2K/00	FS							–	12	22	25	23	NS									
	Gualter Salles (BR)	Dale Coyne Racing Ford Cosworth/Lola B2K/00	FS	20	22																			0
		Dale Coyne Racing Refricentro Ford Cosworth/Lola B2K/00	FS		–	14																		
		Dale Coyne Racing Sports Today Ford Cosworth/Lola B2K/00	FS															–	22	23	19			
	*Jason Bright (AUS)	Della Penna Motorsports DirecTV Toyota/Reynard 2KI	FS	–	–	–	–	–	–	–	–	–	–	–	–	–	–	–	–	–	–	18	–	0

Bold type indicates car still running at finish
* rookie † led most laps p pole position NS did not start ** Points deducted per CART Chief Steward

Pole positions

1	Juan Montoya	7
2	Gil de Ferran	5
3	Helio Castroneves	3
4	Dario Franchitti	2
5 =	Roberto Moreno	1
5 =	Paul Tracy	1
5 =	Alexandre Tagliani	1

Nation's Cup

1	Brazil	332
2	United States	256
3	Canada	226
4	Mexico	165
5	Sweden	135
6	Colombia	126
7	Scotland	92
8	Italy	88
9	Spain	60
10	England	18
11	Japan	13
12	Argentina	2
13	Australia	0

Manufacturer's Championship

1	Ford	335
2	Honda	313
3	Toyota	275
4	Mercedes-Benz	74

Constructor's Championship

1	Reynard	394
2	Lola	312
3	Swift	11

Jim Trueman Rookie of the Year

1	Kenny Bräck	135
2	Oriol Servia	60
3	Alexandre Tagliani	53
4 =	Shinji Nakano	12
4 =	Casey Mears	12
6	Norberto Fontana	2
7	Takuya Kurosawa	1
8	Jason Bright	0

2000 FEDEX CHAMPIONSHIP SERIES

JUAN'S SO SERIOUS ABOUT HIS CHAMPIONSHIP, HE DEFENDS IT THIRTY MILES FROM THE NEAREST TRACK.

TRD TOYOTA RACING DEVELOPMENT

When you see Toyota's newest driver, Juan Montoya of Target Chip Ganassi Racing, alone at the finish line, consider the time he spends alone at the gym. Building the strength he needs to grip the wheel at three G's. And the stamina it takes for a CART champion to raise a ten-pound trophy after a grueling race. www.toyota.com/trd **TOYOTA**

©2000 Toyota Motor Sales, U.S.A., Inc.

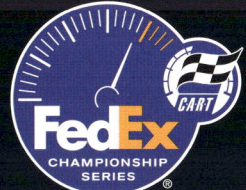

MARLBORO GRAND PRIX OF MIAMI PRESENTED BY TOYOTA, HOMESTEAD–MIAMI SPEEDWAY	72
TOYOTA GRAND PRIX OF LONG BEACH	78
RIO 200, EMERSON FITTIPALDI SPEEDWAY	84
FIRESTONE FIREHAWK 500, TWIN RING MOTEGI	90
BOSCH SPARK PLUG GRAND PRIX PRESENTED BY TOYOTA, NAZARETH SPEEDWAY	96
MILLER LITE 225, THE MILWAUKEE MILE	102
TENNECO AUTOMOTIVE GRAND PRIX OF DETROIT, THE RACEWAY ON BELLE ISLE	108
FREIGHTLINER/G.I. JOE'S 200 PRESENTED BY TEXACO, PORTLAND INTERNATIONAL RACEWAY	114
MARCONI GRAND PRIX OF CLEVELAND PRESENTED BY FIRSTAR, BURKE LAKEFRONT AIRPORT	120
MOLSON INDY TORONTO, EXHIBITION PLACE	126
MICHIGAN 500 PRESENTED BY TOYOTA	132
TARGET GRAND PRIX PRESENTED BY ENERGIZER, CHICAGO MOTOR SPEEDWAY	138
MILLER LITE 200, MID-OHIO SPORTS CAR COURSE	144
MOTOROLA 220, ROAD AMERICA	150
MOLSON INDY VANCOUVER, CONCORD PACIFIC PLACE	156
HONDA GRAND PRIX OF MONTEREY FEATURING THE SHELL 300, LAGUNA SECA RACEWAY	162
MOTOROLA 300, GATEWAY INTERNATIONAL RACEWAY	168
TEXACO/HAVOLINE GRAND PRIX OF HOUSTON	174
HONDA INDY 300, SURFERS PARADISE	180
MARLBORO 500 PRESENTED BY TOYOTA, CALIFORNIA SPEEDWAY	

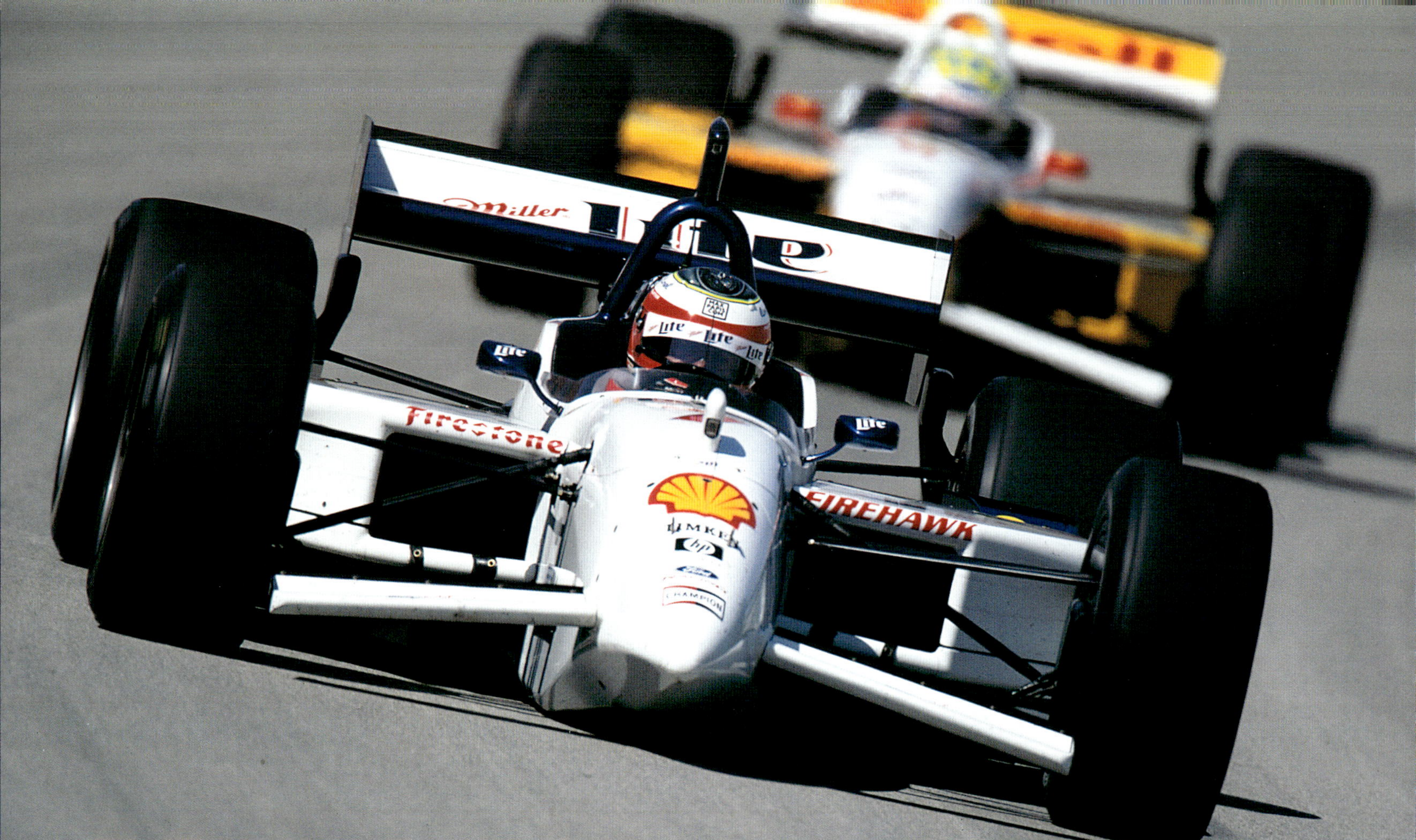

HOMESTEAD

1 - PAPIS

2 - MORENO

3 - TRACY

FEDEX CHAMPIONSHIP SERIES • ROUND 1

Photos: Robert Laberge/Allsport USA

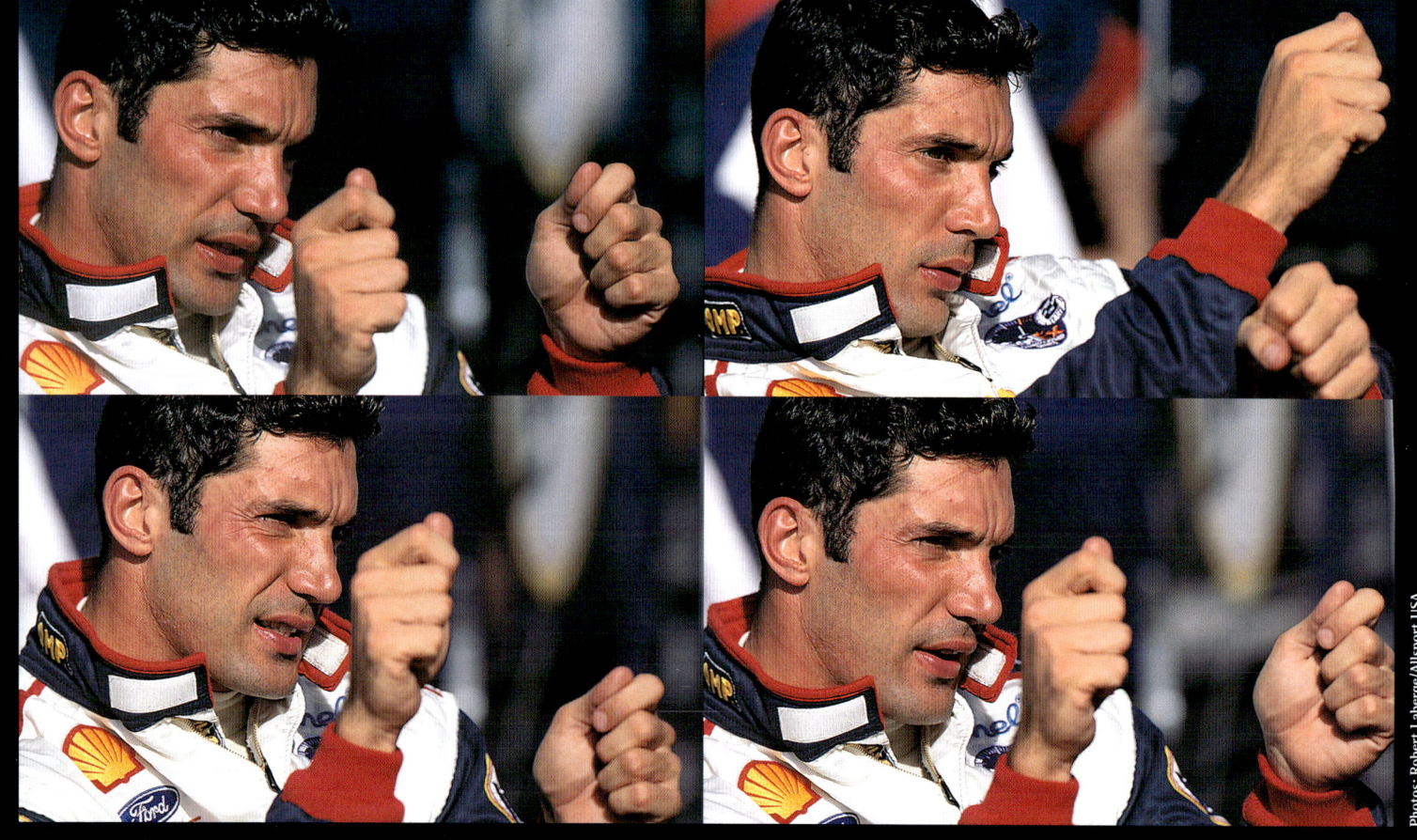

FEDEX CHAMPIONSHIP SERIES • ROUND 1

Team Rahal found the perfect setup for Homestead. Max Papis worked with his engineers to trim the car to perfection, while rookie teammate Kenny Bräck also ran out in front.

Right: Former champions from differing eras, Mario Andretti *(left)* and Alex Zanardi keep an eye on the action during qualifying.

AH, the taste of victory. Max Papis had come so close in the past – at Michigan Speedway in 1999, for example, when he ran out of fuel while leading on the final lap – but the personable Italian finally put the record straight in the CART FedEx Championship Series opener at Homestead-Miami Speedway. His maiden Champ Car win was hugely popular.

Papis displayed the learned patience of a veteran driver. He emerged from the last of two pit stops in second place and, for the next 28 laps, shadowed race leader Paul Tracy's every move. Tracy seemed set to emerge with the first victory of the season, driving a brilliant race for Team KOOL Green after starting a distant 17th, following a troubled practice and qualifying. With only 12 laps to go, a slower car momentarily obstructed Tracy in Turn Four, and that was the opening Papis had waited for so patiently. He carried more momentum off the corner and was able to draft cleanly into the lead before Turn One.

Papis paced himself to the checkered flag, and this time there was no last-minute drama, other than what awaited him in victory circle.

"It's a special day for me because my family and everyone is here with me," said an exuberant Papis, who resides in nearby Miami Beach. "It just feels great, especially coming out of a difficult qualifying situation, when I *almost* hit the wall. I got a lot of congratulations [on his incredible save], but not for what I wanted; I got it right today."

The first CART race of the new millennium fully lived up to expectations. Indeed, Papis became the day's ninth different leader when he took Team Rahal's Miller Lite Ford Cosworth/Reynard 2KI to the front.

"I knew we had a fantastic car," he said. "I just waited for the right opportunity."

Roberto Moreno (Visteon/Patrick Racing Ford/Reynard) finished second, also taking advantage of the traffic situation, which relegated Tracy, aboard his Honda/Reynard, to third.

All four engine manufacturers enjoyed time in the spotlight during the race, with a host of different drivers claiming front-runner status. Defending series champion Juan Montoya quickly displayed the promise of Target/Chip Ganassi Racing's new Toyota/Lola package by vaulting into the lead after passing pole-sitter Gil de Ferran around the outside of Turn One, at the start of the race.

Michael Andretti, twice a winner at Homestead-Miami Speedway, started sixth in Newman/Haas Racing's Big Kmart/Texaco Havoline Ford/Lola, and made a characteristically assertive start, following Montoya around the high line to assume second place as the field streamed onto the back straightaway. Adrian Fernandez (Tecate/Quaker State-Patrick Racing Ford/Reynard) was also on the move, slipping inside de Ferran in Turn Three.

On only his second tour of the 1.502-mile oval, Montoya set what turned out to be the fastest lap of the race (27.826 seconds/194.322 mph), but it was not meant to be his day.

QUALIFYING

A good insight into the intensity of competition in the CART FedEx Championship Series was gained even before qualifying for the first event of the season. In the first official practice session on Friday morning, Patrick Carpentier set the fastest lap (26.590 seconds for an average speed of 203.355 mph) in Jerry Forsythe's Player's Ford Cosworth/Reynard. Later in the day, Tony Kanaan set the pace at 26.437 seconds (204.532 mph) aboard his Hollywood Mercedes/Reynard, fielded by a brand-new team, Mo Nunn Racing. The pace quickened dramatically on Saturday morning when it was the turn of rookie Kenny Bräck to head the timing charts with a lap at 25.815 seconds (209.460 mph). Qualifying, it seemed, was wide open.

Indeed, the one-at-a-time session provided several surprises.

Carpentier's rookie teammate, Alex Tagliani, was the first to make his mark. The young French-Canadian, tenth overall in practice, eclipsed his more experienced partner and eventually wound up an impressive fourth on the starting grid. Adrian Fernandez showed the potency of the Ford/Reynard combination by improving to 26.042 seconds – 0.2 second faster than in practice, despite warmer, windier conditions in the afternoon. Then the Mexican was beaten by Gil de Ferran, who was the first man to dip below the 26-second barrier.

Newman/Haas teammates Christian Fittipaldi and Michael Andretti both tried – and failed – to oust de Ferran. Defending series champion Juan Montoya came within 0.006 second with his Target Toyota/Lola, but still de Ferran held firm.

Bräck, by virtue of being fastest in practice, was the last to take a shot at the Brazilian. He, too, came up short.

"We tried to improve on this morning's setup and we went just a little too far. The car was a little loose," explained the Swede after posting the fifth-fastest time. "Plus, the wind was a factor."

So it was that an emotional de Ferran secured the seventh pole of his Champ Car career in his very first outing for Marlboro Team Penske.

"It's a fantastic sensation right now," said de Ferran. "We put so much into bringing Marlboro Team Penske back up front, and for the first time to be on the pole, you have no idea how I feel. I'm having a hard time putting it into words."

Swiftly gone

NOTABLY absent from the season-opener was the Forsythe Championship Racing team with its factory-assisted Panasonic Swift/Honda and driver Bryan Herta. The saga, which intensified after the Spring Training open test session in February, where the new combination could not match the pace-setters, showed no sign of reaching an early conclusion.

Team owner Jerry Forsythe remained adamant that the team would not race until CART acceded to his wishes and agreed to grant him a third franchise to go along with the pair he owned through his Player's/Forsythe Racing team.

CART regulations, however, restricted all team owners to a maximum of two franchises. CART's public board of directors had previously voted in favor of the principle of changing the rule, but the separate franchise board of directors, comprised of the team owners, subsequently voted down the proposal – at least for the time being.

"He [CART Chairman Andrew Craig] doesn't need to have a meeting [of the team owners]," said Forsythe. "I suggested he send them a letter, like an informal poll, and check either 'Yes' or 'No.' If [they don't vote in my favor] that doesn't give me the chance to come back, it's a moot point, and they've lost a team and an American driver. [But] I remain optimistic that they will make the right decision and we'll be back at the races soon. I can't see why they wouldn't make that decision. It baffles me."

While the posturing continued – and the team members waited anxiously for a decision as to whether or not they would return to the race tracks – the controversy eventually was rendered pointless. Several weeks later, with no resolution in sight, Swift decided to pull the rug from under Forsythe's feet and instead field its own operation in cahoots with Dale Coyne Racing. The new partnership was to make its debut at Motegi in April.

Following the first of only two full-course cautions (when Helio Castroneves' Marlboro Honda/Reynard ground to a halt in Turn Three as a result of engine failure), Montoya met the same misfortune.

"Toyota has done a great job," said an upbeat Montoya, making light of the disappointment. "The engine was very competitive. We did a lot of race simulations and the car was perfect always. It's a shame."

Montoya and Castroneves were soon joined as spectators. Fernandez, who captured the lead from Andretti at the restart, fell victim to an oil leak on lap 50 after 26 laps at the head of the field. At that point, Andretti, too, had been sidelined with engine woes.

Impressive Swedish rookie Kenny Bräck took up the lead in commanding fashion with Team Rahal's Shell Ford/Reynard, but soon it began to look like a race that no one wanted to lead. After six laps at the helm, Bräck slipped to third after being passed by de Ferran during the first round of pit stops, then allowed another rookie, Alex Tagliani, to gain a position by running high in Turn Four. Regaining the lead was not an option, as Bräck also bit the dust.

"We came here to run up front and we definitely did that," declared the Swede after being felled by an oil leak. "There are 20 races in this series so we have a long way to go in the season. I feel good about our team and our chances this year."

Re-enter de Ferran, who dominated the middle stages of the 150-lap Marlboro Grand Prix of Miami. De Ferran took advantage of a brilliant first pit stop by the Marlboro Penske crew to make up for a conservative opening stint. He came under pressure from French-Canadian Tagliani, whose Player's/Forsythe Ford/Reynard closed to within a car length before the pair encountered traffic; but de Ferran's experience shone as he opened up a lead of more than 12 seconds over the next 15 laps.

De Ferran, though, had been running hard instead of concentrating on saving fuel. While his second pit stop [under green-flag conditions] was once again exemplary, moments later he paid the price of not running a leaner fuel mixture and, thus, not being able to extend his fuel range. As the yellow flag came out for Mauricio Gugelmin's Nextel/PacWest Mercedes/Reynard, which had run out of fuel on the back straight, the other contenders made their final pit stops under the caution, and de Ferran was relegated to sixth, where he stayed until the finish.

73

FEDEX CHAMPIONSHIP SERIES • ROUND 1

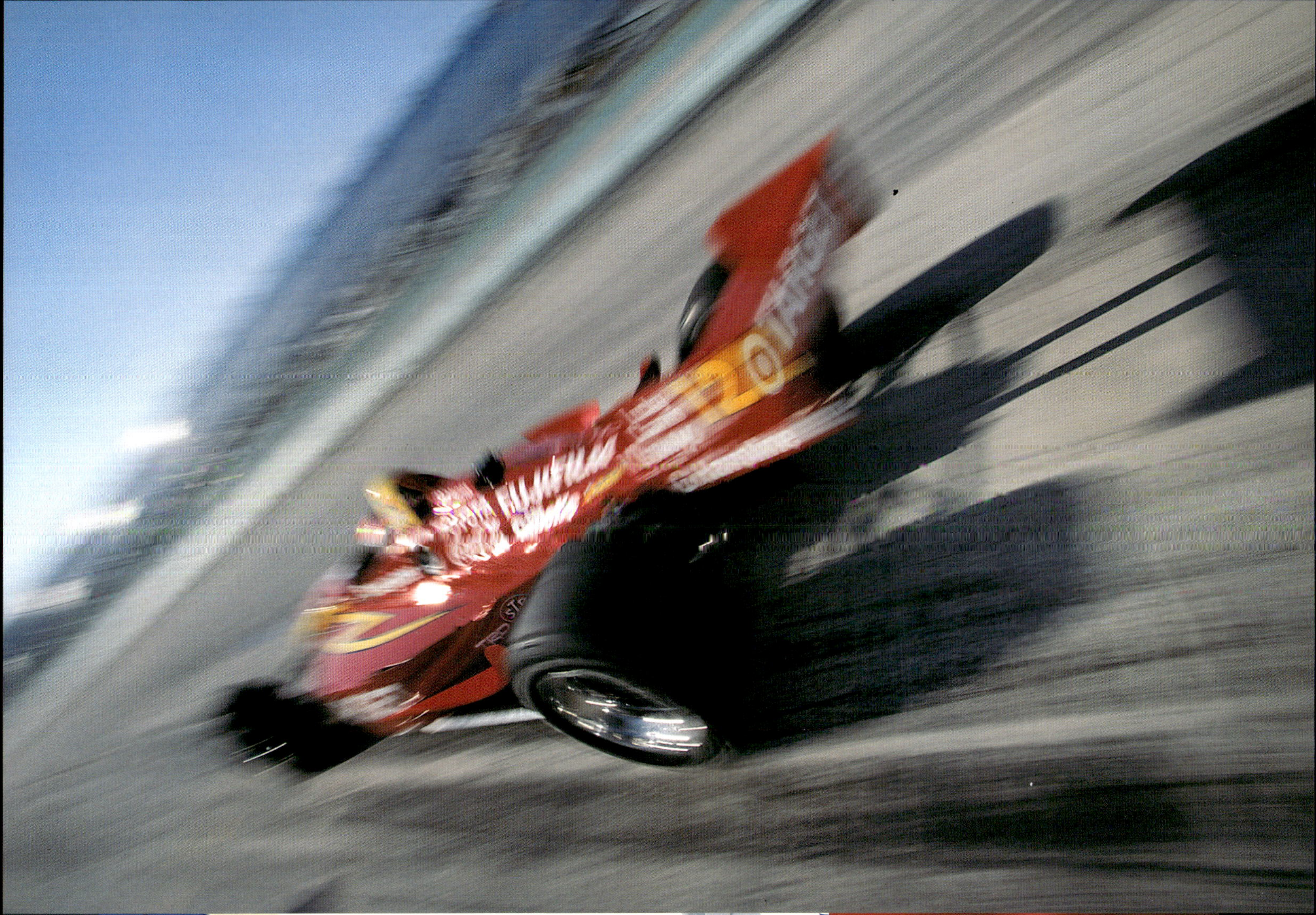

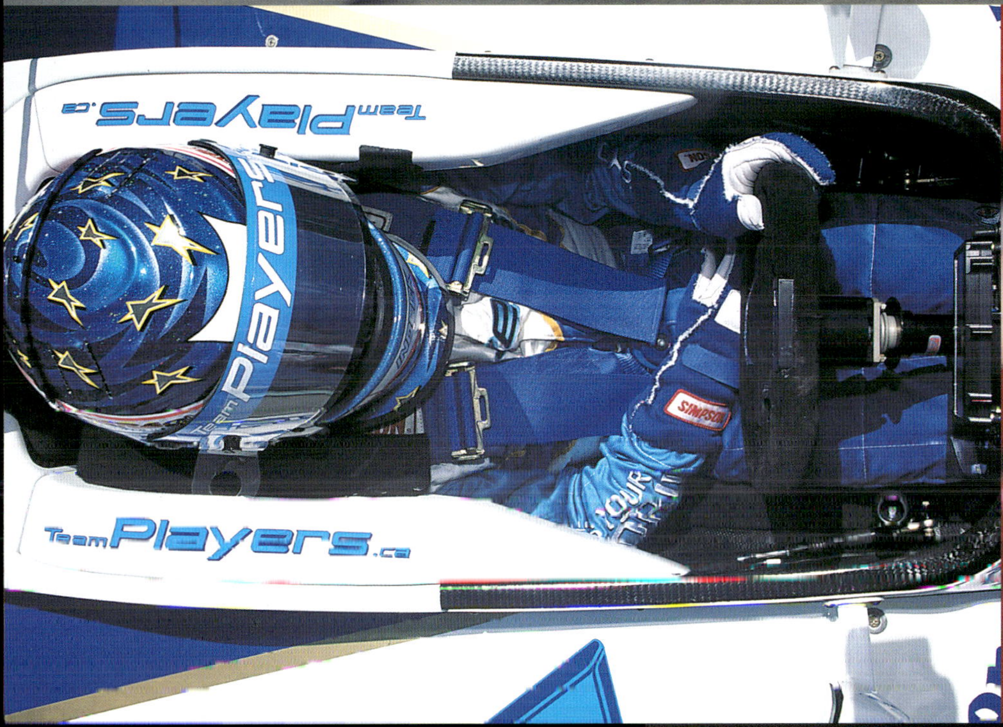

Darrell Ingham/Allsport USA

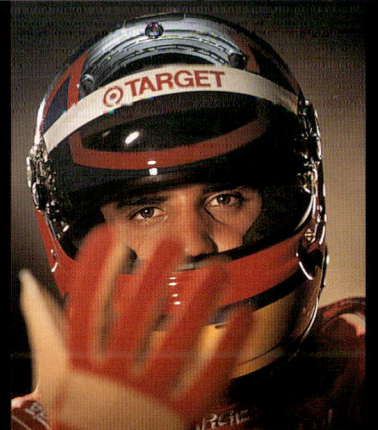

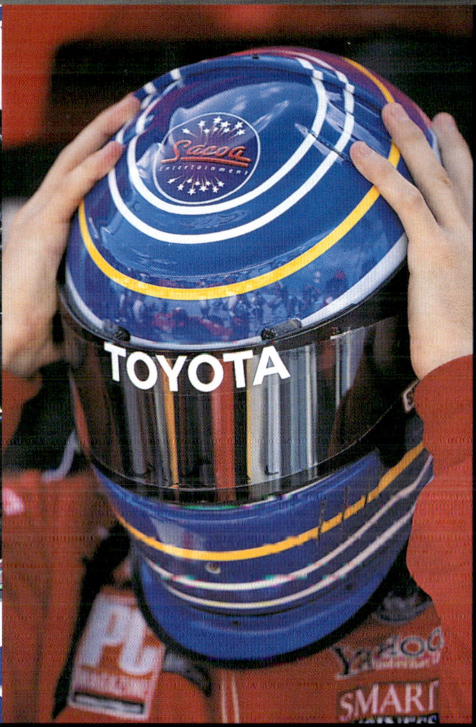

Robert Laberge/Allsport USA

Above left: Making his first scheduled pit stop earlier than the other leading contenders cost Gil de Ferran dearly.

Left: Paul Tracy led from Max Papis and Roberto Moreno...until the leaders encountered traffic in the later stages.

Top: Jimmy Vasser equaled Toyota's best-ever finish, fourth in the Target team's first race with the new RV8E motor.
Andy Lyons/Allsport USA

All dressed up and raring to go: rookies Alex Tagliani *(above left)* and Norberto Fontana *(above)*, plus defending series champion Juan Montoya *(left)*.
Juan Montoya: Jamie Squire/Allsport USA

FEDEX CHAMPIONSHIP SERIES • ROUND 1

Joy on the podium for two of CART's most popular drivers as first-time winner Papis hoists aloft Roberto Moreno.

Maximum Papis

It would be difficult to imagine a more popular winner than Massimiliano Papis. The likeable Italian's first CART victory was well-deserved and long overdue. He had attracted solid support since arriving in the CART series in tragic circumstances following the death of Jeff Krosnoff at Toronto in '96. He earned the ride with Arciero-Wells Racing – and the "Mad Max" moniker – by virtue of some spectacular performances in the Momo Ferrari 333SP sports car owned by American-based fellow countryman Giampiero Moretti.

Papis, who had established his credentials in Europe (including a brief spell in Formula 1), continued to display a never-say-die attitude with the Southern California-based team, which battled long and hard with uncompetitive Toyota engines. There were several rays of hope, including, most notably, a provisional pole in changeable weather conditions in Detroit, then a solid fifth-place finish in Houston toward the end of the '98 season. Papis' results that year brought the offer of a ride with Team Rahal in '99, which he accepted with alacrity.

The significance of stepping into the seat recently vacated by retiring three-time champion Bobby Rahal was not lost on Papis, a keen student of the sport; neither did he allow himself to be distracted by the obvious media attention. Instead, he displayed an intense focus that complemented his off-track joie de vivre. He established himself as a bona fide front-runner as the season progressed and was unfortunate not to find himself in Victory Lane. At Homestead-Miami Speedway, Papis finally put the record straight; but kept a firm grasp on his achievement.

"I feel that this is a great accomplishment for me and all the people who have believed in me," declared Papis. "When I came here [from Europe] in the beginning, it was after a very frustrating time in Formula 1. Then Cal Wells got me a ride at a difficult time with Jeff [Krosnoff]. I always had him in my heart and in my mind everyday. After Cal, I found another special person in Bobby [Rahal]. These guys have played a big part in my career. I also have to thank my family. They gave me the right values to believe in and they came through out there on the track. We built up to this win."

"We started a little bit conservative," he admitted. "The car was a little bit twitchy on the first set of tires. After the first pit stop, the car was a rocket. I was leading the race quite comfortably, and the timing of that yellow was unfortunate. It was a very unlucky break for us, but if you look on the positive side, we ran strong all weekend and we came away with some points. I think it all bodes well for the future."

The lead was assumed, incredibly, by Tagliani, but the rookie's lack of experience cost him dearly, as he was penalized for passing the pace car on his way into the pits. He was banished to the back of the field for the restart, which restricted him to a nonetheless impressive ninth-place finish.

Tony Kanaan also took a turn in the lead, making a fine debut aboard Mo Nunn Racing's Hollywood Mercedes/Reynard, until he was penalized – both for making a pit stop before the pits had been officially opened (the pit lane remains "closed" until all the leaders are lined up behind the pace car) and for exceeding the pit-lane speed limit by a paltry 1 mph. The indiscretion cost him a lap, but he recovered to finish tenth.

It was Tracy out in front at the final restart, hotly pursued by Papis, Moreno, Jimmy Vasser – who had driven a typically canny race in the second Target Toyota/Lola – and Tagliani's teammate, Patrick Carpentier, who had started last after suffering a puncture on the pace lap prior to the start.

For most of the final 40 laps, the top five remained in close formation, until lap 141. From there, it was all Papis.

"I couldn't get him [Tracy] because the turbulence was really moving the car around," explained Papis. "But I pushed really hard to make up the four or five car lengths, so when Paul was held up by the slower car, I was there to take advantage.

"When I crossed the start/finish line, I thought, 'This time I made it.' Last time, how you say, I got shafted, but this time we made it for real."

Papis, who had knocked on the door with two seconds and one third-place finish in 1999, claimed his first Champ Car victory in what was his 60th career start.

"I'm just proud of everyone," said delighted team owner and three-time CART champion Bobby Rahal. "Max did a hell of a job. After Michigan last year – he really 'won' that race – I'm thrilled for him."

It was also a memorable day for second-place finisher Roberto Moreno, who retired the title of "Super Sub" after gaining a well-deserved, full-time ride with Patrick Racing this season.

"I'd like to thank [team owner] Pat Patrick for giving me this opportunity and making us title contenders," Moreno acknowledged. "You don't know how good of a feeling it is after you spend all of this time talking to people and trying to find a ride. It's hard to put into words.

"Max, if you would have run out of fuel this time, I would have pushed you. If you would believe that, you'll believe anything."

Tracy, whose car was handling less than perfectly, was happy with his first podium of the season.

"I didn't have a great car all weekend," related the Canadian. "I had a push condition in the middle of the turns and I was loose coming off, but we got good points coming out of here. From our team's perspective, this weekend was a big success."

Jeremy Shaw

FEDEX CHAMPIONSHIP SERIES • ROUND 1

HOMESTEAD SNIPPETS

- In addition to franchise battles with the CART board of directors, **JERRY FORSYTHE** called a special meeting to decide whether the series would visit the German Lausitzring oval or the new Rockingham Speedway circuit being built in England (with Forsythe as an investor) in 2001. The owners eventually decided to postpone their decision.

- The brand-new **ARCIERO-PROJECT RACING GROUP**, announced just 17 days prior to the first race, performed admirably in its first proper outing with an ex-Player's '99 Mercedes/Reynard. Luiz Garcia Jr. *(right)* was classified 17th, despite lightly clipping the wall and pulling off with damaged right front suspension during the closing stages.

- **JOHN "BILLY" SIMMONDS**, former chief mechanic for Mario Andretti and Newman/Haas Racing, made his return to racing in south Florida. Simmonds, who had been semi-retired for the past two years, running his own business constructing form-fitted seats for race cars, had taken on a new role in charge of the shock absorbers for both Michael Andretti and Christian Fittipaldi.

- **TARGET/CHIP GANASSI RACING** had only three Toyota/Lolas on hand at Homestead. The team's fourth chassis was delivered a few days before the event, too

late for it to be fully race-prepped in time for the season-opener. Fortunately, with Jimmy Vasser and Juan Montoya sharing a backup car during the weekend, the lack of a fourth chassis was never an issue.

- Making a move from Dale Coyne Racing to Bettenhausen Motorsports in 2000, **MICHEL JOURDAIN JR.** had conducted fewer than 1000 miles of testing in his Mercedes/Lola prior to the season-opener. His efforts were further restricted when the likeable Mexican encountered an engine problem during the first practice session.

- In racing, you take **A LITTLE BIT OF LUCK** wherever you can find it. Dario Franchitti's #27 Team KOOL Green car sported Reynard chassis No. 2KI-027. "It was originally going to be Paul's [Tracy's] car," said Franchitti's chief mechanic, Kyle Moyer. "Then we heard from Reynard we were going to have No. 027, so we said, 'We'll take that car, thank you.'"

- PPI Motorsports made several **PERSONNEL CHANGES** following the abrupt departure of former team manager Richard Buck, just a few weeks before the season-opener. Veteran John Dick took over Buck's duties in addition to acting as race engineer for Oriol Servia, while Bharat Narain stepped back from the role of overall crew chief to become chief mechanic on Servia's car after John Stanchina left to pursue a business opportunity of his own.

FEDEX CHAMPIONSHIP SERIES • ROUND 1
MARLBORO GRAND PRIX OF MIAMI PRESENTED BY TOYOTA

HOMESTEAD-MIAMI SPEEDWAY, HOMESTEAD, FLORIDA

MARCH 26, 150 laps of 1.502 miles – 225.30 miles

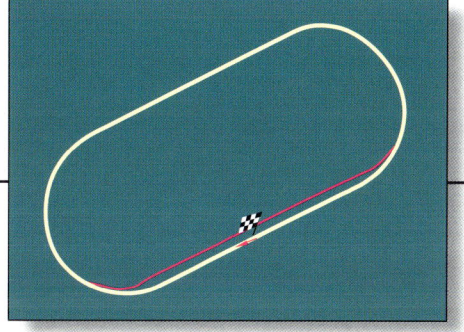

Place	Driver (Nat.)	No.	Team Sponsors Engine/Car	Tires	Q Speed	Q Time	Q Pos.	Laps	Time/Status	Ave. (mph)	Pts
1	Max Papis (I)	7	Team Rahal Miller Lite Ford Cosworth/Reynard 2KI	FS	204.570	26.432s	13	150	1h 22m 01.975s	164.788	20
2	Roberto Moreno (BR)	20	Patrick Racing Visteon Ford Cosworth/Reynard 2KI	FS	206.098	26.236s	7	150	1h 22m 02.595s	164.767	16
3	Paul Tracy (CDN)	26	Team KOOL Green Honda/Reynard 2KI	FS	202.950	26.643s	17	150	1h 22m 05.810s	164.659	14
4	Jimmy Vasser (USA)	12	Target/Chip Ganassi Racing Toyota/Lola B2K/00	FS	205.730	26.283s	10	150	1h 22m 06.429s	164.639	12
5	Patrick Carpentier (CDN)	32	Forsythe Racing Player's/Indeck Ford Cosworth/Reynard 2KI	FS	205.495	26.313s	12	150	1h 22m 06.806s	164.626	10
6	Gil de Ferran (BR)	2	Marlboro Team Penske Honda/Reynard 2KI	FS	208.434	25.942s	1	150	1h 22m 14.394s	164.373	10
7	Christian Fittipaldi (BR)	11	Newman/Haas Big Kmart/Route 66 Ford Cosworth/Lola B2K/00	FS	205.793	26.275s	9	150	1h 22m 16.261s	164.311	6
8	*Shinji Nakano (J)	5	Walker Racing Avex Group Honda/Reynard 2KI	FS	203.861	26.524s	15	150	1h 22m 16.831s	164.292	5
9	*Alexandre Tagliani (CDN)	33	Forsythe Racing Player's/Indeck Ford Cosworth/Reynard 2KI	FS	207.061	26.114s	4	150	1h 22m 27.445s	163.939	4
10	Tony Kanaan (BR)	55	Mo Nunn Racing Hollywood Mercedes/Reynard 2KI	FS	204.153	26.486s	14	149	Running		3
11	Dario Franchitti (GB)	27	Team KOOL Green Honda/Reynard 2KI	FS	201.746	26.802s	22	149	Running		2
12	Cristiano da Matta (BR)	97	PPI Motorsports Pioneer/MCI WorldCom Toyota/Reynard 2KI	FS	201.221	26.872s	23	149	Running		1
13	Mark Blundell (GB)	18	PacWest Racing Motorola Mercedes/Reynard 2KI	FS	203.156	26.616s	16	148	Running		
14	Michel Jourdain Jr. (MEX)	16	Bettenhausen Motorsports Herdez Mercedes/Lola B2K/00	FS	201.829	26.791s	21	147	Running		
15	*Norberto Fontana (RA)	10	Della Penna Motorsports VideoMatch Toyota/Reynard 2KI	FS	201.957	26.774s	19	147	Running		
16	Mauricio Gugelmin (BR)	17	PacWest Racing Nextel Mercedes/Reynard 2KI	FS	202.184	26.744s	18	146	Running		
17	Luiz Garcia Jr. (BR)	25	Arciero-PRG Hollywood/Embratel-21 Mercedes/Reynard 99I	FS	180.204	30.006s	25	132	Accident		
18	*Kenny Bräck (S)	8	Team Rahal Shell Ford Cosworth/Reynard 2KI	FS	206.808	26.140s	5	70	Oil leak		
19	*Oriol Servia (E)	96	PPI Motorsports Telefonica Toyota/Reynard 2KI	FS	201.837	26.790s	20	65	Transmission		
20	Gualter Salles (BR)	34	Dale Coyne Racing Ford Cosworth/Lola B2K/00	FS	205.722	26.204s	11	51	Transmission		
21	Adrian Fernandez (MEX)	40	Patrick Racing Tecate/Quaker State Ford Cosworth/Reynard 2KI	FS	207.634	26.042s	3	49	Oil leak		
22	Michael Andretti (USA)	6	Newman/Haas Big Kmart/Texaco Ford Cosworth/Lola B2K/00	FS	206.579	26.175s	6	37	Oil pressure		
23	Juan Montoya (COL)	1	Target/Chip Ganassi Racing Toyota/Lola B2K/00	FS	208.386	25.948s	2	23	Engine		
24	Takuya Kurosawa (J)	19	Dale Coyne Racing MCI Ford Cosworth/Lola B2K/00	FS	199.065	27.163s	4	11	Electrical		
25	Helio Castroneves (BR)	3	Marlboro Team Penske Honda/Reynard 2KI	FS	205.847	26.268s	8	9	Electrical		

* denotes rookie driver

Caution flags: Laps 11-17, off course/Castroneves; laps 101-110, off course/Gugelmin. **Total:** Two for 17 laps.

Lap leaders: Juan Montoya, 1-21 (21 laps); Adrian Fernandez, 22-47 (26 laps); Kenny Bräck, 48-53 (6 laps); Alexandre Tagliani, 54-55 (2 laps); Mark Blundell, 56-57 (2 laps); Gil de Ferran, 58-98 (41 laps); Tagliani, 99-104 (6 laps); Tony Kanaan, 105-108 (4 laps); Paul Tracy, 109-140 (32 laps); Max Papis, 141-150 (10 laps). **Totals:** de Ferran, 41 laps; Tracy, 32 laps; Fernandez, 26 laps; Montoya, 21 laps; Papis, 10 laps; Tagliani, 8 laps; Bräck, 6 laps; Kanaan, 4 laps; Blundell, 2 laps.

Fastest race lap: Juan Montoya, 27.826s, 194.322 mph on lap 2.

Championship positions: 1 Papis, 20; **2** Moreno, 16; **3** Tracy, 14; **4** Vasser, 12; **5** Carpentier & de Ferran, 10; **7** Fittipaldi, 6; **8** Nakano, 5; **9** Tagliani, 4; **10** Kanaan, 3; **11** Franchitti, 2; **12** da Matta, 1.

1 – TRACY
2 – CASTRONEVES
3 – VASSER

Paul Tracy posted a sensational charge to win for Team KOOL Green after starting way back in 17th.
Jon Ferrey/Allsport USA

Below: The joyful Canadian celebrates by taking a leaf out of WCW pro wrestler "Buff" Bagwell's book.
Robert Laberge/Allsport USA

LONG BEACH

FEDEX CHAMPIONSHIP SERIES • ROUND 2

FEDEX CHAMPIONSHIP SERIES • ROUND 2

A first for Japan

DESPITE gaining a wealth of experience in his Japanese homeland, Dale Coyne Racing's latest Champ Car rookie, Takuya Kurosawa, was something of an unknown quantity prior to the start of the season. But he quickly put himself on the map at Long Beach. With an excellent drive that was aided by Coyne's inspired pit-stop strategy, he became the first Japanese driver to lead a Champ Car event.

Kurosawa ran solidly in the opening stages and, in mid-race, latched onto the rear of Max Papis' Miller Lite Ford/Reynard, running impressively in seventh place when Papis crashed out abruptly on lap 40.

During the ensuing caution, Kurosawa ducked into pit lane. It was a calculated gamble that vaulted his MTCI Ford/Lola into the lead when everyone else pitted during a subsequent full-course caution on lap 54. He did an impressive job out front until lap 61, when Paul Tracy found a way through in Turn One.

By then, Kurosawa was committed to eking out his fuel supply, so was obliged to run a lean mixture. Nevertheless, he turned the 12th-fastest lap of the race and seemed set at least for a top-seven place until Norberto Fontana attempted an impossible move in Turn One that sent Kurosawa down the escape road. After falling to 11th, he was caught up in another incident – this time at the hairpin when Michel Jourdain Jr. clipped the inside wall and spun. Mauricio Gugelmin, running close behind Jourdain, slammed on the brakes in avoidance, and Kurosawa jinked to the inside to avoid the Brazilian. Sadly, in doing so, he, too, clipped the wall with his car's right rear wheel, which broke the suspension.

"It was unlucky," said Kurosawa in broken English. "The crew did a very good job today. It was my first time in a street race. I enjoy."

FEDEX CHAMPIONSHIP SERIES • ROUND 2

QUALIFYING

An exciting final period of qualifying on the revised Long Beach circuit saw Jimmy Vasser and Target/Chip Ganassi Racing teammate Juan Montoya trade fastest times in the waning stages, before Gil de Ferran shot to the top of the charts for Marlboro Team Penske. Ironically using the same Honda/Reynard package discarded by Ganassi at the conclusion of the '99 campaign, de Ferran was justifiably elated after snaring his second consecutive pole.

"That was a pretty nerve-wracking qualifying from my perspective. As soon as we posted a good time, it seemed like everybody else got too close for comfort," said the Brazilian, who admitted to clipping a wall lightly on his fastest lap. Fortunately, there was no damage to his Marlboro Honda/Reynard.

Vasser wound up second on the grid, two tenths of a second shy of de Ferran's best and a similar amount quicker than teammate Montoya.

"I feel a lot more comfortable this season with the new [harder-compound] tires and the Lola chassis," said the Californian. "I think I'm in for a good season."

Adrian Fernandez was fastest of the Ford Cosworth contingent, fourth on the grid with Pat Patrick's Tecate/Quaker State Reynard 2KI after posting the quickest time on Friday.

"We thought we could improve the times more than we did. I made a mistake on my fast lap. I don't want to make a lot of excuses, but I didn't sleep well last night and I couldn't get a good lap together," said Fernandez, who was suffering from a severe case of hives.

Bryan Herta, who took advantage of a fresh set of tires to set the pace during practice on Saturday morning, qualified a strong fifth on his debut for Walker Racing, followed by the two Team Rahal Ford/Reynards of Max Papis and Kenny Bräck.

A winner on the streets of Long Beach already in Toyota Atlantic, rookie Alex Tagliani *(left)* finished a solid fourth in only his second Champ Car start.

Below: Christian Fittipaldi seemed headed for a top-three finish until ending his day with a hasty exit from his Newman/Haas Lola.
Photos: Robert Laberge/Allsport USA

PAUL Tracy once again defined the term "hard charger" as he parlayed a potent mixture of experience, excellent strategy and some plain good fortune into his 16th Champ Car victory, having started in 17th position. The Canadian's sensational effort in the 26th running of the Toyota Grand Prix of Long Beach also moved him into the lead of the CART FedEx Championship Series point standings.

Tracy, who had struggled throughout practice and qualifying with the handling of his #26 Team KOOL Green Honda/Reynard, was the sixth different leader in a race that, like the season-opener, highlighted the amazing unpredictability of the FedEx Series.

"It was a fantastic run for Team KOOL Green," said a delighted Tracy, who made one more pit stop (three in total) than most of his rivals. "The pit strategy the guys came up with was unbelievable. I ran a clean race and we tried to be real conservative with the tires. Starting 17th, the plan was just to stay alive and not get in a wreck."

"Our strategy just seemed to be right at the end."

As at Homestead, Gil de Ferran delivered for Marlboro Team Penske, claiming his second pole position of the season. The Brazilian set off at a hot pace in the opening stages, but, once again, his Honda/Reynard was among the first of the leaders to make a scheduled pit stop, on lap 31. The other front-runners waited at least two more laps before taking on service. By the time they were all back up to speed, de Ferran had been leapfrogged by Roberto Moreno, who played a starring role for Patrick Racing, and Jimmy Vasser, who qualified alongside de Ferran on the front row in Target/Chip Ganassi Racing's steadily improving Toyota/Lola.

Out in the lead at this stage, however, despite having started only 14th in Newman/Haas Racing's Big Kmart/ Texaco Havoline Ford/Lola, was Michael Andretti. The 1991 CART champion had taken advantage of a gamble by his team, making a pit stop during the first caution of the day on lap 11, when Adrian Fernandez crashed his Tecate/Quaker State Ford/Reynard out of fourth place after suffering a catastrophic engine failure on Shoreline Drive.

Andretti took over the lead on lap 35, trailed by Tracy and Christian Fittipaldi in the second Newman/Haas car. Also pursuing a similar strategy were Mark Blundell (Motorola Mercedes/ Reynard), reigning Indy Lights champion Oriol Servia (Telefonica Toyota/ Reynard), Max Papis (Miller Lite Ford/Reynard) and Japanese rookie Takuya Kurosawa (MCI Ford/Lola), who was doing an admirable job of staying tucked in behind the rear wing of the season's first race winner.

Papis finally found a way past Servia in Turn One on lap 40; but his glory lasted only until the next corner, where a complete brake failure sent him spinning into the tire barrier and out of the race.

The ensuing full-course caution saw yet more divergence of pit strategies. Newman/Haas, strangely, elected not to make pit stops. Team KOOL Green, meanwhile, chose the opposite approach and signaled Tracy into pit lane. Blundell, Servia and Kurosawa also took on fuel and fresh tires.

Andretti and Fittipaldi continued to lead at the resumption, chased by Moreno, who had started eighth and drove a brilliant opening stint. The veteran Brazilian passed both Team Rahal Ford/Reynards of Papis and Kenny Bräck in the first few laps, then dispensed with Bryan Herta (driving well as a substitute for the injured Shinji Nakano at Walker Racing) and Vasser in short order.

"Straight away after the start I knew I had a fantastic car," said Moreno. "We were hauling ass."

Both Newman/Haas Ford/Lolas headed for the pits after 48 laps. Fittipaldi, sadly, would go no further. A cracked exhaust bellows caused a major fire in the engine bay while he was stationary in the pit lane. Andretti resumed, only to suffer an identical problem a mere ten laps from the finish.

"The car started losing power and I knew we were in trouble," recounted Andretti.

Moreno regained the lead, chased by the impressive Vasser, who eclipsed teammate Juan Montoya all weekend. (The Colombian ran well in the early stages before retiring when his engine lost power.) De Ferran ran third, ahead of Tracy, who pressured Herta into a quick spin at Turn One on lap 46. Next were Blundell, rookie Alex Tagliani (in one of the Player's/Forsythe Ford/ Reynards), Bräck and Tony Kanaan (Hollywood Mercedes/Reynard). Unfortunately, the latter pair tangled in Turn One while disputing seventh place. Exit both.

The incident on lap 54 ensured another full-course caution, during which everyone ducked into pit lane except Kurosawa and Helio Castroneves. Both had taken on fuel during the previous stoppage, whereupon Castroneves cost himself valuable track position when he incurred a drive-through penalty for exceeding the 50 mph pit-lane limit.

The order for the restart after 58 laps saw Kurosawa leading from Moreno, who looked good for his long overdue maiden Champ Car victory. It was not to be. Shortly after he began to encounter gearbox difficulties.

"If I kept on the throttle, I had gears," related Moreno, "but it took me a few laps to figure out how to handle it."

By the time Moreno had adapted his driving style to cope with the handicap, he had fallen all the way to 11th, although further attrition meant he regained two positions before the finish.

"It was a tough day," summarized Moreno. "We had a really strong car, but then we ran into gearbox problems. It's too bad, but at least I was able to gain some valuable points."

Kurosawa gained a little breathing space as the hobbled Moreno held up his pursuers at the restart, and for seven glorious laps maintained his position at the front to become the first Japanese driver ever to lead a Champ Car race.

Tracy, who saved vital seconds in the pits by electing not to take on fresh tires at his final stop, finally found a way past Kurosawa on lap 62. Castroneves followed in the Canadian's wake, although by this stage he was desperately trying to stretch his fuel load to the finish.

"We were sweating bullets," said Marlboro Team Penske Technical Advisor (and three-time former CART champion) Rick Mears.

Castroneves' break came on lap 64, when the unfortunate Kurosawa, who had been muscled down to a nonetheless very respectable seventh place, was rudely punted off at Turn One by over-ambitious fellow ex-Formula Nippon racer Norberto Fontana (Della Penna Motorsports Toyota/Reynard), who tried to outbrake both Kurosawa and Servia at the same time. Fontana came off worst, ending his race against the wall. Kurosawa was shuffled back to 11th and ultimately went out of the race when he clipped a wall at the hairpin while attempting to avoid a spinning Michel Jourdain Jr.'s Herdez Mercedes/Lola.

Each incident brought out the pace car, after which there remained a

FEDEX CHAMPIONSHIP SERIES • ROUND 2

Bryan Herta *(right)* hopped into Derrick Walker's Honda/Reynard and, without the benefit of any testing, finished fifth.
Robert Laberge/Allsport USA

Below: Jimmy Vasser outshone teammate Juan Montoya all weekend and earned another best-ever result for Toyota.
Jon Ferrey/Allsport USA

four-lap dash to the finish line. Tracy stayed out in front of the depleted field, chased by Castroneves, Vasser, Tagliani, Servia and Herta. De Ferran and Blundell also were in line astern, both having been shuffled backward during a mad scramble at the previous restart. The hobbled Moreno rounded out those runners still on the lead lap.

Castroneves could offer no challenge to Tracy as the race headed toward its climax. Instead he had to work extremely hard to hold off the attentions of Vasser, who drew alongside several times during the frantic closing stages. The young Brazilian kept the door firmly closed and was rewarded with an excellent second-place finish, matching his career best.

"It was really tough, especially having Jimmy all over me," said Castroneves, whose car ran out of fuel on the cool-down lap. "I had to really concentrate a lot not to make any mistakes, and I did it."

Vasser was content to pick up valuable championship points for third.

"I was trying to make an outside pass on Helio, but he did a good job keeping his line and I didn't want to sacrifice 14 points trying to gain two points," said Vasser.

Tagliani showed his Homestead performance was no fluke by finishing a fine fourth, followed by Herta, who snuck past Servia under braking for Turn One on the final lap.

De Ferran has hot on their heels at the finish line, despite struggling with a damaged front wing after rear-ending Vasser during an earlier restart. De Ferran also lost several places on lap 70 when he almost lost control at the exit of the hairpin.

"It was a tough day at the office," said de Ferran after finishing seventh. "But that's the way the chips fell today. Obviously this wasn't the type of finish we were hoping for and it's a shame because the Marlboro car was running well."

Tracy, by contrast, was ecstatic: "We thought if we could just get to the finish, get some points and stay out of trouble, we'd be more than happy with that, so to come away with a win is just fantastic."

Jeremy Shaw

"Super Sub" take two

At the Champ Car drivers' meeting on Saturday at Long Beach, Roberto Moreno officially stepped down from his throne by producing a large Subway sandwich, promptly cutting it into two pieces, and then handing them to Bryan Herta and Memo Gidley as formal recognition of their replacing the Brazilian as "Super Sub."

Moreno had earned the moniker last year, following some impressive drives for the PacWest and Newman/Haas teams while acting as substitute for Mark Blundell and Christian Fittipaldi respectively.

Gidley was drafted in by Player's/Forsythe Racing to replace the injured Patrick Carpentier, who had broken his wrist earlier in the week when he fell down the stairs at his home in Las Vegas. Herta became available when employer Jerry Forsythe made it clear he had no intention of racing again this season with the team formerly known as Tasman Motorsports. He gained his opportunity with Walker Racing after Shinji Nakano suffered a head injury in a crash while testing at Milwaukee a couple of weeks earlier.

Both lived up to "Super Sub" standards, responding with a sensational weekend's work.

Gidley, who hadn't driven a Champ Car since Surfers Paradise the previous fall, was almost immediately on the pace of rookie teammate Alex Tagliani and qualified an impressive tenth, one place ahead of the French-Canadian. He found a way past Helio Castroneves at the start, then latched onto the tail of a close battle between Herta and Kenny Bräck. Gidley even led one lap after displaying remarkable fuel consumption. Unfortunately, a fuel nozzle malfunction during his eventual pit stop on lap 35 meant that only a couple of gallons had been added to his Player's/Indeck Ford/Reynard. Shortly after, Gidley coasted to a halt.

Herta fared rather better. The Californian made the most of his chance by setting the fastest practice time on Saturday morning, then qualifying a fine fifth in Walker's Avex Group Honda/Reynard. He survived a brief off-course excursion to finish in the same position.

FEDEX CHAMPIONSHIP SERIES • ROUND 2

LONG BEACH SNIPPETS

- **FURTHER DEVELOPMENT** at the western end of the temporary race track, in the vicinity of the impressive new Long Beach Aquarium of the Pacific, created a few more modifications since the circuit was reconfigured in 1999, particularly in the area of Turn Five. The changes, which took the track length to 1.968 miles, earned widespread praise from the drivers: "Much, much nicer," said Max Papis, who reckoned the modifications created two new overtaking opportunities.

- Reigning Dayton Indy Lights Champion **ORIOL SERVIA** *(right)* produced a workmanlike performance aboard Cal Wells III's Telefonica Toyota/Reynard. The personable Spaniard recorded his first-ever Champ Car points with a sixth-place finish.

- Dale Coyne Racing battled **AROUND THE CLOCK** to prepare Gualter Salles' #34 Ford/Lola following a heavy crash during practice at Nazareth. The chassis was repaired at Aerodyne in Indianapolis, returning to Coyne's base in Plainfield, Ill., on Monday, whereupon it was totally repainted in the colors of new major sponsor Panasonic before being transported to the West Coast. "It's a miracle the car's here, but it's not running very well," reported Salles on Friday after being troubled by a variety of mechanical gremlins.

- The Toyota Grand Prix of Long Beach effectively became **ROUND TWO** of this year's championship (rather than the originally scheduled round three) when the Bosch Spark Plug Grand Prix Presented by Toyota at Nazareth Speedway, slated for the previous weekend, was postponed due to a snowstorm on race morning!

- Among Lola engineer Duncan McRobbie's **LUGGAGE** on the flight from England to Los Angeles was a package of Brooke Bond Choicest Blend tea, destined for Juan Montoya's English crew chief, Simon Hodgson. "It was recommended by [Lola Technical Director] Frank Dernie," quipped McRobbie. "We did some testing in-house and Choicest Blend was the overall winner. It takes more than a fast car to win races."

- **MAX PAPIS** couldn't match his victory from the season-opener at Homestead, but nonetheless he was pleased after qualifying sixth in Team Rahal's Miller Lite Ford/Reynard. "We have grown up tremendously from last year," said the Italian, "both the team and Ford. We are in another league now. I'm very pleased."

- A press conference was held on Saturday at Long Beach to announce that a **NEW VENUE** would be added to the CART schedule in 2001, at a brand-new temporary circuit being built in Monterrey, Mexico.

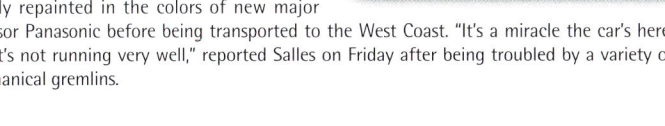

FEDEX CHAMPIONSHIP SERIES • ROUND 2
TOYOTA GRAND PRIX OF LONG BEACH

LONG BEACH STREET CIRCUIT, CALIFORNIA

APRIL 16, 82 laps of 1.97 miles – 161.38 miles

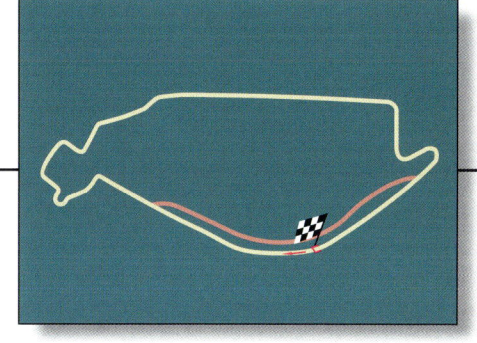

Place	Driver (Nat.)	No.	Team Sponsors Engine/Car	Tires	Q Speed	Q Time	Q Pos.	Laps	Time/Status	Ave. (mph)	Pts.
1	Paul Tracy (CDN)	26	Team KOOL Green Honda/Reynard 2KI	FS	102.918	1m 08.839s	17	82	1h 57m 11.132s	82.626	20
2	Helio Castroneves (BR)	3	Marlboro Team Penske Marlboro Honda/Reynard 2KI	FS	103.555	1m 08.416s	9	82	1h 57m 14.323s	82.588	16
3	Jimmy Vasser (USA)	12	Target/Chip Ganassi Racing Toyota/Lola B2K/00	FS	104.645	1m 07.703s	2	82	1h 57m 14.430s	82.587	14
4	*Alexandre Tagliani (CDN)	33	Forsythe Racing Player's/Indeck Ford Cosworth/Reynard 2KI	FS	103.354	1m 08.549s	11	82	1h 57m 14.916s	82.581	12
5	Bryan Herta (USA)	5	Walker Racing Avex Group Honda/Reynard 2KI	FS	104.170	1m 08.102s	5	82	1h 57m 15.340s	82.576	10
6	*Oriol Servia (E)	96	PPI Motorsports Telefonica Toyota/Reynard 2KI	FS	102.207	1m 09.318s	21	82	1h 57m 16.272s	82.566	8
7	Gil de Ferran (BR)	2	Marlboro Team Penske Marlboro Honda/Reynard 2KI	FS	104.969	1m 07.494s	1	82	1h 57m 16.681s	82.561	8
8	Mark Blundell (GB)	18	PacWest Racing Motorola Mercedes/Reynard 2KI	FS	102.355	1m 09.218s	20	82	1h 57m 18.869s	82.515	5
9	Roberto Moreno (BR)	20	Patrick Racing Visteon Ford Cosworth/Reynard 2KI	FS	103.705	1m 08.317s	8	82	1h 57m 21.057s	82.509	4
10	Mauricio Gugelmin (BR)	17	PacWest Racing Nextel Mercedes/Reynard 2KI	FS	102.945	1m 08.821s	16	81	Running		3
11	Michel Jourdain Jr. (MEX)	16	Bettenhausen Motorsports Herdez Mercedes/Lola B2K/00	FS	101.413	1m 09.861s	22	81	Running		2
12	Luiz Garcia Jr. (BR)	25	Arciero-PRG Hollywood/Embratel-21 Mercedes/Reynard 99I	FS	96.951	1m 13.076s	25	75	Running		1
13	*Takuya Kurosawa (J)	19	Dale Coyne Racing MTCI Ford Cosworth/Lola B2K/00	FS	101.298	1m 09.940s	23	74	Accident		
14	Michael Andretti (USA)	6	Newman/Haas Big Kmart/Texaco Ford Cosworth/Lola B2K/00	FS	103.271	1m 08.604s	14	73	Fire		
15	*Norberto Fontana (RA)	10	Della Penna Motorsports VideoMatch Toyota/Reynard 2KI	FS	102.756	1m 08.948s	18	65	Accident		
16	Tony Kanaan (BR)	55	Mo Nunn Racing Hollywood Mercedes/Reynard 2KI	FS	103.158	1m 08.679s	15	53	Accident		
17	*Kenny Bräck (S)	8	Team Rahal Shell Ford Cosworth/Reynard 2KI	FS	103.744	1m 08.291s	7	53	Accident		
18	Christian Fittipaldi (BR)	11	Newman/Haas Big Kmart/Route 66 Ford Cosworth/Lola B2K/00	FS	103.291	1m 08.591s	13	48	Fire		
19	Juan Montoya (COL)	1	Target/Chip Ganassi Racing Toyota/Lola B2K/00	FS	104.213	1m 07.984s	3	48	Engine		
20	Max Papis (I)	7	Team Rahal Miller Lite Ford Cosworth/Reynard 2KI	FS	104.057	1m 08.086s	6	39	Accident		
21	Memo Gidley (USA)	32	Forsythe Racing Player's/Indeck Ford Cosworth/Reynard 2KI	FS	103.393	1m 08.523s	10	37	Out of fuel		
22	Gualter Salles (BR)	4	Dale Coyne Racing Ford Cosworth/Lola B2K/00	FS	100.937	1m 10.190s	24	34	Turbo		
23	Dario Franchitti (GB)	27	Team KOOL Green Honda/Reynard 2KI	FS	102.665	1m 09.009s	19	23	Accident		
24	Adrian Fernandez (MEX)	40	Patrick Racing Tecate/Quaker State Ford Cosworth/Reynard 2KI	FS	104.178	1m 08.007s	4	10	Accident		
25	Cristiano da Matta (BR)	97	PPI Motorsports Pioneer/MCI WorldCom Toyota/Reynard 2KI	FS	103.328	1m 08.566s	12	10	Engine/accident		

* denotes rookie driver

Caution flags: laps 10-14, accident/Fernandez; laps 15-16, spin/Gugelmin; laps 39-42, accident/Papis; laps 53-57, accident/Bräck & Kanaan; laps 66-69, accident/Fontana; laps 76-77, accident/Kurosawa & Jourdain. **Total.** Six for 20 laps.

Lap leaders: Gil de Ferran, 1-30 (30 laps); Roberto Moreno, 31-33 (3 laps); Memo Gidley, 34 (1 lap); Michael Andretti, 35-47 (13 laps); Moreno, 48-54 (7 laps); Takuya Kurosawa, 55-61 (7 laps); Paul Tracy, 62-82 (21 laps). **Totals:** de Ferran, 30 laps; Tracy, 21 laps; Andretti, 13 laps; Moreno, 10 laps; Kurosawa, 7 laps; Gidley, 1 lap.

Fastest race lap: Gil de Ferran, 1m 09.602s, 101.790 mph on lap 52.

Championship positions: 1 Tracy, 34; **2** Vasser, 26; **3** Papis & Moreno, 20; **5** de Ferran, 18; **6** Castroneves & Tagliani, 16; **8** Herta & Carpentier, 10; **10** Servia, 8; **11** Fittipaldi, 6; **12** Nakano & Blundell, 5; **14** Gugelmin & Kanaan, 3; **16** Franchitti & Jourdain, 2; **18** da Matta, Garcia Jr. & Montoya, 1.

RIO

FEDEX CHAMPIONSHIP SERIES • ROUND 3

FEDEX CHAMPIONSHIP SERIES • ROUND 3

1 – FERNANDEZ
2 – VASSER
3 – TRACY

TWO drivers – one a rookie, the other a veteran – played starring roles when the CART FedEx Championship Series ventured south of the equator to Brazil for the Rio 200. Alex Tagliani started on the pole in only his third race for Player's/Forsythe Racing and maintained control for much of the race. Sadly, a couple of cautions in the late stages exposed the French-Canadian's lack of experience. Tagliani spun off with only ten laps remaining, handing victory to popular Mexican Adrian Fernandez, who parlayed an excellent strategy into a sixth Champ Car triumph in his 108th start.

"This is a well-deserved victory for the team and myself," said Fernandez. "We were strong in qualifying in both the [previous] races this year, but we just couldn't finish. Today we got a little of that back."

Curiously, Fernandez had an awful time in practice and qualifying. He was a dismal 22nd at the end of the first day of practice, and even though race engineer John Ward made some improvements to the setup of Patrick Racing's Tecate/Quaker State Ford Cosworth/Reynard for qualifying, 16th on the grid hardly boded well for race day.

Tagliani, meanwhile, set a torrid pace amid the heat and humidity at Rio de Janeiro's Emerson Fittipaldi Speedway. The Toyota Atlantic graduate remained unflustered at the start, despite an initial wave-off after fellow rookie Oriol Servia lost control of his Telefonica Toyota/Reynard coming off Turn Four. When the green flag finally flew, Tagliani converted his pole into the lead, ahead of fellow front-row qualifier Juan Montoya, and quickly opened up a small advantage over the Target Toyota/Lola. Paul Tracy led the chase in third, but soon came under increasing pressure from yet another rookie, Sweden's Kenny Bräck, who had shown a good turn of pace all weekend aboard Team Rahal's Shell Ford/Reynard.

Bräck slipped ahead in Turn Three on lap 15, and while Tracy briefly regained the advantage, Bräck soon made the pass stick.

By lap 28, Tagliani had extended his margin over Montoya to 2.5 seconds. Such was their superiority that Bräck already was a further six seconds adrift in third. Two laps later, Montoya's challenge was brought to an end by a sudden gearbox failure.

"We were just cruising around, getting good [fuel] mileage. We had plenty of power and were just waiting for the middle of the race to pick it up and go for the win," said the disappointed Colombian, who, after three races, had mustered only one championship point – for securing the pole in the postponed Bosch Spark Plug Grand Prix at Nazareth Speedway. It was a stark contrast to his 1999 campaign.

The first round of pit stops began a half-dozen laps later. Tagliani was among the first to take on service, but duly regained control after Paul Tracy (KOOL Honda/Reynard), Jimmy Vasser

QUALIFYING

By virtue of setting the pace in practice, Alex Tagliani was the last contender to take to the track for qualifying. The 27-year-old French-Canadian had a hard act to follow after defending series and race winner Juan Montoya posted a time some 0.147 second quicker than the previous best set by current FedEx Series points leader Paul Tracy.

"When I got on track, I saw that Juan had a [fastest lap of] 38.6 [seconds]," related Tagliani. "He improved quite a bit from this morning [when Montoya posted a 38.811 in practice]. We weren't expecting him to be so fast. We ran a 38.6 this morning too, but we had a small draft running behind Jimmy [Vasser]."

After Tagliani had turned a 38.8 on his final warmup lap, Player's/Forsythe Vice President, Operations Neil Micklewright told the youngster he needed to step up a little more to secure the pole. Tagliani was up to the task.

"When I came through the first corner, I knew it was going to be a good time," continued Tagliani, who clipped another 0.109 second from Montoya's earlier best. "This isn't really a difficult track to drive, but it's a challenging track for the engineers. This pole is really for the Player's/Forsythe team today."

Montoya was relatively content with second, since his Target Toyota/Lola proved a little too loose for his liking. Tracy remained in third, despite making a slight mistake aboard Team KOOL Green's Honda/Reynard.

"The car has been really good all weekend," said Tracy. "It was good in qualifying, but I messed up on my second lap when I thought I would have been quicker. I got a little loose in Turn One when I got on the throttle a little early, and the car stepped out on me."

Next up was rookie Kenny Bräck, followed by Christian Fittipaldi, who was the best of the Brazilians for the second year in succession – only this time he had to be content with a position on row three rather than the pole.

Adrian Fernandez *(top left)* used all of his experience – and that of Patrick Racing – to emerge with a fine victory in Brazil.
Robert Laberge/Allsport USA

Alex Tagliani slithered high in Turn Four and saw his hopes of victory go up in smoke *(opposite page, right and inset)*, paving the way for Fernandez *(middle left)* to emerge triumphant.
Far left: Darrell Ingham/Allsport USA; opposite page, right and inset: Robert Laberge/Allsport USA; middle left: Jamie Squire/Allsport USA

Kenny Bräck *(left)* was in contention for the win until stalling the engine in Team Rahal's Shell Ford/Reynard.
Robert Laberge/Allsport USA

(in the second Target Toyota/Lola) and Fernandez had all enjoyed a brief taste of the lead.

Tagliani led Bräck by almost ten seconds on lap 40, which was just as well, because the next time around, the youngster unwittingly hit the pit-lane speed-limiter as he rounded Turn Four. By the time he realized his error, Bräck was little more than a second in arrears. The former Indy Racing League champion piled on the pressure for the next ten laps or so, but Tagliani proved up to the challenge.

Respite came on lap 54 in the form of a full-course caution, after a disappointing weekend for Bryan Herta ended when his Avex Group/Walker Racing Honda/Reynard became stranded with a broken transmission.

Surprisingly, most of the field opted to make a pit stop, which meant that they would have to take on service one more time to reach the finish. Not so Tagliani. Michael Andretti (Big Kmart/Texaco Ford/Lola), Tagliani's teammate Memo Gidley, in the second Player's car, and Mark Blundell (Motorola Mercedes/Reynard) also eschewed the opportunity to stop. This quartet duly led at the restart, followed by Fernandez, who had benefited from two super-quick pit stops by Donny Lambert's crew.

Once again, Tagliani asserted his superiority at the restart, pulling away from Andretti at the rate of more than a half-second per lap. It was an impressive performance.

On lap 74, right on schedule, Tagliani made his way into pit lane for his second and final scheduled pit stop. The bad news was that he resumed in tenth. The good news was that all those ahead of him would have to make a third visit to pit lane.

Andretti and Gidley made their final stops two laps later (Blundell already had taken on fuel and fresh tires), which left Bräck in the lead after the Swede had ended a protracted duel with Fernandez by squeezing past under braking for Turn One on lap 72. Bräck romped clear and stretched his lead to over nine seconds before the caution lights flashed again on lap 91, after a fine run by Michel Jourdain Jr. saw the Mexican youngster's Herdez Mercedes/Lola sidelined from seventh place by an engine failure.

The leaders all swept into the pits during the caution, which allowed Tagliani to regain his position at the front of the field. Andretti had fallen a lap behind after being assessed a stop-and-go penalty for an incident in the pits (see sidebar). The unfortunate Gidley was hindered by a turbo wastegate glitch, which cost crucial horsepower, and had been lapped by Bräck shortly before the yellow.

Bräck should have emerged from the pits in second place. Instead, he fell to ninth after stalling the engine as he went to leave his pit box. Fernandez, therefore, inherited second, followed by the ever-consistent Vasser, who had run strongly, but unobtrusively, all afternoon.

When the green flag waved again on lap 98, with ten laps remaining, Vasser challenged Fernandez on the run toward Turn One. Fernandez held his ground.

Tagliani, meanwhile, had taken off into the lead again. Victory, it seemed, was within his grasp. Less than a mile later, however, the youngster left

Right: Roberto Moreno continued his fine early-season form by finishing sixth.

Rookie on the pace

ALEX Tagliani was a revelation in Rio and came tantalizingly close to a stunning victory in only his third Champ Car start. After displaying good form in the opening two races, Tagliani arrived in Brazil placed sixth in the FedEx Series points table. Immediately, he showed that was no fluke by posting the third-quickest time on the opening day of practice.

"Right from my first few laps this morning, I could see the Player's Reynard was really working well," said the rookie driver who hailed originally from the Montreal suburb of Lachenaie, Quebec. "When the Player's crew got the car ready, they were right on with their adjustments. When I came into the pits, all they had to do was some fine-tuning."

Clearly, he had learned humility – as well as pace – during his formative years in the sport. After a lengthy and successful career in karts and ice racing in his native Quebec, young Tagliani graduated through the Spenard/David school at Shannonville, Ontario, and went on to win the Bridgestone FF2000 Racing School Championship. He moved into the ultra-competitive Esso/Protec/BFGoodrich Formula 1600 Series and finished fourth in his rookie season, 1996, before stepping up immediately into Toyota Atlantic.

Tagliani was invited to join the fledgling Player's Atlantic team in '97, spending three seasons with the Indianapolis-based organization and scoring two victories during each campaign. After Greg Moore announced he would be leaving the Player's/Forsythe Champ Car team midway through the '99 season, Tagliani was tabbed for an all-or-nothing shoot-out test with fellow former Player's Atlantic team graduates David Empringham and Lee Bentham.

Each driver was evaluated over two days apiece at Sebring, Florida, and it was Tagliani who gained the nod. Judging by his pace in the first three races of his rookie CART season, the judges made an astute selection.

FEDEX CHAMPIONSHIP SERIES • ROUND 3

Pit-lane penalty

ALMOST two weeks after the Rio 200 – in fact, on the eve of practice for the following race in Japan – CART Chief Steward Kirk Russell announced that Michael Andretti had been excluded from the results in Brazil. The decision was made following a review of the pit-lane incident in which two of Andretti's crew members were injured during a pit stop on lap 76.

Todd Tice sustained a fractured right lower leg and ankle, while John Littlefield suffered a large bruise on his left lower leg. The team had been assessed a stop-and-go penalty at the time of the incident, but subsequently Andretti was stripped of his ninth-place finish.

"After meeting with team representatives and careful review of the facts, I met with the stewards at our first available opportunity and we have chosen to remove the points and awards gained by the #6 car team, thereby having the same effect as exclusion at the time of the event," stated Russell. "The finishing position will remain as part of the event record, but the points and awards will not be redistributed.

"Given the nature and the severity of the incident, we would have excluded the #6 car from the remainder of the event. However, the information available at the time of the event did not support the action.

"We have to make calls based on the best information at the time. However, where safety is concerned, careful investigation of the facts after the event is especially appropriate. My utmost concern is for the safety of the participants, and the teams must understand the seriousness with which we regard these circumstances."

The penalty was not open to appeal. In addition to losing four championship points, Andretti also forfeited prize money totaling $17,500. Instead, the money was donated to CART Charities.

The Brazilian blend. Local drivers (left to right) Luiz Garcia Jr., Helio Castroneves, Gil de Ferran, Cristiano da Matta (kneeling), Mauricio Gugelmin, Tony Kanaan, Roberto Moreno, Tarso Marques and Christian Fittipaldi gave the home crowd plenty to cheer about.

his braking for Turn Four a smidgin too late, slid up into the gray, then looped into a lazy spin. Instinctively, he gunned the throttle, which succeeded only in enveloping the entire race track in a dense cloud of smoke from his tortured Firestone Firehawk tires. Miraculously, there was no major carnage, although Tracy lost his left front wing's end-plate and teammate Dario Franchitti spun while taking avoiding action, falling from seventh to 11th. (Franchitti, incidentally, had earlier survived a spin of his own – in the pit lane!)

Fernandez ducked through gratefully into the lead, while Vasser took evasive action and j-u-s-t squeezed past Tagliani on the outside.

"I lost him in the smoke and I thought he was still rolling down," said Vasser. "So I decided to go for the outside. It was basically a 50-50 chance. It was more luck than anything."

Yellow again. Tagliani's hopes of victory had, quite literally, gone up in smoke. But his eventful day wasn't over. As the race was restarted, with only three laps remaining, Tagliani lost control again – this time at the back of the field after losing two laps while his engine was refired. Sadly, the yellow flags flew once more and, much to the crowd's chagrin, there wasn't enough time for a restart.

"It's very hard," said a chastened Tagliani. "I feel very, very bad for all my guys and for everybody else because the race finished under yellow. I'm really sad for everyone on the Player's team because they gave me a perfect car all weekend, and today we were 'this' close to winning."

Fernandez duly took the checkered flag behind the pace car, followed by Vasser and Tracy, who trundled across the line in third to maintain his championship lead. Cristiano da Matta matched his career-best finish, fourth, after a fine performance in Cal Wells III's Pioneer Toyota/Reynard. Da Matta also earned kudos as the top Brazilian finisher ahead of Christian Fittipaldi (Big Kmart/Route 66 Ford/Lola) and Roberto Moreno (Visteon Ford/Reynard). Blundell, Gidley, Andretti and Bräck completed the top ten.

The sequence of cautions in the late stages ended Vasser's hopes of snatching a maiden victory for Toyota, but he continued the Japanese auto giant's progression, having finished fourth, third and second in the opening three races of the season.

"I thought we had the opportunity for the win for sure," declared Vasser, "but I could never get in the clear. If we keep running in the top five, things are going to come our way and we're going to get that first Toyota victory."

Instead it was Fernandez who emerged to spray the champagne after a typically doughty performance.

"It was a different kind of day for me," related Fernandez, who actually lost a few positions at the start. "I had to work my way through and I made a few passes and had some good pit stops. We ran about 80 laps with the same [set of] tires. That was a big key for us today."

Jeremy Shaw

FEDEX CHAMPIONSHIP SERIES • ROUND 3

RIO SNIPPETS

- The new group of promoters, headed by former Formula 1 and CART series champion Emerson Fittipaldi, drew an estimated **60,000 FANS** on race day – by far the largest crowd in the event's five-year history.

- **ADRIAN FERNANDEZ'S** victory was the sixth of his career, and it earned him the distinction of being the only Champ Car driver to have won races in four different countries and on three different continents. Fernandez's previous successes had come in Toronto, Canada; Twin Ring Motegi, Japan (twice); and two American venues, Mid-Ohio Sports Car Course and California Speedway.

- Briton **MARK BLUNDELL** secured the Budweiser Hard Charger Award for showing the greatest improvement from start to finish in the 25-car field. Blundell, who started 23rd, worked his way through to a promising seventh place finish aboard Bruce McCaw's Motorola/PacWest Mercedes/Reynard.

- **MEMO GIDLEY** took a career-best eighth in his second ride while acting as substitute for the injured Patrick Carpentier. Gidley, after starting 11th on his oval-track debut, worked his way up to third place soon after the halfway mark, behind only teammate Tagliani and Michael Andretti. The gifted American would surely have been in contention for the win if not for a mysterious lack of boost, which blunted his progress in the middle stages.

- **CHRISTIAN FITTIPALDI** was hindered by a lack of straight-line speed compared to some of the other contenders, but soldiered on to a fifth-place finish for Newman/Haas Racing.

- **LUIZ GARCIA JR.** garnered his second championship point in as many races with a steady run to 12th in the fledgling Arciero-Project Racing Group's Hollywood/Embratel Mercedes-Benz/Reynard 99I.

- After taking pole in each of the first two races (and qualifying fifth for the postponed event at Nazareth), **GIL DE FERRAN** *(left)* was never a factor in Brazil. The native of Sao Paulo, Brazil, qualified a disappointing 13th in his Marlboro Team Penske Honda/Reynard and succumbed to a broken exhaust after 79 laps. Teammate Helio Castroneves completed only 22 laps before being sidelined by a gearbox failure.

FEDEX CHAMPIONSHIP SERIES • ROUND 3
RIO 200
EMERSON FITTIPALDI SPEEDWAY, RIO DE JANEIRO, BRAZIL
APRIL 30, 108 laps of 1.864 miles – 201.31 miles

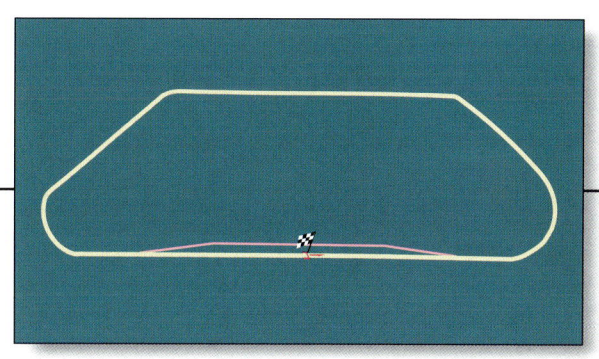

Place	Driver (Nat.)	No.	Team Sponsors Engine/Chassis	Tires	Q Speed	Q Time	Q Pos.	Laps	Time/Status	Ave. (mph)	Pts.
1	Adrian Fernandez (MEX)	40	Patrick Racing Tecate/Quaker State Ford Cosworth/Reynard 2KI	FS	170.354	39.391s	16	108	1h 37m 12.490s	124.256	20
2	Jimmy Vasser (USA)	12	Target/Chip Ganassi Racing Toyota/Lola B2K/00	FS	172.313	38.943s	6	108	1h 37m 13.421s	124.236	16
3	Paul Tracy (CDN)	26	Team KOOL Green Honda/Reynard 2KI	FS	172.757	38.843s	3	108	1h 37m 13.828s	124.228	14
4	Cristiano da Matta (BR)	97	PPI Motorsports Pioneer/MCI WorldCom Toyota/Reynard 2KI	FS	170.233	39.419s	17	108	1h 37m 14.071s	124.223	12
5	Christian Fittipaldi (BR)	11	Newman/Haas Big Kmart/Route 66 Ford Cosworth/Lola B2K/00	FS	172.597	38.679s	5	108	1h 37m 14.846s	124.206	10
6	Roberto Moreno (BR)	20	Patrick Racing Visteon Ford Cosworth/Reynard 2KI	FS	170.900	39.265s	12	108	1h 37m 15.268s	124.197	8
7	Mark Blundell (GB)	18	PacWest Racing Motorola Mercedes/Reynard 2KI	FS	167.454	40.073s	23	108	1h 37m 17.569s	124.148	6
8	Memo Gidley (USA)	32	Forsythe Racing Player's/Indeck Ford Cosworth/Reynard 2KI	FS	170.983	39.246s	11	108	1h 37m 18.994s	124.118	5
9	Michael Andretti (USA)	6	Newman/Haas Big Kmart/Texaco Ford Cosworth/Lola B2K/00	FS	170.574	39.340s	15	107	Running		**4
10	*Kenny Bräck (S)	8	Team Rahal Shell Ford Cosworth/Reynard 2KI	FS	172.610	38.876s	4	107	Running		3
11	Dario Franchitti (GB)	27	Team KOOL Green Honda/Reynard 2KI	FS	171.947	39.026s	8	107	Running		2
12	Luiz Garcia Jr. (BR)	25	Arciero-PRG Hollywood/Embratel-21 Mercedes/Reynard 2KI	FS	no speed	no time	25	104	Running		1
13	*Alexandre Tagliani (CDN)	33	Forsythe Racing Player's/Indeck Ford Cosworth/Reynard 2KI	FS	173.903	38.587s	1	103	Spin		2
14	Gualter Salles (BR)	34	Dale Coyne Racing Refricentro Ford Cosworth/Lola B2K/00	FS	no speed	no time	24	98	Exhaust header		
15	Michel Jourdain Jr. (MEX)	16	Bettenhausen Motorsports Herdez Mercedes/Lola B2K/00	FS	168.366	39.856s	22	90	Engine		
16	Max Papis (I)	7	Team Rahal Miller Lite Ford Cosworth/Reynard 2KI	FS	171.066	39.227s	10	90	Oil line		
17	Gil de Ferran (BR)	2	Marlboro Team Penske Marlboro Honda/Reynard 2KI	FS	170.757	39.298s	13	79	Exhaust		
18	Tony Kanaan (BR)	55	Mo Nunn Racing Hollywood Mercedes/Reynard 2KI	FS	171.617	39.101s	9	69	Gearbox		
19	*Takuya Kurosawa (J)	19	Dale Coyne Racing MTCI Ford Cosworth/Lola B2K/00	FS	169.497	39.590s	19	64	Engine		
20	Bryan Herta (USA)	5	Walker Racing Avex Group Honda/Reynard 2KI	FS	169.369	39.620s	20	61	Gearbox		
21	Mauricio Gugelmin (BR)	17	PacWest Racing Nextel Mercedes/Reynard 2KI	FS	169.104	39.682s	21	53	Engine		
22	Juan Montoya (COL)	1	Target/Chip Ganassi Racing Toyota/Lola B2K/00	FS	173.413	38.696s	2	30	Shift linkage		
23	*Norberto Fontana (RA)	10	Della Penna Motorsports VideoMatch Toyota/Reynard 2KI	FS	169.866	39.504s	18	29	Gearbox		
24	Helio Castroneves (BR)	3	Marlboro Team Penske Marlboro Honda/Reynard 2KI	FS	172.128	38.985s	7	22	Gearbox		
25	*Oriol Servia (E)	96	PPI Motorsports Telefonica Toyota/Reynard 2KI	FS	170.722	39.306s	14	0	Accident		

* denotes rookie driver   ** denotes points subsequently forfeited for a pit-lane infraction, for which a $17,500 fine was levied against the driver

Caution flags: Laps 1-4, accident/Servia; laps 55-60, tow/Herta; laps 91-97, tow/Jourdain; laps 99-104, accident/Tagliani, Bräck, Franchitti & Andretti; laps 105-108, spin/Tagliani. **Total:** Five for 27 laps.

Lap leaders: Alex Tagliani, 1-35 (35 laps); Paul Tracy, 36 (1 lap); Jimmy Vasser, 37 (1 lap); Adrian Fernandez, 38-39 (2 laps); Tagliani, 40-74 (35 laps); Michael Andretti, 75-76 (2 laps); Kenny Bräck, 77-93 (17 laps); Tagliani, 94-99 (6 laps); Fernandez, 100-108 (9 laps). **Totals:** Tagliani, 76 laps; Bräck, 17 laps; Fernandez, 11 laps; Andretti, 2 laps; Vasser 1 lap; Tracy, 1 lap.

Fastest race lap: Alex Tagliani, 39.445s, 170.120 mph on lap 70.

Championship positions: **1** Tracy, 48; **2** Vasser, 42; **3** Moreno, 28; **4** Papis & Fernandez, 20; **6** de Ferran & Tagliani, 18; **8** Castroneves & Fittipaldi, 16; **10** da Matta, 13; **11** Blundell, 11; **12** Herta & Carpentier, 10; **14** Servia, 8; **15** Nakano & Gidley, 5; **17** Andretti & Franchitti, 4; **19** Gugelmin, Bräck & Kanaan, 3; **22** Garcia & Jourdain, 2; **24** Montoya, 1.

MOTEGI

FEDEX CHAMPIONSHIP SERIES • ROUND 4

FEDEX CHAMPIONSHIP SERIES • ROUND 4

Clockwise, from bottom left: Attempts to dry out the track on the originally scheduled race day proved fruitless; Luiz Garcia Jr. donned a native headband for the popular drivers' autograph session; thankfully, the rain clouds moved away and the crowds flocked back one day later for the Firestone Firehawk 500; Michael Andretti is flanked by Dario Franchitti *(left)* and Roberto Moreno on the victory podium; the moment of truth for Andretti as he takes the checkered flag just 0.546 second clear of the pursuing Scotsman.

Andretti back on top

NEWMAN/Haas Racing co-owners Carl Haas and Paul Newman took a calculated gamble following the 1999 campaign by terminating their relationship with Swift Engineering and siding with rival chassis supplier Lola Cars International. The decision renewed a partnership between the British manufacturer and Haas, who had served as Lola's North American importer from the late 1960s until forging his association with Swift in 1997.

Early indications were promising, as Michael Andretti set a string of quick times during winter tests, marking him as one of the strongest preseason favorites for CART FedEx Championship Series honors. Nevertheless, after being dogged by misfortune, Andretti had garnered not so much as a single championship point after three races.

He was an early contender for victory in the opener at Homestead before becoming one of several Ford Cosworth runners to be sidelined by oil leaks. Andretti struggled in qualifying at Long Beach, but took advantage of excellent pit strategy to lead several laps until being felled by a cracked exhaust bellows. Then, in Brazil, he was involved in a pit-lane incident and, although he finished ninth, was later excluded from the results.

Andretti, however, bounced back to prominence by scoring an overdue victory at Twin Ring Motegi in his Ford Cosworth-powered Big Kmart/Texaco Havoline Lola B2K/00.

"The season is far from over," declared the 1991 CART champion. "We have a long way to go. We have 16 races left, which used to be a [full] season for us, so there are many points out there to get."

WHEN the skies opened up on race day at Motegi, Michael Andretti and his Newman/Haas crew found a ray of sunshine. Andretti had seemed poised to start the 201-lap sprint in his backup Big Kmart/Texaco Havoline Ford Cosworth/Lola after his primary car was stricken by a broken throttle position sensor during the shortened final warmup session.

Rain, which had already delayed the start of race-day activities, brought a revised schedule of events, leaving only a small time window for teams to attempt minor adjustments. Andretti's crew chief, Donny Hoevel, had no choice but to resort to the backup car.

Andretti's rainbow appeared moments later. When it rains, it pours, and it did with a vengeance at Twin Ring Motegi, causing a 24-hour postponement of the start of the Firestone Firehawk 500. The delay enabled Hoevel and Co. ample opportunity for repairs. When ill fortune struck the dominant run by Juan Montoya's Target Toyota/Lola in the closing stages of the race, Andretti was there to capitalize.

"I don't know if we'd have had anything for [the Ganassi cars] today, but for once luck went our way," said a relieved Andretti after posting his first championship points of the season. "It was a day when everything went great. It just feels great to get back up here [on the podium]."

Andretti's 39th career win was a solid effort. The veteran driver was in top form on the opening lap, passing four cars around the outside in Turns One and Two, then catapulting past third-place qualifier Jimmy Vasser in Turns Three and Four. Only two obstacles lay ahead – Montoya, whose new single-wastegate Toyota engine had powered him to pole position, and rookie talent Kenny Bräck in Team Rahal's Shell Ford/Reynard.

While Andretti was on the hunt at the front of the field, there were problems at the back as PPI Motorsports' Oriol Servia lost control of his Telefonica Toyota/Reynard in Turn Four. The caution flags waved before the first lap had been completed and brought an end to the Spaniard's day.

It was all Montoya on the ensuing restart. With Bräck avoiding a challenge by Andretti and standing his ground in second place, Montoya was off in the distance. By the time a second caution came, on lap 30 for debris, Montoya had amassed a lead of more than seven seconds. At that moment, yellow was the color of choice for Team KOOL Green teammates Dario Franchitti and Paul Tracy, who had been in danger of going a lap down to the flying Colombian.

The leaders took the opportunity to make their first round of pit stops. Montoya emerged in the lead once again, followed by teammate Vasser. Andretti resumed in third, trailed by Roberto Moreno in Patrick Racing's Visteon Ford/Reynard and Tony Kanaan, who was having a good run aboard Mo Nunn Racing's Hollywood Mercedes/Reynard. It was a costly pit stop for Kenny Bräck, however, who entered in second, but emerged in sixth position.

If the next 40 laps were any indication, it looked as though the day

Photos: Jon Ferrey, Darrell Ingham & Robert Laberge/Allsport USA

FEDEX CHAMPIONSHIP SERIES • ROUND 4

Right: Service is completed by Simon Hodgson's crew, allowing Juan Montoya to rejoin the race after a scheduled pit stop.
Jon Ferrey/Allsport USA

QUALIFYING

A driver with Lady Luck on his side, at least initially, was defending series champion Juan Montoya, who claimed the top spot in qualifying for the Firestone Firehawk 500 after misfortune befell the weekend's pacesetter, Kenny Bräck *(below)*.

Under windy qualifying conditions, Montoya couldn't match his pace from the final practice session, but his second flying lap of 26.237 seconds was enough to secure the Colombian's ninth Champ Car pole in only 25 attempts.

Kenny Bräck's Shell Ford/Reynard had been the car to beat throughout the two days of practice at the superb Twin Ring Motegi facility. The Swede's hopes of his first pole position seemed lost, however, when the rookie suffered a catastrophic engine failure immediately after taking the green flag on his qualifying run. With the minutes ticking away, Team Rahal hurriedly wheeled out the backup car and Bräck *(below)* ventured out for a second qualifying attempt.

He was permitted only one lap in accordance with CART regulations, and while his lap of 26.393 seconds (211.263 mph) did not topple Montoya's Target/Chip Ganassi Toyota/Lola, it was good enough to place Bräck on the front row.

"We kind of suspected that the engine was bad after this morning, but we crossed our fingers and hoped it would be all right," said a relieved Bräck following his eventful afternoon. "Obviously it wasn't, but I can't say enough for the team. To bring out the spare car and have it be close to the setup of the primary car was just fantastic. I think that all we were missing was a new set of tires."

Jimmy Vasser completed a one-three punch by Toyota, securing a position on the inside of the second row with a lap of 26.455 seconds in the other Target car, with Roberto Moreno alongside after a lap of 26.486 seconds in Patrick Racing's Visteon Ford/Reynard.

Gil de Ferran earned honors as the quickest of the Honda contingent, lining up fifth on the grid in the Marlboro Team Penske Reynard. Mauricio Gugelmin was Mercedes-Benz's star, improving from 13th in practice to take seventh on the grid in his Nextel/PacWest Racing Reynard.

Jon Ferrey/Allsport USA

Toyota's maiden win falls by the pit-side

DESPITE what can only be described as a bizarre mishap during Juan Montoya's final pit stop, Toyota gained some satisfaction from clearly making its point at Motegi. Montoya dominated the Firestone Firehawk 500, leading 172 of the first 175 laps. Jimmy Vasser, who left Japan with his second-place ranking in the points standing intact, had an impressive run at the front until being sidelined by mechanical problems. He and teammate Montoya set the two fastest laps of the race, while Cristiano da Matta's second consecutive fourth-place finish vaulted him to fourth in the standings.

But the frustration was evident.

"It's terribly disappointing not to get our first win due to some fluke misfortune," said Jim Aust, Toyota Vice President of Motorsports. "Juan easily had the field covered. He deserved the win today. We know we've got the package to get the job done. All we need now is a little racing luck."

The "fluke" occurred during Montoya's final scheduled stop on lap 174. As the pneumatic hose that operates the onboard airjack system was removed following the tire change, it dislodged the electrical lead to the pop-off valve (which regulates the turbocharger boost pressure to a maximum of 40 inches of mercury per CART regulations) situated on top of the engine.

As Montoya accelerated out of the pits, the pop-off valve was stuck in the open position, thereby robbing him of all turbo boost and, therefore, several hundred horsepower. There was no alternative but to make an additional stop for the lead to be reaffixed. Any hope of Toyota scoring its first victory – ironically at a track owned by Honda – had been thwarted.

Six points for seventh place, plus the bonus marks for pole and leading most laps, seemed scant reward for a brilliant effort by Montoya – and Toyota.

should have belonged to the boys in red, as Montoya and Vasser stretched their advantage to almost half a lap over Andretti and the field.

Their dominance was interrupted on lap 80 when Mark Blundell, fighting an ill-handling Motorola PacWest Mercedes/Reynard, lost control and spun. He emerged unscathed as the leaders headed to the pits for a second round of stops.

Montoya and Vasser maintained control of the race followed by Andretti, who briefly lost third place to Moreno after a slightly slower pit stop, but quickly reclaimed his position.

"That kind of ticked me off a little bit because I had to work to get by him again," said Andretti. "But given everything that we have gone through recently, [the crew] obviously did the right thing [by being more conservative]."

By mid-race, it was a game of follow the leader – except that Montoya was off in the distance again, this time four seconds clear of his teammate. Vasser slowly began to regain some ground, however, and by lap 123 was less than a second behind.

But all was not well with the Toyota/Lola. Moments later, Vasser, who

FEDEX CHAMPIONSHIP SERIES • ROUND 4

had begun the weekend second in the championship point standings, coasted in to a stop. The engine had failed.

"There was a big vibration and I had to shut it off," reported Vasser. "I was pretty much cruising, trying to take care of my car. We had a really good package. It's just one of those unfortunate things."

As the third round of pit stops got under way, Adrian Fernandez parlayed excellent fuel consumption to take the lead for three laps after Montoya's scheduled stop on lap 132, giving his Tecate/Quaker State Ford/Reynard a few minutes in the limelight. Montoya resumed at the front of the pack when Fernandez entered pit lane to refuel on lap 135.

Andretti, meanwhile, was more than ten seconds behind Montoya, followed by Franchitti, who benefited again from great pit stops by Team KOOL Green and a few adjustments to overcome early handling problems.

With 40 laps to go, Montoya led Andretti by 7.4 seconds. Franchitti was a similar distance behind in third. The battle at this point was between the Brazilians for fourth, as Moreno, a further six seconds in arrears, was under pressure from Christian Fittipaldi's Big Kmart/Route 66 Ford/Lola and Cristiano da Matta's Pioneer Toyota/Reynard. Kanaan ran seventh, pursued by points leader Tracy, who had been handicapped during the early stages by excessive oversteer. The only remaining drivers Montoya had not managed to lap were Bräck, who was plagued by a broken weight-jacker and fell to ninth, and Gil de Ferran at the wheel of Marlboro Team Penske's Honda/Reynard.

Timing is everything, and both Fittipaldi and de Ferran saw any hope of a top-five finish slip away when they made their fourth pit stops moments before a full-course yellow as Blundell performed his second pirouette of the day, hitting the wall lightly coming out of Turn Two.

"I just battled handling problems all day," said a frustrated Blundell. "It was only a matter of time before I got too close to the wall. Thankfully, I managed to walk away without any injury."

The yellow brought everyone else into the pits, whereupon Montoya emerged ahead of Andretti and Moreno, who nipped past Franchitti.

To the surprise of everyone, particularly Andretti, Montoya pulled back into pit lane before the restart. In a

Left: Tarso Marques faced a steep learning curve following a last-minute deal to drive the brand-new Ford-powered Swift 011.c.

Below: Dario Franchitti overcame a shaky start to finish in a strong second place.

bizarre turn of events, Montoya's crew had inadvertently wrapped the airjack hose around the pop-off valve during the pit stop and, as he went to rejoin the field, a crucial electrical lead was dislodged, which left his engine drastically short on power. The Target/Chip Ganassi crew made the repair in a matter of seconds, but Montoya slipped from first to eighth and the Toyota top brass watched in despair as any hope of a first victory went out the window.

"I had such a great car today," lamented Montoya, who ended up seventh. "It was so fast; it was just awesome."

At the restart on lap 179, Andretti held the lead followed by Franchitti, who reclaimed second from Moreno. With 12 laps remaining, smoke pouring from the back of Kanaan's Reynard brought out the caution flags once again.

Andretti was on the point, and the only two things that could hamper his claim of victory were a restart and a flying Scotsman.

"I knew the restart was going to be a problem because of all the oil-dry down in [Turns] Three and Four," related Andretti. "I just kept the car above the oil-dry so I would have a good clean line and just try to stand on the throttle when I knew I could stand on it, and hopefully steal a little of Dario's air, and it worked perfect."

Indeed, Andretti took the checkered flag 0.546 second ahead of Franchitti. Under the circumstances, Franchitti was delighted.

"Second is not as good as first, but I'll take it," said Franchitti after posting his first podium finish of the season. "It was a great day for Team KOOL Green and I can't say enough about the Honda engine. But this guy [Andretti] is pretty tough to pass. He's been doing this for awhile and knows exactly where to position the car."

Moreno posted his second podium of the season with his fine run to third, while da Matta claimed his second consecutive fourth-place finish with a superb drive. Bräck followed in fifth, with Tracy earning every bit of his sixth-place result after starting a lowly 20th.

The Canadian strengthened his lead atop the FedEx Series points standings, while Andretti vaulted from nowhere to eighth.

"Finally, we got a break that went our way," said a relieved Andretti, who moved into third on the all-time Champ Car win list with his latest triumph. "I think we could have been up there a few times this year already, but we have just had a lot of bad luck. It just feels really good to break the ice and get back up here."

Jeremy Shaw

FEDEX CHAMPIONSHIP SERIES • ROUND 4

MOTEGI SNIPPETS

• Della Penna Motorsports' rookie driver **NORBERTO FONTANA** did not start the race after crashing heavily in his VideoMatch Toyota/Reynard during the Friday morning practice session. Fontana passed out briefly while being taken to the infield care center. He was transported to a local hospital, where CAT scans confirmed no serious injury. Fontana remained in the hospital overnight for further observation after complaining of some neck discomfort.

• **MEMO GIDLEY** resumed his super-sub duties for Patrick Carpentier, who had broken his wrist in a fall at his home. Gidley posted another fine performance aboard the Player's/Indeck Ford/Reynard, rising from 14th to ninth after the second round of pit stops. Unfortunately, his race was ended by an engine failure in the closing stages.

• **HONDA**, on home ground, breathed a sigh of relief when a last-gasp problem prevented Juan Montoya from scoring a long overdue maiden victory for Toyota. The win by Ford was by far the lesser of two evils. Honda ended the weekend on a high note, however: Franchitti rose from 17th on the grid to finish second, while Tracy left with the championship lead still in hand.

• After severing its ties with Forsythe Championship Racing, **SWIFT ENGINEERING** entered a new association with Dale Coyne Racing and watched intently as young Brazilian Tarso Marques turned the first-ever laps aboard a hastily prepared Ford Cosworth-powered Swift 011.c chassis. While Marques found himself at the bottom of the timing charts, he overcame lengthy pit stops to reach the finish, albeit 15 laps in arrears.

• While Target/Chip Ganassi teammates Juan Montoya and Jimmy Vasser were the only two contenders to lap in the 26s, turning the fastest laps of the race at 26.812 seconds and 26.79 seconds respectively, no fewer than 11 of their **RIVALS** each turned a best lap of between 27.000 and 27.186 seconds. They were, in order, Brack, da Matta, Gidley, Nakano, Tracy, Papis, Fittipaldi, Andretti, Franchitti, Moreno and Kanaan.

• Bryan Herta made the journey to Japan as a possible **SUBSTITUTE** for Shinji Nakano (left), who had suffered a testing accident at Milwaukee on March 31. The Japanese driver passed a fitness test, however, and duly regained his seat at Walker Racing. Nakano ran some quick laps in his Honda/Reynard, but the car suffered from understeer when running with full tanks, which restricted him to a 14th-place finish.

FEDEX CHAMPIONSHIP SERIES • ROUND 4
FIRESTONE FIREHAWK 500

TWIN RING MOTEGI, MOTEGI, JAPAN

MAY 14, 201 laps of 1.549 miles – 311.349 miles

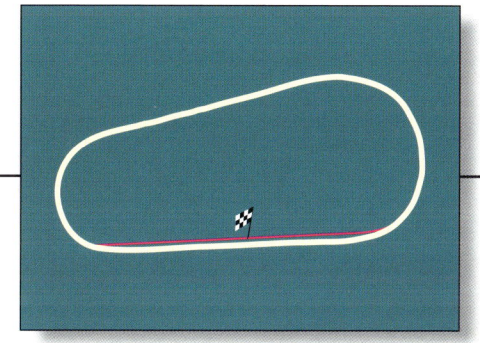

Place	Driver (Nat.)	No.	Team Sponsors Engine/Car	Tires	Q Speed	Q Time	Q Pos.	Laps	Time/Status	Ave. (mph)	Pts.
1	Michael Andretti (USA)	6	Newman/Haas Big Kmart/Texaco Ford Cosworth/Lola B2K/00	FS	209.191	26.657s	8	201	1h 58m 52.201s	157.154	20
2	Dario Franchitti (GB)	27	Team KOOL Green Honda/Reynard 2KI	FS	207.224	26.910s	17	201	1h 58m 52.747s	157.142	16
3	Roberto Moreno (BR)	20	Patrick Racing Visteon Ford Cosworth/Reynard 2KI	FS	210.541	26.486s	4	201	1h 58m 55.026s	157.092	14
4	Cristiano da Matta (BR)	97	PPI Motorsports Pioneer/MCI WorldCom Toyota/Reynard 2KI	FS	207.147	26.920s	19	201	1h 58m 55.743s	157.076	12
5	*Kenny Bräck (S)	8	Team Rahal Shell Ford Cosworth/Reynard 2KI	FS	211.283	26.393s	2	201	1h 58m 56.126s	157.068	10
6	Paul Tracy (CDN)	26	Team KOOL Green Honda/Reynard 2KI	FS	206.671	26.982s	20	201	1h 58m 56.460s	157.061	8
7	Juan Montoya (COL)	1	Target/Chip Ganassi Racing Toyota/Lola B2K/00	FS	212.540	26.237s	1	201	1h 58m 57.053s	157.048	8
8	Max Papis (I)	7	Team Rahal Miller Lite Ford Cosworth/Reynard 2KI	FS	208.300	26.771s	12	200	Running		5
9	Gil de Ferran (BR)	2	Marlboro Team Penske Marlboro Honda/Reynard 2KI	FS	210.335	26.512s	5	200	Running		4
10	Adrian Fernandez (MEX)	40	Patrick Racing Tecate/Quaker State Ford Cosworth/Reynard 2KI	FS	207.826	26.832s	15	200	Running		3
11	Christian Fittipaldi (BR)	11	Newman/Haas Big Kmart/Route 66 Ford Cosworth/Lola B2K/00	FS	210.145	26.536s	6	199	Running		2
12	Michel Jourdain Jr. (MEX)	16	Bettenhausen Motorsports Herdez Mercedes/Lola B2K/00	FS	207.186	26.915s	18	198	Running		1
13	Helio Castroneves (BR)	3	Marlboro Team Penske Marlboro Honda/Reynard 2KI	FS	207.826	26.832s	14	198	Running		
14	*Shinji Nakano (J)	5	Walker Racing Avex Group Honda/Reynard 2KI	FS	208.604	26.732s	11	198	Running		
15	*Alexandre Tagliani (CDN)	33	Forsythe Racing Player's/Indeck Ford Cosworth/Reynard 2KI	FS	208.737	26.715s	10	198	Running		
16	Tony Kanaan (BR)	55	Mo Nunn Racing Hollywood Mercedes/Reynard 2KI	FS	209.112	26.667s	9	189	Engine		
17	Tarso Marques (BR)	34	Dale Coyne Racing Panasonic Ford Cosworth/Swift 011.c	FS	205.635	27.118s	21	186	Running		
18	Memo Gidley (USA)	32	Forsythe Racing Player's/Indeck Ford Cosworth/Reynard 2KI	FS	207.726	26.845s	16	182	Electrical		
19	Mark Blundell (GB)	18	PacWest Racing Motorola Mercedes/Reynard 2KI	FS	203.429	27.412s	22	161	Accident		
20	*Takuya Kurosawa (J)	19	Dale Coyne Racing MTCI Ford Cosworth/Lola B2K/00	FS	202.366	27.556s	23	131	Pit incident		
21	Jimmy Vasser (USA)	12	Target/Chip Ganassi Racing Toyota/Lola B2K/00	FS	210.788	26.455s	3	127	Engine		
22	Mauricio Gugelmin (BR)	17	PacWest Racing Nextel Mercedes/Reynard 2KI	FS	209.379	26.693s	7	42	Exhaust		
23	Luiz Garcia Jr. (BR)	25	Arciero-PRG Hollywood/Embratel-21 Mercedes/Reynard 2KI	FS	201.430	27.604s	24	18	Transmission		
24	Oriol Servia (E)	96	PPI Motorsports Telefonica Toyota/Reynard 2KI	FS	207.989	26.871s	13	0	Accident		
25	*Norberto Fontana (RA)	10	Della Penna Motorsports VideoMatch Toyota/Reynard 2KI	FS	No speed	No time	–	0	Withdrawn		

*denotes rookie driver

Caution flags: Laps 1–6, accident/Servia; laps 32–38, debris; laps 79–84, accident/Jourdain; laps 171–177, accident/Jourdain; laps 192–196, mechanical/Kanaan. **Total:** Five for 29 laps.
Lap leaders: Juan Montoya, 1–132 (132 laps), Adrian Fernandez, 133–135 (3 laps), Montoya, 136–175 (40 laps), Michael Andretti, 176–201 (26 laps). **Totals:** Montoya, 172 laps, Andretti, 26 laps, Fernandez, 3 laps.
Fastest race lap: Juan Montoya, 26.812s, 207.982 mph on lap 73.
Championship positions: 1 Tracy, 58; **2** Vasser & Moreno, 42; **4** Papis & da Matta, 25; **6** Fernandez, 23; **7** de Ferran, 22; **8** Andretti & Franchitti, 20; **10** Tagliani & Fittipaldi, 18; **12** Castroneves, 16; **13** Bräck, 13; **14** Blundell, 11; **15** Herta & Carpentier, 10; **17** Montoya, 9; **18** Servia, 8; **19** Nakano & Gidley, 5; **21** Gugelmin, Jourdain & Kanaan, 3; **24** Garcia, 2.

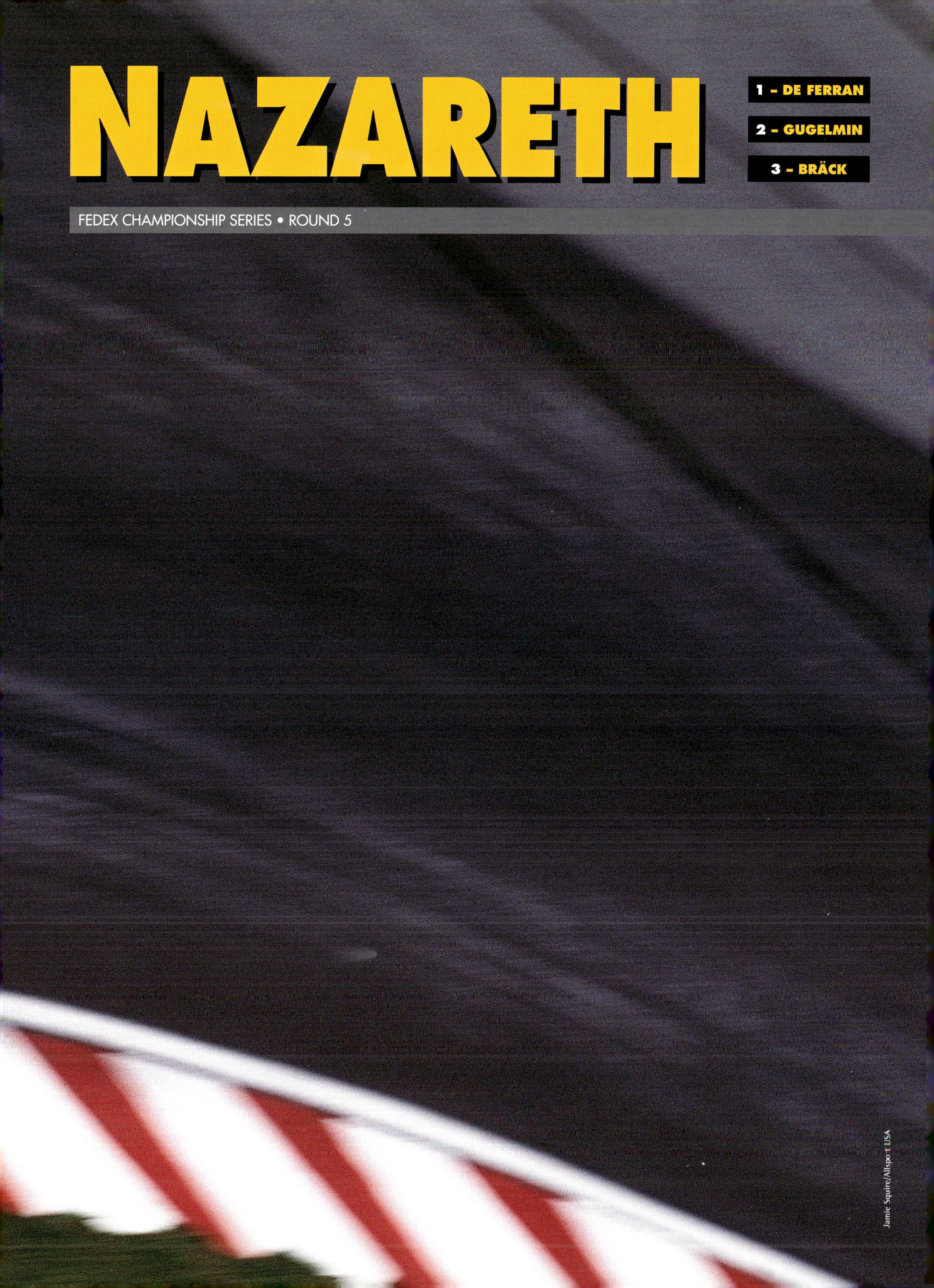

NAZARETH
1 - DE FERRAN
2 - GUGELMIN
3 - BRÄCK
FEDEX CHAMPIONSHIP SERIES • ROUND 5

Jamie Squire/Allsport USA

FEDEX CHAMPIONSHIP SERIES • ROUND 5

QUALIFYING

Juan Montoya secured his second pole in as many visits to the quirky Nazareth Speedway with a typically impressive effort during the traditional single-car qualifying session. Gusty winds saw speeds drop slightly in comparison to the morning practice, when Montoya also turned the fastest lap at 19.121 seconds, an average speed of 178.108 mph. Nevertheless, after Christian Fittipaldi had posted a time to beat of 19.306 seconds (176.401 mph), Montoya required only one flying lap to snatch the inside front-row grid position in Target/Chip Ganassi Racing's Toyota/Lola.

"I tell you what," proclaimed Ganassi, "that kid's something special, isn't he?"

"The wind moved the car a little bit," declared Montoya after claiming his eighth pole in only his 22nd Champ Car start, "but there was a lot of potential to go quicker. Bill [Pappas – race engineer] did a great job. The car was awesome. We did some testing here and I think it really gave us an advantage since we knew where to go with the car right off."

Fittipaldi was content to start second, his smooth driving style proving substantially more effective than his Newman/Haas Racing teammate, Michael Andretti, who could manage no better than 15th – his worst starting position in 13 starts at his hometown race track.

"I was surprised how slow I was," said a disappointed Andretti. "We just haven't got the balance right for my style of driving. Very frustrating."

Helio Castroneves, who started on the front row in '99 for Hogan Racing, had to be content with third this time at the wheel of the rejuvenated Marlboro Team Penske's #3 Honda/Reynard.

"I just wish we could have been a little quicker," said the Brazilian. "That's what I could do today, but you always finish the run and wish you could have maybe run a little quicker."

Teammate Gil de Ferran ended up fifth behind Paul Tracy's similar Team KOOL Green Honda/Reynard.

"It was awfully windy and the car was moving around a little bit – too much for me to get really comfortable in the car," related Tracy.

Kenny Bräck was fastest of the rookie contingent, overcoming a heavy accident on Friday afternoon to set the sixth-fastest time aboard Team Rahal's Shell Ford Cosworth/Reynard.

Robert Laberge/Allsport USA

Penske claims 100th win

WHEN Paul Tracy claimed consecutive victories for Marlboro Team Penske at Nazareth, Rio and Gateway in 1997, it left team owner Roger Penske on the cusp of an astonishing, record-extending 100th Champ Car triumph. At the time, no one would have believed that it would take almost exactly three years to reach the milestone.

In the meantime, as the frustration mounted, Penske's team had been completely revamped. Its own Penske chassis had been replaced by Reynards; the Mercedes-Benz engines were dumped in favor of Hondas; Goodyear's withdrawal meant a switch to Firestone tires; and drivers Tracy and erstwhile teammate Al Unser Jr. had been sent packing, to be replaced by Gil de Ferran and Helio Castroneves.

The management structure, too, had been changed, with Tim Cindric, formerly team manager for Team Rahal, being installed as president of Penske Racing. The one constant was Penske's own belief that eventually his fortunes would turn.

"I really don't know what to say," said Penske during the post-race press conference. "I was worrying about the race. I really wasn't thinking about the 100th win. I guess you had to figure if we won the race, the numbers would take care of themselves.

"Our first win was 30 years ago at Pocono [with Mark Donohue], not too far from here. It's kind of ironic that we would come back here at Nazareth to finally get our 100th win. Our race team is headquartered here in [Reading] Pennsylvania; we've been here for many years.

"Our team has hung together. We've had some downs and ups, ups and downs over the last few years, but I think you've seen we've been able to put the right combination together to where our performance has certainly been competitive."

Indeed so. For a team that had earned just one top-five finish in 1999, the new season witnessed a dramatic turnaround. De Ferran started from pole at Homestead and Long Beach, only to finish sixth on each occasion, while teammate Castroneves enjoyed a fine second-place finish at Long Beach, together with a third-place qualifying run at Nazareth.

"In my mind, it was just a matter of time before we got things right," said de Ferran. "The first few races were a process we had to go through together. I said before the season that I expected the team to get better and better as the season goes on."

FEDEX CHAMPIONSHIP SERIES • ROUND 5

Pages 96/97: Gil de Ferran chose the perfect time to score his first oval victory.

Far left: A blanket of snow forced officials to postpone the original race date.

Below far left: Montoya led the way for Toyota until the second round of pit stops.

Below left: Roger Penske celebrated his milestone 100th win in exuberant style.

THE weather is always a hot topic of conversation when the Champ Cars visit Nazareth Speedway. Mother Nature has a tendency toward unpredictability during springtime in Pennsylvania, and there were more than a few raised eyebrows when Championship Auto Racing Teams announced that its annual Bosch Spark Plug Grand Prix Presented by Toyota would be held on April 9.

Local resident Michael Andretti was among many to express his surprise, even suggesting that snow might not be out of the question. Well, turned out he was right!

Practice and qualifying were held in near-perfect conditions, with temperatures in the 70s, but then a huge cold front blew in from the west. When the crews awoke on race morning, they were greeted by a blanket of white. Officials had no option but to postpone the race.

The conditions were altogether more hospitable when the FedEx Championship Series contenders reconvened some seven weeks later. Nevertheless, the dark cloud that had followed defending series champion Juan Montoya in recent races made another appearance, and the enormously gifted Colombian once again came up short in his effort to score that elusive first victory for Toyota.

Instead, after Montoya had dominated the first half of the 225-lap race, Gil de Ferran emerged to record his first-ever triumph on an oval. More significantly, the Brazilian's patient drive finally brought team owner Roger Penske his long-awaited 100th Champ Car victory.

"I tell you, it is a very special day," said de Ferran. "I have won races before, and Roger has many victories. But for us to win together, for me is almost indescribable."

De Ferran's joy – and relief – was palpable. He drove a fine race aboard Marlboro Team Penske's Honda/Reynard, even though, in the early stages, like everyone else, he had to play second fiddle to Montoya's Target/Chip Ganassi Racing Toyota/Lola.

Montoya took off into the lead at the start, chased by Christian Fittipaldi, who posted a career-best short-oval qualifying effort in Newman/Haas Racing's Big Kmart/Route 66 Ford/Lola. Paul Tracy (KOOL Honda/Reynard) followed in third after ousting the second Marlboro car of Helio Castroneves at the first corner.

Tracy's teammate, Dario Franchitti, wasn't so fortunate, as he lost control approaching the green flag and hit the wall. After a short delay, Montoya took off like a scalded cat. Fittipaldi remained within a second or so until lap 25, but as soon as the leaders began to encounter slower traffic, Montoya made his break.

By lap 36, his lead had grown to almost seven seconds. But then the margin diminished steadily as he came up behind Mark Blundell's Motorola Mercedes/Reynard and spent more than 15 laps bottled up behind the Englishman, who was trying all he knew to remain on the lead lap.

The gap between Montoya and Fittipaldi had been trimmed to around 1.5 seconds by lap 50. Tracy chased hard in third place, followed by Castroneves, who, on lap 72, lost out to teammate de Ferran under braking for Turn Three. Next time around, Max Papis spun his 13th-placed Miller Lite/Team Rahal Ford/Reynard at the exit of Turn One to bring out the yellow flags for a second time.

The ensuing first round of pit stops saw Tracy take advantage of brilliant work by Tony Cotman's crew to leapfrog from third to first, just beating Montoya out of the pits. Montoya set the record straight immediately at the restart, leaving Tracy to fend off Fittipaldi, de Ferran, Bräck and Roberto Moreno, running well again in Pat Patrick's Visteon Ford/Reynard.

Overtaking proved to be all but impossible on the tight, unforgiving 0.946-mile tri-oval, so it wasn't until the next round of pit stops – on lap 118, again under yellow, after Norberto Fontana had spun John Della Penna's VideoMatch Toyota/Reynard into the wall in Turn Two – that the next shuffling of the order came about.

Tony Kanaan (Hollywood Mercedes/Reynard) and Jimmy Vasser (Target Toyota/Lola) elected not to follow the leaders into pit lane and duly emerged in the lead when the race was restarted. Behind, however, Tracy found himself with nowhere to go when Michel Jourdain Jr., running a lap down, lost control of his Herdez Mercedes/Lola coming up for the green. Several others took evasive action, including Montoya, who, having lost several positions in the pits, endured another setback when he ran into the back of Moreno, damaging his Lola's right front wing. Montoya fell to the tail end of the lead lap when he pitted for repairs.

After an extended caution, Kanaan took advantage of track position to lead from de Ferran. The gap between the two Brazilians soon opened to more than a second. Moreno, in third, was unable to match the leading pace, but still remained clear of a battle

Gugelmin runs strong

MAURICIO Gugelmin gave Bruce McCaw's PacWest Racing Group a welcome shot in the arm by finishing a strong second in his Nextel Mercedes/Reynard. It was the first sign of real competitiveness for the latest Mercedes-Benz IC108F engine and the result of a particularly noteworthy performance by the Brazilian, who was among very few drivers to make a significant number of passes on the tricky, slightly-less-than-one-mile oval.

"Today was a great ending, but it was a long day altogether," proclaimed Gugelmin. "Since it was pretty difficult to do an overtaking maneuver, you pretty much had to rely on a banzai move."

Good pit stops also were crucial. After starting 12th, Gugelmin remained in that position, following in the wheel tracks of Jimmy Vasser, until the first round of pit stops on lap 76. He made up two places during the stops, then took advantage of various dramas to move into the top six by lap 137. He was elevated to fourth when Tony Kanaan and Christian Fittipaldi made pit stops during a caution on lap 158, and, on lap 205, usurped Kenny Bräck from third with an opportunistic pass into Turn Three. When Roberto Moreno hit the wall with ten laps remaining, Gugelmin took over in second, then pushed Gil de Ferran all the way to the finish line.

"We made tremendous mileage early in the race and had a little in reserve at the end when it counted," said Gugelmin. "This was only a one-day event, so there were not the Friday and Saturday sessions to put the normal amount of rubber down and you had to be careful. The smart ones made it to the end."

"It is important for us to go on from here and for everyone to realize that we can win races," he continued. "I think we have been unlucky a couple of times this year, but we need to use this as the turning point."

Mauricio Gugelmin charged to a fine second-place finish for the PacWest team.

between Bräck, Fittipaldi and Mauricio Gugelmin (Nextel Mercedes/Reynard).

Jourdain's eventful day ended on lap 155 when a blown engine sent him into the wall in Turn One. There was more drama at the same corner soon after the restart, too, when Castroneves, who was running in 11th (after losing time with a vibration in the early stages, then a drive-through penalty for a pit-lane infraction), tangled with the lapped car of Blundell. There was some initial concern about the Englishman's well-being after a heavy impact. Thankfully, he emerged bruised, but unscathed.

The gamble by Kanaan's crew failed to pay off when he made a pit stop during the caution and fell to the back of the pack. Everyone else benefited from the lengthy caution periods, which ensured that there was no need for an additional pit stop.

De Ferran was in control through the final stages, despite one more interruption when a fine run for Moreno ended against the wall in Turn One, with just ten laps remaining. Troubled by a slow puncture, Moreno elected to press on toward the finish. He paid the price when he found himself off-line while being passed by a charging Gugelmin, who also had found a way past Bräck on lap 206.

"We were just trying to hang on there," said Moreno. "The tire was going down slowly and we thought we would be OK. We had to gamble a little bit because if we would have come in [to the pits], we would have finished [out of the points] anyway."

Moreno's incident paved the way for a three-lap dash to the checkered flag – plenty of time for a last-minute drama, as Roger Penske, watching anxiously in the pits, knew all too well.

"I felt pretty good when there were five laps to go [under caution] and I saw [backmarkers Luiz] Garcia and Tarso [Marques] in between [de Ferran and Gugelmin]," related Penske, "but when they came off Turn Four [for the green], there was Mo on his tailpipe. I couldn't believe it."

Gugelmin, indeed, had pounced immediately past the slower cars and looked set to make a late bid for victory. But de Ferran remained unflustered and made no mistakes, taking the checkered flag 0.815 second clear of his fellow Brazilian.

"Roger kept me informed of the situation over the radio," said de Ferran after earning his fourth Champ Car victory. "He has an amazing knack for keeping me posted and keeping me calm."

A gutsy performance by Gugelmin secured his best result since winning at Vancouver in '97, while rookie Bräck earned a place on the podium for the first time in his Champ Car career after passing Fernandez at the final restart.

Montoya, meanwhile, having fallen as low as 13th, posted a fine comeback to finish fourth – also his best result of the season thus far.

"I was on it today, but bad luck caught us out twice," related Montoya, who led for 110 laps. "Team Target did a great job today getting the nose back on the car, but those last two [cautions] killed us. After we replaced the nose, I was on old tires and the car was getting a bit loose, but when I was running alone, I was fast. It was really good to get some points today."

The unfortunate Fernandez, who had passed both Montoya and Bräck in an opportunist maneuver on lap 206, had to be content with fifth after falling behind both his adversaries at the final restart.

"It wasn't a great day, but it wasn't a bad day either," concluded the Mexican. "We did the best we could with what we had and got some points in the championship. I had a couple of big moments out there, especially in traffic at the end. I lost a couple of positions on the last restart because I couldn't get the power down, and that cost us a podium finish."

Local hero Andretti overcame a lack of boost to finish sixth, ahead of Vasser and Kanaan, who were the last drivers to complete the full 225 laps.

Jeremy Shaw

FEDEX CHAMPIONSHIP SERIES • ROUND 5

NAZARETH SNIPPETS

- Citing a lack of practice time, **WALKER RACING** elected to skip the rescheduled race after being unable to arrange a prior test session for Shinji Nakano, who had been injured in a crash one week prior to the original race date in April.

- The driver previously known as Helio Castro-Neves *(right)* issued a press release prior to the Nazareth race, asking that the **HYPHEN** hereinafter be deleted from his name. "I keep getting called Helio Castro or Helio Neves," explained the newly monikered Castroneves. "I know Catherine Zeta-Jones doesn't seem to have a problem [with a double-barreled name], but I'm not a famous actress!"

- Reigning PPG-Dayton Indy Lights Champion **ORIOL SERVIA** bounced back from two consecutive first-lap spins into retirement by finishing a strong ninth aboard Cal Wells' Telefonica Toyota/Reynard. Servia ran among the leading group all day, despite losing the use of fifth gear at one-quarter distance, which meant he had to rely on sixth for the remainder of the race.

- An unhappy **PAUL TRACY** was penalized on two occasions for passing cars before the green flag at restarts. The series points leader was particularly angry with Luiz Garcia Jr., who finished 11 laps behind and held up the Canadian on more than one occasion. Tracy, who led for eight laps after the first round of pit stops, eventually finished tenth.

- Victory for **GIL DE FERRAN** brought Honda into a tie on points with Ford Cosworth in the battle for the coveted CART Manufacturer's Championship. De Ferran's triumph also lifted Team Brazil back into the overall lead in the CART Nation's Cup standings, breaking a tie with Team USA.

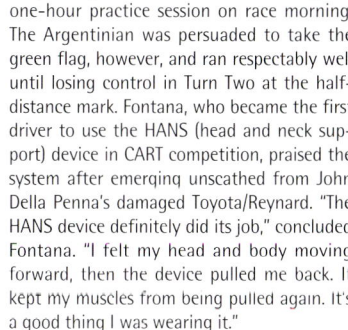

- **NORBERTO FONTANA**, who missed the race at Motegi after a heavy crash during practice, contemplated not starting at Nazareth after complaining of some dizziness following the one-hour practice session on race morning. The Argentinian was persuaded to take the green flag, however, and ran respectably well until losing control in Turn Two at the half-distance mark. Fontana, who became the first driver to use the HANS (head and neck support) device in CART competition, praised the system after emerging unscathed from John Della Penna's damaged Toyota/Reynard. "The HANS device definitely did its job," concluded Fontana. "I felt my head and body moving forward, then the device pulled me back. It kept my muscles from being pulled again. It's a good thing I was wearing it."

- After Juan Montoya was thwarted in his bid for a first win of the season, team owner **CHIP GANASSI** instead was looking forward to the following day's Indianapolis 500: "All I can say is that the fastest car didn't win, but that happens often in this sport. But hey, the weekend is only halfway over for the Target team..."

- Nazareth resident **MICHAEL ANDRETTI** added another venture to his already diverse business portfolio during the race weekend, announcing his new role as co-owner of the locally based Lehigh Valley Xtreme ice hockey team, which competes in the United Hockey League. His other interests include three power sports stores, partnerships in a car dealership, two racing-themed restaurants, three car washes and a distributorship for car-wash equipment.

FEDEX CHAMPIONSHIP SERIES • ROUND 5
BOSCH SPARK PLUG GRAND PRIX PRESENTED BY TOYOTA

NAZARETH SPEEDWAY, NAZARETH, PENNSYLVANIA

MAY 27, 225 laps of 0.946 miles – 212.85 miles

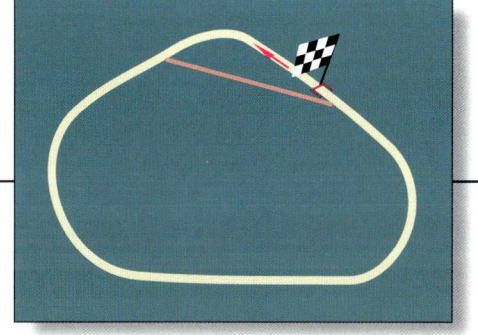

Place	Driver (Nat.)	No.	Team Sponsors Engine/Chassis	Tires	Q Speed	Q Time	Q Pos.	Laps	Time/Status	Ave. (mph)	Pts.
1	Gil de Ferran (BR)	2	Marlboro Team Penske Marlboro Honda/Reynard 2KI	FS	175.628	19.391s	5	225	2h 06m 10.334s	101.219	20
2	Mauricio Gugelmin (BR)	17	PacWest Racing Nextel Mercedes/Reynard 2KI	FS	173.260	19.656s	12	225	2h 06m 11.149s	101.194	16
3	*Kenny Bräck (S)	8	Team Rahal Shell Ford Cosworth/Reynard 2KI	FS	175.465	19.409s	6	225	2h 06m 12.214s	101.194	14
4	Juan Montoya (COL)	1	Target/Chip Ganassi Racing Toyota/Lola B2K/00	FS	176.868	19.255s	1	225	2h 06m 12.442s	101.191	14
5	Adrian Fernandez (MEX)	40	Patrick Racing Tecate/Quaker State Ford Cosworth/Reynard 2KI	FS	174.182	19.552s	9	225	2h 06m 15.052s	101.156	10
6	Michael Andretti (USA)	6	Newman/Haas Big Kmart/Texaco Ford Cosworth/Lola B2K/00	FS	172.392	19.755s	15	225	2h 06m 15.911s	101.144	8
7	Jimmy Vasser (USA)	12	Target/Chip Ganassi Racing Toyota/Lola B2K/00	FS	174.128	19.558s	11	225	2h 06m 17.322s	101.125	6
8	Tony Kanaan (BR)	55	Mo Nunn Racing Hollywood Mercedes/Reynard 2KI	FS	174.664	19.498s	8	225	2h 06m 18.923s	101.104	5
9	*Oriol Servia (E)	96	PPI Motorsports Telefonica Toyota/Reynard 2KI	FS	170.852	19.933s	17	224	Running		4
10	Paul Tracy (CDN)	26	Team KOOL Green Honda/Reynard 2KI	FS	175.891	19.362s	4	224	Running		3
11	Christian Fittipaldi (BR)	11	Newman/Haas Big Kmart/Route 66 Ford Cosworth/Lola B2K/00	FS	176.401	19.306s	2	224	Running		2
12	Tarso Marques (BR)	34	Dale Coyne Racing Panasonic Ford Cosworth/Swift 011.c	FS	no speed	no time	23	222	Running		1
13	Cristiano da Matta (BR)	97	PPI Motorsports Pioneer/MCI WorldCom Toyota/Reynard 2KI	FS	169.644	20.075s	19	221	Running		
14	Roberto Moreno (BR)	20	Patrick Racing Visteon Ford Cosworth/Reynard 2KI	FS	175.393	19.417s	7	214	Accident		
15	Luiz Garcia Jr. (BR)	25	Arciero-PRG Hollywood/Embratel-21 Mercedes/Reynard 2KI	FS	131.475	25.903s	22	214	Running		
16	Helio Castroneves (BR)	3	Marlboro Team Penske Marlboro Honda/Reynard 2KI	FS	175.918	19.359s	3	167	Accident		
17	Mark Blundell (GB)	18	PacWest Racing Motorola Mercedes/Reynard 2KI	FS	170.544	19.969s	18	166	Accident		
18	Michel Jourdain Jr. (MEX)	16	Bettenhausen Motorsports Herdez Mercedes/Lola B2K/00	FS	169.576	20.063s	20	150	Accident		
19	*Alexandre Tagliani (CDN)	33	Forsythe Racing Player's/Indeck Ford Cosworth/Reynard 2KI	FS	172.917	19.695s	13	127	Engine		
20	*Norberto Fontana (RA)	10	Della Penna Motorsports VideoMatch Toyota/Reynard 2KI	FS	164.917	20.741s	21	112	Accident		
21	Patrick Carpentier (CDN)	32	Forsythe Racing Player's/Indeck Ford Cosworth/Reynard 2KI	FS	174.164	19.554s	10	106	Electrical		
22	Max Papis (I)	7	Team Rahal Miller Lite Ford Cosworth/Reynard 2KI	FS	171.619	19.844s	16	71	Accident		
23	Dario Franchitti (GB)	27	Team KOOL Green Honda/Reynard 2KI	FS	172.917	19.695s	14	0	Accident		
24	*Takuya Kurosawa (J)	19	Dale Coyne Racing MTCI Ford Cosworth/Lola B2K/00	FS	no speed	no time	–	0	Withdrawn		

* denotes rookie driver

Caution flags: laps 1-6, accident/Franchitti & da Matta; laps 72-79, accident/Papis; laps 80-84, spin/Garcia; laps 115-128, accident/Fontana; laps 129-136, accident/Jourdain & Tracy; laps 154-165, accident/Jourdain; laps 168-186, accident/Blundell & Castroneves; laps 214-221, accident/Moreno. **Total:** Eight for 80 laps.

Lap leaders: Juan Montoya, 1-76 (76 laps); Paul Tracy, 77-84 (8 laps); Montoya, 85-118 (34 laps); Tony Kanaan, 119-157 (39 laps); Gil de Ferran, 158-225 (68 laps). **Totals:** Montoya, 110 laps; de Ferran, 68 laps; Kanaan, 39 laps; Tracy, 8 laps.

Fastest race lap: Helio Castroneves, 20.600s, 165.320 mph on lap 95.

Championship positions: 1 Tracy, 59; **2** Vasser 48; **3** Moreno & de Ferran, 42; **5** Fernandez, 33; **6** Andretti, 28; **7** Bräck, 27; **8** Papis & da Matta, 25; **10** Montoya, 22; **11** Franchitti & Fittipaldi, 20; **13** Gugelmin, 19; **14** Tagliani, 18; **15** Castroneves, 16; **16** Servia, 12; **17** Blundell, 11; **18** Herta & Carpentier, 10; **20** Kanaan, 8; **21** Nakano & Gidley, 5; **23** Jourdain, 3; **24** Garcia, 2; **25** Marques, 1.

FEDEX CHAMPIONSHIP SERIES • ROUND 6

Left: Fancy a beer? Patrick Carpentier, Juan Montoya and Michael Andretti celebrate with race sponsor Miller's finest rather than the traditional bubbly.

DEFENDING CART FedEx Series champion Juan Montoya dominated proceedings for the third time in a row with Target/Chip Ganassi Racing's #1 Toyota/Lola. Also for the third successive race, inclement weather played a prominent role in the weekend's activities. On this occasion, however, after rain caused the start of the Miller Lite 225 to be postponed for a day, Montoya took control at the Milwaukee Mile oval and was untroubled as he sped to a historic and long overdue first victory for Toyota in Champ Car competition.

"I'm really happy," declared Montoya after scoring the eighth victory of his Champ Car career. "We've been very unlucky in the last few races. I'm really glad to win for Toyota because they've worked so hard. We had the speed all year, but we finally got to the end."

Michael Andretti's Big Kmart/Texaco Havoline Ford Cosworth/Lola finished just over a second behind the defending series champion, while French-Canadian Patrick Carpentier posted a solid third aboard Player's/Forsythe Racing's Ford/Reynard.

Picture-perfect blue skies that prevailed during qualifying gave way to a solid gray on race morning, and even though there was no appreciable rain, a persistent light drizzle precluded any chance of running the race as originally scheduled. Monday morning wasn't much better, with heavy rain causing yet more delays, but finally, at 12.45 pm, the order to fire up the engines was given by Honorary Starter (and former Milwaukee Brewers baseball star-turned-CART Toyota Atlantic team co-owner) Robin Yount.

Montoya set out precisely as he meant to continue, jumping into the lead and leaving outside front-row qualifier Dario Franchitti (Team KOOL Green Honda/Reynard) to come under immediate pressure from Carpentier. The French-Canadian briefly slipped past Franchitti with a brave dive down the inside line into Turn One, only to relinquish the position when Franchitti made a better exit onto the back straightaway.

Gil de Ferran's Marlboro Team Penske Honda/Reynard followed in fourth, ahead of the second KOOL car of series points leader Paul Tracy, who found a way past Christian Fittipaldi's Big Kmart/Route 66 Ford/Lola on the opening lap. Andretti also made a bold early move, vaulting from tenth to seventh inside the opening lap, then ousting his Newman/Haas teammate the next time around.

For the first 15 laps, Franchitti stayed within a second of Montoya. But then the leaders began to encounter traffic. Montoya soon worked his way past Shinji Nakano's Avex Group Honda/Reynard and the Hollywood/Embratel-21 Mercedes/Reynard of Luiz Garcia Jr., but Franchitti, struggling with excessive oversteer, was unable to follow suit. Before long, the gap between the two leaders had ballooned to over three seconds.

On lap 22, Carpentier took advantage of Franchitti's inability to work his way past the slower cars by making a better exit off Turn Four and slipping past the Scotsman with a fine maneuver on the inside into Turn One.

The first caution came five laps later, when Nakano experienced his second incident of the day. The Japanese rookie had crashed heavily during the warmup session, and Derrick Walker's spare car was hurriedly fitted for him. But he was never comfortable and eventually lost control on the exit of Turn Four. This time, fortunately, there was no contact. Nakano continued after a pit stop, but called it quits after 71 laps.

The top nine cars all stayed out on the track during the ensuing caution period. Several other contenders committed themselves to a three-stop strategy and took the opportunity to make their first visit to pit lane. The charge was led by Roberto Moreno's tenth-placed Visteon/Patrick Racing Ford/Reynard. Among those following suit were Helio Castroneves (Marlboro Honda/Reynard), Jimmy Vasser in the second Target Toyota/Lola, Kenny Bräck (Shell/Team Rahal Ford/Reynard) and Moreno's teammate, Adrian Fernandez.

At the restart, Montoya took off into the lead again. Only this time Carpentier gave valiant chase, leaving Franchitti to come under pressure from de Ferran. Andretti followed in sixth, having passed Tracy immediately before the earlier caution.

The two leaders remained tied together until Carpentier peeled off into pit lane after 82 laps. Montoya, despite his prodigious pace, displayed incredible fuel economy and stayed out for two laps more. By now, everyone had made one pit stop, and it was Moreno who found himself in the lead. Vasser followed in second, with Castroneves and Bräck snapping at his heels. But soon they, too, would need more fuel.

Sure enough, Moreno relinquished his advantage on lap 108. Bräck picked up the running and led for seven laps before it became his turn to take on service.

Andretti, meanwhile, had taken advantage of excellent work by Donny Hoevel's crew to emerge from the pits ahead of Montoya. His new-found advantage didn't last long. On lap 101, Montoya slipped past cleanly. Fifteen laps later, that pass was translated once again into the race lead when Bräck came into the pits. Crucially, the Swede cost himself a potential podium finish by stalling the Ford Cosworth engine.

Andretti stayed in touch with Montoya for a while, but then the Colombian began to edge clear. By lap 150, the gap between the two leaders had

QUALIFYING

The wide-open nature of the CART FedEx Championship Series was amply demonstrated during practice for the Miller Lite 225. Juan Montoya set the pace on Friday morning in his Target Toyota/Lola, while Gil de Ferran moved to the top of the charts on Friday afternoon with Marlboro Team Penske's #2 Honda/Reynard. On Saturday morning, it was the turn of Patrick Carpentier's Player's Ford Cosworth/Reynard to assume front-runner status with yet another engine/chassis combination. The situation was finely poised, with the top 16 contenders separated by less than four-tenths of a second.

Blue sky, comfortable temperatures and a slight breeze from the east ensured almost perfect conditions for qualifying, although it came as no surprise to see Montoya move into the premier position with a time of 20.899 seconds (177.769 mph) – a tad faster than anyone else had managed during practice.

Two drivers remained in line to take their turn, but neither Dario Franchitti nor Carpentier could topple Montoya from his perch.

"The car was pretty loose on the first lap," related Franchitti, who produced by far his best qualifying performance of the season aboard Team KOOL Green's Honda/Reynard. "So I waited for the tire pressures to come up and then I stood on it. The second lap was much better than the first. It's nice to be up front again after such a dreadful beginning to the season."

Carpentier, by contrast, set his fastest time on his first flying lap. But then his car developed a severe push. The French-Canadian attempted to compensate by inducing some oversteer, which was spectacular, but slow. He had to be content with third on the grid.

De Ferran set a time just 0.076 second slower than Montoya, but it was good enough for only fourth on the tightly packed grid, ahead of Christian Fittipaldi, who did well to improve from a lowly 16th on the practice charts. Newman/Haas teammate Michael Andretti was five places behind on the grid after hitting the wall heavily on Saturday morning in Turn Four.

Toyota takes its first

TOYOTA'S first-ever Champ Car triumph was achieved in magnificent style by Juan Montoya. It had been a long time coming. The Japanese auto giant first entered the CART fray in 1996, and had little to show for its first four years. The highlight, indeed, had been a fourth-place finish achieved at Nazareth Speedway in 1999 by Cristiano da Matta.

There were some signs of promise as the '99 season progressed, culminating in Scott Pruett's pole-winning effort at Fontana and then the much-publicized liaison with Target/Chip Ganassi Racing. When the new association was formalized, Ganassi said it would be only a matter of time before Toyota developed the winning habit. Clearly, he knew what to expect from the new RV8E engine, which had been designed, built and developed at Toyota Racing Development in Costa Mesa, California.

Sure enough, after displaying a good turn of pace during winter testing, Montoya started on the front row at Homestead and led for 21 laps before his engine failed. Teammate Jimmy Vasser took up the running and finished a creditable fourth. Vasser went on to take third at Long Beach and second in Brazil. Then Montoya dominated the proceedings at both Motegi and Nazareth before circumstances conspired against him in the closing stages.

Incredibly, after six races, Toyota was the only engine manufacturer to have started from the front row each time. And at long last, Montoya delivered that elusive first victory.

"I need to thank all the people who've played a role in this program for four-plus years," said Toyota Vice President of Motorsports Jim Aust. "We really thought we were going to get the win in Motegi and we learned that you don't count laps, you just wait until the checkered flag.

"Juan did a fabulous job today, as did the entire team and everyone at TRD. When we took on the project to design and build the engine entirely in the U.S., we knew it was a formidable challenge, and [this win] has made it all worthwhile."

This page: **Studies in concentration:** *(top to bottom)* Michael Andretti, Roberto Moreno and Adrian Fernandez.

Facing page, top: Paul Tracy failed to score points at Milwaukee, but retained his Fedex Championship lead.

Facing page, bottom: Juan Montoya prepares for action. The Colombian took the pole and dominated the race in Chip Ganassi's Target Toyota/Lola.

FEDEX CHAMPIONSHIP SERIES • ROUND 6

In his second race after suffering an injury, Patrick Carpentier claimed his first podium finish of the season.

grown to two seconds. Carpentier remained in third, with de Ferran a second or so behind. The two KOOL cars ran next, Tracy having moved ahead of Franchitti during the earlier pit stops.

Montoya's mastery of the Milwaukee Mile enabled him once again to display superior fuel mileage than his principal rivals. Of those pursuing a two-stop strategy, Montoya was the last to pull into pit lane – after 170 laps. Fernandez took over the lead, chased by Vasser and Castroneves, who made their third and final pit stops on laps 180 and 179 respectively.

Four laps later, the yellow lights flashed on for only the second time when Tarso Marques crashed his Panasonic Ford/Swift in Turn Two. The caution was perfectly timed for Fernandez, Bräck and Moreno, whose frugal techniques enabled them to make their third pit stops without losing a lap to the leaders.

The order at the final restart, on lap 193, saw Montoya back out in front, ahead of Andretti and de Ferran (who had leapfrogged Carpentier during the earlier second round of pit stops). Fernandez was fifth, only to run high into the "marbles" at Turn Two shortly afterward while attempting to pass the lapped car of Castroneves. That slip cost the unfortunate Fernandez five positions, as he was passed by Bräck, Moreno, Franchitti, Max Papis (Miller Lite Ford/Reynard) and Fittipaldi, who, in contrast to Franchitti, was troubled by excessive push all afternoon.

"I got off line and that was it," related Fernandez. "I thought they cleaned the track [during the caution] and I didn't see the marbles up there and got about a foot higher than I should have, and that got me in the marbles."

The final 32-lap dash to the finish line was largely uneventful. Mauricio Gugelmin (Nextel Mercedes/Reynard), who had lost a lap earlier when he stalled his engine in the pits, was between Montoya and Andretti at the restart, but it made no difference to the outcome. Montoya soon edged away from the Brazilian, who, in turn, was able to motor clear of Andretti.

De Ferran ran third as the race headed toward its climax. Unexpectedly, however, on lap 216, he pulled into pit lane. "We may not have gotten enough fuel at our last scheduled stop and I had to come in for a splash right at the end, just to be sure. It's a real shame," he related, after falling to a disappointing 12th.

Montoya's lead expanded to more than five seconds by lap 205, whereupon he settled into a comfortable rhythm and cruised home to the finish. The gap to Andretti shrank to just 1.015 seconds at the checkered flag, but Montoya's lead was never under serious threat.

A solid weekend's work by Carpentier was rewarded with a third-place finish, while Bräck parlayed his fine economy efforts into a strong fourth, just ahead of Moreno and Franchitti.

Papis followed in the wheel tracks of Franchitti, chased by Fernandez and Fittipaldi, who made up a high-speed train that provided plenty of excitement for the crowd. Tony Kanaan's Hollywood Mercedes/Reynard also remained on the lead lap at the end of a hard-fought and intensely competitive encounter.

Jeremy Shaw

Close racing, but no passing

THE Handford Device, a high-drag, low-downforce rear wing formulated by renowned aerodynamicist Mark Handford, revolutionized Champ Car superspeedway races when it was introduced as a means of curbing the escalation in speeds in 1998. For the 2000 season, CART developed another version – the Handford Device Mk.II – for specific use on the shorter one-mile ovals. However, following races at Nazareth Speedway and the Milwaukee Mile, both of which witnessed plenty of close competition but precious little overtaking, many drivers voiced their displeasure.

"I had a well-balanced car today, especially in the early part of the race," said Tony Kanaan. "But as the wind picked up, the rear end kept getting lighter, and you just couldn't put your foot in the throttle coming out of the turns.

"Running by yourself it was OK, but in traffic, you just couldn't get around anybody. It was frustrating. I gained some positions by really pushing it on cold tires coming out of the pits. Otherwise, there was nothing you could do."

Max Papis also was upset: "Unfortunately, with this new wing, it's just not good racing. I don't enjoy it because there is huge buffeting out there and you take a huge risk when you come into the pits and when you come out. With the new wing, we race more in the pits and on restarts than on the track, and that's not good."

Most vocal of all, perhaps, was runner-up finisher Michael Andretti, who has campaigned all along for CART to retain the superspeedway package used previously on the one-mile ovals. Andretti also had been a proponent of reducing the engines' horsepower.

"I would go back to last year's wings and take a bunch of horsepower away," declared the 1991 CART champion. "Then I think you would have better racing. If you take the horsepower away and limit the downforce, you can drive the car a little more with the throttle, which in my opinion would [ensure] better racing."

FEDEX CHAMPIONSHIP SERIES • ROUND 6

MILWAUKEE SNIPPETS

• Only 23 cars started the race due to the **WITHDRAWAL** of regulars Norberto Fontana and Takuya Kurosawa, both of whom were still suffering from the effects of heavy accidents a week earlier at Nazareth. Fontana's Della Penna Motorsports team did not make the trip to Milwaukee, while Kurosawa pulled out after feeling dizzy during the first practice session on Friday morning.

• **PAUL TRACY** maintained his championship lead, despite finishing out of the points in 15th. Tracy, who started sixth, was running third before making his final pit stop on lap 156. Unfortunately, he was penalized for allowing two wheels to stray outside the yellow line at the pit entrance. The resulting drive-through penalty cost him a lap and any chance of another podium finish.

• Reigning Indy Lights Champion **ORIOL SERVIA** drove another strong race for PPI Motorsports. The likeable Spaniard lost four places on the opening lap after qualifying 15th, but rose to tenth before the first round of pit stops in his Telefonica Toyota/Reynard. Servia enjoyed a good dice with Adrian Fernandez, but eventually strayed up into the gray while trying to pass Michael Andretti after the latter had resumed following a pit stop. Servia lost a couple of laps when he pitted to change tires.

• Alex Tagliani retired from the race due to an **INCIDENT** in the pit lane when an overheated clutch caused his Player's Ford/Reynard to move forward while being refueled. A brief fire ensued but, thankfully, there were no injuries.

• **JUAN MONTOYA** led 179 of the 225 laps, taking his tally of laps led for the season to 482 – or 37 percent of the total. His nearest challenger, Gil de Ferran, had led a total of 139 laps. The Milwaukee win capped a momentous week for Montoya, who, after finishing fourth at Nazareth the previous Saturday, had taken time out from his FedEx Series campaign to dominate the following day's Indy Racing Northern Lights Series Indianapolis 500. The victory also ensured a busy week of interviews and appearances for Montoya and team owner Chip Ganassi.

• Jimmy Vasser's crew had an eventful weekend. The **DRAMAS** began in qualifying, when Vasser got loose in his Target Toyota/Lola and crashed in Turn Four. The car was heavily damaged. Then, on race morning, the backup car was afflicted by a fuel pressure problem during the brief final warmup session. With time running out, Rick Davis' crew wheeled out teammate Juan Montoya's backup car. Vasser had enough time for only one lap. Unable to dial in the car to his liking, he finished just out of the points in 13th.

• **MICHAEL ANDRETTI** (above) failed to finish among the points in Milwaukee, both in 1998 and '99, but prior to that, in 13 races on the historic Wisconsin State Fair Park oval, he had amassed a remarkable tally of 11 top-four placings, including five victories. Andretti came up just short of adding a fifth win in 2000, but was delighted to put his championship challenge back into top gear. "I don't know what it is about this place," he quipped. "Maybe it's the cheese..."

FEDEX CHAMPIONSHIP SERIES • ROUND 6
MILLER LITE 225

THE MILWAUKEE MILE, WEST ALLIS, WISCONSIN

JUNE 5, 225 laps of 1.032 miles – 232.20 miles

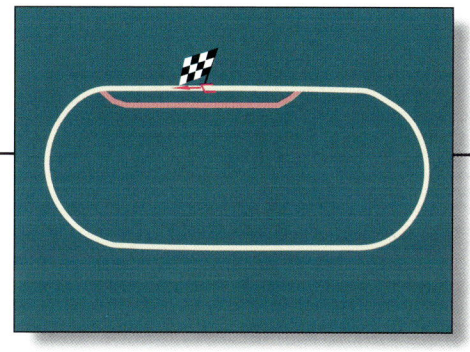

Place	Driver (Nat.)	No.	Team Sponsors Engine/Chassis	Tires	Q Speed	Q Time	Q Pos.	Laps	Time/Status	Ave. (mph)	Pts.
1	Juan Montoya (COL)	1	Target/Chip Ganassi Racing Toyota/Lola B2K/00	FS	177.769	20.899s	1	225	1h 37m 38.526s	142.684	22
2	Michael Andretti (USA)	6	Newman/Haas Big Kmart/Texaco Ford Cosworth/Lola B2K/00	FS	175.743	21.140s	10	225	1h 37m 39.541s	142.660	16
3	Patrick Carpentier (CDN)	32	Forsythe Racing Player's/Indeck Ford Cosworth/Reynard 2KI	FS	177.218	20.964s	3	225	1h 37m 46.983s	142.479	14
4	*Kenny Bräck (S)	8	Team Rahal Shell Ford Cosworth/Reynard 2KI	FS	174.185	21.329s	16	225	1h 37m 53.128s	142.330	12
5	Roberto Moreno (BR)	20	Patrick Racing Visteon Ford Cosworth/Reynard 2KI	FS	176.109	21.096s	7	225	1h 37m 53.685s	142.316	10
6	Dario Franchitti (GB)	27	Team KOOL Green Honda/Reynard 2KI	FS	177.303	20.954s	2	225	1h 37m 54.159s	142.305	8
7	Max Papis (I)	7	Team Rahal Miller Lite Ford Cosworth/Reynard 2KI	FS	175.909	21.120s	9	225	1h 37m 55.726s	142.267	6
8	Adrian Fernandez (MEX)	40	Patrick Racing Tecate/Quaker State Ford Cosworth/Reynard 2KI	FS	173.616	21.399s	19	225	1h 37m 56.425s	142.250	5
9	Christian Fittipaldi (BR)	11	Newman/Haas Big Kmart/Route 66 Ford Cosworth/Lola B2K/00	FS	176.872	21.005s	5	225	1h 37m 57.378s	142.227	4
10	Tony Kanaan (BR)	55	Mo Nunn Racing Hollywood Mercedes/Reynard 2KI	FS	175.510	21.168s	11	225	1h 38m 01.296s	142.132	3
11	Mauricio Gugelmin (BR)	17	PacWest Racing Nextel Mercedes/Reynard 2KI	FS	175.942	21.116s	8	224	Running		2
12	Gil de Ferran (BR)	2	Marlboro Team Penske Marlboro Honda/Reynard 2KI	FS	177.125	20.975s	4	224	Running		1
13	Jimmy Vasser (USA)	12	Target/Chip Ganassi Racing Toyota/Lola B2K/00	FS	174.603	21.278s	14	224	Running		
14	Cristiano da Matta (BR)	97	PPI Motorsports Pioneer/MCI WorldCom Toyota/Reynard 2KI	FS	170.877	21.742s	21	224	Running		
15	Paul Tracy (CDN)	26	Team KOOL Green Honda/Reynard 2KI	FS	176.184	21.087s	6	224	Running		
16	Helio Castroneves (BR)	3	Marlboro Team Penske Marlboro Honda/Reynard 2KI	FS	175.502	21.169s	12	224	Running		
17	Mark Blundell (GB)	18	PacWest Racing Motorola Mercedes/Reynard 2KI	FS	173.778	21.379s	17	224	Running		
18	Michel Jourdain Jr. (MEX)	16	Bettenhausen Motorsports Herdez Mercedes/Lola B2K/00	FS	169.814	21.878s	22	224	Running		
19	*Oriol Servia (E)	96	PPI Motorsports Telefonica Toyota/Reynard 2KI	FS	174.570	21.282s	15	222	Running		
20	Tarso Marques (BR)	34	Dale Coyne Racing Panasonic Ford Cosworth/Swift 011.c	FS	173.745	21.383s	18	180	Accident		
21	Luiz Garcia Jr. (BR)	25	Arciero-PRG Hollywood/Embratel-21 Mercedes/Reynard 2KI	FS	164.317	22.610s	23	115	Oil leak		
22	*Alexandre Tagliani (CDN)	33	Forsythe Racing Player's/Indeck Ford Cosworth/Reynard 2KI	FS	175.386	21.183s	13	108	Pit fire		
23	*Shinji Nakano (J)	5	Walker Racing Avex Group Honda/Reynard 2KI	FS	173.332	21.434s	20	71	Handling		
24	Takuya Kurosawa (J)	19	Dale Coyne Racing MTCI Ford Cosworth/Lola B2K/00	FS	no speed	no time	–	–	Withdrawn		

* denotes rookie driver

Caution flags: Laps 26-30, spin/Nakano; laps 183-192, accident/Marques. Total: Two for 15 laps.

Lap leaders: Juan Montoya, 1-84 (84 laps); Roberto Moreno, 85-107 (23 laps); Kenny Bräck, 108-114 (7 laps); Montoya, 115-170 (56 laps); Adrian Fernandez, 171-186 (16 laps); Montoya, 187-225 (39 laps). Totals: Montoya, 179 laps; Moreno, 23 laps; Fernandez, 16 laps; Bräck, 7 laps.

Fastest race lap: Juan Montoya, 22.345s, 166.258 mph on lap 197.

Championship positions: 1 Tracy, 59; **2** Moreno, 52; **3** Vasser, 48; **4** Montoya & Andretti, 44; **6** de Ferran, 43; **7** Bräck, 39; **8** Fernandez, 38; **9** Papis, 31; **10** Franchitti, 28; **11** da Matta, 25; **12** Carpentier & Fittipaldi, 24; **14** Gugelmin, 21; **15** Tagliani, 18; **16** Castroneves, 16; **17** Servia, 12; **18** Blundell & Kanaan, 11; **20** Herta, 10; **21** Nakano & Gidley, 5; **23** Jourdain, 3; **24** Garcia, 2; **25** Marques, 1.

DETROIT

| 1 – CASTRONEVES |
| 2 – PAPIS |
| 3 – SERVIA |

FEDEX CHAMPIONSHIP SERIES • ROUND 7

Helio Castroneves tails Max Papis against a backdrop of shimmering chainlink fencing.
Robert Laberge Allsport USA

FEDEX CHAMPIONSHIP SERIES • ROUND 7

Rahal takes the helm

THE complexion of Championship Auto Racing Teams Inc., the publicly traded sanctioning body of the FedEx Championship Series, changed dramatically on the first morning of practice in Detroit when chairman and chief executive officer Andrew Craig abruptly tendered his resignation following an impromptu meeting of CART's board of directors. Within a matter of hours, former champion driver-turned-team owner Bobby Rahal *(above left)* had been elected unanimously as interim president and CEO, with long-time friend and associate Jim Hardymon *(above right)*, formerly chief executive of Textron Inc. and, previously, president of Emerson Electric, taking on the role of chairman of the board.

The developments capped a period of mounting tension regarding Craig's future at CART, dating as far back as 1998. It was an open secret that a number – or even most – of CART's team owners had grown dissatisfied with the Englishman's leadership, citing a lack of communication as his main flaw.

For his part, Craig confessed to no regrets at his departure: "Candidly, my heart's not in the job any more, and hasn't been for quite some while. I was getting a bit fed up with [all the politics], and maybe [the owners] were getting fed up with me, too. I pushed for them to bring this to a head."

The choice of Rahal to take over the reins found universal favor in the paddock.

"I think this is a huge day in CART history," summarized team boss Pat Patrick, CART's co-founder and first president. "For the first time since I resigned as head of the company, an owner, someone who is very familiar with the inner workings of the sport, is the CEO of CART. We couldn't have made a better choice."

"I love the sport, and I think everyone who knows me knows that," affirmed Rahal, who identified the finalizing of CART's 2001 schedule and refining the rules to contain speeds and improve the show as his most pressing priorities.

Asked about the potential conflict of interest between continuing as a team owner while assuming the leadership of the sport's governing body, Rahal quipped, "I don't know whether it's a sign of success or not, but my team has been very good at proving to me this year that they don't need me – as was exemplified today when Max [Papis] qualified first and Kenny [Bräck] was third, and I've been in the CART bus all day long."

QUALIFYING

The on-track action during practice and qualifying for the Tenneco Automotive Grand Prix of Detroit played second fiddle to the political machinations going on behind closed doors. Nevertheless, it proved an interesting couple of days.

Appropriately enough, Max Papis snared the provisional pole for Team Rahal on Friday, circulating the demanding 2.346-mile Raceway on Belle Isle in just 1m 13.903s. Helio Castroneves had set the pace in the morning practice session and ended the day second quickest on 1m 14.310s, his Marlboro Honda/Reynard looking extremely sure-footed over the constant surface changes in the tortuous "fountain" section behind the pits.

When the faster of the two qualifying groups took to the track on Saturday, Greg Moore's 1998 track record (1m 13.530s) was ready to bite the dust. Juan Montoya had been comfortably quickest on Saturday morning and soon vaulted to the top of the timing charts, only to be demoted – initially by Castroneves, then by Dario Franchitti, who lowered the benchmark to 1m 13.056s in his KOOL Honda/Reynard.

Montoya's first two attempts to redress the balance came to naught, first when Kenny Bräck hit the wall and caused a red-flag stoppage, then when he tried to carry a bit too much speed into Turn Two and had to abort the lap.

Finally, the defending series champion pulled out all the stops to match Franchitti's time – to the thousandth of a second! – and claim his fourth pole of the year, based on the tie-breaker of next-fastest lap.

Montoya's Firestone Firehawk tires were certainly past their best. Earlier, he had looked on the ragged edge. His eventual pole-winning lap, however, was a model of controlled aggression.

"You gotta be as smooth as you can, that's the fastest way," noted Montoya. "I just gave it everything I had. The car held for a lap."

Castroneves had to make do with a place on the inside of the second row, flanked by Marlboro Team Penske stablemate Gil de Ferran. Papis gridded fifth, while Cristiano da Matta enjoyed a timely return to form in PPI Motorsports' Pioneer/MCI WorldCom Toyota/Reynard, equaling his career-best starting position of sixth.

Right: Dario Franchitti qualified second in Team KOOL Green's Honda/Reynard, only to hit more misfortune on race day.

Below right: Patrick Carpentier enjoyed another strong performance aboard Jerry Forsythe's Team Player's Ford/Reynard.

HELIO Castroneves established a new CART record of seven different winners in as many races by scoring an emotional maiden victory – the 101st for Penske Racing – in the Tenneco Automotive Grand Prix of Detroit.

There was a hint of good fortune as dominant early leader Juan Montoya fell victim to a mechanical failure once again, but that should take nothing away from a fine performance by Castroneves. The 25-year-old Brazilian was a force to be reckoned with all weekend, setting the pace in the first practice session on Friday morning and lining up a strong third on the grid behind perennial sparring partners Montoya and Dario Franchitti. Castroneves shadowed Franchitti's every move in the opening segment of the race, vaulted ahead during the first round of pit stops, then was content to hold a watching brief – behind Montoya – through the middle stages of the 84-lap race. When the Colombian's Target Toyota/Lola was sidelined by a broken drivetrain, Castroneves was perfectly poised to take the win.

"I'm so happy," exclaimed Castroneves after finally finding his composure. "I have to thank so many people – Marlboro, Roger Penske, Honda, Firestone – for supporting me.

"I did it, I did it!"

The first three quarters of the race were all about Montoya, who made full use of his fourth pole of the year to establish an immediate small cushion over Franchitti. The two Marlboro Honda/Reynards of Castroneves and Gil de Ferran held station in third and fourth, chased by two more Brazilians, Cristiano da Matta, showing good form aboard PPI Motorsports' Pioneer/MCI WorldCom Toyota/Reynard, and Christian Fittipaldi (Big Kmart/Route 66 Ford/Lola), who followed da Matta past Max Papis' Miller Lite Ford/Reynard on the opening lap. Kenny Bräck ran eighth in the second Team Rahal entry, ahead of Roberto Moreno (Visteon Ford/Reynard), Michael Andretti (Big Kmart/Texaco Ford/Lola) and Oriol Servia (Telefonica Toyota/Reynard).

Initially, the trio of Montoya, Franchitti and Castroneves made a break from the pursuing pack. The sizeable crowd gathered around Belle Isle Park briefly entertained hopes of a three-way battle for supremacy. Before long, however, Montoya began to stamp his authority on the proceedings, slowly stretching his lead. Franchitti found Castroneves in somewhat closer attendance, while de Ferran, struggling slightly with a loose condition, trailed his teammate. Farther back, the field thinned a little when Bräck crashed (for the third time during the weekend) on lap 11, and da Matta succumbed to an engine failure four laps later.

By the time he peeled into the pit lane for his first scheduled refueling stop, on lap 27, Montoya had eked out an advantage of some three seconds. He resumed with a similarly healthy margin over Castroneves, who benefited from typically slick service from Rick Rinaman's crew to leapfrog ahead of Franchitti. De Ferran, Fittipaldi and Papis continued to round out the top six.

The flurry of pit stops gave rise to a bizarre incident involving Adrian Fernandez. The Mexican, who had started a lowly 14th, outlasted everyone by delaying his visit to the pit lane until lap 31, whereupon a newly discarded visor tear-off slid along the sidepod of his Tecate/Quaker State Ford/Reynard and was ingested into the turbocharger inlet! It would trigger his demise.

"We came out of the pits in eighth place and I tried to put the power down and something was wrong," reported a bewildered Fernandez. "My engineer, John Ward, told me to press the pedal a few times, and I was trying to do that on cold tires going into the corner. Suddenly it went to full power and I spun out."

Behind the serene Montoya, Castroneves settled into a good pace and was able to put some distance between himself and Franchitti. The Scotsman soon had more serious cause for concern, slowing abruptly on lap 47 when a portion of the right front brake duct on his KOOL Honda/Reynard worked loose and became lodged in the front suspension, limiting its travel and adversely affecting the car's handling.

"I didn't know what the problem was, but going down the straight, the car was trying to turn hard right into the wall," related Franchitti. "At first, I thought it was a rear shock absorber, so I slowed down a bit and got passed by a couple of guys. But we knew something else was wrong when we saw the engine temperature go up: the brake duct was blocking the airflow to the radiator."

As the #27 Team KOOL Green car slowly slipped down the order, Montoya's #1 Target/Chip Ganassi Racing entry continued to leave the field in its wake. The defending series champion extended his lead by a couple of tenths of a second each lap. His advantage stood at more than six seconds by the time he rolled into the pits for a fresh complement of fuel and tires on lap 58. Castroneves seemed to have no

FEDEX CHAMPIONSHIP SERIES • ROUND 7

FEDEX CHAMPIONSHIP SERIES • ROUND 7

Spanish rookie Oriol Servia continued his steady progression and claimed his first-ever Champ Car podium finish.

answer. Penske's young charge, however, was unconcerned. He was under firm orders to save fuel and to wait until the race's final stint before mounting a challenge.

"Tim Cindric [strategist and Penske Racing president] kept saying, 'Save fuel, save fuel.' I was very cool, very focused. I didn't have any problems. I had to keep holding and holding, and that's when you make mistakes. Once we had no fuel problem, Tim said, 'Go for it.'"

As it transpired, there was no need. Three laps after his routine stop, Montoya suddenly pulled his Lola back into the pit lane for good, a driveshaft coupling broken.

"It's a shame," shrugged Montoya, not for the first time this season. "The car was great. Everything was going according to plan. I didn't have any warning. The whole package was working beautifully. I thought I had [the race] in my pocket."

Castroneves' reaction when he saw Montoya heading for the pit lane?

"I didn't feel sorry for him because I know how it feels. I have been in that situation many times," he grinned, reflecting on the litany of gremlins that bedeviled him last season at Hogan Racing, costing him a chance of victory on several occasions.

Almost simultaneously there was drama just behind the leaders as Fittipaldi and de Ferran tangled going into the double right-hander before the start/finish straight. The pair had exchanged positions during the recent round of pit stops, when de Ferran had been forced to jam on the brakes upon leaving his pit box as Paul Tracy's KOOL Honda/Reynard made for the stall directly in front of him. The Penske driver was anxious not to lose any further ground to his countryman as they came up to lap the Motorola Mercedes/Reynard of Mark Blundell. When Fittipaldi appeared to misjudge his passing maneuver under braking

Celebration for Castroneves

HELIO Castroneves has been knocking on the door of Victory Circle ever since he joined the Champ Car ranks as a fresh-faced rookie at the beginning of 1998. Two-and-a-half years and 46 races later, the Indy Lights alumnus finally achieved his ambition.

"I'm still looking at myself, pulling my hair and saying, 'Did it really happen?'" beamed an ecstatic Castroneves *(above)*, who all but climbed out of his car as he punched the air in celebration on his cool-down lap. "I knew it would come, but you keep questioning 'when?' and you never believe it."

Castroneves had threatened to win on several occasions for Carl Hogan's team in 1999, only to be thwarted repeatedly by mechanical woes. The move to Marlboro Team Penske over the winter equipped him with the resources, both human and financial, to become a bona fide front-runner. And this time, for once, the amiable Brazilian was on the receiving end of a little good fortune, inheriting the lead when Juan Montoya was stricken by a broken driveshaft at three-quarters distance.

Having adopted a conservative strategy through the middle portion of the race, Castroneves was disappointed to be deprived of the opportunity to take on his rival in a straight fight.

"I was very upset [that I couldn't chase Montoya]. Of course, I like to win this way, because it's easy, but I knew I could catch him. I knew I had a very good car and could race him for it."

A few weeks previously, Castro-Neves, as he was then known, elected to make a subtle change to his name. He had grown tired of being misidentified – of being called Helio Castro or Helio Neves – by fans and media alike. So he removed the "dash" from his name and became simply Helio Castroneves.

"I think it worked," he joked, after scoring his long overdue maiden victory. "I think the dash was slowing me down!"

Not any longer.

for Turn 12, he was promptly hit from behind by de Ferran. All three cars headed directly into the tire wall. De Ferran recovered to finish ninth, a lap down, while an irate Fittipaldi was out on the spot.

"I touched Blundell, but everything was basically under control," claimed Fittipaldi. "What put me into the tire wall was Gil. He braked way too late and ran into the back of me."

Not surprisingly, de Ferran's perspective was slightly different: "Christian got a little sideways, climbed over Mark's right front wheel, and by then I was too freaking close because I didn't want to lose any ground. I locked up in sympathy and basically helped Christian off [the road]."

"If I had backed off, I probably wouldn't have gone off with both of them," admitted de Ferran. "I blame myself for going off. I don't blame myself for taking Christian off."

The incident on lap 61 ensured a full-course caution and promoted a grateful Papis to second place, while Moreno lay third in Pat Patrick's Visteon Ford/Reynard. Had he been able to stay there, the veteran Brazilian would have left Motor City as the championship leader. It was not to be. Soon after the restart, Moreno's day came to an abrupt end when an altercation with the lapped car of Takuya Kurosawa in Turn Four sent him spearing off into the tire barrier.

"The only place I had left was the outside line and I couldn't make the corner," said a disgruntled Moreno.

Later, Kurosawa's newly liveried *Sports Today*/Dale Coyne Racing Ford/Lola was black-flagged for impeding the leaders' progress.

So it was that Servia emerged in third place prior to the final 15-lap dash to the checkered flag. The young Spaniard had moved stealthily up the order, showing a good turn of speed in the Telefonica Toyota/Reynard and making no hint of a mistake.

The closing laps were a mere formality as Castroneves edged steadily clear of Papis who, in turn, pulled away from Servia. Franchitti, meanwhile, soldiered on to a fourth-place finish, aided by the outbreak of incidents and attrition. The two Player's/Forsythe Ford/Reynards of Patrick Carpentier and Alex Tagliani completed the top six, ahead of Jimmy Vasser, who endured a torrid weekend in the second Target Toyota/Lola.

"I just had no grip today," lamented Vasser. "I'm happy we earned some points today, but it was sure an ugly way to do it."

Jeremy Shaw

FEDEX CHAMPIONSHIP SERIES • ROUND 7

DETROIT SNIPPETS

• Mo Nunn **WITHDREW** his Hollywood Mercedes/Reynard from the race after Tony Kanaan suffered a heavy crash at Turn Seven during qualifying and was hospitalized with a broken left arm and two fractured ribs. The talented Brazilian underwent surgery the same evening and was expected to be out of action for six to eight weeks.

• Juan Montoya's pole (the 11th of his Champ Car career in just 27 starts) represented the 69th for **FIRESTONE** (in 96 races) since it rejoined the Champ Car wars in '95. Montoya thereby broke a tie with his predecessor at Target/Chip Ganassi Racing, Alex Zanardi, as the most successful Firestone qualifier in the modern era.

• Pity Dario Franchitti. When asked whether he felt like he was living a **NIGHTMARE** after losing out to Juan Montoya once again on a tie-breaker (remember that he finished equal on points in the '99 FedEx title-chase, only to lose the crown by virtue of scoring only three wins to the Colombian's seven), Franchitti replied calmly, "Yes, it does a bit, but as long as I don't wake up next to him, it's OK!"

• Some fans were **CONFUSED** to see two different driver uniforms sporting the familiar red and white colors of Nextel. In addition to PacWest's regular shoe, Mauricio Gugelmin, the "imposter" was none other than actor Sylvester Stallone, who was busily filming scenes for the movie Driven, due for release in April 2001.

• Max Papis arrived in Motown with a new **RED TINT** to his hair. Obviously, it did no harm, as the flamboyant Italian guided Team Rahal's Miller Lite Ford/Reynard to a second-place finish.

• After encountering a problem during the refueling process on Christian Fittipaldi's car at Milwaukee, Newman/Haas Racing conducted a full analysis and concluded that one of the reasons the vent hose tended to "stick" when being withdrawn from the car after refueling was due to a vacuum effect within the **VENT LINE**. The engineers quickly designed and constructed a revised vent hose, which proved far easier to remove in subsequent tests. Initially, CART refused the team's request to use the non-standard item in Detroit, only to show a change of heart when it was pointed out that the revised item provided absolutely no performance advantage, but was demonstrably safer.

• Takuya Kurosawa lost his **SPONSORSHIP** from MTCI, a Japanese Internet provider, during the brief gap between races at Milwaukee and Detroit, but wasted no time in procuring replacement support from Next Media, a huge Korean-based publishing and broadcasting business. Dale Coyne Racing worked virtually around the clock to repaint its Lolas – and all the pit equipment – in the orange livery of Next's *Sports Today* newspaper (left).

• **ORIOL SERVIA** was one of the stars of the show, recording the first podium finish of his fledgling Champ Car career in his Telefonica Toyota/Reynard. "I came here with a lot of expectations," said the '99 Indy Lights champion. "In Milwaukee, I thought I could fight for the podium, but I ran wide onto the marbles [and fell from contention after making an additional pit stop]. Here, there was a lot of pressure on myself to do well and not make any mistakes."

FEDEX CHAMPIONSHIP SERIES • ROUND 7
TENNECO AUTOMOTIVE GRAND PRIX OF DETROIT

THE RACEWAY ON BELLE ISLE, DETROIT, MICHIGAN

JUNE 18, 84 laps of 2.346 miles – 197.064 miles

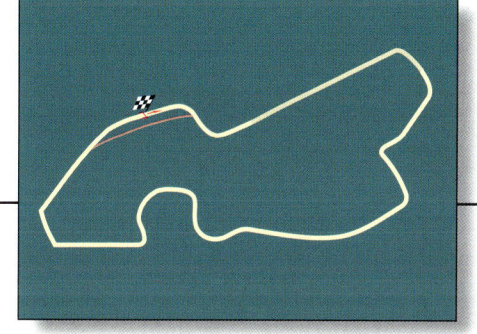

Place	Driver (Nat.)	No.	Team Sponsors Engine/Car	Tires	Q Speed	Q Time	Q Pos.	Laps	Time/Status	Ave. (mph)	Pts.
1	Helio Castroneves (BR)	3	Marlboro Team Penske Marlboro Honda/Reynard 2KI	FS	115.353	1m 13.215s	3	84	2h 01m 23.607s	97.401	20
2	Max Papis (I)	7	Team Rahal Miller Lite Ford Cosworth/Reynard 2KI	FS	114.861	1m 13.529s	5	84	2h 01m 28.022s	97.342	16
3	*Oriol Servia (E)	96	PPI Motorsports Telefonica Toyota/Reynard 2KI	FS	112.944	1m 14.777s	12	84	2h 01m 34.072s	97.261	14
4	Dario Franchitti (GB)	27	Team KOOL Green Honda/Reynard 2KI	FS	115.604	1m 13.056s	2	84	2h 01m 37.244s	97.219	12
5	Patrick Carpentier (CDN)	32	Forsythe Racing Player's/Indeck Ford Cosworth/Reynard 2KI	FS	113.634	1m 14.323s	9	84	2h 01m 48.920s	97.064	10
6	*Alexandre Tagliani (CDN)	33	Forsythe Racing Player's/Indeck Ford Cosworth/Reynard 2KI	FS	112.862	1m 14.831s	14	84	2h 01m 50.009s	97.049	8
7	Jimmy Vasser (USA)	12	Target/Chip Ganassi Racing Toyota/Lola B2K/00	FS	112.797	1m 14.874s	17	84	2h 02m 14.863s	96.720	6
8	Michel Jourdain Jr. (MEX)	16	Bettenhausen Motorsports Herdez Mercedes/Lola B2K/00	FS	112.825	1m 14.856s	16	84	2h 02m 31.647s	96.500	5
9	Gil de Ferran (BR)	2	Marlboro Team Penske Marlboro Honda/Reynard 2KI	FS	115.141	1m 13.350s	4	83	Running		4
10	Tarso Marques (BR)	34	Dale Coyne Racing Panasonic Ford Cosworth/Swift 011.c	FS	111.913	1m 15.466s	21	82	Running		3
11	Mark Blundell (GB)	18	PacWest Racing Motorola Mercedes/Reynard 2KI	FS	112.846	1m 14.842s	15	81	Running		2
12	*Takuya Kurosawa (J)	19	Dale Coyne Racing Sports Today Ford Cosworth/Lola B2K/00	FS	110.439	1m 16.473s	23	81	Running		1
13	Michael Andretti (USA)	6	Newman/Haas Big Kmart/Texaco Ford Cosworth/Lola B2K/00	FS	112.983	1m 14.751s	11	80	Engine		
14	*Norberto Fontana (RA)	10	Della Penna Motorsports VideoMatch Toyota/Reynard 2KI	FS	112.370	1m 15.159s	20	78	Fuel system		
15	*Shinji Nakano (J)	5	Walker Racing Avex Honda/Reynard 2KI	FS	110.507	1m 16.426s	22	78	Running		
16	Mauricio Gugelmin (BR)	17	PacWest Racing Nextel Mercedes/Reynard 2KI	FS	112.785	1m 14.882s	18	78	Running		
17	Roberto Moreno (BR)	20	Patrick Racing Visteon Ford Cosworth/Reynard 2KI	FS	113.311	1m 14.535s	10	65	Accident		
18	Juan Montoya (COL)	1	Target/Chip Ganassi Racing Toyota/Lola B2K/00	FS	115.604	1m 13.056s	1	61	Driveshaft		2
19	Christian Fittipaldi (BR)	11	Newman/Haas Big Kmart/Route 66 Ford Cosworth/Lola B2K/00	FS	113.986	1m 14.093s	8	60	Accident		
20	Paul Tracy (CDN)	26	Team KOOL Green Honda/Reynard 2KI	FS	112.757	1m 14.901s	19	57	Pit incident		
21	Adrian Fernandez (MEX)	40	Patrick Racing Tecate/Quaker State Ford Cosworth/Reynard 2KI	FS	112.889	1m 14.813s	13	31	Turbo		
22	Luiz Garcia Jr. (BR)	25	Arciero-PRG Hollywood/Embratel-21 Mercedes/Reynard 2KI	FS	110.436	1m 16.475s	24	25	Gearbox		
23	Cristiano da Matta (BR)	97	PPI Motorsports Pioneer/MCI WorldCom Toyota/Reynard 2KI	FS	114.787	1m 13.576s	6	14	Engine		
24	*Kenny Bräck (S)	8	Team Rahal Shell Ford Cosworth/Reynard 2KI	FS	114.767	1m 13.589s	7	10	Accident		
25	Tony Kanaan (BR)	55	Mo Nunn Racing Hollywood Mercedes/Reynard 2KI	FS	no speed	no time		0	Withdrawn		

* denotes rookie driver

Caution flags: Laps 31-34, spin/Fernandez; laps 61-64, accident/Fittipaldi, de Ferran & Blundell; laps 66-67, accident/Moreno. **Total:** Three for 10 laps.
Lap leaders: Juan Montoya, 1-58 (58 laps); Roberto Moreno, 59 (1 lap); Montoya, 60 (1 lap); Helio Castroneves, 61-84 (24 laps). **Totals:** Montoya, 59 laps; Castroneves, 24 laps; Moreno, 1 lap.
Fastest race lap: Helio Castroneves, 1m 15.805s, 111.412 mph on lap 78.
Championship positions: 1 Tracy, 59; 2 Vasser, 54; 3 Moreno, 52; 4 Papis & de Ferran, 47; 6 Montoya, 46; 7 Andretti, 44; 8 Franchitti, 40; 9 Bräck, 39; 10 Fernandez, 38; 11 Castroneves, 36; 12 Carpentier, 34; 13 Servia & Tagliani, 26; 15 da Matta, 25; 16 Fittipaldi, 24; 17 Gugelmin, 21; 18 Blundell, 13; 19 Kanaan, 11; 20 Herta, 10; 21 Jourdain, 8; 22 Nakano & Gidley, 5; 24 Marques, 4; 25 Garcia, 2; 26 Kurosawa, 1.

PORTLAND

FEDEX CHAMPIONSHIP SERIES • ROUND 8

FEDEX CHAMPIONSHIP SERIES • ROUND 8

FEDEX CHAMPIONSHIP SERIES • ROUND 8

Pages 114/115: Marlboro Team Penske was the dominant force in Portland: Helio Castronevs took the pole, and teammate Gil de Ferran earned the victory.
Robert Laberge/Allsport USA

Left: De Ferran took advantage of an excellent strategic call by Roger Penske.

Below left: Pole-sitter Castroneves fell to seventh after running out of fuel.

THE Freightliner/G.I. Joe's 200 at Portland International Raceway mirrored the corresponding event in 1999 by providing an absorbing contest of speed, fuel strategy and pit work – in equal measure. And once again it was Gil de Ferran who held all the right cards, parlaying an aggressive three-stop gambit into a perfectly judged victory for Marlboro Team Penske.

"Roger [Penske] called a fantastic race," beamed a delighted de Ferran, who became the first repeat winner of an intensely-fought FedEx Championship Series season.

Fellow Brazilian Roberto Moreno could have made at least an equal claim to the victor's spoils. Confirming his reputation as the best fuel miser in the business, the 41-year-old veteran coaxed remarkable mileage from Pat Patrick's Visteon Ford Cosworth/Reynard, so that he alone was able to go the 112-lap distance on only two pit stops. But for a problem during his final service, Moreno would have overhauled de Ferran when the Penske driver pitted, in accordance with his three-stop routine, 15 laps later. Instead, de Ferran emerged with a narrow advantage, and Moreno was left to give valiant – but vain – chase in the closing laps.

"We had trouble on our second stop getting the fuel [into the car] and that cost us several seconds or it could have been a different story," rued Moreno, who nonetheless was overwhelmed by the realization that he had taken over the championship lead – by a single point from de Ferran – for the first time in his fragmented Champ Car career.

Yet another Brazilian, Helio Castroneves, also played a starring role in the Pacific Northwest. The youngster started from the pole and led the field cleanly into the ultra-tight Festival Curves chicane on the opening lap. Behind, however, chaos erupted. It was triggered when Kenny Bräck tagged Dario Franchitti in the first right-hander, spinning the KOOL Honda/Reynard and creating a logjam in the ensuing left-hander. The oncoming pack scattered in avoidance, with Juan Montoya taking to the dirt on the inside and narrowly missing Bräck's Shell Ford/Reynard as he rejoined. Jimmy Vasser and Max Papis were less fortunate, each sustaining extensive damage and retiring on the spot.

Unsurprisingly, a full-course caution was declared so that the Festival Curves could be cleared. When the green flag waved again, on lap five, Castroneves led a more orderly pro-

QUALIFYING

Any doubts about the extent of Marlboro Team Penske's resurgence were well and truly dispelled during practice and qualifying at Portland International Raceway. The pair of red and white Reynard 2KIs – variously dubbed "Renskes" or "Peynards" in deference to their subtle refinements to the standard customer chassis – appeared tailor made for the scenic Oregonian road circuit's blend of chicanes and long, looping corners. Come Saturday afternoon, the battle for pole position proved to be an in-house affair.

Helio Castroneves and Gil de Ferran traded fastest lap several times during an exciting half-hour final session, before Castroneves, full of confidence on the back of his maiden Champ Car victory in Detroit the previous week, put the matter to rest with a new track record of 57.738 seconds.

"It's just amazing," exclaimed an ecstatic Castroneves *(above)* after clinching his second career pole, and his first on a road course. "What a week, I tell you! After Detroit, now I get the pole here. It's unbelievable!"

De Ferran, who set the pace in Friday's provisional session, came up just 0.082 second short on Saturday, but pronounced himself satisfied after securing the team's first front-row monopoly in 98 races.

Best of the rest was none other than Roberto Moreno. The oldest man in the field had been far from happy with his Visteon Ford/Reynard on Friday, but rebounded strongly in final qualifying thanks to some radical overnight setup changes and a few more judicious adjustments following Saturday morning's free practice.

Dario Franchitti reckoned he "took all the KOOL car would give me" to annex fourth on the grid, while fastest of the Toyota contingent, surprisingly, was reigning Dayton Indy Lights champion Oriol Servia. The likeable Spaniard extracted every ounce of potential from PPI Motorsports' Telefonica-backed Reynard to line up a worthy seventh – one place ahead of reigning series champion Juan Montoya.

"I am learning to get the most out of my tires and that is very important," noted Servia.

A tale of two races

ROGER Penske experienced the thrill of victory and the agony of defeat all in one afternoon at Portland International Raceway. One of his drivers, Gil de Ferran, chalked up the third win in four races for CART's most successful squad, while the other, Helio Castroneves, came away with crumbs after a commanding performance that saw him lead 85 of the 112 laps.

In a strategically-framed, fuel-conscious race, the difference boiled down to pit tactics. Penske, who orchestrated de Ferran's race strategy, out-thought his young team manager Tim Cindric, who held that responsibility for Castroneves.

"Tim and I run our cars independently, based on how the race unfolds," explained The Captain. "Early on I saw that this was not going to be a two-stop race. We had two cars running well, so we had to get out front or be in the same boat as Helio. So we did a short stop on Gil's second stop and then he pulled out a 22-second lead before the third stops. Once we made that move, we knew we were in control."

Castroneves, meanwhile, attempted to pursue an ambitious two-stop strategy, but was forced to relinquish the lead in the closing stages when it became clear he would need to pit for a last minute splash of fuel. Then, to add insult to injury, the #3 Marlboro Honda/Reynard ran dry coming out of the last corner on the final lap, leaving Castroneves to coast across the finish line in seventh.

One week earlier, in Detroit, the emotional Brazilian broke down in tears of joy. This time there were tears of frustration as he sat slumped on the pit wall for all of 15 minutes.

"It's just a shame the way the race finished," said Castroneves after finally recovering his composure. "As I got on the power, everything went dead... Our fuel consumption came up just half a gallon short."

cession into the notorious bottleneck. De Ferran settled into second place, while Christian Fittipaldi nipped inside Moreno for third amid a cloud of tire smoke. On the very next lap, however, Moreno redressed the balance with a neatly executed pass at the same location.

Montoya survived his trip across the dirt to lie fifth, pursued by Cristiano da Matta (Pioneer Toyota/Reynard) and Alex Tagliani (Player's Ford/Reynard), who gained eight positions during the first-corner shenanigans. Michael Andretti (Big Kmart/Texaco Ford/Lola), in eighth, also made up ground. Oriol Servia (Telefonica Toyota/Reynard) wasn't so fortunate, having been bundled back several spots while threading a way through the melee.

The eighth lap saw a change to the leader board as da Matta took advantage of a perfect exit from Turn 12 to breeze past Montoya, no less, under braking for the Festival. A couple of laps later, da Matta repeated the feat to relieve Fittipaldi of fourth place. The Newman/Haas driver was grappling with the handling of his Big Kmart/Route 66 Ford/Lola, having badly flat-spotted his front tires during his earlier maneuver on Moreno. On lap 18, he gave up the unequal struggle and made an early pit stop for fresh rubber.

At the front of the field, Castroneves gradually eked out a sizeable advantage over his teammate. De Ferran, hampered by a touch too much oversteer aboard the #2 Marlboro Honda/Reynard, had his work cut out keeping Moreno at bay. By the time he ducked into the pits for routine service on lap 36, therefore, Castroneves was more than eight seconds to the good.

Nevertheless, there was a long way still to go. In fact, the race distance had been extended since last year's event – from 98 to 112 laps – to reduce the likelihood of a fuel economy run. It was assumed that everyone would now require three refueling stops to reach the finish, whereas in past years they had been able to coast home on just two.

That, at least, was the theory. Moreno and Patrick Racing, however, had other ideas. After stretching his original fuel load one lap farther than anyone else, Moreno employed his economical driving style and judicious fuel mixture settings to similarly good effect in the race's second stint. Perhaps this might be a two-stop race, after all...

At this stage, one half of Marlboro Team Penske was intent upon the same gameplan. Penske Racing president Tim Cindric, calling the strategy for Castroneves, envisaged only one more pit visit for his young charge. By contrast, team owner Roger Penske, who masterminded de Ferran's race from behind the pit wall, elected to commit to a three-stop strategy. It was a pivotal decision.

"It was either make a really tight two-stop run or a much looser three-stop," related de Ferran. "We didn't make any decision prior to the race. We talked and talked and were attempting to go for a two-stop strategy, but Roger changed his mind. I'm like a robot. I don't second-guess his decisions."

Castroneves' lead shrank appreciably during the middle portion of the race, and de Ferran whittled the deficit down to barely one second before the

FEDEX CHAMPIONSHIP SERIES • ROUND 8

Left to right: Papis, Tracy, Fernandez, Andretti, de Ferran, Montoya and Castroneves had one win apiece to their credit prior to arriving in Portland.

second round of pit stops. Clearly, a quick turn-round by Matt Jonsson's crew would be essential to give de Ferran the track position to capitalize on his "all-out" ploy.

Thus, when he pulled into his pit stall at the end of lap 69, de Ferran was held stationary for just 9.6 seconds – the time it took to mount a new set of Firestone radials. The short-fill enabled him to leapfrog Castroneves when the leader took on a full 35-gallon complement of methanol next time around.

Now de Ferran was in the clear: he could richen the fuel mixture, put the hammer down and set about building a large enough cushion to allow for a third stop later on.

"We made a few changes [to the car] at the second stop and, after that, the car was perfect," declared de Ferran. "When Roger told me to go, I knew what to do. I went as fast as I could."

Moreno, meanwhile, had moved up well and made it all the way to lap 74 before appearing in pit lane. If he could muster the same consumption in the race's final segment, he would be home free for the win. Cruelly, Moreno's hard work was undone when the fuel nozzle was knocked inadvertently into the closed position moments before it was inserted into the fuel tank receptacle. As Moreno got under way again, after an agonizing 19.7-second wait, de Ferran, in the midst of his flat-out charge, flashed past.

Turning the fastest laps of the race to that point, de Ferran extended his advantage to more than 22 seconds before pitting for a final time on lap 89. It wasn't enough for him to retain the lead, but he resumed in fourth place, secure in the knowledge that all three drivers in front of him – Castroneves, da Matta and Andretti – would have to stop again for fuel.

Sure enough, at the completion of lap 95, Andretti peeled into pit lane. Da Matta followed suit five laps later.

Castroneves, who had been forced to run a conservative pace in deference to his scheduled two-stop strategy, finally admitted defeat and paused for a splash of methanol on lap 105.

So it was that de Ferran regained control of the race. Moreno, though, was hot on his heels and was poised for a challenge when the leaders ran into traffic, in the shape of an uncooperative Patrick Carpentier, with six laps to go. Carpentier was holding onto tenth position, on the tail end of the lead lap, and seemed determined not to allow the leaders easy passage. Indeed, de Ferran had to lock up his front brakes to avoid contact with the Player's/Forsythe Ford/Reynard in the Festival Curves on the penultimate lap.

"I thought he was letting me go," said a none-too-impressed de Ferran, "but I guess he wasn't."

Carpentier did cede his position farther around the lap, but failed to extend the same courtesy to Moreno, thereby denying the large crowd the prospect of a thrilling finish. Ultimately de Ferran took the checkered flag a comfortable 2.625 seconds clear of his countryman.

Fittipaldi came home third after a spirited recovery drive following his out-of-sequence pit stop, ensuring the first ever all-Brazilian sweep of the podium.

"I really had to earn my money today," commented Fittipaldi. "Basically, after I screwed up at the beginning of the race, there was no other option but to drive every lap like I was on a huge flier."

Likewise Andretti drove a strong race, climbing from 11th on the grid to fourth, but was outpaced by his teammate all weekend. Filling the mirrors of the '91 series champion were da Matta, capping another assured performance for PPI Motorsports, and Bräck, who set fastest lap and went some way to redeeming himself after causing the first-corner mayhem.

Unrelieved misery for Team KOOL Green

TEAM KOOL Green endured a weekend to forget in the Pacific Northwest. After starting a promising fourth, Dario Franchitti was on the receiving end of Kenny Bräck's first-corner antics, then fell foul of the officials due to the slightly unorthodox manner of his recovery.

The Scotsman had been left facing the wrong way following a tap from Bräck's Shell Ford/Reynard in the Festival chicane, and, once the field had filed through, executed a spin-turn to reverse his course – only to stall his engine in the process. The corner workers subsequently pushed the KOOL Honda/Reynard through the chicane short-cut, which serves as an escape road, and the engine refired.

The Portland "ground rules" require marshals to hold any driver who bypasses the Festival Curves for ten seconds before releasing him back onto the circuit proper, to prevent an advantage being gained from "straight-lining" the chicane. Instead, the corner worker in question waved Franchitti on through, whereupon he was promptly assessed a drive-through penalty that dropped him to last on the road and from which he could only salvage a ninth-place finish by the day's end.

An extremely perturbed Barry Green later made his displeasure known to CART chief steward Kirk Russell, who conceded in retrospect that the penalty had been improperly assessed "due to a communications error" between race control and the corner worker. Franchitti, understandably, was in rather a black mood following his brush with officialdom...

Erstwhile championship leader Paul Tracy didn't fare any better. The Canadian languished in 17th on the grid after failing, by his own admission, to arrive at a suitable setup for qualifying. He sustained bent steering in the first-lap fracas, and eventually fell by the wayside on lap 71 after brushing the wall on the exit of Turn 12 and breaking a rear suspension toe-link.

"Team KOOL Green is just having a spell of bad luck and we need to get it turned around," said Tracy, whose third consecutive non-score demoted him to third in the point standings.

Jeremy Shaw/Alex Sabine

FEDEX CHAMPIONSHIP SERIES • ROUND 8

PORTLAND SNIPPETS

• For the second week running, the PPI Motorsports DUO of Cristiano da Matta and Oriol Servia were a force to be reckoned with. Da Matta started ninth after losing the use of fifth gear midway through final qualifying, but made rapid progress in the race and was unlucky not to end up higher than fifth. Servia nursed an ailing gearbox to place eighth.

• Patrick Carpentier was assessed a $10,000 FINE by CART chief steward Kirk Russell for what was termed "failure to follow instructions of officials regarding yielding to the leaders near the close of the race." Admitted Carpentier, who finished tenth, "I should have let the leaders by, but my team kept telling me not to because there were a few cars there that were for position. And we were trying to get as many points as we can."

• JUAN MONTOYA experienced an atypical weekend at PIR. The reigning champion could manage no better than eighth on the grid, and never really got a firm handle on his Target Toyota/Lola. "We've been lucky because we haven't been too [far] off on setup all season, but this weekend we've just had the car on the edge," stated Montoya philosophically. The Colombian's premature exit from the race – this time occasioned by an engine failure – was an all too familiar sight in the 2000 season, however.

• BRYAN HERTA *(above right)* was invited to drive Mo Nunn's Hollywood Mercedes/Reynard while Tony Kanaan recovered from injuries sustained in Detroit. Various mechanical problems robbed Herta of vital track time in the run-up to the race, consigning him to a lowly 20th starting position, but he had made sufficient progress by Sunday to set the fifth-fastest lap.

• The post-race press conference was a few minutes late in starting, so winner GIL DE FERRAN took advantage of the delay to call his home in Fort Lauderdale, Florida, to speak to his children, Luke and Anna. Although most of the conversation was in Portuguese, the words "Daddy won" came through loud and clear in English.

• Dario Franchitti took time off between Detroit and Portland to fly an Airbus A300 SIMULATOR at the FedEx headquarters in Memphis. "It's like the ultimate Playstation," Dario raved. "I got to take off and land the thing. The sensations are incredible...it's too realistic. It costs over $10 million, so I won't be getting one of those for Christmas!"

• A MISERABLE WEEK for Dale Coyne began when a major rock concert at his Route 66 Raceway in Joliet, Ill., featuring 'Nsynch, had to be postponed after the stage set was destroyed by high winds, and continued when the transporter carrying Takuya Kurosawa's Lolas was damaged in a fire en route to the West Coast.

• LUIZ GARCIA JR. enjoyed by far his most competitive showing aboard the Arciero-Project Racing Group's Hollywood Mercedes/Reynard. The Brazilian was shown as high as sixth during practice, and although eventually he qualified a disappointing 22nd, he ran respectably during the race to a 14th-place finish.

FEDEX CHAMPIONSHIP SERIES • ROUND 8
FREIGHTLINER/G.I. JOE'S 200 PRESENTED BY TEXACO

PORTLAND INTERNATIONAL RACEWAY, PORTLAND, OREGON

JUNE 25, 112 laps of 1.967 miles – 220.528 miles

Place	Driver (Nat.)	No.	Team Sponsors Engine/Car	Tires	Q Speed	Q Time	Q Pos.	Laps	Time/Status	Ave. (mph)	Pts.
1	Gil de Ferran (BR)	2	Marlboro Team Penske Marlboro Honda/Reynard 2KI	FS	122.594	57.820s	2	112	2h 00m 46.002s	109.564	20
2	Roberto Moreno (BR)	20	Patrick Racing Visteon Ford Cosworth/Reynard 2KI	FS	122.262	57.977s	3	112	2h 00m 48.627s	109.515	16
3	Christian Fittipaldi (BR)	11	Newman/Haas Big Kmart/Route 66 Ford Cosworth/Lola B2K/00	FS	121.972	58.115s	6	112	2h 00m 54.984s	109.419	14
4	Michael Andretti (USA)	6	Newman/Haas Big Kmart/Texaco Ford Cosworth/Lola B2K/00	FS	120.923	58.619s	11	112	2h 01m 15.733s	109.116	12
5	Cristiano da Matta (BR)	97	PPI Motorsports Pioneer/MCI WorldCom Toyota/Reynard 2KI	FS	121.196	58.487s	9	112	2h 01m 16.072s	109.111	10
6	*Kenny Bräck (S)	8	Team Rahal Shell Ford Cosworth/Reynard 2KI	FS	122.008	58.098s	5	112	2h 01m 16.592s	109.103	8
7	Helio Castroneves (BR)	3	Marlboro Team Penske Marlboro Honda/Reynard 2KI	FS	122.768	57.738s	1	112	2h 01m 19.712s	109.057	8
8	*Oriol Servia (E)	96	PPI Motorsports Telefonica Toyota/Reynard 2KI	FS	121.871	58.163s	7	112	2h 01m 20.471s	108.747	5
9	Dario Franchitti (GB)	27	Team KOOL Green Honda/Reynard 2KI	FS	122.090	58.059s	4	112	2h 01m 28.486s	108.627	4
10	Patrick Carpentier (CDN)	32	Forsythe Racing Player's/Indeck Ford Cosworth/Reynard 2KI	FS	120.841	58.659s	12	111	Running		3
11	*Shinji Nakano (J)	5	Walker Racing Avex Group Honda/Reynard 2KI	FS	118.112	1m 00.014s	21	111	Running		2
12	Adrian Fernandez (MEX)	40	Patrick Racing Tecate/Quaker State Ford Cosworth/Reynard 2KI	FS	121.086	58.540s	10	111	Running		1
13	*Alexandre Tagliani (CDN)	33	Forsythe Racing Player's/Indeck Ford Cosworth/Reynard 2KI	FS	119.430	59.352s	15	110	Out of fuel		
14	Luiz Garcia Jr. (BR)	25	Arciero-PRG Hollywood/Embratel-21 Mercedes/Reynard 2KI	FS	118.020	1m 00.061s	22	110	Running		
15	Tarso Marques (BR)	34	Dale Coyne Racing Panasonic Ford Cosworth/Swift 011.c	FS	118.989	59.572s	18	110	Running		
16	Bryan Herta (USA)	55	Mo Nunn Racing Hollywood Mercedes/Reynard 2KI	FS	118.642	59.746s	20	109	Running		
17	Juan Montoya (COL)	1	Target/Chip Ganassi Racing Toyota/Lola B2K/00	FS	121.593	58.296s	8	87	Engine		
18	Paul Tracy (CDN)	26	Team KOOL Green Honda/Reynard 2KI	FS	119.189	59.472s	17	71	Accident		
19	Mauricio Gugelmin (BR)	17	PacWest Racing Nextel Mercedes/Reynard 2KI	FS	no speed	no time	24	62	Engine		
20	Mark Blundell (GB)	18	PacWest Racing Motorola Mercedes/Reynard 2KI	FS	119.370	59.382s	16	31	Engine		
21	*Norberto Fontana (RA)	10	Della Penna Motorsports DirecTV Toyota/Reynard 2KI	FS	117.773	1m 00.187s	23	24	Gearbox		
22	*Takuya Kurosawa (J)	19	Dale Coyne Racing Sports Today Ford Cosworth/Lola B2K/00	FS	113.633	1m 02.380s	25	10	Clutch cable		
23	Michel Jourdain Jr. (MEX)	16	Bettenhausen Motorsports Herdez Mercedes/Lola B2K/00	FS	118.885	59.624s	19	8	Engine		
24	Jimmy Vasser (USA)	12	Target/Chip Ganassi Racing Toyota/Lola B2K/00	FS	119.597	59.269s	14	1	Accident		
25	Max Papis (I)	7	Team Rahal Miller Lite Ford Cosworth/Reynard 2KI	FS	120.420	58.864s	13	0	Accident		

* denotes rookie driver

Caution flags: Laps 1–3, accident/Papis, Vasser, Franchitti & Fernandez. **Total:** One for 3 laps.

Lap leaders: Helio Castroneves, 1–35 (35 laps); Roberto Moreno, 36 (1 lap); Castroneves, 37–71 (35 laps); Moreno, 72–74 (3 laps); Gil de Ferran, 75–89 (15 laps); Castroneves, 90–104 (15 laps); de Ferran, 105–112 (8 laps). **Totals:** Castroneves, 85 laps; de Ferran, 23 laps; Moreno, 4 laps.

Fastest race lap: Kenny Bräck, 1m 00.345s, 117.465 mph on lap 98.

Championship positions: 1 Moreno, 68; 2 de Ferran, 67; 3 Tracy, 59; 4 Andretti, 56; 5 Vasser, 54; 6 Papis & Bräck, 47; 8 Montoya, 46; 9 Franchitti & Castroneves, 44; 11 Fernandez, 39; 12 Fittipaldi, 38; 13 Carpentier, 37; 14 da Matta, 35; 15 Servia, 31; 16 Tagliani, 26; 17 Gugelmin, 21; 18 Blundell, 13; 19 Kanaan, 11; 20 Herta, 10; 21 Jourdain, 8; 22 Nakano, 7; 23 Gidley, 5; 24 Marques, 4; 25 Garcia, 2; 26 Kurosawa, 1.

CLEVELAND

1 – MORENO
2 – BRÄCK
3 – DA MATTA

FEDEX CHAMPIONSHIP SERIES • ROUND 9

Roberto Moreno was in masterful form at the Burke Lakefront Airport, translating his first-ever pole into his first-ever win.
Robert Laberge/Allsport USA

FEDEX CHAMPIONSHIP SERIES • ROUND 9

Marvelous Moreno

ROBERTO Moreno left his mark on Cleveland, scoring both his first career Champ Car pole position and win. For CART's elder statesman, the road to victory had been a rollercoaster ride of part-time drives and missed opportunities. Throughout his travails, however, the immensely likeable Brazilian displayed the heart of a lion and the determination to persevere.

Entering only his third full season of competition in the CART FedEx Championship Series, Moreno, with the support of his Patrick Racing Visteon Ford/Reynard crew, had emerged as a bona fide championship contender.

"There have been many times in my career that only I believed in myself," he said. "Even my best friends, they say, 'Are you sure you should continue doing that?' It's my love, this sport. It's what I do best in life. As long as my family is secure and healthy, I dedicate my life 100 percent to this."

It had been a long road. After cutting his teeth in the Brazilian karting ranks, Moreno traveled to Europe in 1979 at the behest of close buddy Nelson Piquet (who went on to win three Formula 1 World Championships). Moreno won in Formula Ford, Formula 3, Formula Atlantic and Formula 2, and tried his luck in the Champ Cars in the middle 1980s, including a full campaign with Galles Racing in 1986, which included five top-ten finishes.

Moreno always had his sights set on Formula 1, however, and returned to Europe in '87. He won the Formula 3000 title in dominant fashion one year later and gained some opportunities in Formula 1, but rarely with a front-running team. The exception was in '90, when he shone as teammate to Piquet at Benetton in several races, including a run to second at the Japanese Grand Prix. But again his career faltered.

Moreno drove a wide variety of cars throughout the '90s, and eventually rekindled his Champ Car aspirations in '96, driving a full season with Dale Coyne Racing, highlighted by the team's first and, so far, only podium appearance – third at the inaugural U.S. 500.

He had to be content with a succession of substitute roles for the next couple of years, earning the sobriquet "Super Sub" before finally getting a break with Pat Patrick's team.

"Roberto is young at heart," said Michael Andretti, who had vied with Moreno for the North American Formula Atlantic Championship in 1983. "You wouldn't think he is 41. It doesn't surprise me that he won."

QUALIFYING

With five minutes remaining in the final qualifying session for the Marconi Grand Prix of Cleveland Presented by Firstar, Roberto Moreno found the one-tenth of a second that was needed to propel him to his first career Champ Car pole position. His lap of 57.436 seconds (132.001 mph) eclipsed provisional pole-sitter Mauricio Gugelmin's (Nextel PacWest Mercedes/Reynard) time by 0.102 second. Less than a minute later, however, Moreno found himself sitting in the middle of the track. His spin in Turn Four brought the session to a halt.

"The car was fantastic," Moreno charged. "It was an ace lap. I was actually trying a faster lap after that, and was almost two-tenths faster on the dash of my car when I hit a little bump the wrong way and off I went."

"I tried to go out and get the pole, but Roberto's strategy worked," quipped Andretti, who posted the fourth-fastest time aboard the #6 Big Kmart/Texaco/Havoline Ford/Lola. "I had one of the quickest splits up until he spun."

For Gil de Ferran, the two minutes of qualifying remaining after Moreno's spin were enough to hoist his Marlboro Team Penske Honda/Reynard to a front-row starting position.

"The red flag came out and I still hadn't put in a lap that I felt was representative of the car," de Ferran related. "Luckily, we were able to get that one lap to get us up there."

Mauricio Gugelmin watched as he fell from first to second to third on the starting grid, but still logged his best start of the 2000 season. "This place is very difficult because the conditions are always improving," he said. "I got a pretty good lap in before, but the computer was saying that I was doing pretty good on the last lap. Unfortunately, I ran out of fuel on the last chicane."

Dario Franchitti, who placed his KOOL Honda/Reynard on Friday's provisional pole, ended up sixth on the grid.

"I'm sure we could have done better, but we got screwed up by [Roberto] Moreno's spin," explained the Scotsman. "We were right in the middle of our fastest lap all weekend, but that spin resulted in an untimely red flag."

Right: Kenny Bräck moved to fourth in the points table after finishing second.

Below right: A slipping clutch caused Adrian Fernandez to inadvertently knock over crewman Mike Sales in the pits.

IT was 15 years in the making and, when Roberto Moreno took the checkered flag at Cleveland, it was nothing short of marvelous. Teams up and down pit lane came trackside to unite with the cheers of the fans as Moreno cruised Patrick Racing's Visteon Ford Cosworth/Reynard to the Winner's Circle to claim his maiden victory in the CART FedEx Championship Series.

For the 41-year-old Brazilian, who had made his first Champ Car start back in 1985, albeit only contesting two full seasons, the dream had finally become reality. Moreno had come so close on numerous occasions, including one week earlier at Portland where he was stymied by a poor pit stop and had to be content with second place. Immediately following the win, the emotions of years of hard work and determination surfaced.

"Fantastic," summarized Moreno. "Fantastic. It's just a feeling I cannot describe – almost as good as when my daughters were born. Fantastic."

Moreno was undeniably in top form for Round Nine of the intensely fought championship, a force to be reckoned with on the bumpy Burke Lakefront Airport temporary course in Cleveland, Ohio. After clinching the pole, he led all but nine of the grueling 100 laps and added the one thing missing from his impressive driving curriculum – Champ Car race winner.

"Just imagine, as a comparison, you dream about getting to the moon," said Moreno. "People say, 'You're crazy. How are you going to get to the moon?' And then you push and push and push and push, and eventually you find a way to get there. That's more or less what happened. And when you *get* there, it's just a thrill to be in that position."

While Moreno enjoyed a relatively easy day at the office in the front of the field, many other potential contenders fell by the wayside in a race of surprisingly high attrition that saw just 12 of the 25 starters still running at the finish. The largest skirmish came in the run to the first corner, which in the past has played host to numerous incidents due to the fact that the acres of wide runway funnel into a tight, 130-degree hairpin corner with as many lines as there are combatants.

In an effort to discourage banzai outbraking efforts, CART chief steward Kirk Russell decreed that a series of cones should be placed on the inside of the track, and warned that any driver striking a cone on the run to the first corner would be penalized. The outcome of the cone strategy, if not necessarily the direct result, was a major shunt.

Bryan Herta, aboard Mo Nunn Racing's Hollywood Mercedes/Reynard, was the catalyst as he clipped the rear of Cristiano da Matta's Pioneer Toyota/Reynard which, in turn, sent the Brazilian into Dario Franchitti's KOOL Honda/Reynard. The incident triggered a chain reaction that eliminated Oriol Servia (Telefonica Toyota/Reynard), Takuya Kurosawa (*Sports Today* Ford/Lola) and Dale Coyne Racing teammate Tarso Marques (Panasonic Ford/Swift) on the spot. The fracas also led to the imminent retirements of Helio Castroneves (Marlboro Penske Honda/Reynard) and Michel Jourdain Jr. (Herdez Mercedes/Lola), both of whom sustained holed radiators.

Herta, da Matta (who had qualified a career-best fifth), and Franchitti were able to continue, but subsequent interviews with the "coned start" with those now seated on the sidelines were not, as could be imagined, favorable. However, a few drivers were able to take advantage of the melee at the start, most notably Paul Tracy, who jumped from 17th on the grid to eighth in the second KOOL Honda/Reynard, and Kenny Bräck (Shell Ford/Reynard), who shot from 15th to ninth.

Emerging unscathed were Moreno, Mauricio Gugelmin, who took full advantage of a special Mercedes-Benz qualifying motor to line up third on the grid in his Hollywood/PacWest Reynard, and Gil de Ferran (Marlboro Honda/Reynard). They occupied the top three spots, ahead of Michael Andretti (Big Kmart/Texaco Ford/Lola), Adrian Fernandez (Tecate/Quaker State Ford/Reynard), Tracy, Jimmy Vasser (Target Toyota/Lola), Christian Fittipaldi (Big Kmart/Route 66 Ford/Lola) and Bräck. Following a full-course caution while the debris was swept away, Moreno gradually built a 2.5-second lead over de Ferran, while Gugelmin tumbled down the order and Andretti headed the chase some five seconds adrift of the leaders.

The rash of attrition and problems continued behind Moreno as de Ferran encountered brake trouble and slipped backward before retiring after a coming-together with Gugelmin. Fernandez fell out of the reckoning (but recovered well to finish seventh) when he spun on lap 31, while Tracy's miserable luck continued when his gearbox broke on lap 41. Fittipaldi fared no better, ousted by his second engine failure of the day on lap 58, and Vasser made an early pit stop as part of a

FEDEX CHAMPIONSHIP SERIES • ROUND 9

FEDEX CHAMPIONSHIP SERIES • ROUND 9

Mercedes development engine shows promise

THERE were a few bright spots in the turbulent season experienced by Mercedes-Benz and Ilmor Engineering. The debut of a developmental IC108E engine at Cleveland initially suggested that brighter days might be around the corner. The new-spec motor, of which only one was available, performed well in the back of Mauricio Gugelmin's Nextel/PacWest Reynard, the Brazilian jumping briefly to the top of the timing charts during the final qualifying session on Saturday and ending up a strong third.

"We set ourselves up for one flying lap," said Gugelmin. "It was definitely my fastest and I think good enough for pole, but we ran out of fuel before I got to the line. Despite all that, I am very happy to be in the top three. Mercedes-Benz has done a great job improving the engine, and this is the first step to their reward."

The race, however, brought disappointment. Gugelmin, using a "standard" engine, slipped rapidly down the order due to a lack of straightline speed and, in the closing stages, fading brakes. Eventually, he finished tenth.

"The race was certainly disappointing," said Ilmor USA's Paul Ray, "but it was encouraging to see how well he went in qualifying. At this stage, the development engine is just that – a collection of pieces that we've been working on for some time. We were pretty pleased with it, and Mauricio felt it was a worthwhile improvement. But we're some weeks away from having the parts in any quantity."

"They're all short-life pieces at the moment," he continued. "We haven't been able to test them extensively enough to be sure they'll be OK for a full race distance. We were obviously keen to show the engine's value, which is why we took it to Cleveland, which is noted as being a power circuit."

Unfortunately, the bright spots for Mercedes were few and far between, and led to its withdrawal from competition beyond the 2000 season.

---

three-stop strategy and dropped to the back of the field.

Franchitti and da Matta, meanwhile, were working their respective ways back through the field, and had moved into eighth and ninth by mid-distance.

"In the first half of the race, I was conserving fuel, but I was able to attack when the guy in front of me made a mistake," said da Matta. "I was behind one of the Player's cars [Alex Tagliani] for a long time and when I couldn't pass him, I just decided to save fuel."

Shuffled back from sixth to 11th in the first-corner rumble, Juan Montoya was on the move through the field. He latched onto Bräck's gearbox and steadily moved forward in the Swede's wake. On lap 63, Bräck took advantage of a slip in Turn One by Andretti to move into second place, and Montoya looked set to do the same until making his second pit stop on lap 64.

Moreno remained in complete control, resuming from the pits with a 12-second margin over Bräck on lap 70. Montoya's Target Toyota/Lola emerged ahead of Andretti and immediately began to place Bräck under increasing pressure.

"I tried to keep Montoya behind me, but it wasn't easy because I had to save fuel," related Bräck, who eventually capitulated on lap 74. "I called [Team Rahal general manager and race-day strategist] Scott Roembke a few names and eventually I had to let Juan go. But we got it back so, in the big picture, Scott was right."

Montoya, like teammate Vasser, was indeed committed to a three-stop strategy and, after making his final stop during a full-course yellow caused when Alex Tagliani's Player's Ford/Reynard was stranded by a broken gearbox on lap 79, he resumed in seventh spot, but was unable to make any headway.

For Moreno, the full-course caution depleted what had been a nine-second lead over Bräck. At the green flag on lap 81, however, the Brazilian quickly began refashioning a useful – if not exactly comfortable – lead over Bräck, with Andretti, Franchitti, da Matta, Carpentier and Montoya in hot pursuit. A little too hot for Andretti, as it turned out, for he had been struggling with a loose Lola ever since a first-lap tangle with Gugelmin.

Andretti attempted to go around the outside of Bräck under braking for Turn One on lap 82. It was a futile move that, in fact, resulted in Andretti losing two positions to Franchitti and da Matta. But Franchitti's snake-bitten season continued, and the Scotsman began losing gears at a rapid rate. Da Matta slipped past on lap 92, along with Andretti, while the rest followed suit in the next few laps. Franchitti soon retired with only first gear at his disposal.

Moreno headed into the closing stages with Bräck some three seconds in arrears and da Matta right on the Swede's gearbox. With a clear track ahead of him, about the only thing that stood in the way of Moreno's victory was an unexpected mechanical failure – or the emotions of some three decades of hard work and unflagging determination in the face of sometimes hopeless odds.

On lap 96, the unthinkable nearly happened. Moreno allowed himself to focus on celebrating the coming victory rather than the four laps between himself and the checkered flag. His premature emotional melt-down enabled Bräck to close to within 1.1 seconds on lap 97.

"I was crying," Moreno admitted. "I said, 'OK, I'd better wake up and get going.'"

"It looked like we had a good lead to finish the race," he continued. "So I started to think about things you shouldn't. That gets to you and you can just imagine the emotion inside of me that came out...but I dried out and got going again."

He regained his composure enough to build the margin back to 1.3 seconds, then do all that was necessary to ensure the victory ahead of Bräck and da Matta, who looked set to challenge in the closing stages, only to be forced into fuel conservation mode once more. Still, the young Brazilian finished a close third to secure his career-best result. Andretti soldiered on to finish fourth ahead of Carpentier and Montoya.

For Moreno, whose last taste of victory spoils had been in 1988, while contesting the Formula 3000 Championship, the flag-to-flag win extended his lead in the championship to 22 points over Andretti.

"That's what happens when they give you a good race car," he beamed.

Jeremy Shaw

FEDEX CHAMPIONSHIP SERIES • ROUND 9

CLEVELAND SNIPPETS

• Erstwhile CART FedEx Championship leader **PAUL TRACY** endured yet more disappointment in Cleveland, failing to score points for the fourth race in succession. The Canadian's tale of woe began on Saturday, when the engine in his Team KOOL Green Honda/Reynard expired on the first lap of qualifying. His luck seemed to have taken a turn for the better as he took advantage of a first-corner melee to rise from 15th to sixth on the opening lap, and by one-third distance he was up to fourth, looking set to put his championship challenge back on track. Sadly, just a half-dozen laps after his first pit stop, Tracy's gearbox seized up.

• Ford Cosworth regained **THE LEAD** in the CART Manufacturer's Championship following Roberto Moreno's magnificent weekend. Ford's quest was aided by a disastrous day for Honda, which, for the first time in 83 Champ Car races, dating back to Mid-Ohio in 1995, failed to earn a point-scoring finish.

• Kika Conchesa-Garcia, who handles all media matters and other business arrangements for Marlboro Team Penske star **GIL DE FERRAN**, received a phone call midway through the Friday qualifying session. It was de Ferran's mom, Ziza, calling from her home in São Paulo, Brazil. "She was watching [the live timing] on the Internet and she couldn't see his name," related Garcia, "so she wanted to know what happened." In fact, her son sat out much of the session after misjudging his approach to the final chicane, launching his Honda/Reynard high off the curbing and damaging its suspension.

• Galaxy Latin America, provider of the DirecTV satellite service to Latin America and the Caribbean, became the new primary **SPONSOR** for Della Penna Motorsports' Toyota/Reynard driven by Norberto Fontana. The Argentinian rookie celebrated the arrangement by claiming his first two championship points for an 11th-place finish.

• Newman/Haas Racing was busier than usual following the race-morning warmup, as both Michael Andretti and Christian Fittipaldi suffered **ENGINE FAILURES**, requiring new Ford Cosworth XF motors to be fitted in time for the race.

• Mark Blundell worked with a new **RACE ENGINEER** in Ohio after Guillaume "Rocky" Roquelin took over the duties from Steve Clark. It was the eighth engineering change since Blundell joined the team in 1996.

• CART officials announced a new agreement with "sports and entertainment powerhouse" SFX Sports Group to conduct negotiations with ESPN and ABC Sports concerning its future **TELEVISION** rights. CART's current contract was due to expire following the 2001 season. SFX previously had negotiated deals with sports such as Supercross (motorcycles), Breeder's Cup (horse racing), ATP Tour (tennis) and the U.S. Ski Team on a variety of networks.

FEDEX CHAMPIONSHIP SERIES • ROUND 9
MARCONI GRAND PRIX OF CLEVELAND PRESENTED BY FIRSTAR

BURKE LAKEFRONT AIRPORT, CLEVELAND, OHIO

JULY 2, 100 laps of 2.106 miles – 210.600 miles

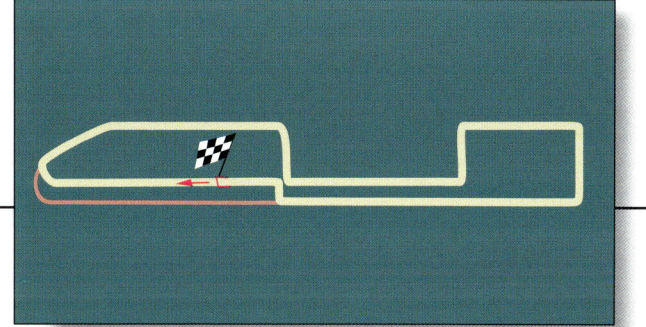

Place	Driver (Nat.)	No.	Team Sponsors Engine/Car	Tires	Q Speed	Q Time	Q Pos.	Laps	Time/Status	Ave. (mph)	Pts.
1	Roberto Moreno (BR)	20	Patrick Racing Visteon Ford Cosworth/Reynard 2KI	FS	123.414	57.436s	1	100	1h 52m 12.092s	112.619	22
2	*Kenny Bräck (S)	8	Team Rahal Shell Ford Cosworth/Reynard 2KI	FS	122.111	58.049s	15	100	1h 52m 12.918s	112.605	16
3	Cristiano da Matta (BR)	97	PPI Motorsports Pioneer/MCI WorldCom Toyota/Reynard 2KI	FS	123.099	57.583s	5	100	1h 52m 14.059s	112.586	14
4	Michael Andretti (USA)	6	Newman/Haas Big Kmart/Texaco Ford Cosworth/Lola B2K/00	FS	123.116	57.575s	4	100	1h 52m 19.654s	112.492	12
5	Patrick Carpentier (CDN)	32	Forsythe Racing Player's/Indeck Ford Cosworth/Reynard 2KI	FS	120.721	58.717s	19	100	1h 52m 20.445s	112.479	10
6	Juan Montoya (COL)	1	Target/Chip Ganassi Racing Toyota/Lola B2K/00	FS	123.060	57.601s	6	100	1h 52m 22.365s	112.447	8
7	Adrian Fernandez (MEX)	40	Patrick Racing Tecate/Quaker State Ford Cosworth/Reynard 2KI	FS	122.834	57.505s	9	100	1h 52m 31.458s	112.296	6
8	Jimmy Vasser (USA)	12	Target/Chip Ganassi Racing Toyota/Lola B2K/00	FS	122.361	57.930s	12	100	1h 52m 31.843s	112.289	5
9	Bryan Herta (USA)	55	Mo Nunn Racing Hollywood Mercedes/Reynard 2KI	FS	122.911	57.671s	7	100	1h 52m 33.293s	112.265	4
10	Mauricio Gugelmin (BR)	17	PacWest Racing Nextel Mercedes/Reynard 2KI	FS	123.195	57.538s	3	100	1h 53m 14.599s	111.583	3
11	*Norberto Fontana (RA)	10	Della Penna Motorsports DirecTV Toyota/Reynard 2KI	FS	119.605	59.625s	22	99	Running		2
12	Mark Blundell (GB)	18	PacWest Racing Motorola Mercedes/Reynard 2KI	FS	121.670	58.259s	16	98	Running		1
13	Dario Franchitti (GB)	27	Team KOOL Green Honda/Reynard 2KI	FS	122.898	57.677s	8	94	Gearbox		
14	Gil de Ferran (BR)	2	Marlboro Team Penske Marlboro Honda/Reynard 2KI	FS	123.225	57.524s	2	87	Accident		
15	*Shinji Nakano (J)	5	Walker Racing Avex Group Honda/Reynard 2KI	FS	120.173	58.985s	21	82	Transmission		
16	*Alexandre Tagliani (CDN)	33	Forsythe Racing Player's/Indeck Ford Cosworth/Reynard 2KI	FS	120.872	58.644s	18	77	Gearbox		
17	Christian Fittipaldi (BR)	11	Newman/Haas Big Kmart/Route 66 Ford Cosworth/Lola B2K/00	FS	122.338	57.941s	13	58	Engine		
18	Max Papis (I)	7	Team Rahal Miller Lite Ford Cosworth/Reynard 2KI	FS	122.121	58.044s	14	49	Driveshaft		
19	Paul Tracy (CDN)	26	Team KOOL Green Honda/Reynard 2KI	FS	121.099	58.534s	17	41	Gearbox		
20	Luiz Garcia Jr. (BR)	25	Arciero-PRG Hollywood/Embratel-21 Mercedes/Reynard 99I	FS	116.670	1m 00.756s	24	17	Engine		
21	Helio Castroneves (BR)	3	Marlboro Team Penske Marlboro Honda/Reynard 2KI	FS	122.802	57.722s	10	3	Accident		
22	Michel Jourdain Jr. (MEX)	16	Bettenhausen Motorsports Herdez Mercedes/Lola B2K/00	FS	120.263	58.941s	20	1	Accident		
23	*Oriol Servia (E)	96	PPI Motorsports Telefonica Toyota/Reynard 2KI	FS	122.598	57.598s	11	0	Accident		
24	Tarso Marques (BR)	34	Dale Coyne Racing Panasonic Ford Cosworth/Swift 011.c	FS	119.249	59.442s	23	0	Accident		
25	*Takuya Kurosawa (J)	19	Dale Coyne Racing Sports Today Ford Cosworth/Lola B2K/00	FS	116.649	1m 00.767s	25	0	Accident		

* denotes rookie driver

Caution flags: Laps 1–5, multi-car accident; laps 12–13, accident/Blundell; laps 78–80, tow/Tagliani. **Total:** Three for 10 laps.

Lap leaders: Roberto Moreno, 1–33 (33 laps); Gil de Ferran, 34–35 (2 laps); Jimmy Vasser, 36–41 (6 laps); Bryan Herta, 42 (1 lap); Moreno, 43–100 (58 laps). Totals: Moreno, 91 laps; Vasser, 6 laps; de Ferran, 2 laps, Herta, 1 lap.

Fastest race lap: Juan Montoya, 59.625s, 123.364 mph on lap 76.

Championship positions: 1 Moreno, 90; **2** Andretti, 68; **3** de Ferran, 67; **4** Bräck, 63; **5** Tracy & Vasser, 59; **7** Montoya, 54; **8** da Matta, 49; **9** Papis & Carpentier, 47; **11** Fernandez, 45; **12** Franchitti & Castroneves, 44; **14** Fittipaldi, 38; **15** Servia, 31; **16** Tagliani, 26; **17** Gugelmin, 24; **19** Herta & Blundell, 14; **20** Kanaan, 11; **21** Jourdain, 8; **22** Nakano, 7; **23** Gidley, 5; **24** Marques, 4; **25** Garcia & Fontana, 2; **27** Kurosawa, 1.

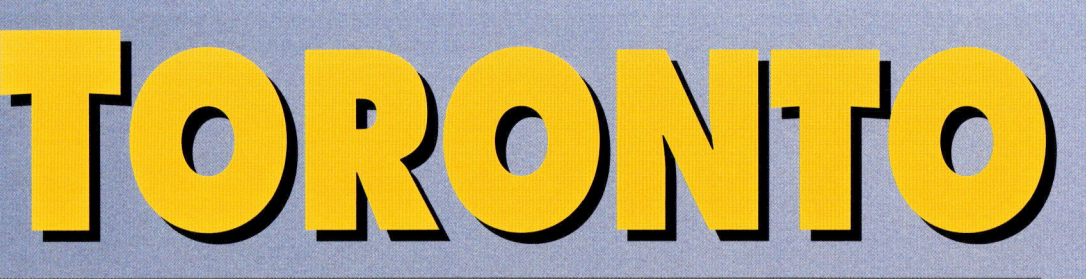

TORONTO

FEDEX CHAMPIONSHIP SERIES • ROUND 10

1 – ANDRETTI
2 – FERNANDEZ
3 – TRACY

FEDEX CHAMPIONSHIP SERIES • ROUND 10

Andretti closes in

MICHAEL Andretti has accumulated a remarkable record on the challenging Exhibition Place temporary circuit in Toronto. He has started lower than sixth on the grid in only two of his 14 appearances, and now has no fewer than nine podium finishes to his credit, including six victories.

"I don't know what it is about this place," said Andretti, "but I love the track. It seems to suit my style. I love [the city of] Toronto also. It's always a good feeling to come here and an even better one to win here."

Even team co-owner Carl Haas *(below, congratulating Michael)* was impressed.

"We've had a lot of good times in Toronto, and Michael did a great, great job," said Haas. "The whole crew did. It was a tough race, very close. You didn't see much passing, but I guarantee you it was a very difficult race for everybody."

Andretti's latest triumph was notable for several reasons, including the fact that it elevated him to within two points of FedEx Championship Series leader Roberto Moreno as the title-chase reached its halfway stage.

"This helps a lot for the championship," said Andretti, who started the season among the hot favorites, but failed to score any points from the first three races. Since then, he has finished all but one of the seven races among the top six.

"All we've got to do is just keep finishing and continue to do the job we've been doing the last few races, and we should be OK," said Andretti.

The 40th victory of his career also moved him ahead of Al Unser into sole possession of third place on the all-time list of Champ Car winners. Only A.J. Foyt, the all-time leader with 67 wins, and Mario Andretti, with 52 wins, have been more successful.

"It's gettable," said the younger Andretti of his father's tally. "That's going to be one of the biggest motivations of my career – to beat dad's record."

FEDEX CHAMPIONSHIP SERIES • ROUND 10

Pages 126/127: After failing to finish three straight races, Toronto native Paul Tracy placed third for Team KOOL Green.
Robert Laberge/Allsport USA

Left: Michael Andretti used all of his vast experience to excellent effect.

Below left: Fernandez, Andretti and Tracy enjoy the customary podium celebrations.

Below: Early leader Cristiano da Matta was unfortunate to finish fourth.

RISING sophomore star Cristiano da Matta took advantage of a slip by Brazilian countryman Helio Castroneves on the opening lap and held onto a slim lead for most of the Molson Indy Toronto. But this wasn't to be his day. Instead, wily veteran Michael Andretti emerged to score his second win of the season for Newman/Haas Racing – and the 40th of his career.

It was a masterful performance by Andretti, 37, who was content to run third in the opening stages, then picked up one position at each of his two pit stops. Thereafter, his Big Kmart/Texaco Havoline Ford Cosworth/Lola was never seriously threatened en route to an amazing sixth triumph at the challenging Exhibition Place temporary circuit.

"It was just a perfect day" said Andretti. "I'm just so happy to get my 40th here in Toronto, because it's been so good to me."

QUALIFYING

Final qualifying for the Molson Indy Toronto provided a tremendous spectacle for the huge and enthusiastic crowd. There was no clear-cut favorite. Christian Fittipaldi had set the pace on Friday morning in Newman/Haas Racing's Big Kmart/Route 66 Ford Cosworth/Lola, while Dario Franchitti's KOOL Honda/Reynard emerged fastest in provisional qualifying – after a heavy thunder shower left the circuit drenched for the first group of contenders. A third different engine/chassis combination led the timing charts during practice on Saturday morning, Juan Montoya being quickest aboard Target/Chip Ganassi Racing's #1 Toyota/Lola.

Times were substantially faster in the final qualifying period, and after the first group it was Kenny Bräck who led the way with a lap at 57.984s aboard Team Rahal's Shell Ford/Reynard. Two more contenders, Michael Andretti (in the second Newman/Haas Ford/Lola) and Helio Castroneves (Marlboro Honda/Reynard) traded the top position for the opening 15 minutes, before Castroneves put the issue beyond doubt with a lap of 57.200s.

"I was in the zone," smiled Castroneves. "I didn't have any traffic and everything went really well."

Cristiano da Matta, too, was delighted after overcoming some braking difficulties on the first day to qualify a career-best second for Cal Wells III's PPI Motorsports team.

"I'm happy to see the team and me progressing the way we are right now," said da Matta. "I think we need to just keep working as we have been working since the beginning of the season, and the good results and race wins are going to come."

Andretti ended up third on the grid, his best starting position of the season thus far, and was joined on row two by Montoya. Franchitti's hopes of maintaining his 100 percent record of front-row starts in his fourth visit to Toronto came unstuck in the final session, when he tried to carry a little too much speed into Turn Eight and ended up in the tire barrier. The Scotsman's time remained good for fifth, though, ahead of Fittipaldi and Bräck, who was the fastest rookie once again.

Molstar Sports and Entertainment did its usual fine job of promotion in the cosmopolitan provincial capital city, and once some early-morning rain clouds had cleared, another record-breaking crowd of 72,976 was treated to near perfect weather conditions for the 2 pm start.

Castroneves made full use of his second pole of the season to lead into the first corner, chased by da Matta's Pioneer Toyota/Reynard and second-row starters Andretti and Juan Montoya. At the end of Lake Shore Boulevard, however, Castroneves overshot his braking mark and immediately lost his advantage. Da Matta was the grateful beneficiary of the error.

"I tried to go really, really late on the brakes," related da Matta. "Helio went a little deeper than me and about lost it."

Somehow, Castroneves retrieved a huge sideways slide and resumed in second, just ahead of Andretti, who also locked up his brakes.

"Helio got in really hard" said Andretti. "It wasn't his fault. It was like ice down there. I was all out of shape, and obviously the other guys must've felt the same thing, because they all got into each other."

Montoya's Target Toyota/Lola, indeed, had been shadowing Andretti on the outside line, only to be knocked into a spin by perennial rival Dario Franchitti, whose KOOL Honda/Reynard snapped first one way, then the other as the Scotsman fought for control. The impact ensured that, for the third race in a row, the first lap was completed under a full-course caution.

"I don't know what happened," related Franchitti. "I got on the brakes pretty hard and the back end swung around on me. I'm disappointed that we got tangled up. I feel bad for Juan – bad for us both."

Kenny Bräck takes a breather during qualifying for the Molson Indy Toronto.

As usual, fuel conservation – plus the ability to stay out a little longer and take advantage of a clear track to turn a fast lap or two – was crucial to the outcome of the race. Andretti vaulted ahead of da Matta, while Fernandez's characteristic miserly consumption enabled him to emerge from the pits with a tenuous lead over Andretti. But could he hold on? Fernandez scrabbled around Turn One ahead of his rival, then maintained a defensive line all the way down Lake Shore Boulevard. But Andretti's tires already were up to optimum temperature, which enabled him to brake deeper than the Mexican and wrest the lead with a bold maneuver around the outside line at Turn Three.

Franchitti and Montoya made it back to the pits, but no farther.

After four laps behind the pace car, da Matta took off into the lead, chased by Castroneves, Andretti and Newman/Haas teammate Christian Fittipaldi. Kenny Bräck (Shell Ford/Reynard) ran fifth ahead of Adrian Fernandez (Quaker State/Tecate Ford/Reynard), who overtook Gil de Ferran's Marlboro Honda/Reynard at the restart in Turn One. De Ferran was forced wide at the exit of the corner, losing two more positions to Paul Tracy (KOOL Honda/Reynard) and Oriol Servia (Telefonica Toyota/Reynard). Mauricio Gugelmin's Nextel Mercedes/Reynard rounded out the top ten.

The only other change of position among the leaders prior to the first round of pit stops came on lap 26, when Servia squeezed past Tracy under braking for Turn Three. Servia soon edged clear of the Canadian and, by lap 34, had reduced a sizeable deficit to Fernandez to little more than a couple of car lengths. The first stops came just two laps later, under yellow due to a clash between Tarso Marques (Panasonic Ford/Swift) and Norberto Fontana (DirecTV Toyota/Reynard) in Turn Eight.

The interruption saw important changes at the head of the field. Da Matta remained in front, but Andretti took advantage of excellent service by Donny Hoevel's Newman/Haas crew to edge out Castroneves. Fernandez, Servia and the rest also gained a position when Fittipaldi, who was leaving the pits in company with his teammate, rear-ended de Ferran, who was on his way to his own pit stall.

"[Andretti] wouldn't let me in, so I lifted to get in behind him and – bang! – I got hit so hard that it lifted the back end of the car into the air," related de Ferran. Incredibly, it was the third time in as many races in Toronto that the pair had been involved in a pit-lane miscue. This time, Fittipaldi's day was done, suspension broken.

The middle stint of the race was a struggle for da Matta, who was running on worn tires and was unable to match his earlier pace. In addition to suffering problems in transmitting his Toyota engine's power to the ground, da Matta began to experience fading brakes. He came under increasing pressure from Andretti, and soon there was a huge train of cars lined up in their wake, comprising Fernandez, Tracy, Bräck, de Ferran, Alex Tagliani (who had moved impressively from 19th in his Player's/Forsythe Ford/Reynard), Jimmy Vasser (Target Toyota/Lola), Max Papis (Miller Lite Ford/Reynard), Patrick Carpentier (in the second Player's car) and Roberto Moreno. (The championship leader had lost a few positions immediately prior to the earlier caution, when his Visteon Ford/Reynard was inadvertently punted into a spin in Turn One by an over-zealous Tagliani.)

The pressure on da Matta was intense, yet the 1998 Indy Lights Champion looked like a seasoned veteran as he calmly held onto his lead.

"It was a struggle on old tires," he admitted. "I have led many races before; it's not the first time. I've done it many times; I'm not going to make a silly mistake."

Even so, Andretti was hoping that da Matta would crack.

"I was just pushing him really hard," said the 1991 CART champion, "trying to make him make a mistake. He made a couple, but not enough to take advantage of, so I thought, 'OK, I'll just leave it up to my pit crew.'"

Andretti's patience paid off. On lap 74, da Matta was the first of the leaders to make his second pit stop. Bräck and Papis followed suit on the same lap. Andretti, Tagliani and de Ferran stopped one lap later. Tracy and Vasser stayed out until lap 76, Carpentier until lap 77. Patrick Racing teammates Fernandez and Moreno remained out until laps 78 and 79 respectively.

CART spreads its wings

AS part of its continuing worldwide expansion, Championship Auto Racing Teams, Inc., sanctioning body for the FedEx Championship Series, confirmed three new race venues for the 2001 season during the days leading up to the Molson Indy Toronto. Two of the additions will be in Europe – at brand-new ovals under construction at Lausitz, Germany, and Rockingham, England. Texas Motor Speedway, situated near Dallas/Fort Worth, also will play host to a Champ Car event.

After negotiations lasting several years, there had been speculation that the CART team owners might decide to visit only one of the European ovals. Nevertheless, interim CART president and CEO Bobby Rahal visited both facilities for the formal announcements.

"We are well aware of the huge following our sport has in Europe," said Rahal, "and we're excited about these two new races. We're looking forward to bringing the world's fastest form of circuit racing to Rockingham and the Lausitzring."

Virtually everyone involved in the series was bullish about the European foray – none more so, predictably, than British drivers Mark Blundell and Dario Franchitti.

"I think the atmosphere will be something that has not been experienced in the UK for a long, long time," declared Blundell. "This formula is so exciting and I think English race fans are in for a real treat.

"It will just be fantastic to be in front of a home crowd again. It was one of the things I really used to look forward to when I was in Formula 1, and now I can experience that feeling again. Obviously, running in your home country creates extra pressure with all the attention from family, friends, media and sponsors, but it's all worth it."

Franchitti was equally excited about the prospect: "Brilliant," he exclaimed. "It's great for the sport to go in front of the fans in Europe. I think it's awesome. The fan base in Europe is massive. It's going to be an excellent show, and I think the fans will really get into it."

"I just knew I had to take advantage of his cold tires," said Andretti. "I knew I could trust Adrian; he's great to race with. And that was it. The rest of the race it was just a case of not making a mistake."

Andretti, indeed, was flawless. Others were less so. Servia, for example, lost his chance of a podium finish when he spun in Turn Five while attempting to pass Fernandez on lap 44. The Spaniard resumed several laps in arrears and, due to the high rate of attrition, gained a couple of championship points after being classified 11th. Fellow rookie Bräck also threw away valuable points when he "outbraked myself" at Turn Three while following Tagliani on lap 88.

Tracy, meanwhile, despite brushing the wall in Turn Two immediately after the first restart, produced another workmanlike performance to claim third – his series-leading (along with Moreno) fourth podium of the year. Da Matta had to make do with fourth.

"It's a little bit disappointing [after leading a race-high 73 laps]," he admitted, "but it was pretty good to lead the race. We're getting closer and closer to the race win. When you put yourself closer to the front, things start to happen your way. I think, sooner or later, everything's going to come our way."

Tagliani took an excellent fifth after a tigering drive, while de Ferran claimed sixth ahead of Carpentier, Papis, Vasser and Bräck. Series leader Moreno looked set for another good finish, running fifth after the final round of pit stops, but soon was stricken by a failing gearbox. Eventually, he lost all drive on lap 100.

Moreno's misfortune played into the hands of Andretti: "It was perfect timing to make up some ground on Roberto, because he had some problems and that's how you win championships, by taking advantage of other people's problems. We just have to keep it up to the end of the season."

Jeremy Shaw

FEDEX CHAMPIONSHIP SERIES • ROUND 10

TORONTO SNIPPETS

• Marlboro Team Penske's **GIL DE FERRAN** drove a subdued race to sixth, feeling somewhat less than fully fit. "My neck was ready to fall off, so I just tried to hang in there," said the Brazilian, referring to a crash during qualifying on Friday and another incident in testing one week earlier in Chicago.

• Gil de Ferran's teammate, **HELIO CASTRONEVES**, also had an eventful weekend, which began with a bizarre failure on Friday morning, in which the entire plenum chamber literally blew off the top of the motor and ended up in the middle of the race track! Castroneves came back to win the pole, but lost the lead on the opening lap and later retired from the race following another mishap in the engine department.

• **ORIOL SERVIA** once again was impressive in PPI Motorsports' Telefonica Toyota/Reynard. The reigning Indy Lights champion rose from 11th to fifth at the expense of the likes of Gil de Ferran and Paul Tracy, before coming to grief in a breathtaking – if ultimately flawed – effort to wrest fourth place from Adrian Fernandez. The Spaniard thrust his car down the inside of Fernandez under braking for Turn Three – with just a few hairs' width between his right-side tires and the wall, and between his left-side tires and Fernandez. The Mexican held his ground as the two accelerated up the hill to Turn Five, whereupon Servia promptly spun into the tire barrier. "I guess that's why they have the category called 'rookie,'" quipped the Spaniard, who lost four laps, but continued to finish 11th and set fifth-fastest lap of the race in the process.

• With the blessing of Ric Moore, father of Greg Moore, who tragically lost his life in a crash at the '99 season finale, Paul Tracy wore a special **BELL HELMET**, created by noted helmet artist Troy Lee in the design and colors used by Moore. Prior to being used in the race, the helmet was auctioned at a pre-event gala and fetched an impressive CDN$45,000 for the Greg Moore Foundation.

• Two-time former CART champion **ALEX ZANARDI** enjoyed a two-day test aboard Mo Nunn Racing's Hollywood Mercedes/Reynard at Sebring, Florida, during the weekend, between races at Cleveland and Toronto. Rumors that he might drive in Toronto proved unfounded, however, and once again Bryan Herta sat in for the injured Tony Kanaan. The Brazilian, meanwhile, pronounced himself ready to make a return to the cockpit at Michigan Speedway, following intensive physiotherapy and a session in a 125cc shifter kart under the supervision of CART medical adviser Dr. Terry Trammell.

• "TAG" **TAGUCHI**, who oversees all of Toyota's business dealings in Canada, the United States and Mexico, was in Toronto for meetings and made a surprise visit to the CART paddock area on Sunday morning. Taguchi stopped by to see all of the teams using Toyota power, of course, as well as noted Toyota dealer Roger Penske.

• **MOVIE STARS** Sylvester Stallone (*pictured with Luiz Garcia Jr.*) and Burt Reynolds were much in evidence during the weekend as filming of *Driven*, a major motion picture centered on the FedEx Championship Series (and due for release in April 2001), moved into high gear.

FEDEX CHAMPIONSHIP SERIES • ROUND 10
MOLSON INDY TORONTO

EXHIBITION PLACE, TORONTO, ONTARIO, CANADA

JULY 16, 112 laps of 1.721 miles – 192.752 miles

Place	Driver (Nat.)	No.	Team Sponsors Engine/Car	Tires	Q Speed	Q Time	Q Pos.	Laps	Time/Status	Ave. (mph)	Pts.
1	Michael Andretti (USA)	6	Newman/Haas Big Kmart/Texaco Ford Cosworth/Lola B2K/00	FS	109.562	57.666s	3	112	2h 00m 02.313s	98.248	20
2	Adrian Fernandez (MEX)	40	Patrick Racing Tecate/Quaker State Ford Cosworth/Reynard 2KI	FS	108.826	58.056s	9	112	2h 00m 08.840s	98.159	16
3	Paul Tracy (CDN)	26	Team KOOL Green Honda/Reynard 2KI	FS	108.242	58.369s	12	112	2h 00m 11.431s	98.124	14
4	Cristiano da Matta (BR)	97	PPI Motorsports Pioneer/MCI WorldCom Toyota/Reynard 2KI	FS	109.804	57.539s	2	112	2h 00m 17.283s	98.045	13
5	*Alexandre Tagliani (CDN)	33	Forsythe Racing Player's/Indeck Ford Cosworth/Reynard 2KI	FS	107.500	58.772s	19	112	2h 00m 23.935s	97.954	10
6	Gil de Ferran (BR)	2	Marlboro Team Penske Marlboro Honda/Reynard 2KI	FS	108.847	58.045s	8	112	2h 00m 26.663s	97.917	8
7	Patrick Carpentier (CDN)	32	Forsythe Racing Player's/Indeck Ford Cosworth/Reynard 2KI	FS	107.897	58.556s	17	112	2h 00m 29.480s	97.879	6
8	Max Papis (I)	7	Team Rahal Miller Lite Ford Cosworth/Reynard 2KI	FS	108.135	58.427s	14	112	2h 00m 31.353s	97.854	5
9	Jimmy Vasser (USA)	12	Target/Chip Ganassi Racing Toyota/Lola B2K/00	FS	108.165	58.411s	13	112	2h 00m 41.051s	97.723	4
10	*Kenny Bräck (S)	8	Team Rahal Shell Ford Cosworth/Reynard 2KI	FS	108.961	57.984s	7	112	2h 00m 49.242s	97.612	3
11	*Oriol Servia (E)	96	PPI Motorsports Telefonica Toyota/Reynard 2KI	FS	108.350	58.311s	11	108	Running		2
12	Luiz Garcia Jr. (BR)	25	Arciero-PRG Hollywood/Embratel-21 Mercedes/Reynard 2KI	FS	no speed	no time	25	105	Running		1
13	Roberto Moreno (BR)	20	Patrick Racing Visteon Ford Cosworth/Reynard 2KI	FS	108.107	58.442s	16	99	Gearbox		
14	*Shinji Nakano (J)	5	Walker Racing Avex Honda/Reynard 2KI	FS	106.980	59.058s	21	56	Electrical		
15	Mauricio Gugelmin (BR)	17	PacWest Racing Nextel Mercedes/Reynard 2KI	FS	108.646	58.152s	10	45	Engine		
16	Helio Castroneves (BR)	3	Marlboro Team Penske Marlboro Honda/Reynard 2KI	FS	110.455	57.200s	1	45	Exhaust header		1
17	Christian Fittipaldi (BR)	11	Newman/Haas Big Kmart/Route 66 Ford Cosworth/Lola B2K/00	FS	109.027	57.949s	6	37	Accident		
18	Bryan Herta (USA)	55	Mo Nunn Racing Hollywood Mercedes/Reynard 2KI	FS	107.871	58.570s	18	36	Exhaust		
19	Michel Jourdain Jr. (MEX)	16	Bettenhausen Motorsports Herdez Mercedes/Lola B2K/00	FS	107.045	59.022s	20	36	Engine		
20	*Norberto Fontana (RA)	10	Della Penna Motorsports DirecTV Toyota/Reynard 2KI	FS	106.741	59.190s	22	33	Accident		
21	Tarso Marques (BR)	34	Dale Coyne Racing Panasonic Ford Cosworth/Swift 011.c	FS	106.727	59.198s	23	33	Accident		
22	Mark Blundell (GB)	18	PacWest Racing Motorola Mercedes/Reynard 2KI	FS	108.133	58.428s	15	19	Engine		
23	*Takuya Kurosawa (J)	19	Dale Coyne Racing *Sports Today* Ford Cosworth/Lola B2K/00	FS	103.944	1m 00.783s	24	8	Exhaust		
24	Juan Montoya (COL)	1	Target/Chip Ganassi Racing Toyota/Lola B2K/00	FS	109.066	57.928s	4	1	Accident		
25	Dario Franchitti (GB)	27	Team KOOL Green Honda/Reynard 2KI	FS	109.044	57.940s	5	1	Accident		

* denotes rookie driver

Caution flags: Laps 1–3, accident/Montoya & Franchitti; laps 35–38, accident/Fontana & Marques. **Total:** Two for 7 laps.

Lap leaders: Cristiano da Matta, 1–73 (73 laps); Michael Andretti, 74 (1 lap); Adrian Fernandez, 75–77 (3 laps); Roberto Moreno, 78–79 (2 laps); Andretti, 80–112 (33 laps). **Totals:** da Matta, 73 laps; Andretti, 34 laps; Fernandez, 3 laps; Moreno, 2 laps.

Fastest race lap: Michael Andretti, 1m 00.045s, 105.221 mph on lap 86.

Championship positions: 1 Moreno, 90; 2 Andretti, 88; 3 de Ferran, 75; 4 Tracy, 73; 5 Bräck, 66; 6 Vasser, 63; 7 da Matta, 62; 8 Fernandez, 61; 9 Montoya, 54; 10 Carpentier, 53; 11 Papis, 52; 12 Castroneves, 45; 13 Franchitti, 44; 14 Fittipaldi, 38; 15 Tagliani, 36; 16 Servia, 33; 17 Gugelmin, 24; 18 Herta & Blundell, 14; 20 Kanaan, 11; 21 Jourdain, 8; 22 Nakano, 7; 23 Gidley, 5; 24 Marques, 4; 25 Garcia 3; 26 Fontana, 2; 27 Kurosawa, 1.

Far left: The action was intense from the moment the green flag flew.
Robert Laberge/Allsport USA

Top: Tarso Marques unwittingly assisted Juan Montoya's quest for victory.
Robert Laberge/Allsport USA

Above middle: It could hardly be closer as Montoya edges Andretti at the finish line.
Craig Jones/Allsport USA

Above: All smiles for podium finishers Franchitti, Montoya and Andretti.
Robert Laberge/Allsport USA

Left: Chip Ganassi celebrates his 34th victory in partnership with Target Stores.
Craig Jones/Allsport USA

FEDEX CHAMPIONSHIP SERIES • ROUND 11

FEDEX CHAMPIONSHIP SERIES • ROUND 11

Left: Kyle Moyer's crew goes to work for third-place finisher Dario Franchitti.
Robert Laberge/Allsport USA

Below left: Memo Gidley made a welcome Champ Car return with John Della Penna.
Darrell Ingham/Allsport USA

Below: A surprisingly small crowd was on hand for what was a truly spectacular race.
Darrell Ingham/Allsport USA

QUALIFYING

It is said that the only qualifying spot that matters at Michigan is the first one, and only then because you receive a championship point for it. But that didn't keep the drivers from making it tough for Paul Tracy, forcing him to post a record speed of 234.933 mph to claim his first pole position since 1997 and his first since joining Team KOOL Green in '98.

"It's a boost for the whole team," said Tracy, who edged Michael Andretti and Christian Fittipaldi for the top spot. "I owe it to the engineering staff, especially [Technical Director] Tino Belli who has done a fantastic job, and all the work they've done over the winter in the wind tunnel."

Tracy had to work hard for the pole after Newman/Haas Racing turned in surprisingly strong qualifying runs. Although practice speeds had topped the 238-mph mark in the morning (with Tracy quickest of all at 238.933 mph), most expected that, running alone without the benefit of drafting, qualifying speeds would be in the 232-mph range. But when Fittipaldi nailed a 234.269-mph lap before the qualifying session was even halfway through, it was clear the predictions would fall short of the mark.

"We had some very small mechanical problems with the car in practice, so we didn't get to run a lot either day, but we were happy with the car anyway," said Fittipaldi. "I expected to be in the top five or six, but I didn't think pole would be that quick. I thought it would be maybe a high 231 or 232."

After Fittipaldi's surprise laps, a host of drivers tried and failed to match or better the Brazilian's speed before Andretti whistled around at 234.267 mph to make it an all-Newman/Haas front row – temporarily.

Tracy's teammate Dario Franchitti's effort meant that just two teams would comprise the front two rows, as the green-and-white cars of TKG would sandwich the black Ford/Lolas after Franchitti took the fourth qualifying spot. Gil de Ferran claimed fifth for Marlboro Team Penske, followed by the Target/Chip Ganassi Racing Toyota/Lolas of Jimmy Vasser and Juan Montoya.

IN shorter, less demanding races all season, Juan Montoya had been strong; yet trouble and misfortune always seemed to find a way of catching up with his Target Toyota/Lola. But when the ante was upped to 500 miles, Montoya's cards all fell the right way.

The defending series champ backed up his Indianapolis 500 win with a victory in one of the most thrilling CART FedEx races in recent memory, claiming the 500-miler at Michigan Speedway by a scant 0.04 second over a charging Michael Andretti.

With 30 miles to go, Montoya and Andretti (Big Kmart/Texaco Ford/Lola) broke away from an eight-car lead pack and turned the race into a two-car affair. They swapped the lead a couple of dozen times in the last 14 laps before staging a nail-biter of a finish, sweeping across the finish line in wheel-to-wheel formation, with Montoya inches behind the lapped car of Tarso Marques – but, more importantly, narrowly ahead of Andretti.

"Michael was pushing me up in the last corner and I could see Tarso moving up," said Montoya, who finished second to Tony Kanaan at Michigan last year by 0.032 second. "I wasn't going to lift; if I had to, I was gonna bump him and give him a little push. Fortunately, he gave me a little bit of a tow and I thought, 'Whew. That was close.' I lost by the same amount last year, so I'm happy to win this one."

Coincidentally, Montoya and Andretti also were locked in combat through the opening stages of the 250-lap Michigan 500 Presented by Toyota. While pole-sitter Paul Tracy was content to run a conservative pace in his KOOL Honda/Reynard, Montoya and Andretti took off at the front of the field and traded positions several times each lap. It was an astonishing sight, first one driver and then the other taking advantage of the prodigious draft afforded by the Handford Device rear wing.

As the race settled down, several other drivers took a turn out in front of the pack. Tracy, Kenny Bräck, Christian Fittipaldi, Adrian Fernandez, Helio Castroneves, Oriol Servia, Alex Tagliani and Max Papis each led at least one lap, while Dario Franchitti and Patrick Carpentier were in close contention most of the day, along with Cristiano da Matta and Gil de Ferran. One by one, though, several of the potential contenders fell by the wayside.

Bräck, Tagliani and Fittipaldi all crashed out of the race. Bräck found his Shell Ford/Reynard pinched between Fittipaldi's Big/Kmart/Route 66 Ford/Lola and the wall coming off Turn Two on lap 98. Tagliani lost control of his Player's/Indeck Ford/Reynard in Turn Four on lap 161, shortly after taking the lead. Later, Fittipaldi

Send in the crowds

IT is a curious anomaly that a pair of NASCAR Winston Cup races at Michigan Speedway each year attract capacity crowds – despite the fact that the venue does not lend itself to particularly close competition between the 3500lb behemoths. Indeed, such is the popularity of the stock car events that the track's seating capacity has been raised substantially in recent years. By contrast, the Champ Car races at the International Speedway Corporation's two-mile, high-banked oval, set among the scenic Irish Hills vacation area of southern Michigan, have tended to provide sensational action – witness two of the three closest finishes in CART history – yet draw only mediocre attendances.

CART's first 500-mile race of the new millennium lived up to expectations in every conceivable way, with glorious weather conditions and a thrilling finish. Sadly, it was witnessed by a crowd estimated at around 50,000 – or less than one-third capacity.

According to Michigan Speedway president Gene Haskett, the track has spent a total of $1 million on promoting the CART races over the past three years. But for some reason, the public has not responded.

"I'm a huge fan of open-wheel racing," said Haskett, "and I have to say that was one of the best – if not *the* best – races I have ever seen. I don't know what we have do to get more people in here."

Third-place finisher Dario Franchitti was equally perplexed: "I don't understand [why the crowd figure wasn't higher]. You watch some other races here and the place is packed, and the racing isn't nearly as interesting. I don't understand it. Explain it to me somebody, please."

In the weeks leading up to event, there had been increasing speculation that CART might not return to Michigan after the current contract expires following the 2001 season. Haskett, however, firmly denied the reports: "The race will go on," he declared. "I've talked to [CART interim CEO] Bobby [Rahal]. He wants it back. It's pretty hard to walk away from an event like this. You gotta build on the equity you have in open-wheel racing, and places like here and Milwaukee have a lot of equity."

FEDEX CHAMPIONSHIP SERIES • ROUND 11

Welcome returnee Tony Kanaan, his arm still in a splint, shares a joke with fellow Brazilian Christian Fittipaldi.
Robert Laberge/Allsport USA

took a wild ride through the grass amid a traffic jam on the back straightaway.

A pit incident put paid to da Matta's chances after a strong performance in the Pioneer/WorldCom Toyota/Reynard, while de Ferran – who had suffered a broken finger when he was hit by debris from Bräck's accident – retired his Marlboro Honda/Reynard after contact with Michel Jourdain Jr.'s Herdez Mercedes/Lola. The learning curve for the rookie Servia became a little steeper as the Spaniard removed his Telefonica Toyota/Reynard from contention with a couple of pit-lane violations.

De Ferran's teammate, Castroneves, made his bid for the win by trying to outrun those who were content to run a lean fuel mixture and a conservative pace as the race headed toward its climax. The strategy failed to pan out. Although Castroneves stretched his lead in the Marlboro Honda/Reynard to over ten seconds with only 30 laps remaining, it was not enough to enable him make an extra pit stop and still retain the lead.

Fittipaldi's dramatic spin on lap 221 also took care of Fernandez's hopes following an eventful afternoon. The Mexican had battled back after losing two laps when, embarrassingly, he spun exiting the pits on lap 39 and blunted the nosecone of Patrick Racing's Tecate/Quaker State Ford/Reynard. Running at the tail of the lead pack when Tagliani crashed, he stopped for fuel on the lap before the restart and, given his typically superb fuel mileage, was poised to win the race by running to the finish on just one more stop.

While the other leaders stopped between laps 205 and 210, Fernandez stretched his run to 213, but the fruits of the strategy soured with Fittipaldi's flight through the infield. The caution meant that everyone – save Castroneves, Montoya and Tracy – had enough fuel to make the finish. Those three stopped during the Fittipaldi yellow to take on enough methanol to run full-rich to the finish, dropping near the tail of the dwindling pack as a result.

Fernandez remained up front, but a fateful gear choice meant he couldn't match the speed of the leaders. He was left to watch as Andretti, Franchitti and Max Papis stormed into the lead.

"My car was fast, but it wasn't fast enough for the guys who qualified up front," said Fernandez, who finished sixth. "I didn't have enough straightaway speed."

When the green flags waved for the final time, on lap 230, Andretti immediately jumped into the lead, while Montoya came rocketing through the field after his splash-and-go pit stop. Castroneves' car developed a push, which prevented him from posing a serious threat in the waning stages, while Tracy was unable to make any progress after becoming caught behind slower cars on the restart.

It took Montoya all of five laps to commandeer second place, whereupon he and Andretti staged a breakaway of their own.

"I knew it was going to be important to try to get away from the rest of the group," said the American. "It came down to Juan and myself working together, and I think we both knew we needed to break away, so we really worked together where we were leapfrogging away from the rest of the pack. We knew then it was going to be between the two of us."

From lap 240 onward, the pair were never separated by more than half a car's length. Behind them, Franchitti dispatched Papis for a clear third place and a bird's-eye view of one of the greatest finishes in Champ Car history.

Andretti and Montoya took the white flag absolutely tied together as Marques' Panasonic Ford/Swift loomed on the horizon. At first, everything went Andretti's way, as he dropped in behind Montoya through Turns One and Two, in preparation for an attack in Turn Three.

"I was able to get him to do exactly as I wanted," said Andretti. "I allowed him to go by into Turn One and I knew I wanted to get a draft going into Turn Three and get a run on him."

Then Marques came into play. Trying to stay out of the way, he chose the ultra high line and unwittingly played into Montoya's hands.

"I came off Turn Four really strong," said Andretti. "In fact, I pulled [Juan] a little bit because we were behind Tarso. I thought Tarso was going to help me because normally his line had been down low, but for some reason he decided to stay high.

"I got a little tow from him initially, and then all of a sudden he went really high, up by the wall. So then I started fighting for the tow and Juan was stuck right there and neither of us was backing off. I was hoping that Tarso would move over – half a car width and I'd have won the race. But he stayed up real high trying to stay out of the way, but by doing that he allowed Juan to get a tow and that was the difference."

"You just try to go as fast as you can, even if you had to bump him [Marques] – but not too much," said Montoya. "It was fun. It's fun [racing] with guys you can trust. It's no fun with guys you can't trust."

Speaking of which, Franchitti was hoping that history would repeat itself.

"I didn't think anything would happen," he said. "But I was right behind them in Japan [in '99 when Andretti and Montoya banged wheels at 200 mph in practice and crashed]. I was hoping for a little bit of deja vu, but it didn't happen."

Instead, Franchitti had to settle for third after his strongest performance to date on a superspeedway, while Carpentier added another chapter to a quietly impressive season by coming home fourth ahead of Castroneves and Fernandez. Tracy finished seventh, the last driver on the lead lap.

Papis, too, had been in the thick of the action, battling back and forth with Franchitti for third place until the engine in his Miller Lite Ford/Reynard let go with fewer than ten miles left. Well, at least his demise wasn't as heart-wrenching as 12 months earlier, when he ran out of fuel on the final lap with victory in sight.

Jeremy Shaw/Eric Mauk

Back in the saddle

DEFENDING Michigan 500 champion Tony Kanaan, who had missed the previous three races due to injuries suffered in Detroit, was finally given clearance to drive Mo Nunn Racing's Hollywood Mercedes/Reynard at Michigan Speedway following a brief shakedown run on Thursday under the supervision of CART medical advisor Dr. Terry Trammell.

"I feel absolutely great," said a beaming Kanaan afterward. "This is a wonderful feeling to be back in my race car.

"I tried not to get too excited about coming back. Last night, I went to bed at a normal hour, but I woke up this morning as if it was going to be just another day in the office. But when they strapped me into the car and fired up the motor, chills ran up and down my spine. It was great."

On Friday evening, Kanaan expressed himself relatively content after posting a best practice lap of 229.241 mph (31.408 seconds), good enough for 20th on the day.

"The good news is that I feel absolutely great in the race car," said the upbeat Brazilian, who ran very few laps on Friday after suffering an engine failure. "The arm and the ribs were not even an issue today out on the track."

Once again, the Mercedes-Benz engine wasn't up to par in comparison to the Ford Cosworth, Honda and Toyota competition, although, after qualifying 18th, Kanaan moved up into the top ten before being forced out of the race after only 69 laps.

"I was having a really good time out there," said Kanaan. "I had a good race car and I was moving my way up the order pretty steadily. But once we got into the top ten, our water temperature got a little high and we just couldn't seem to fix the problem. We didn't want to risk anything happening out there on the track, so we retired the car.

"Otherwise, it's great to be back. Ten days ago, I couldn't drive at all. A week ago, I was driving a go-kart. And today, here I am defending my championship in the Michigan 500. It's unfortunate the day had to end the way it did, but hey, that's racing."

FEDEX CHAMPIONSHIP SERIES • ROUND 11

MICHIGAN SNIPPETS

• Juan Montoya's **MARGIN** of victory over Michael Andretti was the third closest finish in CART history after Portland in '97, when Mark Blundell edged Gil de Ferran by 0.027 second, and the '99 Michigan 500, when Tony Kanaan headed Montoya by 0.032 second. The sum of the margins of victory in the last three Champ Car races at Michigan Speedway totals a mere 0.331 second.

• Christian Fittipaldi came in for some **CRITICISM** after the race, not least from Kenny Bräck, who crashed heavily on the back straightaway after making contact with the Brazilian. "There is a lot of side-by-side racing over 500 miles, and everyone has to leave room for each other," said Bräck. "Many people did that. There was nothing I could do when somebody drives into the side of my car. I don't know if his mirror fell off or his spotter fell asleep, but he didn't see me and it was a big hit. We had a car that could have won this race."

• Newman/Haas **TEAMMATES** Michael Andretti *(right)* and Christian Fittipaldi both wore the Head And Neck Support (HANS) system, which was used for the first time in Champ Car competition by Norberto Fontana at Nazareth.

• Japanese rookie **TAKUYA KUROSAWA** did not start the race after being involved in a huge crash during qualifying. "He's sore from head to toe," reported Dale Coyne Racing team manager Bernie Myers, "but he has no broken bones. It was a big hit. The car did its job [to protect him]. The way the gearbox and the back end crumbled really absorbed a lot of the impact."

Robert Laberge/Allsport USA

• Formula 1 veteran **JOHNNY HERBERT** was seen in conversation with a variety of team owners, pursuing opportunities to join the CART ranks for 2001 after learning that his contract with Jaguar would not be renewed.

• Cristiano da Matta ended his day in the pits after a **MISCOMMUNICATION** with right-front tire changer Bharat Naran during a routine stop. The driver thought he had been released to leave the pits, but dropped the clutch before the fuel line had been disconnected. Fueler Chris Moschetto was knocked over but, fortunately, did not suffer any substantial injury.

• **MEMO GIDLEY** made a welcome return to the cockpit, having been invited to drive John Della Penna's DirecTV Toyota/Reynard in place of the accident-prone Norberto Fontana. Gidley acquitted himself well in his first-ever superspeedway race, although his efforts were hindered by the lack of a cockpit-controlled weight-jacker (used as a means of altering the car's mechanical balance to compensate for the shrinking fuel load during a long run). After a manual adjustment to the chassis late in the race, Gidley ran with the leaders and even outran Helio Castroneves to un-lap himself at one point.

• Paul Tracy's qualifying run was aided by a **ONE OFF ENGINE** from Honda, featuring a single turbo wastegate arrangement similar to that first introduced by Toyota at Twin Ring Motegi in May. Tracy had tested the trick Honda at Michigan in June, ran competitive speeds and was rewarded for his testing work with a new track record, breaking the mark of 234.665 mph set by Jimmy Vasser in '96 before the advent of the Handford Device.

FEDEX CHAMPIONSHIP SERIES • ROUND 11
MICHIGAN 500 PRESENTED BY TOYOTA

MICHIGAN SPEEDWAY, BROOKLYN, MICHIGAN

JULY 23, 250 laps of 2 miles – 500 miles

Place	Driver (Nat.)	No.	Team Sponsors Engine/Car	Tires	Q Speed	Q Time	Q Pos.	Laps	Time/Status	Ave. (mph)	Pts.
1	Juan Montoya (COL)	1	Target/Chip Ganassi Racing Toyota/Lola B2K/00	FS	228.931	30.963s	7	250	2h 48m 49.790s	177.694	20
2	Michael Andretti (USA)	6	Newman/Haas Big Kmart/Texaco Ford Cosworth/Lola B2K/00	FS	230.990	30.687s	2	250	2h 48m 49.830s	177.693	16
3	Dario Franchitti (GB)	27	Team KOOL Green Honda/Reynard 2KI	FS	229.562	30.878s	4	250	2h 48m 51.411s	177.665	14
4	Patrick Carpentier (CDN)	32	Forsythe Racing Player's/Indeck Ford Cosworth/Reynard 2KI	FS	228.393	31.036s	9	250	2h 48m 51.895s	177.657	12
5	Helio Castroneves (BR)	3	Marlboro Team Penske Marlboro Honda/Reynard 2KI	FS	227.185	31.201s	13	250	2h 48m 52.920s	177.639	11
6	Adrian Fernandez (MEX)	40	Patrick Racing Tecate/Quaker State Ford Cosworth/Reynard 2KI	FS	227.586	31.146s	12	250	2h 48m 53.633s	177.626	8
7	Paul Tracy (CDN)	26	Team KOOL Green Honda/Reynard 2KI	FS	231.307	30.645s	1	250	2h 48m 56.676s	177.573	7
8	*Oriol Servia (E)	96	PPI Motorsports Telefonica Toyota/Reynard 2KI	FS	225.954	31.371s	15	249	Running		5
9	Max Papis (I)	7	Team Rahal Miller Lite Ford Cosworth/Reynard 2KI	FS	227.725	31.127s	11	247	Engine		4
10	Memo Gidley (USA)	10	Della Penna Motorsports DirecTV Toyota/Reynard 2KI	FS	221.146	32.053s	21	247	Running		3
11	Luiz Garcia Jr. (BR)	25	Arciero-PRG Hollywood/Embratel-21 Mercedes/Reynard 2KI	FS	216.678	32.714s	23	246	Running		2
12	Tarso Marques (BR)	34	Dale Coyne Racing Panasonic Ford Cosworth/Swift 011.c	FS	212.609	33.340s	24	246	Running		1
13	Mauricio Gugelmin (BR)	17	PacWest Racing Nextel Mercedes/Reynard 2KI	FS	222.144	31.909s	20	241	Engine		
14	Christian Fittipaldi (BR)	11	Newman/Haas Big Kmart/Route 66 Ford Cosworth/Lola B2K/00	FS	230.600	30.739s	3	220	Accident		
15	Michel Jourdain Jr. (MEX)	16	Bettenhausen Motorsports Herdez Mercedes/Lola B2K/00	FS	220.308	32.175s	22	162	Engine		
16	*Alexandre Tagliani (CDN)	33	Forsythe Racing Player's/Indeck Ford Cosworth/Reynard 2KI	FS	228.732	30.990s	8	160	Accident		
17	Cristiano da Matta (BR)	97	PPI Motorsports Pioneer/WorldCom Toyota/Reynard 2KI	FS	226.315	31.321s	14	142	Pit incident		
18	Gil de Ferran (BR)	2	Marlboro Team Penske Marlboro Honda/Reynard 2KI	FS	229.368	30.904s	5	140	Suspension		
19	Mark Blundell (GB)	18	PacWest Racing Motorola Mercedes/Reynard 2KI	FS	223.046	31.780s	17	131	Engine		
20	*Shinji Nakano (J)	5	Walker Racing Avex Group Honda/Reynard 2KI	FS	222.311	31.885s	19	104	Drivetrain		
21	Jimmy Vasser (USA)	12	Target/Chip Ganassi Racing Toyota/Lola B2K/00	FS	229.153	30.933s	6	102	Gearbox		
22	*Kenny Bräck (S)	8	Team Rahal Shell Ford Cosworth/Reynard 2KI	FS	228.180	31.065s	10	97	Accident		
23	Roberto Moreno (BR)	20	Patrick Racing Visteon Ford Cosworth/Reynard 2KI	FS	224.551	31.567s	16	97	Gearbox		
24	Tony Kanaan (BR)	55	Mo Nunn Racing Hollywood Mercedes/Reynard 2KI	FS	222.661	31.835s	18	61	Engine		
25	*Takuya Kurosawa (J)	19	Dale Coyne Racing *Sports Today* Ford Cosworth/Lola B2K/00	FS	no speed	no time	–	–	Withdrawn		

* denotes rookie driver

Caution flags: Laps 39-45, spin/Fernandez; laps 82-87, debris; laps 98-105, accident/Bräck & Fittipaldi; laps 161-169, accident/Tagliani; laps 221-228, accident/Fittipaldi. **Total:** Five for 38 laps.

Lap leaders: Juan Montoya, 1-16 (16 laps); Michael Andretti, 17-18 (2 laps); Montoya, 19-21 (3 laps); Helio Castroneves, 22-33 (12 laps); Kenny Bräck, 34 (1 lap); Christian Fittipaldi, 35-37 (3 laps); Adrian Fernandez, 38-39 (2 laps); Bräck, 40-50 (11 laps); Fittipaldi, 51-56 (6 laps); Bräck, 57-61 (5 laps); Andretti, 62-67 (6 laps); Castroneves, 68 (1 lap); Andretti, 69-78 (10 laps); Fittipaldi, 79-81 (3 laps); Max Papis, 82-88 (7 laps); Castroneves, 89 (1 lap); Papis, 90-91 (2 laps); Bräck, 92 (1 lap); Castroneves, 93-100 (8 laps); Montoya, 101-106 (6 laps); Castroneves, 107-126 (20 laps); Andretti, 127-129 (3 laps); Castroneves, 130 (1 lap); Andretti, 131-133 (3 laps); Castroneves, 134 (1 lap); Andretti, 135-140 (6 laps); Montoya, 141 (1 lap); Fittipaldi, 142 (1 lap); Fernandez, 143-144 (2 laps); Andretti, 145-154 (10 laps); Alexandre Tagliani, 155 (1 lap); Andretti, 156 (1 lap); Tagliani, 157-160 (4 laps); Castroneves, 161-164 (4 laps); Montoya, 165-170 (6 laps); Paul Tracy, 171-173 (3 laps); Castroneves, 174-176 (3 laps); Tracy, 177-181 (5 laps); Castroneves, 182-204 (23 laps); Oriol Servia, 205-206 (2 laps); Andretti, 207-209 (3 laps); Fernandez, 210-213 (4 laps); Castroneves, 214-224 (11 laps); Fernandez, 225-229 (5 laps); Andretti, 230-237 (8 laps); Montoya, 238-240 (3 laps); Andretti, 241 (1 lap); Montoya, 242 (1 lap); Andretti, 243-246 (4 laps); Montoya, 247-248 (2 laps); Andretti, 249 (1 lap); Montoya, 250 (1 lap). **Totals:** Castroneves, 85 laps; Andretti, 58 laps; Montoya, 39 laps; Bräck, 18 laps; Fernandez, 13 laps; Fittipaldi, 13 laps; Papis, 9 laps; Tracy, 8 laps; Tagliani, 5 laps; Servia, 2 laps.

Fastest race lap: Juan Montoya, 31.162s, 231.051 mph on lap 232.

Championship positions: 1 Andretti, 104; **2** Moreno, 90; **3** Tracy, 80; **4** de Ferran, 75; **5** Montoya, 74; **6** Fernandez, 69; **7** Bräck, 66; **8** Carpentier, 65; **9** Vasser, 63; **10** da Matta, 62; **11** Franchitti, 58; **12** Papis & Castroneves, 56; **14** Fittipaldi & Servia, 38; **16** Tagliani, 36; **17** Gugelmin, 24; **18** Herta & Blundell, 14; **20** Kanaan, 11; **21** Jourdain & Gidley, 8; **23** Nakano, 7; **24** Marques & Garcia, 5; **26** Fontana, 2; **27** Kurosawa, 1.

CHICAGO

FEDEX CHAMPIONSHIP SERIES • ROUND 12

1 - DA MATTA
2 - ANDRETTI
3 - DE FERRAN

FEDEX CHAMPIONSHIP SERIES • ROUND 12

Da Matta's moment

CRISTIANO da Matta's father, Antonio, was an 11-time Brazilian touring-car champion, and it was virtually preordained that the diminutive youngster from Belo Horizonte would seek a career in the sport. The young da Matta gained a successful grounding in South American karting, then continued his learning curve in Europe, competing in Formula 3 and F3000, before following in the footsteps of former karting buddies Tony Kanaan, Helio Castroneves and Gualter Salles by moving to North America in 1997. After Kanaan won the Indy Lights Championship in '97, da Matta assumed his ride with Tasman Motorsports and lived up to expectations by claiming the team's fourth championship in five attempts.

Then he served a solid Champ Car apprenticeship with Arciero-Wells Racing in 1999, showing flashes of the brilliance to come in the 2000 season. He took a new Toyota engine program and meshed with race engineer Iain Watt nearly from the first day to give the engine manufacturer some landmark qualifying efforts and finishes.

Team owner Cal Wells III split with the Arciero family after five years to run instead under the PPI Motorsports banner in 2000, but that made little difference to da Matta, 26, who continued his steady progress by earning three top-five finishes in the four events prior to Chicago. He finished a career-best third in Cleveland, despite spinning in the first corner, and led 73 of the 112 laps in Toronto before losing the handling on his Pioneer/WorldCom Toyota/Reynard and coming home in fourth. His maiden victory finally came in his 32nd Champ Car start.

"I was never really worried about getting my first win," related da Matta. "I knew we were always running in the top five and my experience is that if you can run consistently in the top five, one day the door will open. Everything fell my way today."

The win capped six years of futility for team owner Cal Wells. The popular da Matta victory was the first for Wells after 167 Champ Car starts.

Left: Toyota continued its marvelous form on the ovals as Cristiano da Matta scored an overdue and extremely popular victory.
Robert Laberge/Allsport USA

Below far left: The Target Grand Prix once again attracted a large and enthusiastic crowd to Chicago Motor Speedway.
Darrell Ingham/Allsport USA

Below left: The little man with the big grin celebrates his maiden Champ Car success
Donald Miralle/Allsport USA

CRISTIANO da Matta, despite his Brazilian heritage, does not practice Santeria, or any other religion that allows him to see into the future. However, after his driving days are done, a job as a prognosticator may not be that far fetched. One day after predicting the Target Grand Prix would resemble a Formula 1 race, where pit strategy and quality overtaking maneuvers ruled the day, rather than the mind-boggling number of drafting passes of a Handford Device-era superspeedway race, the diminutive driver earned his first Champ Car win in a race that ran largely as he predicted.

The day on which the win came may lend further credence to da Matta's cosmic ties, as he claimed his breakthrough victory a few hours after fellow Brazilian and former housemate Rubens Barrichello scored his first F1 triumph in Germany.

"I couldn't watch the [F1] race because it was a little too early [due to the seven-hour time difference]," said da Matta. "I was, of course, happy to see Rubens win his first race. I shared the same house with him back in '96 when I was racing Formula 3000 in Europe, and I know how much he worked to get to this point and I know how happy he was today."

Da Matta had been making serious overtures toward grabbing that elusive first win, placing fourth or higher in three of the four races prior to Chicago, but the former Indy Lights champion proved that sometimes in racing it is all about being in the right place at the right time.

Although he ran a strong pace throughout the race after qualifying fifth, it was his last pit stop that put da Matta in the lead for the final 50 miles. While Juan Montoya and Michael Andretti hammered around at the front, stretching their fuel mileage, da Matta brought the Pioneer/WorldCom Toyota/Reynard in for his third and last stop on lap 162.

The pitwork by PPI Motorsports was good rather than exceptional. But the timing of the pit stop was such that da Matta returned to a mile oval with a dozen other cars on it...and nothing but wide-open spaces ahead.

"When I came back out, the track ahead of me was clear," he said. "So I ran the next five or six laps like it was qualifying. They [Montoya and Andretti] were in traffic at the time. I think that was the difference."

The timing of the pit stop threw the spotters off as well. After Andretti and Montoya made their final pit stops, and then circulated around behind the pace car after a lap-171 caution flag for Patrick Carpentier's crash, Andretti's "eye-in-the-sky" (situated high atop the main grandstand) told him

QUALIFYING

Juan Montoya displayed his mastery of the superspeedway ovals by winning handsomely at Michigan Speedway. He proved to be no less adept on the one-mile variety, completing a hat trick on the small ovals by winning the pole at Chicago Motor Speedway and repeating the top qualifying spots earned at Nazareth and Milwaukee.

The defending race and series champion moved to the top of the timing charts during practice, circulating the 1.029-mile oval at 22.061 seconds (167.916 mph). He was, therefore, the final runner to take to the track during qualifying, which was held in cloudy conditions and with a stiffening breeze from the east.

Montoya had his work cut out to beat the 22.133-second (167.370 mph) lap set by Marlboro Team Penske's Helio Castroneves, but he was up to the task. On his first flying lap, Montoya stopped the clocks at 22.107 seconds (167.567 mph), smashing the track record. His pole assured, Montoya immediately lifted off and coasted his Target Toyota/Lola B2K/00 into the pits to a rapturous reception from team owner Chip Ganassi.

"It's great to win the pole for the Target Grand Prix, and to get the [bonus championship] point," said Montoya. "We need to get some points to win this championship. We were very unlucky at the beginning of the year with some failures, but we knew it was going to be that way with the new engine and chassis. Now we've got those sorted out and we know we need to score as many points as possible."

All four engine manufacturers were represented within the top two rows of the grid. Castroneves' Marlboro Honda/Reynard started alongside on the front row, with Mercedes-Benz and Ford Cosworth sharing row two through the efforts of Tony Kanaan and top rookie Kenny Bräck. The third-place run for Kanaan was the best of the year by a Mercedes-powered machine on an oval and equaled Mauricio Gugelmin's effort at Cleveland as the overall best of the season. It also capped a rough road to recovery for the 1997 Indy Lights champ, who suffered a broken arm during qualifying at Belle Isle.

Cristiano da Matta was disappointed with fifth after posting quick times all weekend with his Pioneer/WorldCom Toyota/Reynard, while 1999 Chicago pole-sitter Max Papis couldn't repeat the feat and started sixth in his Miller Lite Ford/Reynard.

FEDEX CHAMPIONSHIP SERIES • ROUND 12

Above: Oriol Servia made a hasty exit from his Telefonica car following a brief methanol fire during a botched pit stop.
Robert Laberge/Allsport USA

Right: Tony Kanaan ran impressively in third place until the gearbox failed in Mo Nunn's Hollywood Mercedes/Reynard.
Donald Miralle/Allsport USA

Far right: Kenny Bräck leads the lapped car of Memo Gidley, followed by Jimmy Vasser, Michel Jourdain and the rest soon after Juan Montoya made his first pit stop.
Donald Miralle/Allsport USA

not to worry about the #97 car in front of him.

"I don't know where he came from! When we had that last yellow, my crew read off the guys who had to pit. They said Bräck had to pit and somebody else, and then they said Cristiano," related Andretti. "I said, 'All right!' So then the first two went in and I said, 'Hey, Cristiano didn't go in. What's up?' They came back and said, 'Well, we were wrong. He's gonna stay out.' And I thought, 'Oh, no.'"

Before the surprise, Montoya and Andretti had accounted for their share of passes in a renewal of their epic duel at Michigan. Montoya had jumped to an early lead the old-fashioned way, by qualifying on pole and bolting ahead of Helio Castroneves, Tony Kanaan and da Matta at the start. Andretti, on the other hand, relied on pit strategy and typically aggressive driving as he worked his way into contention after qualifying a dismal 15th. When the engine in Mark Blundell's Motorola Mercedes/Reynard scattered on lap 18, Andretti was alone among the potential contenders to head for the pits.

"We were ready to do whatever was the opposite of what the leaders did, because we were so far back," said Andretti. "We pitted, they didn't and it put us off-sequence. Then the way the yellows fell for us was just perfect, and the next thing you know, we're in second place."

Andretti moved all the way up to fourth when everyone, save for Bräck, Jimmy Vasser and Michel Jourdain Jr., pitted during a yellow caused by a thermonuclear explosion in the engine bay of Castroneves' Marlboro Honda/Reynard, which sent the Belle Isle winner to the garage. At that point, Team KOOL Green's Paul Tracy and Dario Franchitti re-enacted their Houston problem from a year ago, spinning into the Turn One wall after getting together on lap 75, sending the field into pit lane en masse. It was then that Andretti emerged in second behind Montoya after Bräck stalled as he attempted to leave his pit.

The two leaders played a game of cat-and-mouse over the next 50 miles, saving fuel and tires, all the while reeling in the tail end of the lead lap featuring Adrian Fernandez and Bräck. When Montoya lost the front end of his car in Fernandez's wake exiting Turn Four on lap 144, Andretti pounced, slicing through on the run to Turn One. Montoya regrouped, then counterattacked as the American did all he could to lap the unyielding Fernandez.

HANS device protects Fittipaldi

CHRISTIAN Fittipaldi kept a dubious streak alive when he lost control of Newman/Haas Racing's Big Kmart/Route 66 Ford/Lola during practice on Friday morning and backed the car hard into the Turn Two wall. The rear end of his car was destroyed in the crash, which occurred as the driver ran by himself through the turn.

Fittipaldi was knocked unconscious by the impact which, according to CART rules, made him ineligible to drive in the Target Grand Prix, making the 2000 season the fourth consecutive campaign that would see the Brazilian miss at least one event due to injury.

"I remember being slightly aware that I was in a race car, then I thought I was away from the race track and then back," said Fittipaldi. "I didn't like it at all. Compared to the other times I was unconscious, this was totally different, since I could hear and see certain things, but wasn't sure if I was dreaming. I have no idea what happened. The car just swung around and I was just a passenger."

Fittipaldi's legacy of pain started in 1997 when he missed seven events after breaking his leg in a crash at Surfers Paradise. He missed the Milwaukee event in '98 after an accident during practice left him with a mild concussion and, in '99, set the stage for Roberto Moreno's career revival as he left the seat open for the former Formula 1 pilot for five events after suffering a subdural hematoma following a Gateway testing crash.

The good news is that the nephew of F1 great Emerson Fittipaldi had learned something from those injuries, which likely protected him in Chicago. He was one of the first drivers to wear the HANS (head and neck support) device on a regular basis and, according to CART's Dr. Terry Trammell, the apparatus helped save Fittipaldi from serious injury on the Cicero oval.

Wailing down the backstraight on lap 162, Montoya pinned Andretti behind Fernandez and reclaimed the lead.

"We were both trying to save fuel, you could tell, and we both ran some pretty good times, so it was good," said Andretti. "Then he got a little out of shape in traffic and I was able to pass him, then a few laps later I had to get out of the throttle and he took advantage of it. That's what it's about. He's a hard racer, man. He doesn't back off, and I don't back off, but it was good racing and we took care of each other."

The battle between Montoya and Andretti ended as da Matta trundled around behind the pace car with Montoya in tow, when the Target Toyota/Lola simply stopped exiting Turn Two.

"I don't know what happened," said the '99 Chicago winner. "The car was running well all day – we were really fast. I thought this was going to be like last year, but it didn't happen. The car just stopped. I went to give it power, and nothing happened."

That put Andretti back in second place with just Jourdain's lapped car between him and da Matta. Jourdain had run well all day, but fell off the lead lap after a pair of leisurely pit stops, owing to the fact that several crew members were playing unaccustomed roles thanks to illness among the regulars.

Trying to get the jump on Jourdain at the green flag on lap 182, an over-eager Andretti all but lost it in Turn Four. By the time he recovered, da Matta had checked out. Da Matta put a full straightaway's distance between himself and Jourdain on that lap, and although Andretti succeeded in getting around the Herdez machine on lap 183, the damage was done as da Matta loped away to as much as a five-second margin. Andretti chipped away a couple of seconds of the lead when da Matta closed on Mauricio Gugelmin's Nextel Mercedes/Reynard and was forced to run in the turbulent air for several laps, but the Motegi winner never posed a serious threat to the leader. When eventually da Matta lapped the courteous Championship Drivers Association president with five laps remaining, he knew the race was his.

"Michael was turning similar lap times to mine, and I knew when he got close he'd have the same problems I was having," said da Matta. "But when I passed Mauricio, it was time for extra relaxation."

Less than two minutes later, da Matta crossed the finish line 1.69 seconds ahead of Andretti, and it was time for some extra celebration.

"It's very good to win a race again," said the 1998 Indy Lights champion. "It's been since Vancouver, '98 – almost two years. So it's good to refresh in your mind what it is to win a race, how good it is, because that's what makes you work harder, because it's an amazing feeling. And when you remember how it is like, you just want to do it again and again."

Although attention focused on da Matta and Andretti, Gil de Ferran capped a workmanlike drive from tenth on the grid to take third, less than a second adrift of the Newman/Haas Ford/Lola, despite driving with a broken left index finger (suffered a week before at Michigan).

"We had a good start to the race and I just slowly picked my way through the traffic," he said. "I made some good passes of lapped cars and some good passes for position. It was a great day, actually."

Bräck recovered from his stall to finish fourth ahead of Fernandez, while Roberto Moreno came home in sixth place, the last driver to go the full 225 laps, and leave Chicago 22 points adrift of Andretti in the race for the FedEx Championship.

Jeremy Shaw/Eric Mauk

FEDEX CHAMPIONSHIP SERIES • ROUND 12

CHICAGO SNIPPETS

• There were a few moments of **TENSION** midway through practice on Saturday afternoon after defending series (and race) champion Juan Montoya was held up unwittingly by Helio Castroneves in Turn Four. Montoya responded with a not altogether friendly hand gesture, whereupon Castroneves promptly retaliated in kind. "He started to show me his hand, but I tried to say, 'I'm having a hard time here, don't piss me off,'" explained Castroneves, who was in the middle of a long run, simulating race conditions, and was struggling with the handling of his car. "I think it was just a misunderstanding. It's just racing, you know? I think everything's OK."

• Takuya Kurosawa's place in Dale Coyne Racing's Sports Today Ford/Lola was taken by **GUALTER SALLES** after the Japanese rookie was sidelined by a nagging lower back injury that had been aggravated by his crash at Michigan Speedway. Salles (right) didn't have much luck, being sidelined by a major gearbox problem just eight laps into Friday afternoon's practice session, then being forced out of the race early following an incident with Memo Gidley.

• Max Papis announced a helmet design **CONTEST** to commemorate his new commercial sponsorship arrangement with Nutella hazelnut spread. Visitors to the MaxPapis.com web site were able to enter the contest by submitting a helmet design and filling out a contest questionnaire. Papis would wear an Arai helmet adorned with the winning design (painted by noted helmet artist Troy Lee) in the CART season finale at Fontana.

• Former F3000 standout and Williams F1 test driver **MAX WILSON** was an interested visitor to the Target Grand Prix, as efforts to field the new Sigma Champ Car team for the 2001 season continued. "We are hoping to take delivery of our first chassis [Lola] in August and our engine [Ford XF] in September, and be testing by the end of September," said Wilson.

• The entire **TOYOTA** contingent – Target/Chip Ganassi Racing, PPI Motorsports and Della Penna Motorsports – was equipped during practice and qualifying with the same "SST" (single-sided turbo) RV8E engines that were used in qualifying both at Motegi and Michigan. The motors produced a little more horsepower than the "conventional" twin-wastegate setup and were also slightly lighter. Originally, da Matta intended to race the SST motor as well, but finally elected not to do so following the race-morning warmup.

• There had been some serious **CONCERNS** about the suitability of the Handford Device Mk.II rear wing for the one-mile Chicago Motor Speedway oval, especially following a pair of processional races at Nazareth and Milwaukee. CART duly arranged for a back-to-back test with the more traditional superspeedway-type wing in Chicago a few weeks before the race, whereupon the drivers decided after all that the original (Mk.II) plan would be best.

• Race day dawned with heavy cloud cover and persistent light **RAIN**, which caused the start of the Champ Car warmup practice session to be delayed. Fortunately, the weather gods cooperated and the race was run on schedule. Then, less than 15 minutes after the race had been concluded, the precipitation returned.

FEDEX CHAMPIONSHIP SERIES • ROUND 12
TARGET GRAND PRIX PRESENTED BY ENERGIZER
CHICAGO MOTOR SPEEDWAY, CICERO, ILLINOIS
JULY 30, 225 laps of 1.029 miles – 231.525 miles

Place	Driver (Nat.)	No.	Team Sponsors Engine/Car	Tires	Q Speed	Q Time	Q Pos	Laps	Time/Status	Ave. (mph)	Pts.
1	Cristiano da Matta (BR)	97	PPI Motorsports Pioneer/WorldCom Toyota/Reynard 2KI	FS	166.266	22.280s	5	225	2h 01m 23.727s	114.432	20
2	Michael Andretti (USA)	6	Newman/Haas Big Kmart/Texaco Ford Cosworth/Lola B2K/00	FS	163.477	22.660s	15	225	2h 01m 25.417s	114.405	16
3	Gil de Ferran (BR)	2	Marlboro Team Penske Marlboro Honda/Reynard 2KI	FS	165.102	22.437s	10	225	2h 01m 26.246s	114.392	14
4	*Kenny Bräck (S)	8	Team Rahal Shell Ford Cosworth/Reynard 2KI	FS	166.602	22.235s	4	225	2h 01m 26.511s	114.388	12
5	Adrian Fernandez (MEX)	40	Patrick Racing Tecate/Quaker State Ford Cosworth/Reynard 2KI	FS	162.005	22.866s	19	225	2h 01m 28.413s	114.202	10
6	Roberto Moreno (BR)	20	Patrick Racing Visteon Ford Cosworth/Reynard 2KI	FS	164.100	22.574s	13	225	2h 01m 29.276s	114.188	8
7	Mauricio Gugelmin (BR)	17	PacWest Racing Nextel Mercedes/Reynard 2KI	FS	163.290	22.686s	16	224	Running		6
8	Jimmy Vasser (USA)	12	Target/Chip Ganassi Racing Toyota/Lola B2K/00	FS	165.205	22.423s	9	224	Running		5
9	*Alexandre Tagliani (CDN)	33	Forsythe Racing Player's/Indeck Ford Cosworth/Reynard 2KI	FS	165.309	22.409s	8	223	Running		4
10	Memo Gidley (USA)	10	Della Penna Motorsports DirecTV Toyota/Reynard 2KI	FS	161.468	22.942s	20	223	Running		3
11	Michel Jourdain Jr. (MEX)	16	Bettenhausen Motorsports Herdez Mercedes/Lola B2K/00	FS	162.282	22.827s	18	207	Engine		2
12	Juan Montoya (COL)	1	Target/Chip Ganassi Racing Toyota/Lola B2K/00	FS	167.567	22.107s	1	177	Engine		3
13	*Shinji Nakano (J)	5	Walker Racing Avex Group Honda/Reynard 2KI	FS	159.955	23.159s	22	172	Gearbox		
14	Patrick Carpentier (CDN)	32	Forsythe Racing Player's/Indeck Ford Cosworth/Reynard 2KI	FS	164.779	22.481s	12	170	Accident		
15	*Oriol Servia (E)	96	PPI Motorsports Telefonica Toyota/Reynard 2KI	FS	164.093	22.575s	14	160	Pit incident		
16	Tony Kanaan (BR)	55	Mo Nunn Racing Hollywood Mercedes/Reynard 2KI	FS	167.340	22.137s	3	146	Gearbox		
17	Luiz Garcia Jr. (BR)	25	Arciero-PRG Hollywood/Embratel-21 Mercedes/Reynard 2KI	FS	no speed	no time	23	99	Engine		
18	Tarso Marques (BR)	34	Dale Coyne Racing Panasonic Ford Cosworth/Swift 011.c	FS	no speed	no time	24	84	Electrical		
19	Paul Tracy (CDN)	26	Team KOOL Green Honda/Reynard 2KI	FS	165.419	22.394s	7	75	Accident		
20	Dario Franchitti (GB)	27	Team KOOL Green Honda/Reynard 2KI	FS	164.874	22.468s	11	74	Accident		
21	Helio Castroneves (BR)	3	Marlboro Team Penske Marlboro Honda/Reynard 2KI	FS	167.370	22.133s	2	35	Engine		
22	Gualter Salles (BR)	19	Dale Coyne Racing Sports Today Ford Cosworth/Lola B2K/00	FS	161.117	22.992s	21	25	Accident		
23	Mark Blundell (GB)	18	PacWest Racing Motorola Mercedes/Reynard 2KI	FS	163.060	22.718s	17	18	Engine		
24	Max Papis (I)	7	Team Rahal Miller Lite Ford Cosworth/Reynard 2KI	FS	165.641	22.364s	6	0	Engine		
25	Christian Fittipaldi (BR)	11	Newman/Haas Big Kmart/Route 66 Ford Cosworth/Lola B2K/00	FS	no speed	no time	–	–	Withdrawn		

* denotes rookie driver

Caution flags: Laps 10-24, debris; laps 26-31, accident/Gidley & Salles; laps 36-42, tow/Castroneves; laps 75-81, accident/Tracy & Franchitti; laps 102-114, tow/Garcia; laps 171-181, accident/Carpentier. **Total:** Six for 50 laps.

Lap leaders: Juan Montoya, 1-37 (37 laps); Kenny Bräck, 38-79 (42 laps); Montoya, 80-144 (65 laps); Michael Andretti, 145-161 (17 laps); Montoya, 162-170 (9 laps); Bräck, 171-174 (4 laps); Cristiano da Matta, 175-225 (51 laps). **Totals:** Montoya, 111 laps; da Matta, 51 laps; Bräck, 46 laps; Andretti, 17 laps.

Fastest race lap: Adrian Fernandez, 23.714s, 156.212 mph on lap 171.

Championship positions: 1 Andretti, 120; **2** Moreno, 98; **3** de Ferran, 89; **4** da Matta, 82; **5** Tracy, 80; **6** Fernandez, 79; **7** Bräck, 78; **8** Montoya, 77; **9** Vasser, 68; **10** Carpentier, 65; **11** Franchitti, 58; **12** Papis & Castroneves, 56; **14** Tagliani, 40; **15** Fittipaldi & Servia, 38; **17** Gugelmin, 30; **18** Herta & Blundell, 14; **20** Kanaan & Gidley, 11; **22** Jourdain, 10; **23** Nakano, 7; **24** Marques & Garcia, 5; **26** Fontana, 2; **27** Kurosawa, 1.

While Alex Zanardi performed donuts to commemorate his race wins, Helio Castroneves has developed his own signature celebration – fence hanging.
Jon Ferrey/Allsport USA

FEDEX CHAMPIONSHIP SERIES • ROUND 13

FEDEX CHAMPIONSHIP SERIES • ROUND 13

Left: Christian Fittipaldi overcame the effects of his accident in Chicago by earning a strong third-place finish.
Robert Laberge/Allsport USA

Below left: Daryl Fox's crew performs routine service for Mark Blundell.
Jon Ferrey/Allsport USA

ANY doubt about the potency of the rejuvenated Marlboro Team Penske organization was well and truly dispelled by a dominating performance throughout the Miller Lite 200 weekend. Indeed, its superiority at the Mid-Ohio Sports Car Course brought back memories of the Penske juggernaut that swept all before it throughout much of the 1970s and '80s, and most recently earned 12 wins from 16 races in 1994.

Either Helio Castroneves or Gil de Ferran topped the timing charts in every session, and while de Ferran took the pole, for the third time wearing the Penske colors, it was teammate Castroneves who emerged ahead on race day. The 25-year-old Brazilian scored his second win of the year – and reached another milestone for Honda in Champ Car competition – despite the after-effects of a debilitating viral infection that had struck him earlier in the week.

"I'm very proud to be able to deliver Honda's 50th Champ Car win; they have been a key part in the success of Marlboro Team Penske," said a joyful Castroneves, who celebrated just like he did after his maiden success in Detroit, by leaping out of his car and jumping onto the catch-fencing across the track from the pits to share his celebration with the fans.

"I also have to thank Steve [Olvey – CART director of medical service] and all the CART medical staff, who helped me with my recent illness," continued Castroneves. "They kept me hydrated and I've felt better and better all weekend."

The Honda/Reynard was clearly the technical package of choice on the twisting, undulating parkland venue, as indicated by the fact that Dario Franchitti qualified third in his similar Team KOOL Green machine. Kenny Bräck broke the stranglehold briefly by diving past Franchitti on the opening lap, but clearly the Swede's Shell Ford Cosworth/Reynard was not fast enough to stay there. De Ferran and Castroneves romped away at a second per lap, and it took Franchitti only until lap four to find a way past into third place under braking for the Esses.

The Scotsman was able to keep the two red-and-white cars in sight, losing only another second during the next 15 laps as Bräck and teammate Max Papis (Miller Lite Ford/Reynard) fell farther behind. Sadly, Franchitti's run of misfortune continued unabated as an electrical glitch caused a gradual loss of power. He made the first of several unscheduled pit stops on lap 18. The problem was fixed eventually,

QUALIFYING

Timing proved to be everything during final qualifying. Helio Castroneves seemed to have the upper hand in the Penske team after setting the fastest time during practice, both on Friday and Saturday, only for Gil de Ferran to turn the tables in qualifying.

After claiming the provisional pole on Friday, a scant 0.015 second faster than Castroneves, de Ferran, surprisingly, remained unbeaten in the final session. There was more than a hint of good fortune, however, as the lap times had begun to tumble inside the final five minutes. De Ferran himself edged to within a couple of tenths of his previous best, quickest on the day, only to lose control in Turn One and spin backward into the tire barrier. The #2 Marlboro Honda/Reynard came to rest upside down in the gravel trap. With time running out, de Ferran's pole was assured, albeit somewhat ignominiously.

"The track was a bit slick today," reckoned de Ferran, "making it tough to get a quick time. When I [began] my last lap, the rear wheels seized up on the entry to Turn One and the car started to slide, at which point I was practicing accident control techniques!"

The incident came just as Castroneves was preparing to mount his own challenge for the pole.

"Unfortunately, the red flag came out and I was unable to improve my time [from Friday]," said Castroneves. "But these things happen in racing and we are just glad that Gil is OK, and that it will be an all-Marlboro front row."

Dario Franchitti also was on a quick lap as the red flag was displayed, costing him a chance of taking the coveted pole position for Team KOOL Green.

Rookie Kenny Bräck performed impressively on his first visit to Mid-Ohio since competing in a Barber Saab Pro Series event way back in 1993. Fourth represented an excellent effort for the Swede, two places ahead of teammate Max Papis. The two Team Rahal Ford/Reynards were split by Christian Fittipaldi's Big Kmart/Route 66 Ford/Lola. Cristiano da Matta, fresh from his Chicago victory, was fastest of the Toyota contingent, seventh in PPI Motorsports' Pioneer/WorldCom Toyota/Reynard.

A milestone weekend

TWO of Champ Car racing's staunchest technical supporters, Firestone and Honda, reached significant milestones at Mid-Ohio. First to do so was Firestone, which, through the efforts of Marlboro Team Penske's Gil de Ferran *(above)*, recorded its 100th pole in open-wheel competition since rejoining the fray in 1995 after a 21-year sabbatical. Parker Johnstone, who retired from driving at the conclusion of the 1998 season and subsequently began a new career as analyst for ABC Sports and ESPN's television coverage of the CART FedEx Championship Series, set the ball rolling at Michigan International Speedway in 1995.

"We are thrilled to take our 100th modern-era pole since we returned to the top forms of racing in 1995," said Firestone Racing project supervisor Joe Barbieri. "That's a very significant accomplishment when you consider 80 of those poles came in head-to-head competition with another tire manufacturer [Goodyear]."

Helio Castroneves, meanwhile, earned his place in the record books by scoring Honda's 50th Champ Car win. The achievement came four months after teammate Gil de Ferran claimed Penske Racing's 100th Champ Car triumph at Nazareth Speedway.

"That's fair," declared Castroneves. "What a great day for Marlboro Team Penske and our friends at Honda."

"We're very proud of our record," added Honda Performance Development general manager Robert Clarke. "We've come a long way since [an ignominious beginning in] 1994. From Indianapolis in '96 on, it was pretty clear that we'd figured it out, but it was difficult to show it that year because we only had one full-time car with Andre Ribeiro and a part-time car with Scott Goodyear at Tasman Motorsports.

"In '96 we won the first race of the season with Jimmy Vasser and it sort of took off from there. The only let-down was in '97 when our drivers finished 1-2-3 in the CART Championship, but we finished second in the Manufacturer's Championship because we didn't win enough races."

but by then he was two laps in arrears. Adding insult to injury, on lap 55, Franchitti tangled unwittingly with Jimmy Vasser, who was running 11th, at Turn Two. Both were forced out of the race.

"I was just sitting behind Jimmy," related Franchitti. "I didn't want to make a move on him because he was two laps ahead and I didn't want to screw up his race. Jimmy made a mistake coming out of Turn One, dropping a wheel on the curb, and I got close behind him. I was so close to him [that] I lost downforce, and then when I got on the brakes, I locked them up and got into him.

"I feel really bad for Jimmy. We talked about it when we got out of our cars. He was saying, 'I know you didn't mean to do it,' trying to make me feel better. It's the last thing I wanted to do. I feel sorry for Jimmy; I feel sorry for Team KOOL Green because we had a good car today, maybe good enough to win the race."

Bräck regained third place following Franchitti's earlier problem, chased by Christian Fittipaldi (Big Kmart/Route 66 Ford/Lola), who had found a way past Papis on lap 18. Fittipaldi's Newman/Haas teammate, Michael Andretti, ran sixth ahead of Cristiano da Matta (Pioneer Toyota/Reynard), Patrick Carpentier (Player's Ford/Reynard), Adrian Fernandez (Tecate/Quaker State Ford/Reynard) and Vasser (Target Toyota/Lola), whose teammate, Juan Montoya, made a rare mistake when he lost control and spun out of ninth place at Turn 11 on lap 14.

"In the beginning of the [race] we had some good handling and I thought we were going to be good," said the defending series (and race) champion. "As the run went on, the car started sliding and getting harder to handle."

Montoya rejoined at the back of the pack and survived another off-course excursion in Turn One before ending his day when he ran out of fuel after completing 43 laps.

"I was preparing to pit [one lap later], and right past the start/finish line I was out of fuel. It hurts [in the championship chase], but that is how racing goes," said a philosophical Montoya.

De Ferran and Castroneves remained tied together at the front of the field until de Ferran peeled off into the pit lane for his first routine pit stop after 29 laps. Castroneves, however, had managed to conserve some fuel while running in the wake of his teammate, and was able to complete one more lap before taking on service. It was a crucial advantage.

Robert Laberge/Allsport USA

Max Papis finished fourth for locally based (in Hilliard, Ohio) Team Rahal.

"When Gil pitted, Tim [Cindric – strategist] told me to go for it," said Castroneves. "I went full [rich on the] fuel [mixture] and really went for it. The guys did a fantastic job in the pit stop, too."

In fact, Castroneves rejoined the track with a handsome five-second advantage over de Ferran, which he extended to more than 16 seconds before de Ferran made his second and final pit visit on lap 55. The youngster's lead was negated by a couple of full-course cautions in the closing stages, but Castroneves was unperturbed and finally took the checkered flag some 4.425 seconds clear of de Ferran. Still, the effects of his illness meant this was no walk in the park.

"It was hard work today," said Castroneves. "I didn't say a word [on the radio] the whole race, saving my energy. I was really trying to keep focused."

While the leading pair of Penske Reynards disappeared into the distance, all eyes were centered on the battle for third between Bräck and Fittipaldi. The Swede made his final pit visit on lap 57, while Fittipaldi stayed out two laps longer. Bräck's stop, furthermore, was slightly longer than usual due to a refueling problem, which cost him any hope of a podium finish. Thus Fittipaldi emerged with a handy advantage, which he maintained to the end.

"The Penske machines were superior today," noted Fittipaldi. "They really got their act together here. I thought it was going to be like Portland, where they qualified well, but didn't dominate the race as much. That wasn't the case today. My hat's off to them. I'm happy I won the race of the rest."

Papis also took advantage of a late final pit stop to jump ahead of teammate Bräck.

"We couldn't race with the Penske cars, but I felt I could have finished third," reckoned the Italian. "I got caught in traffic at the end, or I might have had a good chance to catch Christian. Our Miller Lite car was very good on the longer runs. We were able to run consistent laps and our second pit stop was very quick. This was good for our team after [disappointments in] the recent races."

Bräck held on for fourth and could take solace from the fact that his sixth top-six finish moved him to fourth in the points table.

"I think we were just racing for third today," said Bräck. "The Penske cars were in another class. But overall it's not bad for my first time here [at Mid-Ohio]. This place is not easy to drive. The elevation changes and the off-camber corners make it tough on a driver."

"We moved to fourth in points, which is good, but I still want to win races," declared Bräck. "That's my goal this year."

Fernandez, after starting 12th in Patrick Racing's Tecate/Quaker State Ford/Reynard, displayed his usual excellent fuel economy and was delighted to manage a couple of on-track passes on Vasser and Carpentier. Sixth place was his reward.

Carpentier, too, drove well, claiming seventh for Player's/Forsythe Racing ahead of Andretti, who lost ground in the middle stages when his engine's boost disappeared mysteriously.

"I was all over Max [Papis] and then something happened to the boost," said Andretti. Fortunately, the problem rectified itself during the late caution, and Andretti was able to hold onto eighth place ahead of Alex Tagliani in the second Player's car. Thereby Andretti maintained his lead in the CART FedEx Championship Series, 19 points clear of de Ferran with seven races remaining.

On this day, however, de Ferran had to give best to his fellow countryman and teammate.

"I had a good start and stayed in front of Helio," said de Ferran, "but I could tell he was very strong. I also had some issues to deal with, locking up the front brakes and things like that, but in the end, he was quicker than me today, especially in lapped traffic."

Jeremy Shaw

CART announces substantial changes for 2001

CHAMPIONSHIP Auto Racing Teams, Inc., sanctioning body for the FedEx Championship Series, took the opportunity at Mid-Ohio to announce some dramatic alterations to its weekend schedule and testing policies that would come into effect for the 2001 season. First of all, the CART franchise board (comprised of the individual team owners) voted virtually to eliminate in-season testing and permit a maximum of 20 test days for a two-car team (and 14 days for a one-car team) during the off-season, which was defined as running from November 13, 2000 to March 1, 2001. (Current regulations allowed a total of 36 days of testing for a two-car team, 20 of which could be run "in-season." One-car outfits were permitted 24 days of testing.)

Exceptions would be allowed for "special circumstances," such as driver injuries or additional tire or engine tests, which would be controlled under the direction of CART.

In addition, the 2001 regulations called for four hours of practice on Friday during race weekends and the elimination of Friday qualifying sessions on the road courses.

"Fans are at the core of our racing – they are what the sport is all about," declared CART's interim president and CEO Bobby Rahal. "These initiatives are designed to provide more track time that is meaningful for our fans, sponsors, manufacturers and teams. I credit our team owners for working together to make this happen."

"By doing this, it not only delivers more value to fans, but it also reduces the wear and tear on all the people who make this happen every week – the race team crews and officials who are so important to CART and the FedEx Championship Series. With the increase to 22 races [in 2001], reducing our testing schedule was an important step for CART and its race teams."

Added Hal Whiteford, CART's president of racing operations, "Importantly, from a fan's perspective, we are expanding the amount of track time for the Champ Cars each Friday. The emphasis on development is reflected in the increase to four hours of Friday practice time and the elimination of Friday qualifying. The new rules move much of the important development work in front of the fans for the first time."

FEDEX CHAMPIONSHIP SERIES • ROUND 13

MID-OHIO SNIPPETS

• While moving forward on testing restrictions for the 2001 season, the CART franchise board did not reach any final decisions on **ENGINE RULES** for the future. Prior to the Mid-Ohio race weekend, interim president and CEO Bobby Rahal indicated a belief that some resolution would be reached regarding an initiative to curb the escalation in speeds for 2001 by reducing engine power – most likely by reducing turbo boost. The four engine manufacturers had all either signed or initialed a letter stating that boost should be reduced from 40 inches to 38 inches in 2001, and from 38 inches to 34 inches in 2002, before introducing an all-new 1.8-liter turbocharged engine in 2003. No ratification was forthcoming, however.

• **CHRISTIAN FITTIPALDI** returned to action after skipping the Chicago race due to a crash during practice in the Windy City. The Brazilian admitted to feeling "very stiff and sore" in the shoulder area, but rebounded impressively to qualify fifth and finish third in Newman/Haas Racing's Big Kmart/Route 66 Ford Cosworth/Lola.

• Helio Castroneves *(above right)*, Gil de Ferran *(above left)* and Christian Fittipaldi combined to ensure another all-Brazilian sweep of the podium and further enhance Team Brazil's lead in the **CART NATION'S CUP** standings over Team USA to 50 points, 223–173.

• Paul Tracy, Alex Tagliani, Cristiano da Matta and Tony Kanaan were embroiled in a **BATTLE** for ninth, just behind Michael Andretti, until lap 70, when Tagliani inadvertently tipped Tracy into a spin at the Esses. Kanaan was unable to avoid Tracy (although the Brazilian resumed a lap in arrears), while da Matta joined Tracy on the sidelines when he was forced off into the gravel trap.

• Prior to the start of the Miller Lite 200, interim CART president and CEO – and three-time former champion – Bobby Rahal presented race fan Thomas Boehland with a Reynard 96I Champ Car chassis, which he had earned in the Miller Lite "Get The Goods" online auction. Boehland, from Hopkins, Minnesota, was the **HIGHEST BIDDER** at $39,091. The car, which until recently had been adorning the roof of the Miller Brewing Company's headquarters in Milwaukee, Wisconsin, was autographed by Rahal and Team Rahal co-owner David Letterman.

• The Champ Car **"SILLY SEASON"** hit full stride during the Mid-Ohio race weekend when two of the FedEx Championship's star drivers, Michael Andretti and Jimmy Vasser, confirmed that they were on the verge of leaving their respective teams. Andretti was the first to confirm his free agency after Newman/Haas Racing team co-owner Carl Haas apparently told him earlier in the week that he was not prepared to meet his financial demands for their relationship to be continued. Vasser, meanwhile, learned that Chip Ganassi intended to buy out the final year of a three-year contract that had been signed at the end of the '98 season.

• **MICHEL JOURDAIN JR.** experienced another weekend to forget. His Herdez Mercedes/Lola was stricken by a broken exhaust header during qualifying on Friday and, more seriously, during the final warmup practice on race morning, when the hapless Mexican trailed into the pits with the rear end well and truly ablaze. He was forced into the backup car for the race and was running just outside the points, in 13th, when the engine failed again with only six laps remaining.

FEDEX CHAMPIONSHIP SERIES • ROUND 13
MILLER LITE 200

MID-OHIO SPORTS CAR COURSE, LEXINGTON, OHIO

AUGUST 13, 83 laps of 2.258 miles – 187.414 miles

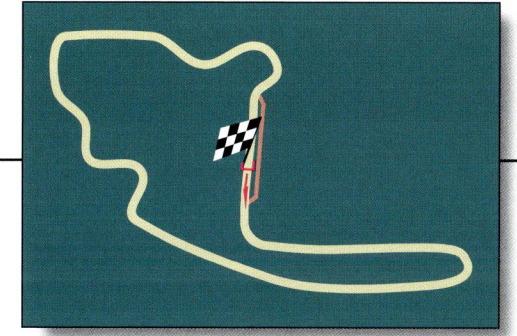

Place	Driver (Nat.)	No.	Team Sponsors Engine/Car	Tires	Q Speed	Q Time	Q Pos.	Laps	Time/Status	Ave. (mph)	Pts.
1	Helio Castroneves (BR)	3	Marlboro Team Penske Marlboro Honda/Reynard 2KI	FS	124.366	1m 05.362s	2	83	1h 44m 59.029s	106.558	21
2	Gil de Ferran (BR)	2	Marlboro Team Penske Marlboro Honda/Reynard 2KI	FS	124.394	1m 05.347s	1	83	1h 45m 03.454s	106.483	17
3	Christian Fittipaldi (BR)	11	Newman/Haas Big Kmart/Route 66 Ford Cosworth/Lola B2K/00	FS	123.235	1m 05.962s	5	83	1h 45m 04.941s	106.458	14
4	Max Papis (I)	7	Team Rahal Miller Lite Ford Cosworth/Reynard 2KI	FS	123.076	1m 06.047s	6	83	1h 45m 07.116s	106.421	12
5	*Kenny Bräck (S)	8	Team Rahal Shell Ford Cosworth/Reynard 2KI	FS	123.527	1m 05.806s	4	83	1h 45m 07.890s	106.408	10
6	Adrian Fernandez (MEX)	40	Patrick Racing Tecate/Quaker State Ford Cosworth/Reynard 2KI	FS	122.289	1m 06.472s	12	83	1h 45m 08.623s	106.396	8
7	Patrick Carpentier (CDN)	32	Forsythe Racing Player's/Indeck Ford Cosworth/Reynard 2KI	FS	122.438	1m 06.391s	9	83	1h 45m 09.075s	106.388	6
8	Michael Andretti (USA)	6	Newman/Haas Big Kmart/Texaco Ford Cosworth/Lola B2K/00	FS	122.536	1m 06.338s	8	83	1h 45m 09.835s	106.375	5
9	*Alexandre Tagliani (CDN)	33	Forsythe Racing Player's/Indeck Ford Cosworth/Reynard 2KI	FS	121.594	1m 06.852s	16	83	1h 45m 10.358s	106.366	4
10	*Oriol Servia (E)	96	PPI Motorsports Telefonica Toyota/Reynard 2KI	FS	121.239	1m 07.048s	17	82	Running		3
11	Roberto Moreno (BR)	20	Patrick Racing Visteon Ford Cosworth/Reynard 2KI	FS	121.721	1m 06.782s	15	82	Running		2
12	Memo Gidley (USA)	10	Della Penna Motorsports DirecTV Toyota/Reynard 2KI	FS	119.387	1m 08.088s	23	82	Running		1
13	Tony Kanaan (BR)	55	Mo Nunn Racing Hollywood Mercedes/Reynard 2KI	FS	121.013	1m 07.173s	19	82	Running		
14	Mark Blundell (GB)	18	PacWest Racing Motorola Mercedes/Reynard 2KI	FS	121.201	1m 07.069s	18	82	Running		
15	Michel Jourdain Jr. (MEX)	16	Bettenhausen Motorsports Herdez Mercedes/Lola B2K/00	FS	119.093	1m 08.256s	24	76	Engine		
16	Paul Tracy (CDN)	26	Team KOOL Green Honda/Reynard 2KI	FS	122.058	1m 06.598s	14	69	Accident		
17	Cristiano da Matta (BR)	97	PPI Motorsports Pioneer/WorldCom Toyota/Reynard 2KI	FS	122.697	1m 06.251s	7	69	Accident		
18	Tarso Marques (BR)	34	Dale Coyne Racing Panasonic Ford Cosworth/Swift 011.c	FS	119.982	1m 07.750s	22	62	Driveshaft		
19	*Shinji Nakano (J)	5	Walker Racing Avex Group Honda/Reynard 2KI	FS	120.713	1m 07.340s	20	59	Broken wheel		
20	Mauricio Gugelmin (BR)	17	PacWest Racing Nextel Mercedes/Reynard 2KI	FS	122.184	1m 06.529s	13	57	Engine		
21	Jimmy Vasser (USA)	12	Target/Chip Ganassi Racing Toyota/Lola B2K/00	FS	122.370	1m 06.428s	11	54	Accident		
22	Dario Franchitti (GB)	27	Team KOOL Green Honda/Reynard 2KI	FS	123.792	1m 05.665s	3	52	Accident		
23	Gualter Salles (BR)	19	Dale Coyne Racing Sports Today Ford Cosworth/Lola B2K/00	FS	120.222	1m 07.615s	21	47	Spin		
24	Juan Montoya (COL)	1	Target/Chip Ganassi Racing Toyota/Lola B2K/00	FS	122.411	1m 06.406s	10	43	Out of fuel		
25	Luiz Garcia Jr. (BR)	25	Arciero-PRG Hollywood/Embratel-21 Mercedes/Reynard 2KI	FS	117.010	1m 09.471s	25	5	Engine		

* denotes rookie driver

Caution flags: Laps 61–65, spin/Nakano; laps 70–73, accident/Tracy, Kanaan & da Matta. **Total:** Two for 9 laps.
Lap leaders: Gil de Ferran, 1–28 (28 laps); Helio Castroneves, 29–83 (55 laps). **Totals:** Castroneves, 55 laps; de Ferran, 28 laps.
Fastest race lap: Dario Franchitti, 1m 08.162s, 119.257 mph on lap 20.
Championship positions: 1 Andretti, 125; **2** de Ferran, 106; **3** Moreno, 100; **4** Bräck, 88; **5** Fernandez, 87; **6** da Matta, 82; **7** Tracy, 80; **8** Montoya & Castroneves, 77; **10** Carpentier, 71; **11** Vasser & Papis, 68; **13** Franchitti, 58; **14** Fittipaldi, 52; **15** Tagliani, 44; **16** Servia, 41; **17** Gugelmin, 30; **18** Herta & Blundell, 14; **20** Gidley, 12; **21** Kanaan, 11; **22** Jourdain 10; **23** Nakano, 7; **24** Marques & Garcia, 5; **26** Fontana, 2; **27** Kurosawa, 1.

ROAD AMERICA

1 – TRACY

2 – FERNANDEZ

3 – BRÄCK

FEDEX CHAMPIONSHIP SERIES • ROUND 14

FEDEX CHAMPIONSHIP SERIES • ROUND 14

Left: Paul Tracy bounced back from early difficulties to win easily at Elkhart Lake.
Jon Ferrey/Allsport USA

Below left: Tracy's bravura left even the other podium finishers, Kenny Bräck and Adrian Fernandez, in the shadows.
Robert Laberge/Allsport USA

Below: Christian Fittipaldi, Dario Franchitti and Jimmy Vasser run in close proximity on the back straightaway
Robert Laberge/Allsport USA

QUALIFYING

Dario Franchitti had tried nearly everything in his power to win a pole in the 2000 season, but had done no better than close all year long. He tied Juan Montoya down to the thousandth of a second at Detroit, but had to start on the outside of the front row, owing to the fact that Montoya's second-fastest lap was the quicker of the two. At Mid-Ohio, he was on his way to a pole-winning lap when a red flag voided his time only 50 yards shy of the finish line.

So taking his first pole of the 2000 FedEx Championship at Road America with a lap record time of 1m 39.866s was all the sweeter to Franchitti.

"It feels good to get the pole," he said. "This time there was no tie, no red flags to take it away."

Ironically, perhaps, Franchitti's first pole lap in 2000 was far from perfect.

"I made a big mistake in Turns One and Two," he said. "I was overdriving the car, trying to carry too much speed into One and Two. In did a big tank slapper coming off Turn One...I thought I was going to hit the wall. It's funny, on television it all looks so smooth, but I can assure you, it's not the case."

But bobble or not, Franchitti carded a lap that was 0.278 second better than Gil de Ferran achieved in his similar Honda/Reynard. Like Franchitti, de Ferran had a major scare – half spinning the Marlboro entry in Turn Five on one of his hot laps. Unlike the Scot, however, Friday's provisional pole-winner was unable to overcome his mistake.

Alexandre Tagliani backed up his fourth-place performance in provisional qualifying by whittling 0.222 second off Friday's best to slot into third on the grid at 1m 40.260s, his best qualifying run since taking pole at Rio.

Michael Andretti was a disgruntled fourth fastest, slowed up by Oriol Servia and Helio Castroneves on his best lap, while Adrian Fernandez took fifth on the grid in his Patrick Racing Ford/Reynard. Castroneves came through to qualify sixth, having abandoned his primary Marlboro Honda/Reynard in favor of the backup.

WHATEVER semblance of order there had been in the CART FedEx Championship standings was scrambled as if thrown in a blender at Road America. Attrition was the name of the game at the fabled road course, with components breaking like matchsticks almost from the drop of the green flag. Only ten of the 25 starters crossed the finish line, the top two point scorers, Michael Andretti and Gil de Ferran, being banished to the sidelines inside the first 20 laps. Indeed, de Ferran completed only a single lap before his gearbox failed.

"It's a huge disappointment for the entire Marlboro Team Penske to leave this race without any points," said de Ferran after posting his fourth DNF of the season. "I don't know what happened. All of a sudden I got a box full of neutrals. It's really too bad this had to happen at this time in the championship battle because we usually don't have these kinds of problems."

Paul Tracy's race threatened to follow the same path as de Ferran's. The Canadian slipped back immediately from his third-row starting spot as his Team KOOL Green Honda/Reynard refused to answer the bell. The engine stalled directly after the start of the race, and Tracy's engineers hurriedly radioed instructions to the stricken driver to reset his onboard computer to overcome a stuck throttle sensor; but by then he had fallen to the back of the field. Undaunted, he began a sensational charge that was to take him to Victory Lane.

"It's always satisfying to win, but this has to rank right up there as one of the top victories of my career," said Tracy after notching his 17th Champ Car triumph. "I really had to race for it, and when you do it with the odds stacked against you, it feels really good. I just kept driving as hard as I could. I guess I was just in the zone."

Tracy benefited from the attrition as he marched through the field, making up ground as his competitors fell by the wayside. Five cars were felled by gearbox problems alone, with fuel pumps, CV joints, exhaust headers and driveshafts claiming other victims.

The driveshaft malady ended a promising run for Alex Tagliani in the Player's/Forsythe Ford Cosworth/Reynard. The French-Canadian made a spectacular start from the second row of the grid, drafting past pole-sitter Dario Franchitti's KOOL Honda/Reynard and the similar Marlboro-sponsored car of fellow front-row starter Gil de Ferran on the run to the first corner. Once out in front, Tagliani piled on the pressure impressively and opened a clear lead of almost two seconds on the very first lap.

Franchitti pursued the fleeing machine of Tagliani, followed by Adrian Fernandez (Tecate/Quaker State Ford/Reynard), who also made a fine start from row three. Andretti ran fourth at the end of lap one, chased by Juan Montoya, who vaulted like Sergei Bubka from 12th on the grid in his Target Toyota/Lola. Next time around, Montoya slipped past Andretti and began to make advances on Fernandez for third.

Andretti soon fell away from this battle, and on lap seven was passed by

151

FEDEX CHAMPIONSHIP SERIES • ROUND 14

Never say never

THERE were many reasons why Memo Gidley (left) would not soon forget the Motorola 220 weekend at Elkhart Lake's Road America circuit. Firstly, he belied his sophomore status by standing up in the drivers' meeting to chastise his fellow pilots for halting qualifying repeatedly by running off course and causing red flags, then, to his embarrassment, brought a halt to Sunday's warmup by losing control of his DirecTV Toyota/Reynard in Turn 12.

In the race itself, Gidley tore through the back of the field, climbing from 18th to 12th in the opening laps, before indulging in another agricultural excursion in Turn Three on his out-lap following his first pit stop. Although he dropped to 20th place in the process, Gidley tightened his belts and saved some face by carving his way back to a career-best sixth place at the checkered flag. The finish capped a run of four consecutive points-paying placings since he had taken over the Della Penna Motorsports ride from Norberto Fontana.

It was the best finish for John Della Penna's hardworking team since Richie Hearn also placed sixth at Vancouver in 1999. Hearn had garnered the team's best-ever finish, fifth, at Michigan Speedway in 1998.

"I knew we had a good car, but we weren't able to show how good it was until the start of the race," said Gidley. "I was going outside, inside, down this side – it was hectic. When I came around at the end of the second lap, I was in 12th place...

"I always go into a weekend thinking I could win. That's the mindset. As you start practicing, maybe you're 15th and you think, 'Well, I can still win.' Every session can beat you down just a bit more, but I never give up."

Top left: Kenny Bräck charged hard in the late stages, despite a slight misfire.
Jon Ferrey/Allsport USA

Far left: There was heartbreak for Alex Tagliani, halted by a broken driveshaft.
Robert Laberge/Allsport USA

Above: Gil de Ferran surveys the timing charts during Saturday morning practice.
Robert Laberge/Allsport USA

Left: Memo Gidley's helmet was as striking as his performance at Road America.
Darrell Ingham/Allsport USA

FEDEX CHAMPIONSHIP SERIES • ROUND 14

Ganassi and Vasser to part company

CHIP Ganassi and Jimmy Vasser put an end to weeks of speculation, announcing officially that Vasser would be leaving the Target/Chip Ganassi Racing machine at the end of the season. The two sat down in front of the press to quash rumors, but never really said anything particularly illuminating.

Ganassi refused to name a replacement for Vasser, who had secured the first of Ganassi's record-setting four consecutive CART championship crowns in 1996. He even went so far as to claim, "I haven't even thought about that yet."

"Target said, '[Do] whatever it takes,'" continued Ganassi. "'Do the right thing, but make sure you take care of Jimmy,' and that's what we're doing."

All Vasser *(right)* would say was that he had no intention of retiring and that he was actively shopping around for a ride for the 2001 season. He also confirmed that he would contemplate a future in the Indy Racing Northern Lights Series or even follow the lead set in 1999 by Scott Pruett, who switched to the NASCAR Winston Cup circuit.

"I'm going to look at all my options," he said. "There will be other series in those options, but right now this [CART] is where my heart is, and I'm going to focus my energies in this paddock and see what I can come up with."

Ganassi, meanwhile, said he had no time frame for announcing Vasser's replacement, and all he would say of any consequence was, "I look for heart. I think that's a big thing. It started with Jimmy and went on with Alex [Zanardi, '97 and '98 champion] and ['99 title-holder Juan] Montoya. I like guys with a lot of heart. Talent helps, but there's a lot of guys with a lot of talent; you need heart as well."

Below: Road America offers some of the greatest viewing in the country – including the quaintly named Hurry Downs section.
Robert Laberge/Allsport USA

his Newman/Haas teammate, Christian Fittipaldi. Kenny Bräck (Shell Ford/Reynard) ran seventh in front of Cristiano da Matta (Pioneer Toyota/Reynard) and Roberto Moreno (Visteon Ford/Reynard).

Helio Castroneves threatened to follow his Team Penske mate to the sidelines early on as he allowed his left-side wheels to stray onto the grass under braking for Turn Three and slid straight on into the gravel trap. He was lucky, having built enough momentum to carry him through the trap and onto the grass beyond. The Mid-Ohio winner was able to rejoin at the back of the field.

The order at the front remained unchanged until the first round of pit stops. Franchitti was the first of the leaders to stop, after 15 laps of the Elkhart Lake circuit, along with Fernandez, Montoya, Fittipaldi and Bräck. Tagliani relinquished his lead one circuit later and was joined in the pit lane by Andretti, while Moreno used his customary excellent fuel mileage to extend his run for another pass.

Wisely Montoya's crew elected to put a little less than a full tank of fuel aboard the #1 Toyota/Lola, which enabled him to leapfrog Fernandez and Franchitti as he exited pit lane. Cold tires were of no concern to the Colombian, who snapped off one of his patented, super-quick out-laps, during which he outbraked Tagliani into Turn 12 to take the lead. By lap 23, Montoya had extended his advantage to more than nine seconds.

"The first laps were so good today," said Montoya. "I was pushing the car hard early on and moving forward, and then we started to try and conserve fuel."

Montoya was first to make his second pit stop, pulling in on lap 28. He rejoined in seventh, but became one of the quintet who would be left with what de Ferran earlier called "a box full of neutrals" as he, too, succumbed to a broken transmission.

"The problem was sudden," he related. "The car was working perfectly, and then it wouldn't shift up. It's disappointing to not finish, but now we know that we are capable of leading races on a road course and winning the races."

Franchitti also had been stricken by gearbox woes, falling from third to 11th between laps 20 and 22. He soldiered on, taking advantage of the high rate of attrition to rise as high as fifth, until his transmission failed altogether with 12 laps remaining.

Montoya's demise handed the lead back to Tagliani, who led defending race-winner Fittipaldi by 11 seconds before the Brazilian made his second pit stop, on lap 31. Fittipaldi would not be seen on the track again, falling victim to a broken exhaust header.

Meanwhile, Tracy was reprising his Long Beach victory charge, rising from 23rd to 15th before his first pit stop, on lap 15, then continuing his march by moving to eighth before the second round of pit stops. Just prior to his second stop, Tracy had closed up onto the battle for third place, which raged between Fittipaldi, Fernandez, Moreno, Bräck and Jimmy Vasser.

Tracy passed Bräck immediately before taking on service on lap 30, then squeezed past Fernandez on lap 34 on the approach to Turn One. After Moreno stretched his fuel load once again to lead a couple of laps before pulling into pit lane on lap 34, Tracy was up into second place. And he continued to make steady inroads on Tagliani's advantage, chewing up the Canadian rookie's lead like a Doberman. The gap shrank from 7.4 seconds on lap 34 to 6.2 the next time around, then to 5.0 and 3.6 on successive laps.

On lap 38, though, Tagliani lost yet another golden opportunity to taste victory champagne, coasting to a halt near the Carousel turn with a broken driveshaft.

So it was that Tracy's magnificent comeback drive was transformed into the race leadership. He made his third and final pit stop on lap 46, relinquishing his hard-fought advantage to Patrick's perennial late-stoppers Fernandez and Moreno (who stretched his methanol until lap 51). Tracy, though, was in control. He extended his margin over Fernandez to as much as 10.6 seconds before backing off during the final couple of laps and taking the checkered flag 7.450 seconds ahead of the field.

"We overcame adversity throughout the weekend," said Tracy, alluding to an incident that saw him stranded in the gravel trap toward the end of the first qualifying session on Friday. "And today – after the first lap – everything was perfect. The crew gave me awesome stops, and Barry Green and the engineers called a smart race."

In addition, Tracy drove as close to a perfect race as possible in moving himself to within 25 points of series-leader Andretti.

"All wins are great," said Tracy, "but this one is especially sweet."

Fernandez was equally delighted to finish second, which put him fourth in the series standings, only 22 points behind Andretti. Bräck continued to show that he was more than just an oval expert, driving a smart race to record his seventh top-five finish of an impressive rookie campaign.

Moreno was one of the few who could make a balky gearbox hold up, surviving a problematic third gear to finish fourth and shift his championship challenge back into high gear after a string of disappointments, while Vasser drove a strong race to finish in fifth after starting a lowly 16th in the second of Target/Chip Ganassi Racing's Toyota/Lolas.

"We started the season out very strong with consistent points, and I think if we can get on a roll now, the top three is still in sight for the championship," said the '96 champion.

Jeremy Shaw/Eric Mauk

FEDEX CHAMPIONSHIP SERIES • ROUND 14

ROAD AMERICA SNIPPETS

• Target/Chip Ganassi Racing's Lolas were fitted with the same "catfish" **FRONT-WING** configuration that was introduced at Mid-Ohio (and tested previously at Road America). Juan Montoya was pleased with the new design, which helped the car's balance and enabled him to lead the race. Teammate Jimmy Vasser finished fifth in his similar car. Newman/Haas Racing, meanwhile, tried yet another kind of nose wing that had more than a passing resemblance to the team's '99 Swift.

• **FUEL CONSERVATION** was the name of the game at Elkhart Lake, many drivers concentrating more on stretching mileage than on passing competitors. Mo Nunn Racing's Tony Kanaan was one of the protagonists who was less than pleased with the way the race was run. "That was not fun," he said. "It was not racing. It was all about fuel economy. You can't drive the car, the car drives you."

• After completing 42 laps, Cristiano da Matta was **DISQUALIFIED** from 13th place as the result of an incident during his first pit stop. Da Matta (right) struck PPI Motorsports' right rear tire changer, Robby Maschhaupi, injuring his left knee. CART allowed da Matta to continue, but after reviewing the incident, excluded him retrospectively at the time of the pit stop. He was classified 22nd.

• While the FedEx Series cars were pounding around in Wisconsin, under-employed racer Bryan Herta traveled **OVERSEAS** to give German fans a taste of what they might expect to see in 2001. Herta ran exhibition laps at the grand opening of the EuroSpeedway oval in front of an estimated crowd of 100,000. The former Laguna Seca winner drove a Walker Racing Honda/Reynard on a track that he compared to the "roval" at Rio in terms of layout.

• The Herdez/Bettenhausen Motorsports team embarked on an ambitious **DEVELOPMENT** program during the race weekend at Road America, testing new nose-wing configurations, different wheelbase dimensions and new combinations of rear suspension geometry on Michel Jourdain Jr.'s Mercedes/Lola B2K/00. "We've gone from survival to moving forward again," said technical director Tom Brown. "Hopefully, you'll see us begin to creep forward into respectability."

• **GUALTER SALLES** suffered a huge accident at the notorious Kink during practice on Friday morning. Dale Coyne Racing's spare Ford/Lola was still in component form following a crash at Chicago Motor Speedway, but the crew worked late into the evening to complete the rebuild so that the amiable Brazilian could resume action on Saturday morning.

• Just one race after claiming its 100th pole since returning to major league open-wheel racing in 1995, **FIRESTONE** secured its 100th race win and marked the event by donating $10,000 to the winning driver's favorite charity. Paul Tracy chose the Greg Moore Foundation as the beneficiary of Firestone's largesse.

FEDEX CHAMPIONSHIP SERIES • ROUND 14
MOTOROLA 220

ROAD AMERICA, ELKHART LAKE, WISCONSIN

AUGUST 20, 55 laps of 4.048 miles – 222.640 miles

Place	Driver (Nat.)	No.	Team Sponsors Engine/Car	Tires	Q Speed	Q Time	Q Pos.	Laps	Time/Status	Ave. (mph)	Pts.
1	Paul Tracy (CDN)	26	Team KOOL Green Honda/Reynard 2KI	FS	144.741	1m 40.682s	7	55	1h 37m 53.681s	136.457	20
2	Adrian Fernandez (MEX)	40	Patrick Racing Tecate/Quaker State Ford Cosworth/Reynard 2KI	FS	144.886	1m 40.581s	5	55	1h 38m 01.131s	136.284	16
3	*Kenny Bräck (S)	8	Team Rahal Shell Ford Cosworth/Reynard 2KI	FS	144.318	1m 40.977s	9	55	1h 38m 02.517s	136.252	14
4	Roberto Moreno (BR)	20	Patrick Racing Visteon Ford Cosworth/Reynard 2KI	FS	144.184	1m 41.071s	11	55	1h 38m 17.260s	135.911	12
5	Jimmy Vasser (USA)	12	Target/Chip Ganassi Racing Toyota/Lola B2K/00	FS	143.231	1m 41.743s	16	55	1h 38m 27.630s	135.673	10
6	Memo Gidley (USA)	10	Della Penna Motorsports DirecTV Toyota/Reynard 2KI	FS	142.941	1m 41.950s	18	55	1h 39m 28.245s	134.295	8
7	Max Papis (I)	7	Team Rahal Miller Lite Ford Cosworth/Reynard 2KI	FS	143.634	1m 41.458s	15	55	1h 39m 33.819s	134.169	6
8	Tony Kanaan (BR)	55	Mo Nunn Racing Hollywood Mercedes/Reynard 2KI	FS	143.129	1m 41.816s	17	54	Running		5
9	Helio Castroneves (BR)	3	Marlboro Team Penske Marlboro Honda/Reynard 2KI	FS	144.844	1m 40.610s	6	54	Running		4
10	*Oriol Servia (E)	96	PPI Motorsports Telefonica Toyota/Reynard 2KI	FS	143.886	1m 41.280s	14	54	Running		3
11	Mark Blundell (GB)	18	PacWest Racing Motorola Mercedes/Reynard 2KI	FS	142.402	1m 42.336s	20	48	Gearbox		2
12	Dario Franchitti (GB)	27	Team KOOL Green Honda/Reynard 2KI	FS	145.924	1m 39.866s	1	43	Gearbox		2
13	*Alexandre Tagliani (CDN)	33	Forsythe Racing Player's/Indeck Ford Cosworth/Reynard 2KI	FS	145.350	1m 40.260s	3	37	Driveshaft		1
14	Christian Fittipaldi (BR)	11	Newman/Haas Big Kmart/Route 66 Ford Cosworth/Lola B2K/00	FS	144.425	1m 40.902s	8	31	Exhaust header		
15	Juan Montoya (COL)	1	Target/Chip Ganassi Racing Toyota/Lola B2K/00	FS	144.147	1m 41.097s	12	30	Gearbox		
16	Mauricio Gugelmin (BR)	17	PacWest Racing Nextel Mercedes/Reynard 2KI	FS	144.222	1m 41.044s	10	20	Engine		
17	Michel Jourdain Jr. (MEX)	16	Bettenhausen Motorsports Herdez Mercedes/Lola B2K/00	FS	142.289	1m 42.417s	21	19	Fuel pump		
18	Michael Andretti (USA)	6	Newman/Haas Big Kmart/Texaco Ford Cosworth/Lola B2K/00	FS	145.146	1m 40.401s	4	17	CV joint		
19	Gualter Salles (BR)	19	Dale Coyne Racing Sports Today Ford Cosworth/Lola B2K/00	FS	139.538	1m 44.436s	25	16	Engine		
20	Patrick Carpentier (CDN)	32	Forsythe Racing Player's/Indeck Ford Cosworth/Reynard 2KI	FS	142.484	1m 42.277s	19	15	Accident		
21	*Shinji Nakano (J)	5	Walker Racing Avex Group Honda/Reynard 2KI	FS	141.201	1m 43.206s	23	15	Gearbox		
22	Cristiano da Matta (BR)	97	PPI Motorsports Pioneer/WorldCom Toyota/Reynard 2KI	FS	144.056	1m 41.161s	13	14	Pit incident		
23	Tarso Marques (BR)	34	Dale Coyne Racing Panasonic Ford Cosworth/Swift 011.c	FS	141.338	1m 43.106s	22	3	Accident		
24	Luiz Garcia Jr. (BR)	25	Arciero-PRG Hollywood/Embratel-21 Mercedes/Reynard 2KI	FS	140.929	1m 43.405s	24	2	Engine		
25	Gil de Ferran (BR)	2	Marlboro Team Penske Marlboro Honda/Reynard 2KI	FS	145.504	1m 40.154s	2	1	Gearbox		

* denotes rookie driver

Caution flags: None.

Lap leaders: Alexandre Tagliani, 1-16 (16 laps); Roberto Moreno, 17 (1 lap); Juan Montoya, 18-28 (11 laps); Tagliani, 29-32 (4 laps); Moreno, 33-34 (2 laps); Tagliani, 35-37 (3 laps); Paul Tracy, 38-45 (8 laps); Adrian Fernandez, 46 (1 lap); Moreno, 47-50 (4 laps); Tracy, 51-55 (5 laps). **Totals:** Tagliani, 23 laps; Tracy, 13 laps; Montoya, 11 laps; Moreno, 7 laps; Fernandez, 1 lap.

Fastest race lap: Paul Tracy, 1m 42.334s, 142.404 mph on lap 44.

Championship positions: 1 Andretti, 125; **2** Moreno, 112; **3** de Ferran, 106; **4** Fernandez, 103; **5** Bräck, 102; **6** Tracy, 100; **7** da Matta, 82; **8** Castroneves, 81; **9** Vasser, 78; **10** Montoya, 77; **11** Papis, 74; **12** Carpentier, 71; **13** Franchitti, 60; **14** Fittipaldi, 52; **15** Tagliani, 45; **16** Servia, 44; **17** Gugelmin, 30; **18** Gidley, 20; **19** Blundell & Kanaan, 16; **21** Herta, 14; **22** Jourdain, 10; **23** Nakano, 7; **24** Marques & Garcia, 5; **26** Fontana, 2; **27** Kurosawa, 1.

VANCOUVER
FEDEX CHAMPIONSHIP SERIES • ROUND 15

1 – TRACY
2 – FRANCHITTI
3 – FERNANDEZ

FEDEX CHAMPIONSHIP SERIES • ROUND 15

QUALIFYING

Team KOOL Green was in a class of its own at Vancouver. Dario Franchitti was fastest in every official session, and after trading times with teammate Paul Tracy during the all-important final half-hour of qualifying, the 27-year-old Scotsman secured his second pole in as many races by a margin of just 0.088 second.

"That was sweet," said a delighted Franchitti. "The car was good and I didn't make the most of it on the first set of tires. The second set, I got the tires up to temperature and really went for it."

Franchitti's pole – the tenth of his career – was all the more pleasing for the fact that it was achieved virtually in the back yard of his late close friend, Greg Moore, from nearby Maple Ridge, B.C., who tragically lost his life in a crash during the 1999 season finale at California Speedway.

"It's a special race, being Greg's home town and him not being here," said Franchitti. "I try to win every race, but I'd say there's probably a little extra incentive this weekend. Today was particularly satisfying. It felt good."

A red-flag interruption with only a few minutes remaining – when Christian Fittipaldi's Big Kmart/Route 66 Ford Cosworth/Lola ground to a halt with a broken drive train tripod joint – perhaps worked in Franchitti's favor, since by then the Scotsman had been confined to the pits with a bent rear suspension.

"I'm not sure what happened," related Franchitti. "I don't think I hit the wall, but all of a sudden the car was crabbing down the straight. Let's just say the red was fairly well timed!"

Not so for teammate Tracy. Immediately prior to the final red flag, he had been on a particularly quick lap. "I was up two-tenths [of a second] halfway round and then the red came out," declared the Canadian.

Marlboro Team Penske pairing Gil de Ferran and Helio Castroneves ensured an amazing top-four sweep for the Honda/Reynard combination. Best of the rest was defending series champion Juan Montoya, who found a substantial amount of speed on Saturday in his Target/Chip Ganassi Racing Toyota/Lola, vaulting to fifth on the grid ahead of Fittipaldi and Cristiano da Matta in the Pioneer Toyota/Reynard.

Pages 165/166: Paul Tracy speeds beneath Jim Swintal's twin checkered flags to score a popular Canadian victory.
Robert Laberge/Allsport USA

Right: Dario Franchitti is frantically push-started by his crew – but teammate Paul Tracy is already through into the lead.
Donald Miralle/Allsport USA

Below right: Franchitti and Tracy take a moment to reflect on the circumstances of a one-two finish for Team KOOL Green.
Robert Laberge/Allsport USA

DARIO Franchitti posted a classy performance in the Molson Indy Vancouver. After gaining his second pole in successive races, the personable Scotsman took off into a convincing lead with Team KOOL Green's Honda/Reynard and seemed assured of a long overdue victory when he pulled into pit lane for his second and final routine pit stop of the day. But Lady Luck hadn't finished weaving her miserable spell on a desperately disappointing Y2K campaign, and Franchitti stalled the engine as he attempted to rejoin.

Kyle Moyer's crew leapt into action and quickly pushed Franchitti back into the fray, but not before he had relinquished the advantage to teammate Paul Tracy. And a prior agreement between the pair meant that Franchitti was obliged to maintain station in the closing stages.

"I probably had enough to pass Paul, especially on cold tires, but a deal's a deal and that's the way it goes," said a philosophical Franchitti.

Tracy, by contrast, was elated after claiming his third win of the season – and second in a row – to vault back into the championship reckoning.

"It was a fantastic day for everybody at Team KOOL Green," declared Tracy. "I don't know if I had the outright speed to beat Dario, but we stayed close and, at the pit stop, Dario had a problem."

"I'd say I was happy, but I was also disappointed for him," added Tracy magnanimously. "He had the measure of the field today and I don't know that we'd have been able to beat him."

Pleasant weather conditions and the prospect (duly fulfilled) of a Canadian victory attracted a huge crowd to the Concord Pacific Place temporary circuit, and there was plenty of action in the early stages to keep them entertained. Franchitti leapt away into the lead at the start, chased by Tracy and the two Marlboro Team Penske Honda/Reynards of Gil de Ferran and Helio Castroneves. Juan Montoya also maintained his starting position, fifth in his Target Toyota/Lola. Behind, Cristiano da Matta (Pioneer Toyota/Reynard) immediately found a way past Christian Fittipaldi's Big Kmart/Route 66 Ford/Lola.

The yellows waved shortly thereafter, however, when Patrick Carpentier was punted off ignominiously at the Science World Chicane by Player's/Forsythe teammate Alex Tagliani. Carpenter was not impressed. Mark Blundell also was involved in the melee. Almost immediately after the restart, Michel Jourdain Jr., having passed Mexican countryman Adrian Fernandez, ran into the back of Tony Kanaan's Hollywood Mercedes/Reynard in Turn One. Caution again.

At the next restart, Tagliani was punted inadvertently into a spin at Turn One by Fernandez.

"I have to apologize to Tagliani," said Fernandez. "I went too deep and he went on his line, which he should have done, but I just hit him. It was my fault."

Fernandez continued unscathed, while Tagliani lost a lap.

When the race finally settled into a proper rhythm, Franchitti began to stretch out an advantage over Tracy who, in turn, was under no pressure from de Ferran. Castroneves, meanwhile, couldn't quite match his countryman's pace and struggled to remain ahead of Montoya and da Matta.

Franchitti made his first pit stop on lap 40, rejoining well clear of his teammate. De Ferran led a couple of laps before making his first fuel stop, whereupon smart strategy by Target/Chip Ganassi Racing saw Montoya take on only a partial load of fuel – a little over 21 gallons – which enabled him to nip ahead of the Brazilian. Even worse, de Ferran was assessed a drive-through penalty for straying over the yellow line marking the edge of the pit lane between Turns One and Two. The infraction cost him all hope of a top-three finish.

Teammate Castroneves also was out of luck, as a suspension failure on lap 44 sent him spinning down the escape road at Turn Six.

In common with Montoya, a strategic gamble paid off for Fernandez, who had been among several drivers to take on fuel during the early series of cautions. Ditto Memo Gidley, who had been called in on lap six by team owner John Della Penna, then posted a fine charge that took him from 23rd to 13th in just nine laps. He ran third after the leaders made their first in-sequence stops, and dropped only to ninth when he resumed after taking on scheduled service on lap 45. Sadly, after seeming set for at least a seventh-place finish, Gidley succumbed to a gearbox failure with 14 laps to go.

Fernandez, who had made his first pit stop on lap 12, took over in third after Gidley made his visit to pit lane.

All the while, Team KOOL Green maintained its dominant form.

"We were quite comfortable up front, running reasonable [lap] times and saving fuel," related Franchitti. "Everything was looking pretty good."

Then came another caution, on lap 52, when Shinji Nakano crashed Derrick Walker's Avex Group Honda/Reynard heavily in Turn Seven. The two leaders took the opportunity to make their second and final pit stops. Neither Franchitti nor Tracy took on fresh tires. In a roundabout way, that was to prove Franchitti's downfall.

The sticky rubber and a different procedure for the pit-lane speed-limiter, which had been introduced recently by Honda, caught out Franchitti, whose engine died as he attempted to leave his pit.

"When you try to spin the wheels, it just limits the revs and stalls the car," explained Franchitti. "I told them [Honda] it was going to happen. And it did, unfortunately."

Franchitti's crew scrambled to push-start the #27 car, but by then Tracy was already through into the lead.

Montoya remained in third after Ganassi left it just a little too late to call in the Colombian for a second pit stop on lap 52. By the time Ganassi had made the decision, Montoya was past the pit entrance. Rather than stop on the following lap, under caution, which would have dropped Montoya to the back of the pack, Ganassi elected to go with track position.

Montoya chased valiantly after the two green cars at the restart. He established the fastest lap of the race on lap 65, closing onto the tail of Franchitti, but two laps later he was parked by the side of the track. A detailed inspection later revealed that there were still

FEDEX CHAMPIONSHIP SERIES • ROUND 15

Team harmony

THERE was a certain amount of snickering within the paddock area after Dario Franchitti and Paul Tracy qualified their two KOOL Honda/Reynards alongside each other on the front row of the grid. Would there be a repeat, some cynics wondered, of previous incidents between the pair – at Gateway and Houston a couple of years ago, for example, and at Chicago just a couple of months earlier. But this time the teammates behaved impeccably – even after Tracy passed Franchitti during the final round of pit stops.

In fact, the two drivers had developed a plan for just such an eventuality.

"We agreed that we'd fight it out until the last pit stop," revealed Franchitti, "then whoever was ahead would stay there."

"I knew I wasn't allowed to pass him [back], but I was pushing him, just keeping him honest," continued Franchitti with a grin. "I don't know whether he trusted me, but..."

For a short while, even Tracy began to wonder: "He was pressuring me, so I was just asking [on the radio], 'Hey, is this what the deal is?' Barry came on the radio and told me we had a deal and not to worry about Dario."

Indeed so. "We had an agreement and I would've expected the same from Paul," recounted the honorable Scotsman. "In the past, when we've had the agreement, the guy in front was generally quicker. That wasn't the case today, but it didn't make any difference.

"I definitely had my best chance to pass Paul at the restarts, but an agreement is an agreement and I'm at ease with that. It's better to have a one-two finish than have a Chicago finish again [where the pair collided and eliminated each other]."

Added Tracy with a chuckle, "Typically, we're going to race until the final pit stop, and in the past we've had our incidents before the last stop!"

159

FEDEX CHAMPIONSHIP SERIES • ROUND 15

Patience is the key

PRIOR to the Molson Indy Vancouver, the top six contenders in the CART FedEx Championship Series were separated by 25 points. Following a sensational – and sensationally popular – victory by Canada's very own Paul Tracy, however, the top five contenders were blanketed by a mere 11 marks after 15 races.

Michael Andretti continued to lead the way on 126 points, despite not finishing in British Columbia when his Newman/Haas Ford/Lola ran out of fuel with two laps remaining. Tracy leapt from sixth all the way to second on 120 points, ahead of Adrian Fernandez (117), Gil de Ferran (116) and Roberto Moreno (115). Kenny Bräck lay sixth on 106 points as the championship headed toward its exciting climax following yet another race of changing fortunes.

"A lot can happen in a two-hour race like this, so the main thing in this type of racing is that you have to be patient," declared Fernandez after a strong third-place finish. "Sometimes people don't have the patience, and that's what we managed to achieve in the last few races – patience, be fast and have good [pit] stops and strategy."

"The team is working fantastic and we've been able to make the right calls," he continued. "The preparation of the car is fantastic. I think what it will take [to win the title] is to just keep scoring [points] – finish in the top five from now on and hopefully another one or two wins and we're going to be close. Paul is on a roll, but hopefully we'll score some wins in the next five races."

Tracy, too, fully intended to stick by the formula that had served him so well thus far. Asked in the post-race press conference whether he might consider changing his usual hard-charging tactics, Tracy replied emphatically to the contrary. "To win this championship, you're going to have to charge and go out and win it," he said. "That's what we were able to do today and last [race at Road America], and we've got the confidence and the momentum to take the bull by the horns and take it where we want to go. You can't cruise around and hope to win the championship."

Below: Patience, good pit stops and an excellent strategy allowed Adrian Fernandez to finish third.

two-and-a-quarter gallons of fuel on board – a faulty fuel pump was named as the culprit. Regardless, Montoya was out and yet more valuable points had slipped away.

Da Matta took over in third. He, too, elected not to make a second pit stop under yellow. In fact, his team had determined that he could run the distance with only one pit visit – as long as there was another caution in the late stages. There was, in fact, on lap 69, while Montoya's car was towed to a safe location. But the interruption was brief.

"We just needed two more laps of yellow and we would've made it home," said team owner Cal Wells III later. "It was a safe bet, to be honest with you."

But not safe enough. The gamble failed to pay off. Da Matta was forced to make a second pit stop with four laps left, relegating him to seventh.

Incredibly, Andretti's team also took a gamble on fuel strategy. The championship leader stuck to an ultra-conservative pace and was in eighth place when he ran out of fuel with two laps remaining.

"The telemetry told us that we had enough fuel to go the distance," related a furious Andretti afterward. "We had been running lean since the start of the race and were going slower than most of the guys because we were going for a one-stop strategy. That turned out to be a mistake because we should have finished fourth or fifth with a two-stop strategy."

Patrick Racing, meanwhile, called the perfect race. Fernandez was directed into the pits as soon as strategist/race engineer John Ward saw the severity of Nakano's crash on lap 51 – even before the full-course caution had been ordered by Race Control. In truth, there was also a measure of good fortune, since Fernandez was due for a pit stop anyway. The upshot, however, was that he lost only two positions, and was able to claim a magnificent third-place finish. Not bad after starting 15th.

"Fantastic," said Fernandez. "I'm very happy because we didn't have the [speed] all weekend. We were struggling to get some grip in the back of the car, and today we did what we always do – we were patient and waited to see what we needed to do."

Patience also paid off for Tracy, who maintained a conservative pace to the finish and was rewarded with his second win in as many races. After the cool-down lap, Tracy played to the crowd with a spectacular series of tire-smoking donuts in Turn One.

"For the last five laps, I could see everybody jumping up and down in the grandstands and it was really emotional," said Tracy. "It was a time to celebrate with my countrymen."

Jeremy Shaw

FEDEX CHAMPIONSHIP SERIES • ROUND 15

VANCOUVER SNIPPETS

• Pre-race ceremonies included *(right)* the **RETIREMENT** of car #99 from the Champ Car, Indy Lights and Toyota Atlantic ranks in memory of local hero Greg Moore. The #14 of all-time win leader A.J. Foyt is the only other car number to have been retired from CART competition. One of Moore's helmets was bought by actor Richard Dean Anderson (star of the popular television series *McGyver* and a frequent competitor in the Toyota Pro-Celebrity race at Long Beach) for an impressive CDN$57,000 at a pre-event raffle during a gala dinner to benefit the Greg Moore Foundation.

• The forecast of rain showers for the Vancouver area on race day did not deter many spectators. Thankfully, the precipitation did not materialize and a **BUMPER CROWD** of 63,677, up from 60,938 in '99, ensured a strong three-day attendance totaling 155,937.

• **HONDA'S** third victory in a row and its second one-two finish in three races saw the 1999 CART Manufacturer's Champion close to within seven points (255-248) of long-time pace-setter Ford Cosworth.

• **ROBERTO MORENO** chased hard after the two Team KOOL Green Honda/Reynards in the closing stages, but, unfortunately, already was a full lap in arrears after electing not to change tires during his first pit stop on lap 41. "I think it was the first time this year that our strategy didn't pay off," said Moreno, who finished tenth and fell from second to fifth in the point standings. "We took a chance and it didn't pay off."

• After attending some meetings in Toronto earlier in the week, former Champ Car star **TEO FABI** decided he was too close to miss the opportunity of catching up with many of his old friends. "I was halfway here, so I figured I might as well come on over to Vancouver," said Fabi, who, with younger brother Corrado, has taken responsibility for his family's Italian-based mining business. "It's been fun. I see a lot of the same people. It's a really good atmosphere."

• Gualter Salles stood down from Dale Coyne Racing's *Sports Today* Ford/Lola after three **DISAPPOINTING RACES** while substituting for Takuya Kurosawa, who required back surgery to repair an old injury that had been aggravated in his crash at Michigan Speedway. Alex Barron was invited to drive the car for the final five races of the season, and despite having not driven a Champ Car for almost a full year, acquitted himself respectably en route to a 13th-place finish.

• The Herdez/Bettenhausen Motorsports team held a **SURPRISE** 24th birthday celebration for Michel Jourdain Jr. prior to final qualifying. Fellow drivers Juan Montoya, Jimmy Vasser and Memo Gidley made brief appearances, but, unfortunately, neither Lady Luck nor the CART Safety Team gave the talented Mexican a break. After posting the 14th-fastest time during practice, Jourdain's Herdez Mercedes/Lola ground to a halt without even completing a timed lap in final qualifying. Even worse, the CART Safety Team elected not to tow his car back to the pit lane. Jourdain, therefore, had no opportunity to defend his 12th position on the provisional grid.

FEDEX CHAMPIONSHIP SERIES • ROUND 15
MOLSON INDY VANCOUVER
CONCORD PACIFIC PLACE, VANCOUVER, BRITISH COLUMBIA, CANADA
SEPTEMBER 3, 90 laps of 1.781 miles – 160.290 miles

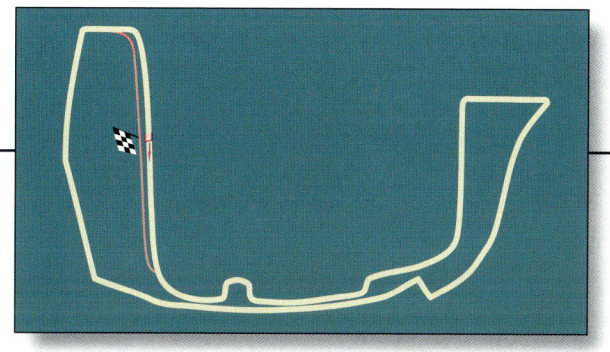

Place	Driver (Nat.)	No.	Team Sponsors Engine/Car	Tires	Q Speed	Q Time	Q Pos.	Laps	Time/Status	Ave. (mph)	Pts.
1	Paul Tracy (CDN)	26	Team KOOL Green Honda/Reynard 2KI	FS	105.989	1m 00.493s	2	90	1h 53m 06.024s	85.034	20
2	Dario Franchitti (GB)	27	Team KOOL Green Honda/Reynard 2KI	FS	106.144	1m 00.405s	1	90	1h 53m 06.408s	85.029	18
3	Adrian Fernandez (MEX)	40	Patrick Racing Tecate/Quaker State Ford Cosworth/Reynard 2KI	FS	103.480	1m 01.960s	15	90	1h 53m 25.055s	84.796	14
4	Christian Fittipaldi (BR)	11	Newman/Haas Big Kmart/Route 66 Ford Cosworth/Lola B2K/00	FS	104.425	1m 01.399s	6	90	1h 53m 25.638s	84.789	12
5	Gil de Ferran (BR)	2	Marlboro Team Penske Marlboro Honda/Reynard 2KI	FS	105.470	1m 00.791s	3	90	1h 53m 26.137s	84.783	10
6	Jimmy Vasser (USA)	12	Target/Chip Ganassi Racing Toyota/Lola B2K/00	FS	103.943	1m 01.684s	11	90	1h 53m 26.583s	84.777	8
7	Cristiano da Matta (BR)	97	PPI Motorsports Pioneer/WorldCom Toyota/Reynard 2KI	FS	104.235	1m 01.511s	7	90	1h 53m 37.972s	84.636	6
8	Max Papis (I)	7	Team Rahal Miller Lite Ford Cosworth/Reynard 2KI	FS	104.076	1m 01.605s	9	90	1h 53m 51.466s	84.469	5
9	*Kenny Bräck (S)	8	Team Rahal Shell Ford Cosworth/Reynard 2KI	FS	103.436	1m 01.986s	16	90	1h 53m 51.856s	84.464	4
10	Roberto Moreno (BR)	20	Patrick Racing Visteon Ford Cosworth/Reynard 2KI	FS	104.037	1m 01.628s	10	89	Running		3
11	*Oriol Servia (E)	96	PPI Motorsports Telefonica Toyota/Reynard 2KI	FS	103.800	1m 01.769s	12	89	Running		2
12	Michael Andretti (USA)	6	Newman/Haas Big Kmart/Texaco Ford Cosworth/Lola B2K/00	FS	104.220	1m 01.520s	8	88	Out of fuel		1
13	Alex Barron (USA)	19	Dale Coyne Racing *Sports Today* Ford Cosworth/Lola B2K/00	FS	100.245	1m 03.959s	24	87	Running		
14	Tony Kanaan (BR)	55	Mo Nunn Racing Hollywood Mercedes/Reynard 2KI	FS	103.516	1m 01.938s	14	85	Running		
15	Luiz Garcia Jr. (BR)	25	Arciero-PRG Hollywood/Embratel-21 Mercedes/Reynard 2KI	FS	100.072	1m 04.070s	25	84	Running		
16	Memo Gidley (USA)	10	Della Penna Motorsports DirecTV Toyota/Reynard 2KI	FS	101.289	1m 03.300s	21	77	Gearbox		
17	Juan Montoya (COL)	1	Target/Chip Ganassi Racing Toyota/Lola B2K/00	FS	104.669	1m 01.256s	5	67	Fuel pump		
18	*Alexandre Tagliani (CDN)	33	Forsythe Racing Player's/Indeck Ford Cosworth/Reynard 2KI	FS	102.209	1m 02.730s	19	63	Handling		
19	*Shinji Nakano (J)	5	Walker Racing Avex Group Honda/Reynard 2KI	FS	100.846	1m 03.578s	22	49	Accident		
20	Helio Castroneves (BR)	3	Marlboro Team Penske Marlboro Honda/Reynard 2KI	FS	104.753	1m 01.207s	4	43	Accident		
21	Mauricio Gugelmin (BR)	17	PacWest Racing Nextel Mercedes/Reynard 2KI	FS	103.771	1m 01.786s	13	14	Accident		
22	Tarso Marques (BR)	34	Dale Coyne Racing Panasonic Ford Cosworth/Swift 011.c	FS	100.521	1m 03.784s	23	14	Accident		
23	Michel Jourdain Jr. (MEX)	16	Bettenhausen Motorsports Herdez Mercedes/Lola B2K/00	FS	103.306	1m 02.064s	17	11	Accident		
24	Patrick Carpentier (CDN)	32	Forsythe Racing Player's/Indeck Ford Cosworth/Reynard 2KI	FS	102.699	1m 02.131s	18	3	Accident		
25	Mark Blundell (GB)	18	PacWest Racing Motorola Mercedes/Reynard 2KI	FS	102.136	1m 02.775s	20	3	Accident		

* denotes rookie driver

Caution flags: Lap 1, yellow start; laps 4-9, accident/Blundell & Carpentier; laps 12-14, accident/Jourdain; laps 17-19, accident/Tagliani; laps 51-60, accident/Nakano; laps 68-70, tow/Montoya. **Total:** Six for 22 laps.

Lap leaders: Dario Franchitti, 1-40 (40 laps); Gil de Ferran, 41-42 (2 laps); Franchitti, 43-52 (10 laps); Paul Tracy, 53-90 (38 laps). **Totals:** Franchitti, 50 laps; Tracy, 38 laps; de Ferran, 2 laps.

Fastest race lap: Juan Montoya, 1m 01.538s, 104.189 mph on lap 65.

Championship positions: 1 Andretti, 126; 2 Tracy, 120; 3 Fernandez, 117; 4 de Ferran, 116; 5 Moreno, 115; 6 Bräck, 106; 7 da Matta, 88; 8 Vasser, 86; 9 Castroneves, 81; 10 Papis, 79; 11 Franchitti, 78; 12 Montoya, 77; 13 Carpentier, 71; 14 Fittipaldi, 64; 15 Servia, 46; 16 Tagliani, 45; 17 Gugelmin, 30; 18 Gidley, 20; 19 Blundell & Kanaan, 16; 21 Herta 14; 22 Jourdain, 10; 23 Nakano, 7; 24 Marques & Garcia, 5; 26 Fontana, 2; 27 Kurosawa, 1.

FEDEX CHAMPIONSHIP SERIES • ROUND 16

LAGUNA SECA

FEDEX CHAMPIONSHIP SERIES • ROUND 16

Left: Helio Castroneves was in imperious form at Laguna Seca Raceway, taking his third victory for Marlboro Team Penske.

Below left: Situated high in the hills overlooking Monterey Bay, Laguna Seca Raceway offers spectacular viewing.

Below right: CART officials Wally Dallenbach, Lon Bromley, Kirk Russell and Bobby Rahal assess some changes to the tire barriers at the famed Corkscrew.

QUALIFYING

Two dramatic days of qualifying saw Helio Castroneves fastest in each of the half-hour sessions. The 25-year-old Brazilian duly claimed his second pole of the year for Marlboro Team Penske. Unusually, his best time was set on Friday, when track conditions were at their best following a lengthy delay caused by a frightening accident that befell Patrick Carpentier. Temperatures were a little warmer on Saturday, and, despite the drivers' best efforts, very few were able to improve on their previous best.

The top three places remained unchanged, assuring Castroneves' teammate, Gil de Ferran, a place on the outside of the front row in his identical Marlboro Honda/Reynard. Dario Franchitti was confident of finding a little more speed from his similar KOOL Honda/Reynard, only to leave his braking a fraction too late at the final corner, Turn 11.

"It was frustrating," said Franchitti. "I felt I had a car today to be quicker."

The real star of qualifying was Bryan Herta, who bounced back from an enforced exile and overcame a mechanical failure on Friday to post the fastest practice time on Saturday morning with Jerry Forsythe's Ford Cosworth/Reynard. Herta was second only to Castroneves in the final afternoon session, and even though he was in the first, "slower" group, his time was good enough for a position on the outside of the second row on the grid.

"I really, really enjoyed it, and I felt like I got everything out of the car," said Herta. "There's still more we can do to make the car better, so we'll keep working and see what happens [in the race]. It's a good place to start, and I'm really pleased."

Juan Montoya lost time with a driveshaft failure on Saturday morning, so was relatively content to qualify fifth in his Target Toyota/Lola. Kenny Bräck equaled Montoya's best with Team Rahal's Shell Ford/Reynard, while Mauricio Gugelmin gave the beleaguered PacWest team a much-needed boost by setting the seventh-fastest time in his Nextel Mercedes/Reynard.

THE Honda Grand Prix of Monterey Featuring the Shell 300 was not the greatest race of the season – unless one looked at it from the perspective of Marlboro Team Penske and, in particular, Helio Castroneves. In much the same way as the previous week's race at Vancouver had been dominated by Team KOOL Green, so Roger Penske's brigade of similar Honda-powered Reynards proved an unstoppable force at Laguna Seca Raceway. Castroneves qualified fastest, ahead of teammate Gil de Ferran, and led all but two of the 83 laps in a processional affair that, due to the timing of the second round of pit stops, which coincided with the day's only full-course caution, also developed into a fuel economy run.

"What a great day for Marlboro Team Penske," declared a delighted Castroneves after gaining his third victory of the season. "At the beginning of the race, I knew there wouldn't be a lot of yellow flags so we would have to conserve fuel. I was really 'in the zone' today and I'm so proud of the effort everyone has put forth to achieve these results."

De Ferran was equally delighted after finishing a close second ahead of Team KOOL Green's Dario Franchitti, who enabled Honda to complete a podium sweep at its namesake race and snatch the lead of the coveted CART Manufacturer's Championship from Ford Cosworth.

Perfect California weather conditions greeted the 26 runners for the start at high noon, and Castroneves lost no time in asserting his superiority. De Ferran tucked in behind under braking for the first corner, followed by Franchitti and Juan Montoya (Target Toyota/Lola), who muscled around the outside of a massively impressive Bryan Herta's Forsythe Championship Racing Ford/Reynard at the Turn Two hairpin. Kenny Bräck, who, ironically, had replaced Herta following the '99 season aboard Team Rahal's Shell Ford/Reynard, ran fifth ahead of Mauricio Gugelmin, who performed well again in PacWest Racing's Nextel Reynard and was comfortably quickest of the Mercedes-Benz contingent.

The leading quartet remained close together for the first seven laps or so, whereupon Castroneves began to stretch his advantage. The margin was out to 2.8 seconds before the Brazilian made his first pit stop, on lap 28. Montoya ran two more laps before taking on service, which enabled him to jump from fourth to second ahead of de Ferran and Franchitti. The defending champion gradually edged closer to the race leader, whittling the deficit from 4.2 seconds on lap 30 to less than two seconds on lap 42. By then, Castroneves was having to contend with some lapped traffic.

"My only scary time came when I approached the backmarkers," stated Castroneves. "Some of them were very difficult to pass and I thought, 'Oh boy, you'd better be careful now, Juan's coming.' But I just tried to remain calm."

But Montoya's challenge disintegrated during the second round of pit stops, which came on lap 47 during a full-course caution to remove Roberto Moreno's Visteon Ford/Reynard from a dangerous location in Turn Five. The Brazilian had spun off while attempting to pass Max Papis for 14th place. The leaders duly made their way into pit lane, where Montoya encountered a problem with his Target Toyota/Lola's air jack and fell to eighth before resuming. The status quo, meanwhile, had been restored, with de Ferran and Franchitti in second and third, despite a near collision in pit lane.

"It was my one chance to move up all day," said Franchitti. "My guys gave me a tremendous stop and I could see Gil up ahead on pit lane. Roger [Penske] sent him as I was halfway alongside and he just kept coming out, coming out. It was either back off or take the hit.

"I don't know whether it was Roger's or Gil's fault, but we have etiquette on the track; we should have some in the pit lane as well."

"Roger said, 'Go,' I dropped the clutch and the thing went into a big tank-slapper," said de Ferran in his defense. "It took me all the way out to the pit wall, and when I got to the end of pit lane, I looked in my mirrors and saw Dario and thought, 'Oops.'

"Dario pulled alongside of me while we were behind the pace car and I tried to signal my apologies, and as soon as the race was over I apologized to him."

The timing and length of the caution, which continued until lap 54, offered those who had pitted under the yellow the opportunity to go the distance without another stop – assuming they conserved fuel to the max.

"I talked to the team and they said just do the [fuel] numbers, and I thought, 'This is impossible. It's absurd,'" said Castroneves. "Then I did a couple of laps and opened a small gap, and I realized the other guys were in the same boat, so I have to stay in the same boat, too.

"But it's tough. When you're not driving hard, it gives you time to see

Drivers on the verge of a walkout

CART faced the distinct possibility of a drivers' walkout following a spectacular accident suffered by Patrick Carpentier during the first qualifying session on Friday afternoon. The French-Canadian allowed his Player's Ford/Reynard's left rear wheel to stray onto the dirt on the approach to the right-handed Turn Four, lost control and spun backward into the gravel trap. Rather than arresting Carpentier's progress, however, the raised leading edge of the gravel trap merely launched his car into the air. It flew for several yards before impacting the tire barrier – still going backward at a high velocity – and then, amazingly, vaulted clear over the safety fence before coming to rest, upside-down, on the other side!

Incredibly, Carpentier escaped injury, but his fellow drivers were incensed that a long list of safety concerns that had been presented to the track – and to CART – prior to the race weekend (following the fatal accident that befell Gonzalo Rodriguez one year earlier) had not been addressed.

The qualifying session was stopped after Carpentier's crash, and all the drivers, led by Championship Drivers Association chairman Mauricio Gugelmin, took part in a closed-door meeting. CART president of racing Hal Whiteford was invited into the meeting and was able to allay some of the drivers' fears by confirming that he would call a halt to the proceedings until some improvements could be made. Interim CART CEO and president Bobby Rahal, however, nearly caused a riot when he suggested that the drivers should get on with their business.

Fortunately, sanity – and Whiteford – prevailed. The gravel traps were re-groomed, several tire barriers were repositioned, and qualifying was resumed after a two-hour delay.

In the closing minutes of the following morning's practice session, Paul Tracy spun his Team KOOL Green Honda/Reynard in almost precisely the same location as Carpentier. Tracy was not at all happy that the gravel trap did not appear to slow his errant car appreciably, although at least he remained virtually at ground level, and the tire wall did its job in preventing serious damage to either Tracy or his car.

FEDEX CHAMPIONSHIP SERIES • ROUND 16

Above: **Helio Castroneves celebrates his third victory in typically exuberant style.**
Robert Laberge/Allsport USA

Left: **Juan Montoya crests the rise at the top of the hill leading into the Corkscrew.**
Jon Ferrey/Allsport USA

Above left: **Dario Franchitti ensured a clean sweep of the podium for Honda.**
Jon Ferrey/Allsport USA

Far left: **Maintaining control of a 900hp Champ Car while plunging downhill through the Corkscrew is no mean feat.**
Robert Laberge/Allsport USA

Main photopgraph: **Second place vaulted Gil de Ferran into the championship lead.**
Robert Laberge/Allsport USA

FEDEX CHAMPIONSHIP SERIES • ROUND 16

everything. You have to concentrate very hard not to make a mistake."

All the while, de Ferran was hard on the heels of his young countryman.

"It becomes a question of how fast can you drive and still save fuel," said de Ferran, "and can I push Helio into driving harder so he will have fuel problems later on? So you try to push him into making a mistake or using more fuel. He didn't, and he won."

Rebuffed in his efforts to pass de Ferran in pit lane, Franchitti resigned himself to third place ahead of Herta, who earned kudos for being the highest placed Ford finisher. Bräck was equally happy, and somewhat philosophical, after claiming fifth.

"It was a pretty uneventful race for me really," said the Swede. "I tried to get a run on Bryan through Turn Eight early on and got into a real tank-slapper. I lost about one-and-a-half to two seconds, and the rest of the race was a bit of a fuel conservation run.

"Still, I feel pretty good about today. We lost to the two Penskes that are outstanding, one of the Green cars that are very good on the road courses and the 'King of Laguna' [Herta]. So that's not bad for my first time here."

Bräck's seventh top-five finish of his rookie campaign kept him well in the running for the FedEx Championship, only 16 points short of first place. Aside from him and de Ferran, however, the other main title contenders had days ranging from disappointing to miserable.

Erstwhile championship leader Michael Andretti, who suffered from a stomach bug all weekend, finished a fruitless 14th after a costly miscalculation on pit-stop strategy saw the Newman/Haas team opt not to stop during the mid-race full-course caution. The move gained Andretti considerable track position, moving him up to fourth at one stage, but subsequently

Herta returns in style

BRYAN Herta (above) and his Forsythe Championship Racing Team made a stunning return to action at Laguna Seca Raceway. After sitting out the first 14 races due to a falling-out with Swift Engineering, then a dispute with CART over franchise issues, team owner Jerry Forsythe decided to give Herta an opportunity to chase his third victory in as many years at the challenging Californian road course. Accordingly, Forsythe arranged for the loan of a Ford Cosworth-powered Reynard 2KI from the sister Player's/Forsythe organization.

The decision was made rather late, which meant there was time for only one brief shakedown test at Putnam Park, near Indianapolis, a week or so before the Honda Grand Prix of Monterey. Furthermore, Herta was denied the opportunity of qualifying on the first day by a fuel system glitch. The team – and Ford engineers – worked hard to find a cure, but to no avail. Herta didn't even complete a lap.

Remarkably, Herta bounced back on Saturday morning in sensational style, setting the fastest practice time at 1m 08.748s. The fact that he had failed to post a time on Friday meant that he would be consigned to the "slower" group on Saturday afternoon, but Herta refused to allow that to cloud his mind and turned in a magnificent effort that elevated him to fourth place on the grid. When no one else improved on their Friday times during the "faster" group of second-day qualifiers, a place on the second row of the grid was assured.

Herta's incredible record of qualifying on the front row on *every* visit to Laguna Seca, dating back through Formula Ford, Barber Saab and Indy Lights, was at an end, but he was still delighted with the result.

"I'm real pleased with where we are right now," said Herta. "We're way ahead of where I thought we'd be."

He ran better than expected on race day, too, maintaining his position as the fastest Ford contender and finishing in a fine fourth place.

"I'm really happy," he said. "It's a great sense of relief and satisfaction. In some ways, it was a risk coming here because I have such a good record [at Laguna Seca], and if we didn't perform to expectations, a lot of people would have been disappointed. With this finish, I think we exceeded expectations. Given the limited time we ran, the car was great."

he made his second stop under green-flag conditions and fell out of the points as a result.

Paul Tracy, who arrived in California placed second in the points, failed to take advantage of a fine strategic call by Team KOOL Green. Curiously, he struggled for pace all weekend, but after stopping for a splash and go right before the end of the caution, he worked his way back to ninth before misjudging his attempt to wrest a position from Oriol Servia in Turn Two on the very last lap. The miscue relegated him to 11th. Ironically, eighth place was Tracy's for the taking, as Servia ran out of fuel half a lap from home...

Moreno, of course, failed to score following his rare error, while his Patrick Racing teammate, Adrian Fernandez, struggled home in 12th with his oversteering Tecate/Quaker State Ford/Reynard.

Roger Penske's men, meanwhile, made the most of their day in the sun. Castroneves, by virtue of his maximum score (having added the bonus points for pole and most laps led), moved into contention for the championship for the first time, lying just 29 points shy of the new points leader – none other than de Ferran, who led the standings for the first time in his career. It was the first time atop the points table for Marlboro Team Penske since Tracy led the way at Toronto in 1997. Typically, however, de Ferran kept his feet firmly on the ground.

"It's fantastic to be leading, but our job is not finished," said de Ferran. "It's not time to be tapping ourselves on the back. Now we have to concentrate on the next few races and do as good a job if not better. I think we will have to win a race or even two before the season is over. So it's important we keep our heads down and not get too excited."

Jeremy Shaw

FEDEX CHAMPIONSHIP SERIES • ROUND 16

LAGUNA SECA SNIPPETS

- For the fifth straight year, Jimmy Vasser and Laguna Seca Raceway hosted a **CHARITY** golf tournament prior to the race weekend that raised over $150,000 to benefit the Monterey Bay Boys and Girls Club and the Greg Moore Foundation.

- **MERCEDES-BENZ** confirmed persistent paddock rumors on Saturday morning at Laguna Seca when it released a formal statement to the effect that it would cease its Champ Car involvement at the end of the season. "We have had to re-evaluate our motorsport strategy from 2001 onwards in order to meet higher targets in the Formula 1 World Championship, where eight manufacturers will be competing beginning in 2003," explained Jurgen Hubbert, the DaimlerChrysler board member responsible for all motorsports activities.

- Despite the fact that a year still remained on his contract, **MARK BLUNDELL** was informed by PacWest Racing Group owner Bruce McCaw prior to the race weekend that his services would not be required for the 2001 season.

- CART officials announced that the current breed of 2.65-litre turbocharged **ENGINES** would be required to run at reduced intake manifold (turbocharger) pressure for the 2001 and 2002 seasons prior to a new engine formula being introduced in 2003. The current boost limit of 40 inches would be lowered to 37 inches in 2001, and 34 inches in 2002. The change was expected to reduce power from around 900 hp to 775 hp.

- Marlboro Team Penske's Honda/Reynard 2KIs ran revised front **SUSPENSION** components at Laguna Seca following the failure that had sent Helio Castroneves spinning into the wall one week earlier in Vancouver. "Things like that shake the organization to the core," admitted technical director Nigel Beresford, "because we could have injured the drivers. We just made a mistake. In that situation, everyone just does whatever it takes and works around the clock to replace everything. Literally, within 12 hours of the accident, we'd redesigned the part and we were cutting metal [to build replacements]."

- Notwithstanding a miserable streak of misfortune, which culminated in a terrifying accident during practice on Friday, Patrick Carpentier maintained his keen **SENSE OF HUMOR** following an inspired drive that saw him rise impressively from 18th place on the grid to ninth at the finish line. "It was a pretty good race, but I'm also very happy to end the day with four wheels on the ground and the sun shining on top of the car, not on the undertray," quipped the amiable French-Canadian.

- Gil de Ferran became the fourth different driver to take the lead in the CART FedEx Championship Series **POINT STANDINGS** during the 2000 season when he slipped ahead of erstwhile pace-setter Michael Andretti by virtue of his second-place finish.

FEDEX CHAMPIONSHIP SERIES • ROUND 16
HONDA GRAND PRIX OF MONTEREY FEATURING THE SHELL 300

LAGUNA SECA RACEWAY, MONTEREY, CALIFORNIA

SEPTEMBER 10, 83 laps of 2.238 miles – 185.754 miles

Place	Driver (Nat.)	No.	Team Sponsors Engine/Car	Tires	Q Speed	Q Time	Q Pos.	Laps	Time/Status	Ave. (mph)	Pts.
1	Helio Castroneves (BR)	3	Marlboro Team Penske Marlboro Honda/Reynard 2KI	FS	118.969	1m 07.722s	1	83	1h 46m 11.800s	104.949	22
2	Gil de Ferran (BR)	2	Marlboro Team Penske Marlboro Honda/Reynard 2KI	FS	118.792	1m 07.823s	2	83	1h 46m 12.754s	104.933	16
3	Dario Franchitti (GB)	27	Team KOOL Green Honda/Reynard 2KI	FS	118.225	1m 08.148s	3	83	1h 46m 14.442s	104.906	14
4	Bryan Herta (USA)	77	Forsythe Championship Racing Ford Cosworth/Reynard 2KI	FS	117.995	1m 08.281s	4	83	1h 46m 16.219s	104.876	12
5	*Kenny Bräck (S)	8	Team Rahal Shell Ford Cosworth/Reynard 2KI	FS	117.542	1m 08.544s	6	83	1h 46m 16.958s	104.864	10
6	Juan Montoya (COL)	1	Target/Chip Ganassi Racing Toyota/Lola B2K/00	FS	117.542	1m 08.544s	5	83	1h 46m 19.101s	104.829	8
7	Mauricio Gugelmin (BR)	17	PacWest Racing Nextel Mercedes/Reynard 2KI	FS	117.432	1m 08.608s	7	83	1h 46m 26.614s	104.706	6
8	Jimmy Vasser (USA)	12	Target/Chip Ganassi Racing Toyota/Lola B2K/00	FS	117.374	1m 08.642s	9	83	1h 46m 32.697s	104.606	5
9	Patrick Carpentier (CDN)	32	Forsythe Racing Player's/Indeck Ford Cosworth/Reynard 2KI	FS	116.009	1m 09.450s	18	83	1h 46m 33.409s	104.594	4
10	Christian Fittipaldi (BR)	11	Newman/Haas Big Kmart/Route 66 Ford Cosworth/Lola B2K/00	FS	117.400	1m 08.627s	8	83	1h 46m 34.092s	104.583	3
11	Paul Tracy (CDN)	26	Team KOOL Green Honda/Reynard 2KI	FS	116.938	1m 08.898s	13	83	1h 46m 35.022s	104.568	2
12	Adrian Fernandez (MEX)	40	Patrick Racing Tecate/Quaker State Ford Cosworth/Reynard 2KI	FS	116.069	1m 09.414s	17	83	1h 46m 35.304s	104.563	1
13	Mark Blundell (GB)	18	PacWest Racing Motorola Mercedes/Reynard 2KI	FS	115.695	1m 09.638s	21	83	1h 46m 37.112s	104.534	
14	Michael Andretti (USA)	6	Newman/Haas Big Kmart/Texaco Ford Cosworth/Lola B2K/00	FS	117.074	1m 08.818s	11	83	1h 46m 37.981s	104.520	
15	Cristiano da Matta (BR)	97	PPI Motorsports Pioneer/WorldCom Toyota/Reynard 2KI	FS	116.225	1m 09.321s	15	83	1h 46m 38.474s	104.512	
16	Max Papis (I)	7	Team Rahal Miller Lite Ford Cosworth/Reynard 2KI	FS	116.836	1m 08.958s	14	83	1h 46m 56.651s	104.214	
17	*Oriol Servia (E)	96	PPI Motorsports Telefonica Toyota/Reynard 2KI	FS	117.105	1m 08.800s	10	82	Out of fuel		
18	Tarso Marques (BR)	34	Dale Coyne Racing Panasonic Ford Cosworth/Swift 011.c	FS	114.797	1m 10.183s	23	82	Running		
19	Memo Gidley (USA)	10	Della Penna Motorsports DirecTV Toyota/Reynard 2KI	FS	113.686	1m 10.869s	26	82	Running		
20	Luiz Garcia Jr. (BR)	25	Arciero-PRG Hollywood/Embratel-21 Mercedes/Reynard 2KI	FS	114.111	1m 10.605s	25	81	Out of fuel		
21	Alex Barron (USA)	19	Dale Coyne Racing *Sports Today* Ford Cosworth/Lola B2K/00	FS	114.764	1m 10.203s	24	81	Running		
22	Tony Kanaan (BR)	55	Mo Nunn Racing Hollywood Mercedes/Reynard 2KI	FS	117.008	1m 08.857s	12	69	Clutch/brakes		
23	*Alexandre Tagliani (CDN)	33	Forsythe Racing Player's/Indeck Ford Cosworth/Reynard 2KI	FS	116.104	1m 09.393s	16	55	Electrical		
24	Michel Jourdain Jr. (MEX)	16	Bettenhausen Motorsports Herdez Mercedes/Lola B2K/00	FS	115.862	1m 09.538s	20	46	Accident		
25	Roberto Moreno (BR)	20	Patrick Racing Visteon Ford Cosworth/Reynard 2KI	FS	115.863	1m 09.537s	19	45	Accident		
26	*Shinji Nakano (J)	5	Walker Racing Avex Honda/Reynard 2KI	FS	114.828	1m 10.164s	22	45	Turbo wastegate		

* denotes rookie driver

Caution flags: Laps 47–53, accident/Moreno, Tagliani & Jourdain. **Total:** One for 7 laps.
Lap leaders: Helio Castroneves, 1–27 (27 laps); Juan Montoya, 28–29 (2 laps); Castroneves, 30–83 (54 laps). **Totals:** Castroneves, 81 laps; Montoya, 2 laps.
Fastest race lap: Gil de Ferran, 1m 11.034s, 113.422 mph on lap 25.

Championship positions: **1** de Ferran, 132; **2** Andretti, 126; **3** Tracy, 122; **4** Fernandez, 118; **5** Bräck, 116; **6** Moreno, 115; **7** Castroneves, 103; **8** Franchitti, 92; **9** Vasser, 91; **10** da Matta, 88; **11** Montoya, 85; **12** Papis, 79; **13** Carpentier, 75; **14** Fittipaldi, 67; **15** Servia, 46; **16** Tagliani, 45; **17** Gugelmin, 36; **18** Herta, 26; **19** Gidley, 20; **20** Blundell & Kanaan, 16; **22** Jourdain, 10; **23** Nakano, 7; **24** Marques & Garcia, 5; **26** Fontana, 2; **27** Kurosawa, 1.

FEDEX CHAMPIONSHIP SERIES • ROUND 17

Left: After his third win of the season, Juan Montoya is joined on the podium by Patrick Carpentier *(left)*, who equaled his career best, and Roberto Moreno.

Overleaf: Target/Ganassi teammates Juan Montoya and Jimmy Vasser lead the KOOL pair, Dario Franchitti and Paul Tracy, at the start of the Motorola 300.
Darrell Ingham/Allsport USA

JUAN Montoya started on the pole at Gateway International Raceway and ultimately scored his third win of the season. But the defending series champion was eclipsed throughout much of an exciting Motorola 300 by Michael Andretti, who qualified a disappointing 15th, then rapidly worked his way to the front. Andretti had lapped everyone bar the Colombian when the engine in his Big Kmart/Texaco Ford Cosworth/Lola failed abruptly with only 50 miles remaining.

Montoya took full advantage as he stroked Target/Chip Ganassi Racing's Toyota/Lola to the checkered flag well clear of Patrick Carpentier's Player's Ford/Reynard. Montoya's tenth victory of his Champ Car career came at a record average speed of 155.519 mph in a race that was slowed only briefly by one full-course caution.

"I don't know how many races I've lost this year for different reasons, so it's nice to have someone else give me one," said Montoya with a wry smile.

Carpentier drove impressively, having regained the lead lap during the closing stages, to equal his career-best finish. Roberto Moreno, also equipped with a Ford-powered Reynard, took a strong third aboard Patrick Racing's Visteon entry.

Montoya and his Target teammate, Jimmy Vasser, took off into the lead at the start of the 236-lap race, having qualified alongside each other on the front row of the grid. The two Team KOOL Green Honda/Reynards of Dario Franchitti and Paul Tracy led the chase at the end of lap one, having already exchanged positions, while Carpentier followed in fifth until being passed by Tony Kanaan's Hollywood Mercedes/Reynard on lap two.

Montoya quickly stretched out a slight lead in the opening stages, then was content to settle into a comfortable rhythm, circulating the 1.27-mile oval in the high 27-second range. Soon, though, his Lola began to lose its balance, and as he coped with increasing oversteer, Vasser was able to inch closer.

The American's first few attempts to pass his teammate were rebuffed. Finally, he found a way through on lap 29, but was unable to put any significant distance between himself and his pursuer. Indeed, only a dozen laps later, Montoya returned the favor, taking advantage of some slower traffic and driving boldly around the outside of Vasser between Turns Three and Four.

Franchitti and Tracy also exchanged places a couple of times in the early stages, whereupon Franchitti, like Montoya, suffered from a severe loose condition and elected to make a pit stop after only 32 laps. The Scotsman rejoined a lap in arrears, only to be forced out by a gearbox failure.

Tracy, meanwhile, kept the pressure on the Target cars until he became embroiled in a close tussle with Carpentier, which allowed the two leaders to extend their advantage. Kanaan, too, ran well until being blocked inadvertently by a slower car on lap 34, which cost him valuable momentum and caused him to slip from fourth to tenth in the space of just three laps.

Vasser and Montoya continued to trade the lead prior to the first round of pit stops, which began when Helio Castroneves (Marlboro Honda/Reynard), Cristiano da Matta (Pioneer Toyota/Reynard) and Kanaan relinquished ninth, tenth and 11th places on lap 59. Gil de Ferran, in the second Marlboro car, had elevated himself from 14th to sixth before making his first pit visit on lap 60. Andretti, too, had made excellent progress, rising from 15th to fifth by lap 51. The 1991 CART champion made his first pit stop after 61 laps.

Vasser pulled into pit lane one lap later, while Adrian Fernandez (Tecate/Quaker State Ford/Reynard) and Kenny Bräck (Shell Ford/Reynard) displayed their customary fuel efficiency by stopping on laps 64 and 65 respectively. Most frugal of all, though, were Montoya and Carpentier, who stayed out until lap 66 before taking on service for the first time. The strategy didn't really work in Montoya's favor. He retained the lead, but Andretti already had a good head of steam after his earlier pit stop and pounced effortlessly around the outside as Montoya headed into Turn Three on cold tires.

Andretti proceeded to drive away in the lead, stretching his advantage to almost four seconds inside just ten laps. By lap 91, the gap had grown to 7.7 seconds.

"The car was working really good, but it got very loose late in the runs," said Montoya, who lost second place to Tracy on lap 121.

Montoya regained the point when Andretti and Tracy made their second pit stops after 123 laps. Montoya's team, curiously, kept their man out for another seven laps before calling him in for fuel and fresh tires. By the time he resumed, Montoya was back in third place, almost six seconds adrift of Tracy and a further 11 seconds behind runaway leader Andretti. A front wing adjustment provided the desired effect, however, and Montoya quickly narrowed the gap between himself and Tracy before retaking second place on lap 161.

Everyone else already was a lap down to the flying Andretti. Not that the battles going on behind the three leaders were any less intense. In fact, da Matta had moved up to fourth, chased by Castroneves and da Matta's PPI Motorsports teammate, Oriol Servia (Telefonica Toyota/Reynard), who had moved impressively and unobtrusively to sixth. Next were de Ferran, Max Papis (Miller Lite Ford/Reynard), Patrick Racing teammates Moreno and Fernandez, then Carpentier and Vasser, both of whom stretched their fuel load as long as they could before making their second visits to pit lane.

Tracy was lapped by Andretti on lap 167. Sixteen laps later, Andretti made

QUALIFYING

Max Papis and Cristiano da Matta were the two pace-setters following the conclusion of practice for the Motorola 300 on Saturday morning, but neither could offer any real opposition to Juan Montoya in the traditional single-car qualifying session.

After posting the third-fastest lap in practice, Montoya *(above)* benefited from a substantial improvement by his Target/Chip Ganassi Racing teammate, Jimmy Vasser, who, running 14th in the usual inverted order due to an electronic glitch in practice, posted a lap some three-tenths better than his previous best. None of the next nine qualifiers was able to eclipse Vasser's best, and Montoya himself, the acknowledged master of qualifying, only managed to do so by a slim 0.015-second margin.

"The car had a lot of understeer [in practice]," related Montoya. "We did some changes before qualifying and the car was a lot better. I had to lift quite a bit in Turn Three, but I was still able to put in a good speed and get the pole, so it's good."

Vasser was content after securing his first front-row starting position since round two at Long Beach in the second Target Toyota/Lola. Paul Tracy, only 15th quickest in practice, also posted a dramatic improvement, moving to third on the grid, just ahead of the similar Team KOOL Green Honda/Reynard of Dario Franchitti.

Patrick Carpentier was fastest of the Ford-powered cars, fifth in Jerry Forsythe's Player's/Indeck Reynard, followed by the quickest of the Mercedes runners, Tony Kanaan, in Morris Nunn's Hollywood-backed Reynard.

Da Matta reported that his car went loose in Turn Three, restricting the Pioneer/WorldCom Toyota/Reynard to tenth on the starting grid behind Adrian Fernandez (Tecate/Quaker State Ford/Reynard), Alex Tagliani (Player's Ford/Reynard) and Helio Castroneves (Marlboro Honda/Reynard). A bitterly disappointed Papis found himself way back in 14th.

"When I had my warmup laps, I thought I was going to have a good lap," related the Italian, "but I just had a very big push in the turns. I had to get off the throttle twice in the corners. The car just pushed and pushed toward the wall."

Adieu Gateway

A MONTH or so prior to the Motorola 300, Championship Auto Racing Teams officials confirmed that the FedEx Championship Series would not return to Gateway International Raceway for the 2001 season. Disappointing crowd figures were cited as one of the reasons for the elimination of the Gateway event. Thus, after only four events, the 1.27-mile oval, situated in Madison, Illinois, just across the Mississippi River from St. Louis, Missouri, would be consigned to the Champ Car history books.

Two of the first three events had been dogged by inclement weather, including a massive storm in 1998, which caused qualifying to be canceled. This time around, ironically, the race was run in spectacularly pleasant fall conditions. Unfortunately, with the National Football League Super Bowl champions St. Louis Rams playing their arch rivals, the San Francisco 49ers, and the Major League Baseball Cardinals hosting the Chicago Cubs, both within five miles of the race track and with a combined attendance estimated at 110,000 – not to mention the first weekend of the Sydney Summer Olympics on the television – the Motorola 300 was up against some pretty stiff competition for sports fans. Although some predicted a crowd of less than 15,000, seasoned observers rated the turnout in the 25–30,000 range.

At least Gateway's four races did produce one memorable statistic: four different drivers, engine manufacturers and chassis shared the spoils of victory. A Mercedes/Penske emerged triumphant in the first visit to Madison in 1997, when Paul Tracy scored Roger Penske's 99th Champ Car success on Memorial Day weekend. One year later, Alex Zanardi scored a fine win in Target/Chip Ganassi Racing's Honda/Reynard. In '99, it was the turn of Michael Andretti, who scored a notable victory from behind aboard Newman/Haas Racing's Ford Cosworth-powered Swift chassis. Finally, Juan Montoya completed the remarkable sequence by taking the win in Ganassi's Toyota/Lola.

169

FEDEX CHAMPIONSHIP SERIES • ROUND 17

Misfortune for Andretti

MICHAEL Andretti gave no indication of what was to come in the race when he qualified a lowly 15th in Newman/Haas Racing's Big Kmart/Texaco Havoline Ford Cosworth/Lola B2K/00. The grid position equaled his worst of the season (in fact, he was 15th also at Rio, Nazareth and Chicago).

"We are making life difficult for ourselves by not qualifying well," noted Andretti, who was seeking a second successive victory at Gateway International Raceway to regain some momentum in his quest for the FedEx Championship. "We won from 11th place last year, but this is obviously going to be a little more challenging."

"We had too much push in the qualifying setup, but the car is good in race trim," he continued. "We have been working on that and the car feels OK. We stumbled onto something this morning [in practice] that should be good for the race [setup], so that keeps us optimistic."

Sure enough, Andretti began his forward march soon after the green flag, making up two places on the opening lap, then passing both Helio Castroneves and Roberto Moreno inside the next two laps. Alex Tagliani was a tougher nut to crack, but once past the French-Canadian on lap 36, Andretti continued to make progress and was up to fifth on lap 51.

Andretti continued to charge in the wake of an excellent first pit stop, passing Juan Montoya for the lead soon after the Colombian emerged from pit lane. He never looked back. Sadly, a brilliant performance was concluded 40 laps too soon by an engine failure.

"The guys did a great job today," praised Andretti. "It would have been a real treat for them to win this one after a bad stint [in which he had earned only six points from the previous four races], but I guess we're snake-bitten right now."

The only good news for Andretti was that neither of his main title rivals, Paul Tracy and Gil de Ferran, scored well. Still, he noted, "A win would have put us in the lead [of the championship], and that hurts."

Below: Patrick Carpentier is hounded by Tony Kanaan during the very early stages.

his third and final pit stop. Everything was going according to plan.

Just three laps later, however, an ominous wisp of smoke showed at the rear of Andretti's Lola. Almost immediately, he radioed to his crew to say he was losing power. An exhaust header had broken. Andretti was advised to stay out on the track, but it came as no great surprise when his engine blew just prior to the completion of lap 196.

"We were just one car shy of lapping the entire field, and that would have been a great boost for the team," said a distraught Andretti. "It's a huge, huge, huge loss because of the championship. This one is right up there as one of biggest losses of my career because of the championship."

Indeed, a victory would have moved him back atop the standings. Similarly, Tracy was unfortunate when his hopes of reclaiming the series points lead evaporated after a gearbox problem caused him to slide up into the Turn Four wall on lap 207.

"When I downshifted going into the turn, the gearbox started locking up, and I slid into the gray and brushed the wall," explained Tracy, who was forced out of the race by a bent lower wishbone in the right rear suspension. "I really feel bad for Team KOOL Green because we had a really good car and we were hanging around the top three all day."

The incident brought out the caution flags for the first and only time. Montoya was a lap clear of the entire field at the restart, although Carpentier had emerged in second place, thanks to his team's strategy, which required only a relatively brief splash of fuel when he made his final pit stop on lap 200. Moreno ran in third ahead of da Matta, Servia, Papis, and Vasser, followed by de Ferran and Castroneves in the two Marlboro cars.

Carpentier charged past Montoya at the restart, but the race leader remained cool.

"I knew Patrick was a lap behind me," related Montoya. "I saw him coming up so fast and thought it would be really silly to stuff the car into the wall."

"I had a little too much push in the middle of the race, but we just cracked on a bit of front wing and the car was neutral. It was fast, fast, fast," confirmed Carpentier, who proceeded to set a series of rapid laps. "I was trying as hard as I could in case [Montoya] had a problem or made a mistake, but it was pretty impossible."

The Canadian was content with a second-place finish. Moreno was equally delighted with third, ending a sequence of disappointing results that had seen him score only 25 points from the previous seven races. Moreno's fifth podium appearance vaulted him to second place in the championship reckoning with three races remaining.

Da Matta and Servia ensured a successful day for Cal Wells' PPI Motorsports team, claiming fourth and fifth ahead of Papis, who was charging along in the closing stages, but wasn't able to find a way past the two Toyota-powered cars. Vasser was frustrated to finish seventh after running so well in the early stages, while de Ferran, Castroneves, Fernandez and Bräck also were in close contention at the end of a very entertaining race.

Jeremy Shaw

Robert Laberge/Allsport USA

FEDEX CHAMPIONSHIP SERIES • ROUND 17

GATEWAY SNIPPETS

- **JIMMY VASSER** experienced more frustration in the race when, after falling from first to fourth following his first pit stop, he spent a large portion of his second stint in the wheel tracks of Alex Tagliani's lapped Ford/Reynard. Eventually, Vasser finished an unrepresentative seventh after another tardy pit stop.

- There was good news and bad news for **FORD COSWORTH**. First, the bad news. Michael Andretti's brilliant drive was for naught when his XF engine failed. The good news was that the Honda-powered cars had a disappointing day. Both Team KOOL Green cars failed to finish, while the Marlboro Penske entries trailed home in eighth and ninth places. Thus, only one week after relinquishing its lead in the CART Manufacturer's Championship, Ford regained the advantage from Honda by a score of 285 to 274.

- **QUOTE** of the weekend came from Juan Montoya after ESPN pit reporter Gary Gerould reflected on the Colombian's spin into the wall at Turn Two during practice on Friday and asked whether he was ever scared in the face of an impending accident. "You don't get scared when you hit the wall," responded Montoya. "You get scared when the car is pointing in the wrong direction!"

Jon Ferrey/Allsport USA

- Roberto Moreno was thoroughly **ELATED** after finishing third. "I had a terrible warmup," he said, grinning broadly. "I did two laps and came in [to the pits] and said, 'I can't drive it!' So afterwards, we sat down, talked about it and went back to how the car was on Friday, and it worked. The car handled really well and was quite fast. Plus, Jim McGee did a great strategy again. It's fantastic! The team put me up front and kept me there. It's just a great day."

- **ORIOL SERVIA** (below) earned his second-best finish of the season when he brought PPI Motorsports' Telefonica Toyota/Reynard home in fifth place right behind teammate Cristiano da Matta. Servia's performance was all the more meritorious for the fact that he had been obliged to start the race in his backup car, which had not turned a wheel previously during the weekend, following the discovery of a substantial fuel leak after the warmup practice session on race morning.

- Memo Gidley and Luiz Garcia Jr. also were forced to start in their **BACKUP CARS** following a collision in the final minute of the morning warmup. Both Gidley's DirecTV/Della Penna Motorsports Toyota/Reynard and Garcia's Hollywood/Arciero-Project Racing Group Mercedes/Reynard were damaged badly. Unlike Servia and PPI, however, their races did not have happy endings. Garcia lasted only seven laps before his engine failed, while Gidley completed 76 laps before abandoning his mount due to handling difficulties.

- In the knowledge that Juan Montoya would be switching to Formula 1 for the 2001 season, and Jimmy Vasser already had been told to seek alternative employment, Chip Ganassi confirmed that he was due to test four prospective **REPLACEMENTS** – Formula 3000 front-runners Bruno Junqueira and Nicolas Minassian, Indy Lights star Casey Mears and Toyota Atlantic series leader Buddy Rice – at Firebird Raceway in Arizona during the week immediately following the race at Gateway.

FEDEX CHAMPIONSHIP SERIES • ROUND 17
MOTOROLA 300

GATEWAY INTERNATIONAL RACEWAY, MADISON, ILLINOIS

SEPTEMBER 17, 236 laps of 1.27 miles – 299.72 miles

Place	Driver (Nat.)	No.	Team Sponsors Engine/Car	Tires	Q Speed	Q Time	Q Pos	Laps	Time/Status	Ave. (mph)	Pts.
1	Juan Montoya (COL)	1	Target/Chip Ganassi Racing Toyota/Lola B2K/00	FS	180.334	25.353s	1	236	1h 55m 38.003s	155.519	21
2	Patrick Carpentier (CDN)	32	Forsythe Racing Player's/Indeck Ford Cosworth/Reynard 2KI	FS	179.182	25.516s	5	236	1h 55m 49.807s	155.255	16
3	Roberto Moreno (BR)	20	Patrick Racing Visteon Ford Cosworth/Reynard 2KI	FS	177.498	25.758s	11	235	Running		14
4	Cristiano da Matta (BR)	97	PPI Motorsports Pioneer/WorldCom Toyota/Reynard 2KI	FS	178.044	25.679s	10	235	Running		12
5	*Oriol Servia (E)	96	PPI Motorsports Telefonica Toyota/Reynard 2KI	FS	175.347	26.074s	18	235	Running		10
6	Max Papis (I)	7	Team Rahal Miller Lite Ford Cosworth/Reynard 2KI	FS	176.634	25.884s	14	235	Running		8
7	Jimmy Vasser (USA)	12	Target/Chip Ganassi Racing Toyota/Lola B2K/00	FS	180.227	25.368s	2	235	Running		6
8	Gil de Ferran (BR)	2	Marlboro Team Penske Marlboro Honda/Reynard 2KI	FS	177.099	25.816s	13	235	Running		5
9	Helio Castroneves (BR)	3	Marlboro Team Penske Marlboro Honda/Reynard 2KI	FS	178.100	25.671s	9	235	Running		4
10	Adrian Fernandez (MEX)	40	Patrick Racing Tecate/Quaker State Ford Cosworth/Reynard 2KI	FS	178.782	25.573s	7	235	Running		3
11	*Kenny Bräck (S)	8	Team Rahal Shell Ford Cosworth/Reynard 2KI	FS	177.216	25.799s	12	235	Running		2
12	Christian Fittipaldi (BR)	11	Newman/Haas Big Kmart/Route 66 Ford Cosworth/Lola B2K/00	FS	175.785	26.009s	17	235	Running		1
13	Tony Kanaan (BR)	55	Mo Nunn Racing Hollywood Mercedes/Reynard 2KI	FS	178.866	25.561s	6	234	Running		
14	*Alexandre Tagliani (CDN)	33	Forsythe Racing Player's/Indeck Ford Cosworth/Reynard 2KI	FS	178.301	25.642s	8	233	Running		
15	Tarso Marques (BR)	34	Dale Coyne Racing Panasonic Ford Cosworth/Swift 011.c	FS	170.788	26.770s	23	231	Running		
16	Michel Jourdain Jr. (MEX)	16	Bettenhausen Motorsports Herdez Mercedes/Lola B2K/00	FS	173.333	26.377s	21	231	Running		
17	Alex Barron (USA)	19	Dale Coyne Racing *Sports Today* Ford Cosworth/Lola B2K/00	FS	176.233	25.943s	16	222	Running		
18	Paul Tracy (CDN)	26	Team KOOL Green Honda/Reynard 2KI	FS	179.294	25.500s	3	212	Accident		
19	Mauricio Gugelmin (BR)	17	PacWest Racing Nextel Mercedes/Reynard 2KI	FS	no speed	no time	24	198	Engine		
20	Michael Andretti (USA)	6	Newman/Haas Big Kmart/Texaco Ford Cosworth/Lola B2K/00	FS	176.307	25.932s	15	196	Engine		1
21	*Shinji Nakano (J)	5	Walker Racing Avex Group Honda/Reynard 2KI	FS	171.828	26.608s	22	78	Handling		
22	Memo Gidley (USA)	10	Della Penna Motorsports DirecTV Toyota/Reynard 2KI	FS	174.864	26.146s	19	76	Handling		
23	Mark Blundell (GB)	18	PacWest Racing Motorola Mercedes/Reynard 2KI	FS	174.811	26.154s	20	64	Engine		
24	Dario Franchitti (GB)	27	Team KOOL Green Honda/Reynard 2KI	FS	179.196	25.514s	4	62	Gearbox		
25	Luiz Garcia Jr. (BR)	25	Arciero-PRG Hollywood/Embratel-21 Mercedes/Reynard 2KI	FS	no speed	no time	25	7	Engine		

* denotes rookie driver

Caution flags: Laps 209-213, accident/Tracy. **Total:** One for 5 laps.

Lap leaders: Juan Montoya, 1-28 (28 laps); Jimmy Vasser, 29-41 (13 laps); Montoya, 42-47 (6 laps); Vasser, 48-61 (14 laps); Montoya, 62-66 (5 laps); Michael Andretti, 67-123 (57 laps); Montoya, 124-130 (7 laps); Patrick Carpentier, 131-132 (2 laps); Andretti, 133-196 (64 laps); Carpentier, 197-199 (3 laps); Montoya, 200-236 (37 laps). **Totals:** Andretti, 121 laps; Montoya, 83 laps; Vasser, 27 laps; Carpentier, 5 laps.

Fastest race lap: Patrick Carpentier, 26.770s, 170.788 mph on lap 218.

Championship positions: 1 de Ferran, 137; **2** Moreno, 129; **3** Andretti, 127; **4** Tracy, 122; **5** Fernandez, 121; **6** Bräck, 118; **7** Castroneves, 107; **8** Montoya, 106; **9** da Matta, 100; **10** Vasser, 97; **11** Franchitti, 92; **12** Carpentier, 91; **13** Papis, 87; **14** Fittipaldi, 68; **15** Servia, 56; **16** Tagliani, 45; **17** Gugelmin, 36; **18** Herta, 26; **19** Gidley, 20; **20** Blundell & Kanaan, 16; **22** Jourdain, 10; **23** Nakano, 7; **24** Marques & Garcia, 5; **26** Fontana, 2; **27** Kurosawa, 1.

HOUSTON

1 – VASSER
2 – MONTOYA
3 – DE FERRAN

FEDEX CHAMPIONSHIP SERIES • ROUND 18

FEDEX CHAMPIONSHIP SERIES • ROUND 18

QUALIFYING

Gil de Ferran took another step toward the 2000 CART FedEx Championship by claiming the Houston pole in one of his first laps of final qualifying. The Brazilian laid down a quick lap of 58.757 seconds in the Marlboro Team Penske Honda/Reynard, then spent the rest of his session in a vain attempt to better the time.

But while he could not go any faster, neither could the remainder of the field. The Brazilian duly gained his fourth pole of the season ahead of Dario Franchitti and Jimmy Vasser.

"It was a pretty exciting qualifying session," said de Ferran. "I managed to get one clear lap on my first set of tires. With one lap in the bank, I could push harder. The car was not that bad, so I waited until the final ten minutes when the track conditions would be at their best.

"I tried hard on my second set of tires, but I never quite managed to equal my best time. On my best lap I encountered traffic with Patrick [Carpentier] and that was it for my tires. Then it was just a matter of waiting...and it turned out OK."

Franchitti's run for the top spot was hampered by having to serve an eight-minute penalty for bringing out a red flag in the closing moments of Friday's qualifying session. To make matters worse, he found his KOOL Honda/Reynard was not quite as sharp as it had been when he took the provisional pole at 59.434 seconds.

"We knew we were limited in our time," said Franchitti. "Actually we spent most of our time trying to get out of traffic so we could get a clear lap. On the first set of tires, we had a bit of understeer; the second set was better, but the car was not that great. I was driving over the limit and dragging the car around for a lap or two to get a time."

Vasser showed the depth of the Target/Ganassi team by putting an untested backup car on the second row after burying his primary car in the Turn One tire wall on his first hot lap of qualifying. He ran back to his pits – at the head of pit lane – where the 12X Toyota/Lola was waiting, and stuck it into third place on the grid, just a tick behind Franchitti.

Helio Castroneves was a scant 0.002 second behind Vasser after also serving an eight-minute penalty, while Michael Andretti jumped from tenth on Friday's run to fifth.

Vasser back in the saddle

JIMMY Vasser went out on the Houston streets with a renewed sense of purpose as his 2001 job hunt began, but his victory was one part determination, one part veteran savvy, and a final part of long-overdue good fortune.

Vasser had often been as fast as his celebrated teammate, Juan Montoya, during the season, but on more than one occasion, when the team employed two different pit strategies, it tended to work, not intentionally, to his detriment. Take Indianapolis, for example, where the strategy left Vasser out of contention while Montoya went on to win. A one-stop strategy in Houston, however, paid off with a ride to Victory Lane.

The win came at a most opportune time, increasing interest in the 1996 CART champion only weeks after he had been told that his services would not be required at Target/Chip Ganassi Racing in 2001. But that wasn't all that was on his mind.

"My friend Alex [Zanardi] gets on at me every time I don't win a race, so this one's for Alex," noted a delighted Vasser.

As it turns out, the win wasn't the only thing that would be for Vasser's former Ganassi teammate.

"Alex Zanardi gave me his helmet from his final CART win at Surfers Paradise, then I gave my helmet from my last win – our last race together – at Fontana in 1998 to Bobby Rahal because it was the last race of his career," Vasser recalled. "I didn't realize that Alex really wanted that helmet. He keeps calling me about it, but I'm sure Bobby doesn't want to give it up. Lately I've been thinking I might never be able to give [Alex] another one. So my mind was wandering on the final few laps. I know Alex does commentary on the CART races for Italian television, so I have to confess I was thinking about him on the final couple of laps."

Left: Jimmy Vasser towered over the opposition en route to a deserved victory.
Jon Ferrey/Allsport USA

Below far left: Juan Montoya had to settle for second best behind his teammate.
Robert Laberge/Allsport USA

Below left: Jimmy Vasser celebrates his long overdue success in cowboy country.
Robert Laberge/Allsport USA

THE most successful teams in the last ten years of CART competition waged an old-fashioned Texas Shootout at the Texaco/Havoline Grand Prix of Houston, as the event was all about Marlboro Team Penske and Target/Chip Ganassi Racing. The recent rulers of the division fought an epic duel that, effectively, was settled by fuel strategy and full-course cautions.

Penske's Gil de Ferran led most of the race after starting from the pole aboard his Marlboro Honda/Reynard. However, at the end of a mainly processional, but nonetheless interesting, 100-lap battle, it was Target/Ganassi's Jimmy Vasser who emerged with a long overdue and hugely popular victory after a weekend of inspired effort in his Toyota/Lola. The win was Toyota's fifth triumph of the season and its first on a road or street circuit.

"I've gone about a year-and-a-half [without a win], since the end of '98 [at Fontana]," noted a delighted Vasser. "We've been in position to win a couple, but we haven't managed to pull it off."

After a year of questionable luck, Vasser was the beneficiary of a timely caution flag on lap 74, which threw the Penske strategy of running away from the field out the window. De Ferran had been consuming fuel at a prodigious rate in building a 16.5-second lead over Vasser, figuring that everyone would have to stop a second time for fuel.

"That yellow came a couple of laps too soon for me," lamented de Ferran. "It's always a gamble when you do that [strategy], because if you catch a yellow early, there's a risk it won't work out for you. That's what happened for us today."

The gap was wide and becoming wider when the yellows flew, waving as an excellent effort by Tarso Marques ended with a driveline failure, leaving his Panasonic Ford/Swift stranded on the exit of Turn One.

De Ferran quickly ducked into the pits when the yellow flags came out, but by the time he had taken on the required amount of methanol, the Ganassi machines of Vasser and Montoya – which had been running lean and did not need to pit – flashed by and left him in third place. But at that stage the situation did not appear too bleak for de Ferran, as the Target cars still needed to run a lean fuel mixture, compromising horsepower, to reach the finish. The Brazilian pole-sitter, though, could run flat out and, with 20-odd laps remaining, seemed to be in good shape.

But fate smiled on the Ganassi camp when, almost immediately after the restart, there was a huge melee in Turn Seven, triggered when Alex Tagliani (Player's Ford/Reynard) punted Michael Andretti's Big Kmart/Texaco Ford/Lola from behind. Both cars spun into the tire barriers, causing a chain reaction accident that involved Oriol Servia, Kenny Bräck, Shinji Nakano and the lapped Cristiano da Matta.

"Honestly, Michael got a lot of wheelspin coming off of Turn Six," explained Tagliani. "I made a move to pass him at Turn Seven, then decided not to pass. I don't know why, but I didn't stop as good as he did. I was on the marbles maybe and I hit a bump in the road, and I kept on braking, braking, braking and thinking, 'Come on Michael, step on the throttle.' And then my nose touched his rear wheel and spun him around.

"It was a stupid accident. I was not making a move to pass. I made a move, then decided not to pass. It was a move to put pressure on him, and unfortunately it really hurt his place in the championship. I feel very bad. You know, Michael has a strange reputation as a guy who blocks in qualifying, but on Saturday, I tell you, he was the one guy who I had no trouble with. He could have blocked me easily and, me being a rookie, nobody would have listened much to my complaints, but every time I was behind him, he gave me room."

Andretti was philosophical about the shunt.

"What can I say," he shrugged. "I was turning into the corner and BOOM! He drove right into the back of me. He probably hit that bump and locked his brakes and drove into me.

"This definitely hurt us in the championship. The front-runners will need to run into some trouble in the last two races. I'm not going to make any predictions on our chances in the last two races at this point. At some point, though, our luck has to turnaround."

The benefits of the caution were two-fold for the Ganassi cars. First, the lengthy clean-up from the crash meant that they could meander at a leisurely pace behind the pace car, saving precious fuel. Second, de Ferran's tires picked up some excess rubber from the track and, once the green flag flew, he was unable to maintain the same pace as before.

"In the middle of the race, my car was very, very good and I was happy with the machine at that point," related de Ferran. "But that second yellow was long enough to give everybody a little bit of a cushion on the fuel

FEDEX CHAMPIONSHIP SERIES • ROUND 18

Marques shines in the Swift

TARSO Marques started 11th in the Ford-powered Panasonic Swift and rose as high as seventh, highlighting that climb with a bold outbraking maneuver to relieve Alexandre Tagliani of eighth place on lap 42. The run ended 28 circuits early when the transmission gave up on lap 72, but the likeable Brazilian was suitably encouraged by his performance.

"The car was really good during the race, especially after the pit stop," reported Marques. "Unfortunately, we lost the transmission, although I don't exactly know why. It's a shame because the car was really fast, and I passed a lot of cars and had fun.

"My engineer said that we would be strong here and more competitive, and it really happened. We've improved a lot the balance of the car. This track is even for everybody because you don't need the same amount of downforce as the other tracks, so we knew we would be bit more competitive this weekend."

Marques served notice with Friday's practice that he could be a force, running 14th fastest and topping the first group for a while before the clutch cable gave way. Hoping to keep the run going, the team tried to bump-start the car, leading to a gearbox failure.

A new transmission installed, the team rolled out for qualifying and took the point in the first group of runners, whereupon Marques overcooked it and hit the wall while trying to find even more speed on a subsequent lap.

"I was trying too hard. I was trying way too hard, and lost it, unfortunately," he said. "The good news is there wasn't too much damage."

The team's strong run came as little surprise to the man who had been slated to run a Swift all season for Forsythe Championship Racing, Bryan Herta, who said that he expected the team to be in its element on the tight Houston course.

"I'm not terribly surprised by the speed," said Herta. "When we tested before the season at Firebird, I think we set the quickest time of anyone. The car has good mechanical grip, which is what you need at places like here [at Houston] or at Firebird; it's the aerodynamic grip that it's lacking."

Left: Gil de Ferran consolidated his championship lead by finishing in third place behind the two Target cars.
Robert Laberge/Allsport USA

Below: Tarso Marques and the Swift chassis posted by far their most impressive performance of the season.
Robert Laberge/Allsport USA

Bottom, left to right: Bobby Golasinski's crew performs typically efficient service on Spanish rookie Oriol Servia's car.
Jon Ferrey/Allsport USA

FEDEX CHAMPIONSHIP SERIES • ROUND 18

[consumption]. Juan was a little bit stronger, and I picked up some rubber on my tires and I wasn't able to push as hard as before."

The fuel saved during the caution allowed Vasser and Montoya to ratchet up their fuel mixture as well, and while they could not go full rich, the yellow-flag laps gave them both enough of a margin to increase their pace and stay ahead of the now struggling de Ferran.

The race shaped up as an intramural battle between the two Target cars as both edged away initially from de Ferran. But then, with a dozen laps or so remaining, it was Montoya's turn to struggle. The tires of the #1 car went away as the final laps ticked off, allowing de Ferran to reel in the defending series champion as Vasser rode off into the Texas sunset.

"The weekend has been pretty tough for us," said Montoya. "We couldn't really get the car right all weekend, but I'm pleased for Jimmy. He had a good car and did a great job today."

De Ferran closed on Montoya in the final stages, but could not find a way around and eventually settled for third. However, the view of Montoya's last laps kept de Ferran entertained on his way to that final podium spot.

"He was sliding around pretty good; it was pretty spectacular to watch," related de Ferran, who was almost overcome with exhaustion at the finish. "It was tough. I had to push so hard, you wouldn't believe. I was OK until I took the checkered flag and I guess I must have relaxed a bit, and I thought, 'Phew, I'm not going to be able to make it back to the pits.'"

Paul Tracy spent another 2000 street race clawing his way to the front after starting mid-pack in Team KOOL Green's #26 Honda/Reynard, but he did it with aplomb, ending his day in fourth and keeping his championship hopes alive. The valuable points moved him to within 19 marks of de Ferran with two events remaining.

"We had a good car, not a great car," said Tracy. "We're still in the [championship] hunt and second's better than fourth. There are still two races to go and I'm looking forward to it."

Tracy fared better than teammate Dario Franchitti, who suffered the latest in a litany of first-lap problems that ended his day without the Scotsman even working up a sweat. Franchitti didn't get the start he wanted from the outside of the front row, then clipped the wall solidly at the exit of Turn Six. He slipped back a number of positions on the opening lap, and was sidelined for good when his right front suspension failed, causing him to crash at Turn One on lap two.

De Ferran's teammate, Helio Castroneves, overcame a problem during his first pit stop to finish fifth ahead of Christian Fittipaldi and Adrian Fernandez, who once again used an excellent pit strategy to rise from 16th to seventh. Shinji Nakano ended a ten-race scoring drought and matched his career-best finish – at the season opener at Homestead – with an eighth-place run. Oriol Servia made it back-to-back rookies in the top ten by coming home ninth, while Tony Kanaan carried the Mercedes-Benz banner to the tenth spot. Roberto Moreno stayed in the hunt, collecting two more points with an 11th-place finish, while Alex Barron gained his first point of the season, piloting the Dale Coyne Racing *Sports Today* Ford/Lola to 12th.

Jeremy Shaw/Eric Mauk

Below: Shinji Nakano equaled his best finish of the season for Walker Racing.

FEDEX CHAMPIONSHIP SERIES • ROUND 18

HOUSTON SNIPPETS

• **BRYAN HERTA** was hoping to follow his Laguna Seca success by running in the Texaco/Havoline Grand Prix of Houston with Forsythe Championship Racing. The team had been busy preparing the same Ford/Reynard that he had guided to a fourth-place finish at Laguna Seca, before owner Gerald Forsythe decided against entering due to financial constraints.

• **JIMMY VASSER** (right) divulged over the weekend at Houston that he was exploring another option for the 2001 season, as he was set to test a Team Sabco NASCAR Winston Cup stock car at Lakeland Speedway in Florida. A large stake in Team Sabco had been purchased by Ganassi during the 2000 season, and former Winston Cup champion crew chief Andy Graves (who also oversaw Ganassi's successful Indy 500 foray) had been hired to run the operation.

• Chip Ganassi called on officials to inspect the uneven TIRE TRACKS left by the Honda/Reynards of Marlboro Team Penske in the pit stalls adjacent to Target/Ganassi, speculating that the Penskes were using a form of traction control. "I told everybody to just look at the tire marks," said Ganassi. "They tell the story." Roger Penske wasn't impressed: "He says, 'Look at the tire tracks.' What does he think I am? Some kind of dummy?"

• **CHIP GANASSI** did not attend the first day of Houston practice as a result of taking part in ceremonies at Pittsburgh's famed Three Rivers Stadium, which was hosting the final Pirates baseball game in its 30-year history before being demolished to make way for parking lots for the city's new baseball and football stadia. Ganassi, a minority owner of the Pirates, joined the other team owners in singing "Take Me Out to the Ballgame" during the seventh-inning stretch.

• In a curious coincidence, **SHINJI NAKANO** virtually mirrored the performance of his Japanese countryman, Naoki Hattori, whose high point during a desperately disappointing '99 Champ Car season came at Houston, where he qualified a season-best seventh. One year later, Nakano emerged fastest of the first group of qualifiers on Friday, then took Walker Racing's Avex Group Honda/Reynard to the fifth-fastest time on Saturday morning. Nakano couldn't match that form in final qualifying and slipped to 18th on the grid, but rebounded well in the race to finish a strong eighth.

• Each of the two Newman/Haas Racing Ford/Lolas sprouted a distinctive **"SNORKEL"** on top of its left-hand sidepod on race day. The new appendage was there for a reason, of course – to improve engine cooling – and had been developed in testing during the previous week at Sebring.

• A few days before setting out for Houston, team owner **BARRY GREEN** announced that he would run a third Honda/Reynard in 2001, with Motorola sponsorship, for Michael Andretti.

• Second-generation driver **CASEY MEARS** put himself in line for his Champ Car debut after testing a Team Rahal Ford/Reynard at California Speedway in the week before the Houston race. The Indy Lights front-runner covered over 400 miles and lapped at an impressive 227 mph.

• Former Champ Car driver **DAVY JONES** was a welcome visitor to the George R. Brown Convention Center, which once again acted as the focal point for the weekend's activities. Jones, who had suffered serious injuries when he crashed an IRL car in early 1997, was promoting his latest business venture, Houston-based Davy Jones KartZone, due to open in early 2001.

Jon Ferrey/Allsport USA

FEDEX CHAMPIONSHIP SERIES • ROUND 18
TEXACO/HAVOLINE GRAND PRIX OF HOUSTON
HOUSTON, TEXAS
OCTOBER 1, 100 laps of 1.527 miles – 152.025 miles

Place	Driver (Nat.)	No.	Team Sponsors Engine/Car	Tires	Q Speed	Q Time	Q Pos.	Laps	Time/Status	Ave. (mph)	Pts.
1	Jimmy Vasser (USA)	12	Target/Chip Ganassi Racing Toyota/Lola B2K/00	FS	93.420	58.844s	3	100	1h 59m 02.370s	76.626	20
2	Juan Montoya (COL)	1	Target/Chip Ganassi Racing Toyota/Lola B2K/00	FS	93.235	58.961s	6	100	1h 59m 04.284s	76.605	16
3	Gil de Ferran (BR)	2	Marlboro Team Penske Marlboro Honda/Reynard 2KI	FS	93.558	58.757s	1	100	1h 59m 04.687s	76.601	16
4	Paul Tracy (CDN)	26	Team KOOL Green Honda/Reynard 2KI	FS	92.822	59.223s	9	100	1h 59m 05.099s	76.597	12
5	Helio Castroneves (BR)	3	Marlboro Team Penske Marlboro Honda/Reynard 2KI	FS	93.417	58.846s	4	100	1h 59m 10.709s	76.536	10
6	Christian Fittipaldi (BR)	11	Newman/Haas Big Kmart/Route 66 Ford Cosworth/Lola B2K/00	FS	92.966	59.131s	7	100	1h 59m 17.689s	76.462	8
7	Adrian Fernandez (MEX)	40	Patrick Racing Tecate/Quaker State Ford Cosworth/Reynard 2KI	FS	92.045	59.723s	16	100	1h 59m 19.647s	76.441	6
8	*Shinji Nakano (J)	5	Walker Racing Avex Group Honda/Reynard 2KI	FS	91.865	59.840s	18	100	1h 59m 23.785s	76.397	5
9	*Oriol Servia (E)	96	PPI Motorsports Telefonica Toyota/Reynard 2KI	FS	92.067	59.709s	15	100	1h 59m 28.197s	76.350	4
10	Tony Kanaan (BR)	66	Mo Nunn Racing Hollywood Mercedes/Reynard 2KI	FS	92.814	59.228s	10	100	1h 59m 33.822s	76.290	3
11	Roberto Moreno (BR)	20	Patrick Racing Visteon Ford Cosworth/Reynard 2KI	FS	92.209	59.617s	14	99	Running		2
12	Alex Barron (USA)	19	Dale Coyne Racing Sports Today Ford Cosworth/Lola B2K/00	FS	90.635	1m 00.652s	23	99	Running		1
13	Michael Andretti (USA)	6	Newman/Haas Big Kmart/Texaco Ford Cosworth/Lola B2K/00	FS	93.317	58.909s	5	98	Running		
14	Cristiano da Matta (BR)	97	PPI Motorsports Pioneer/WorldCom Toyota/Reynard 2KI	FS	92.725	59.285s	12	97	Running		
15	*Kenny Bräck (S)	8	Team Rahal Shell Ford Cosworth/Reynard 2KI	FS	92.572	59.383s	13	79	Accident		
16	*Alexandre Tagliani (CDN)	33	Forsythe Racing Player's/Indeck Ford Cosworth/Reynard 2KI	FS	92.937	59.150s	8	77	Accident		
17	Tarso Marques (BR)	34	Dale Coyne Racing Panasonic Ford Cosworth/Swift 011.c	FS	92.750	59.269s	11	72	Tripod joint		
18	Michel Jourdain Jr. (MEX)	16	Bettenhausen Motorsports Herdez Mercedes/Lola B2K/00	FS	90.173	1m 00.963s	24	61	Engine		
19	Patrick Carpentier (CDN)	32	Forsythe Racing Player's/Indeck Ford Cosworth/Reynard 2KI	FS	91.862	59.842s	19	54	Engine		
20	Mark Blundell (GB)	18	PacWest Racing Motorola Mercedes/Reynard 2KI	FS	91.107	1m 00.338s	20	50	Withdrawn		
21	Memo Gidley (USA)	10	Della Penna Motorsports DirecTV Toyota/Reynard 2KI	FS	90.985	1m 00.419s	22	47	Withdrawn		
22	Luiz Garcia Jr. (BR)	25	Arciero-PRG Hollywood/Embratel-21 Mercedes/Reynard 2KI	FS	87.231	1m 03.019s	25	46	Drivetrain		
23	Mauricio Gugelmin (BR)	17	PacWest Racing Nextel Mercedes/Reynard 2KI	FS	91.075	1m 00.359s	21	44	Accident		
24	Max Papis (I)	7	Team Rahal Miller Lite Ford Cosworth/Reynard 2KI	FS	92.020	59.739s	17	6	Throttle linkage		
25	Dario Franchitti (GB)	27	Team KOOL Green Honda/Reynard 2KI	FS	93.421	58.843s	2	1	Accident		

* denotes rookie driver

Caution flags: Laps 2-5, accident/Franchitti & Carpentier; laps 7-11, accident/Papis & Gidley; laps 54-56, accident/da Matta; laps 73-76, tow/Marques; laps 78-82, accident/Nakano, Andretti, Bräck, Tagliani & Servia. **Total:** Five for 21 laps.

Lap leaders: Gil de Ferran, 1-46 (46 laps); Jimmy Vasser, 47-51 (5 laps); de Ferran, 52-74 (23 laps); Vasser, 75-100 (26 laps). **Totals:** de Ferran, 69 laps; Vasser, 31 laps.

Fastest race lap: Michael Andretti, 1m 00.219s, 91.287 mph on lap 92 (record).

Championship positions: 1 de Ferran, 153; **2** Tracy, 134; **3** Moreno, 131; **4** Andretti & Fernandez, 127; **6** Montoya, 122; **7** Bräck, 118; **8** Castroneves & Vasser, 117; **10** da Matta, 100; **11** Franchitti, 92; **12** Carpentier, 91; **13** Papis, 87; **14** Fittipaldi, 76; **15** Servia, 60; **16** Tagliani, 45; **17** Gugelmin, 26; **18** Herta, 26; **19** Gidley, 20; **20** Kanaan, 19; **21** Blundell, 16; **22** Nakano, 12; **23** Jourdain, 10; **24** Marques & Garcia, 5; **26** Fontana, 2; **27** Kurosawa & Barron, 1.

SURFERS PARADISE

FEDEX CHAMPIONSHIP SERIES • ROUND 19

FEDEX CHAMPIONSHIP SERIES • ROUND 19

1 – FERNANDEZ

2 – BRÄCK

3 – VASSER

QUALIFYING

The first half-hour of Saturday's qualifying session was tedious in the extreme, due to a variety of interruptions. The final five minutes provided a sensational climax, however, as Juan Montoya and Gil de Ferran waged a terrific battle for the pole.

After stoppages due to an errant track banner, blown from its moorings by strong winds, and the misfortunes of Newman/Haas teammates Christian Fittipaldi (who crashed) and Michael Andretti (stranded by a broken gearbox), the session was extended beyond the normal 30 minutes to ensure the minimum allotment of 20 minutes of green-flag running.

As time ticked away, Montoya vaulted to the top of the timing charts with the fastest lap of the weekend thus far, 1m 31.924s. Then de Ferran eclipsed Montoya's best with a faster lap at 1m 31.827s. Elation in the Marlboro Team Penske pit lasted only for a few moments, however, before Montoya lowered the benchmark still further to 1m 31.722s.

"I was pushing as hard as I could," said a delighted Montoya after clinching his series-high seventh pole of the year and the 14th of his Champ Car career. "It's my last road course here [in CART before switching to Formula 1 for the 2001 season] and it's good to be on pole."

De Ferran took the reversal in his stride, despite the fact that it cost him one potentially vital point in his quest for the CART Championship title.

"Every point counts," noted de Ferran. "One extra point would have given me a 20-point lead [in the championship] instead of 19, so it's important. It would have been nice, but if it didn't happen, it didn't happen. It's OK."

Dario Franchitti, the '99 pole-sitter at Surfers Paradise, had to be content with third on the grid in his KOOL Honda/Reynard after improving his previous best by more than 1.3 seconds in the waning moments of the session. Teammate Paul Tracy qualified fourth in his identical car, followed by Jimmy Vasser in the second Target Toyota/Lola, Andretti (Big Kmart/Texaco Ford/Lola) and Tony Kanaan aboard his Hollywood Mercedes/Reynard.

Main photograph: **Paul Tracy (26) and Michael Andretti squeak through unscathed as Juan Montoya and Gil de Ferran tangle.**
Robert Laberge/Allsport USA

Above: **De Ferran waits in vain as the Penske crew attempts to repair his car.**
Darrell Ingham/Allsport USA

Far left and left: **Paul Tracy unwittingly tips Max Papis into a spin as Adrian Fernandez leads from Kenny Bräck and Alex Barron at the restart on lap 48.**
John Morris/M-Pix

THE CART FedEx Championship Series was finely poised as the competitors gathered on the Gold Coast of Queensland, Australia, for the Honda Indy 300. Incredibly, after 18 races, no fewer than nine drivers still held a legitimate hope of claiming the title. By the end of a weekend of rapidly changing fortunes, that number had been whittled down to only a handful.

Gil de Ferran still led the way, despite being involved in an accident at the first corner with pole-sitter Juan Montoya. As a result of the various shenanigans, Adrian Fernandez emerged as de Ferran's nearest challenger after scoring a textbook victory. The Mexican had struggled all weekend to find a workable setup for Pat Patrick's Tecate/Quaker State Ford Cosworth/Reynard, but, after starting 15th, he took advantage of typically excellent strategy to emerge as a surprise, although nonetheless deserving, victor for the second time in 2000.

"It's not nice to qualify so far back, but it's just fantastic that this series offers you the opportunity to win from the back," said a delighted Fernandez. "Everyone is so closely matched and the Patrick team has just done a fantastic job all season."

Kenny Bräck moved to within 19 points of de Ferran following a fine second-place finish – his fourth podium appearance of the season – in Team Rahal's Shell Ford/Reynard.

Of the other title hopefuls, Michael Andretti suffered another engine failure when looking good for a victory, eliminating the 1991 champion from contention, while Paul Tracy also seemed set to make significant inroads on de Ferran's points advantage until being involved in a couple of incidents. Roberto Moreno, meanwhile, uncharacteristically threw away a great opportunity by crashing on cold tires at a restart in the late stages. At least Tracy and Moreno remained alive in the overall reckoning, which is more than can be said for Montoya, Helio Castroneves, who needed more than a sixth-place finish, and Jimmy Vasser, for whom a robust third-place finish proved to be not quite enough.

The unpredictable nature of the FedEx Series was highlighted within moments of the start when de Ferran, who qualified second in his Marlboro Honda/Reynard and needed only a solid finish virtually to clinch the title, inadvertently clipped the rear of Montoya's Target Toyota/Lola as they approached the braking area for the first chicane.

"I was driving hard into the first turn and felt someone touch me from behind," said Montoya, who made heavy contact with the wall. "It's a shame because we have been running so strong lately and I really felt that I had a good car for today."

De Ferran limped back to the pits with a broken suspension, but was unable to resume. Dario Franchitti, who had started third, also was eliminated after being hit accidentally by Vasser as the melee unfolded.

After four laps under caution while the debris was cleared, Franchitti's teammate, Paul Tracy, inherited the lead in the second Team KOOL Green Honda/Reynard. The Canadian took off at a prodigious rate at the front of the field. One lap after the restart, Tracy was a full 3.3 seconds clear of Andretti's Big Kmart/Texaco Ford/Lola. Next time around, the gap was 6.6 seconds, then 7.3 seconds.

Soon the margin to Andretti stabilized at around nine seconds, but only until lap 12, when suddenly Tracy came to a halt at the Queensland Turn,

181

FEDEX CHAMPIONSHIP SERIES • ROUND 19

Top left: Roberto Moreno's title hopes took a beating following a rare miscue.
Jamie Squire/Allsport USA

Above: Luiz Garcia Jr. steered clear of trouble to claim his fifth top-12 finish.
Jamie Squire/Allsport USA

Right: Juan Montoya was philosophical after his title hopes were finally quashed.
Robert Laberge/Allsport USA

Top right: Kenny Bräck once again drove well to secure his fourth podium finish.
Robert Cianflone/Allsport USA

Far right: Michel Jourdain Jr. earned his best result of the year, seventh.
Robert Laberge/Allsport USA

Lord of the flyaways

A FORTUITOUS, but nonetheless well-earned, victory at Surfers Paradise gained Adrian Fernandez *(above)* a place in the record books, as he became the first driver to win races on all four continents that are visited by the CART FedEx Championship Series. Along the way, the 35-year-old Paradise Valley, Arizona-based Mexican had earned an enviable reputation for versatility.

Fernandez secured his first checkered flag on the streets of Toronto, Canada, in 1996 while driving for Steve Horne's Tasman Motorsports team. After a dreadfully disappointing '97 campaign with the uncompetitive Lola chassis, Fernandez switched to U.E. "Pat" Patrick's team and recorded the second triumph of his career when the series made its inaugural visit to the impressive Twin Ring Motegi oval in Japan. Fernandez added another win at the Mid-Ohio road course during the '98 season, then scored a repeat victory in Japan in '99 and capped off the season by claiming the $1 million bonus for a magnificent success in the Marlboro 500 Presented by Toyota at California Speedway.

The 2000 season completed his remarkable feat by bringing another pair of wins, firstly at the unique "roval" in Rio de Janeiro, Brazil, and, most recently, the challenging Surfers Paradise street circuit, where he took advantage of an excellent strategic call by Patrick Racing after posting another disappointing performance in qualifying. Consistency and reliability proved equally crucial to his success.

"I tell you, you have to finish to be able to win," said Fernandez. "Patrick Racing has struggled the second half of the season, both [teammate Roberto] Moreno and myself, to qualify up front. We know we can win races if we can qualify at the front, but we continue to fight even when we don't, and we get great fuel consumption.

"My team reckoned I could do the mileage to get to the end [after his second pit stop], and any yellows could help us. It was a risk, but it was a calculated risk, and at the end, of course, those yellows helped us."

Look on the Bright side

LOCAL driver Jason Bright endured a baptism of fire at Surfers Paradise when he became the first Australian since Gary Brabham in 1994 to compete in his home country's round of the CART FedEx Championship Series. Bright, 27, acquitted himself extremely well and was running a fine fifth *(above)* before becoming an innocent victim in a wreck with just 15 laps remaining.

In common with most of his peers, Bright began his career in karting. After recording numerous successes, he went on to dominate the 1995 Fordcare Australian Formula Ford Championship by winning eight of the 16 races. He set his sights on a future in the Champ Cars in 1996 when, at age 22, he traveled overseas and finished a close second in the U.S. F2000 National Championship. Bright also easily claimed Rookie of the Year honors. The hoped-for graduation into Indy Lights failed to materialize, however, so he returned home to race in the Aussie equivalent, Formula Holden.

Bright won the title in '97 and parlayed that success into a ride in his country's most prestigious series, V8 Supercars. The following year, he won the biggest race on the calendar, the world-renowned FAI 1000 at Bathurst.

All the while, however, Bright hankered after a return to open-wheel racing. His dream came true at the beginning of the new millennium when he joined defending champion team Dorricott Racing in the Dayton Indy Lights Championship. He secured his first victory at Portland in June, then cemented a deal through former CART team owner Carl Hogan to join Della Penna Motorsports (replacing Memo Gidley for the weekend) for his Champ Car debut at Surfers Paradise.

Bright's preparations, however, consisted of only one brief test at Putnam Park, near Indianapolis. To make matters worse, both official practice sessions for the Honda Indy 300 were interrupted by rain.

"If I could have dreamed up my worst nightmare, this would have been it," said Bright. Nevertheless, he knuckled down to the task, took all the distractions of being a hometown hero in his stride, and posted an impressive drive that was ended when Max Papis slowed abruptly in front of him to avoid a spinning Roberto Moreno.

"I'm disappointed we dropped out," said Bright, "but I'm happy it wasn't a silly mistake on my behalf. It was just one of those things."

Right: The wall-lined Surfers Paradise street circuit has absolutely no room for error.

producing the second full-course caution of the afternoon.

"The throttle stuck wide open going into the braking zone," related Tracy, who lost almost a complete lap before he was able to reset the onboard computer and get a push-start from the CART Safety Team.

Now Andretti led from Vasser and Christian Fittipaldi in the second Newman/Haas Ford/Lola. Tony Kanaan ran fourth in Mo Nunn's Hollywood Mercedes/Reynard, but soon began to slip into the clutches of PPI teammates Cristiano da Matta and Oriol Servia.

Andretti made the first of two scheduled pit stops on lap 24. Vasser stayed out for one more lap before pulling into pit lane. The later stop, together with excellent service from Ricky Davis' team, enabled Vasser to emerge from the pits ahead of Andretti.

Ahead of them both, though, were eight other cars that had taken the opportunity to make pit stops – and therefore commit themselves to a three-stop strategy – during the earlier caution periods. Kenny Bräck emerged as the new leader, pursued at a distance by fellow rookie Alex Tagliani (Player's/Forsythe Ford/Reynard) and Alex Barron, who had risen to third aboard Dale Coyne Racing's *Sports Today* Ford/Lola. Fernandez followed closely in fourth, while Tracy had already worked his way back up to fifth place by virtue of some typically bold maneuvers.

The gap between Bräck and Tagliani remained fairly steady at around four seconds until the second round of pit stops, which began on lap 36 when Bräck pulled into pit lane. Tagliani attempted to go one more lap, but, cruelly, never made it around to the pits. The telemetry suggested that he should have been able to get back with a little over a gallon to spare. It wasn't enough of a margin. The French-Canadian's fine run was over.

Tracy, Fernandez and Barron made their second stops, on schedule, after 37 laps. They resumed in tenth, 11th and 12th, albeit with their positions shuffled dramatically. Fernandez was ahead of Barron, while Tracy had leapfrogged both Ford-powered cars.

Vasser took over at the front of the field, chased by Andretti and Fittipaldi. Da Matta had moved up to fourth in his Pioneer Toyota/Reynard ahead of Bräck, Servia and Kanaan. At this stage, everyone, it seemed, would have to make one more visit to pit lane. But there was more drama just around the corner.

On lap 39, Andretti's day was ended by a massive engine failure. At virtually the same time, Shinji Nakano, who had run as high as sixth in Derrick Walker's Avex Group Honda/Reynard, also ground to a halt with a similar problem. Caution again.

The interruption came at the wrong time for Vasser, who had just passed the pits when the order was given to display the double yellow flags. In order not to disadvantage the race leader, the officials called for the pits to be closed, which worked against many other contenders, including da Matta, who had to wait for the field to pack up behind the pace car before the pit lane was reopened.

All except Fernandez, Barron, Moreno, Max Papis (Miller Lite Ford/Reynard) and Jason Bright (DirecTV Toyota/Reynard) made their final fuel stops, under caution, on lap 42. This sextet led the pack in anticipation of the restart on lap 44, whereupon Moreno hit the wall at the exit of the Honda Hairpin.

"I had to come off the throttle and I just lost it when I got back onto it again," related Moreno sheepishly.

Papis, running right behind the Brazilian, lifted off the throttle abruptly when Moreno hit the wall. Following closely, Bright was caught unawares and ran into the back of the Miller Lite Reynard. Bright was out on the spot, marking the end of a solid Champ Car debut.

After another delay, the next attempt at a restart saw Papis, Bräck and Tracy all vying for the same piece of asphalt going into the first chicane. In the confusion that followed, Papis was sent spinning and several cars took evasive action over the curbing, including Servia, who vaulted from ninth to fifth.

Then Tracy made an attempt to dive past Servia into the WorldCom Chicane on the Esplanade, only to run wide over the curbs at the exit and be passed again by Servia. The pair raced side by side toward the Foster's Chicane, where neither was prepared to give way. Again, Tracy left his braking until the very last moment and lunged ahead. Servia, though, in attempting to give Tracy room, succeeded only in making stout contact with the rear end of Tracy's Reynard, which was sent spinning into the barriers.

Exit two more contenders.

And still the action wasn't over! After yet another full-course caution, Fittipaldi and Vasser clashed while disputing fourth place at Conrad Jupiters Corner. Fittipaldi was forced out, while Vasser continued minus much of his Lola's right front wing.

The various interruptions – which ensured that the race would be concluded at the two-hour limit, rather than after the originally scheduled 65 laps – played right into the hands of Fernandez, who was assured of being able to make the finish without a final pit stop. Barron, too, was looking good for a second-place finish until, cruelly, his engine failed with only five laps to go.

Therefore Bräck inherited second ahead of Vasser. Da Matta followed in fourth after a good drive, while Patrick Carpentier (Player's Ford/Reynard) rounded out the top five, despite making a trip into an escape road during the early stages.

Jeremy Shaw

FEDEX CHAMPIONSHIP SERIES • ROUND 19

SURFERS SNIPPETS

- **ADRIAN FERNANDEZ** became the tenth different driver to win at Surfers Paradise during the event's ten-year history, joining an illustrious group comprising John Andretti (who won the inaugural Gold Coast race in 1991), Emerson Fittipaldi, Nigel Mansell, Michael Andretti, Paul Tracy, Jimmy Vasser, Scott Pruett, Alex Zanardi and Dario Franchitti.

- A **DISASTROUS** day for Honda saw Helio Castroneves (who took sixth) as the engine manufacturer's only finisher. By contrast, Ford Cosworth's fifth victory of the season – and, surprisingly, its first since Toronto in July – was enough to eke out a commanding 16-point lead in the coveted CART Manufacturer's Championship standings with just one race to go.

- Champ Car racing's popularity was amply demonstrated by the fact that a **RECORD** race day attendance of 107,785 pushed the weekend total to an astonishing 269,890 – an increase of seven percent over the 1999 figure.

- **ROBERTO MORENO** was not feeling his best when practice began on Friday morning, the legacy of a brief, but gut-wrenching, ride with the Royal Australian Air Force's Roulette aerobatic team the previous afternoon. Admitted Moreno, "After about 15 minutes, I told the pilot I'd had enough and to please land the plane."

Robert Laberge/Allsport USA

- Ferrari Formula 1 driver Rubens Barrichello was a **SURPRISE VISITOR** to the Honda Indy 300, preferring to spend the weekend in Surfers Paradise en route to the Malaysian Grand Prix rather than going back to Brazil in the wake of teammate Michael Schumacher's World Championship-clinching drive one week earlier at Suzuka, Japan.

- One of the best performances during the Honda Indy 300 was posted by **ALEX BARRON** (left), who took advantage of excellent strategy by Dale Coyne and a strong pace to run as high as second before his *Sports Today* Ford/Lola suffered an engine failure only five laps from the finish. "It's an unbelievable feeling, said a crestfallen Barron. I can't even explain it, because my Champ Car career has been very frustrating. I just hope this was a sign for the future in terms of the way we ran on the race track."

- Luiz Garcia Jr. struggled all weekend to get up to **SPEED** in Andreas Leberle's Arciero-Project Racing Group Mercedes/Reynard. In fact, Memo Gidley was invited to hop aboard the Hollywood-backed car for the warmup on Sunday morning, but politely declined the opportunity due to a lack of familiarity with the car.

FEDEX CHAMPIONSHIP SERIES • ROUND 19
HONDA INDY 300

SURFERS PARADISE, QUEENSLAND, AUSTRALIA

OCTOBER 15, 59 laps of 2.795 miles – 164.905 miles

Place	Driver (Nat.)	No.	Team Sponsors Engine/Car	Tires	Q Speed	Q Time	Q Pos.	Laps	Time/Status	Ave. (mph)	Pts.
1	Adrian Fernandez (MEX)	40	Patrick Racing Tecate/Quaker State Ford Cosworth/Reynard 2KI	FS	106.665	1m 34.333s	17	59	2h 01m 14.605s	81.607	21
2	*Kenny Bräck (S)	8	Team Rahal Shell Ford Cosworth/Reynard 2KI	FS	107.207	1m 33.856s	12	59	2h 01m 14.929s	81.603	16
3	Jimmy Vasser (USA)	12	Target/Chip Ganassi Racing Toyota/Lola B2K/00	FS	108.133	1m 33.052s	5	59	2h 01m 18.664s	81.561	14
4	Cristiano da Matta (BR)	97	PPI Motorsports Pioneer/WorldCom Toyota/Reynard 2KI	FS	107.315	1m 33.761s	10	59	2h 01m 19.418s	81.553	12
5	Patrick Carpentier (CDN)	32	Forsythe Racing Player's/Indeck Ford Cosworth/Reynard 2KI	FS	107.273	1m 33.798s	11	59	2h 01m 19.836s	81.548	10
6	Helio Castroneves (BR)	3	Marlboro Team Penske Marlboro Honda/Reynard 2KI	FS	107.645	1m 33.474s	8	59	2h 01m 24.945s	81.491	8
7	Michel Jourdain Jr. (MEX)	16	Bettenhausen Motorsports Herdez Mercedes/Lola B2K/00	FS	106.722	1m 34.282s	16	59	2h 01m 25.614s	81.484	6
8	Tony Kanaan (BR)	55	Mo Nunn Racing Hollywood Mercedes/Reynard 2KI	FS	108.002	1m 33.165s	7	59	2h 01m 30.375s	81.430	5
9	*Oriol Servia (E)	96	PPI Motorsports Telefonica Toyota/Reynard 2KI	FS	106.975	1m 34.059s	14	59	2h 01m 32.786s	81.403	**4
10	Mauricio Gugelmin (BR)	17	PacWest Racing Nextel Mercedes/Reynard 2KI	FS	106.460	1m 34.514s	18	59	2h 01m 33.186s	81.399	3
11	Mark Blundell (GB)	18	PacWest Racing Motorola Mercedes/Reynard 2KI	FS	105.473	1m 35.399s	22	59	2h 01m 33.328s	81.397	2
12	Luiz Garcia Jr. (BR)	25	Arciero-PRG Hollywood/Embratel-21 Mercedes/Reynard 2KI	FS	101.957	1m 38.689s	25	58	Running		1
13	Tarso Marques (BR)	34	Dale Coyne Racing Panasonic Ford Cosworth/Swift 011.c	FS	105.176	1m 35.668s	23	57	Running		
14	Alex Barron (USA)	19	Dale Coyne Racing *Sports Today* Ford Cosworth/Lola B2K/00	FS	106.411	1m 34.558s	19	54	Engine		
15	Christian Fittipaldi (BR)	11	Newman/Haas Big Kmart/Route 66 Ford Cosworth/Lola B2K/00	FS	107.626	1m 33.490s	9	51	Accident		
16	Max Papis (I)	7	Team Rahal Miller Lite Ford Cosworth/Reynard 2KI	FS	106.892	1m 34.132s	15	48	Accident		
17	Paul Tracy (CDN)	26	Team KOOL Green Honda/Reynard 2KI	FS	108.981	1m 32.328s	4	47	Accident		
18	*Jason Bright (AUS)	10	Della Penna Motorsports DirecTV Toyota/Reynard 2KI	FS	104.343	1m 36.432s	24	44	Accident		
19	Roberto Moreno (BR)	20	Patrick Racing Visteon Ford Cosworth/Reynard 2KI	FS	100.100	1m 34.035s	20	43	Accident		
20	Michael Andretti (USA)	6	Newman/Haas Big Kmart/Texaco Ford Cosworth/Lola B2K/00	FS	108.051	1m 33.123s	6	38	Engine		
21	*Shinji Nakano (J)	5	Walker Racing Avex Group Honda/Reynard 2KI	FS	105.947	1m 34.972s	21	38	Engine		
22	*Alexandre Tagliani (CDN)	33	Forsythe Racing Player's/Indeck Ford Cosworth/Reynard 2KI	FS	107.015	1m 34.459s	13	36	Out of fuel		
23	Gil de Ferran (BR)	2	Marlboro Team Penske Marlboro Honda/Reynard 2KI	FS	109.576	1m 31.827s	2	1	Accident		
24	Juan Montoya (COL)	1	Target/Chip Ganassi Racing Toyota/Lola B2K/00	FS	109.701	1m 31.722s	1	0	Accident		1
25	Dario Franchitti (GB)	27	Team KOOL Green Honda/Reynard 2KI	FS	109.299	1m 32.059s	3	0	Accident		

* denotes rookie driver ** denotes points subsequently forfeited for on-track infractions, for which a $20,000 fine was levied against the driver

Caution flags: Laps 1-2, accident/Franchitti, de Ferran & Montoya; laps 11-12, tow/Tracy; laps 39-43, tow/Nakano; laps 44-47, accident/Moreno; laps 48-51, accident/Tracy. **Total:** Five for 19 laps.

Lap leaders: Paul Tracy, 1-11 (11 laps); Michael Andretti, 12-23 (12 laps); Jimmy Vasser, 24-25 (2 laps); Kenny Bräck, 26-35 (10 laps); Alexandre Tagliani, 36 (1 lap); Vasser, 37-42 (6 laps); Adrian Fernandez, 43-59 (17 laps). **Totals:** Fernandez, 17 laps; Andretti, 12 laps; Tracy, 11 laps; Bräck, 10 laps; Vasser, 8 laps; Tagliani, 1 lap.

Fastest race lap: Jimmy Vasser, 1m 34.959s, 105.962 mph on lap 23.

Championship positions: 1 de Ferran, 153; **2** Fernandez, 148; **3** Tracy & Bräck, 134; **5** Moreno & Vasser, 131; **7** Andretti, 127; **8** Castroneves, 125; **9** Montoya, 123; **10** da Matta, 112; **11** Carpentier, 101; **12** Franchitti, 92; **13** Papis, 87; **14** Fittipaldi, 76; **15** Servia, 64; **16** Tagliani, 45; **17** Gugelmin, 39; **18** Herta, 26; **19** Kanaan, 24; **20** Gidley, 20; **21** Blundell, 18; **22** Jourdain, 16; **23** Nakano, 12; **24** Garcia, 6; **25** Marques, 5; **26** Fontana, 2; **27** Kurosawa & Barron, 1.

FONTANA

FEDEX CHAMPIONSHIP SERIES • ROUND 20

FEDEX CHAMPIONSHIP SERIES • ROUND 20

1 - FITTIPALDI
2 - MORENO
3 - DE FERRAN

G. de FERRAN

Above: Cool and collected. Gil de Ferran sits in his Marlboro Honda/Reynard before the most momentous day of his racing life.
Jon Ferrey/Allsport USA

Far left: Persistent drizzle caused the race to be postponed by almost 24 hours.
Jon Ferrey/Allsport USA

Left: Gil de Ferran is choked with emotion after finally achieving his goal of winning the CART FedEx Championship.
Robert Laberge/Allsport USA

QUALIFYING

Those who thought the speeds were too high at Michigan Speedway earlier in the year had a whole new argument after Fontana qualifying; but Gil de Ferran didn't seem to mind as he inched closer to the CART FedEx Championship by setting a new closed course record lap of 241.428 mph to take the pole for the Marlboro 500 Presented by Toyota.

De Ferran's e-ticket ride eclipsed Mauricio Gugelmin's existing record lap of 240.942 mph (set in qualifying for the 1997 Marlboro 500). More importantly, it comfortably topped Newman/Haas Racing's Michael Andretti and Christian Fittipaldi for the pole position and the single championship point that went with it.

The pole gave de Ferran a six-point lead over Adrian Fernandez, and widened the gap to 20 over Paul Tracy and Kenny Bräck, who still carried title hopes into Monday's race. The point also eliminated long-shot Roberto Moreno from title contention.

"It is very pleasing to have established a new record, but the most important thing is to have the extra point because you never know when you'll need it. It could buy us some extra cushion," said de Ferran. "To be honest, it was not too difficult. The car was not sliding, there was no understeer and I was sitting on the right rear tire a little bit. The car was spot on. I thought, 'There's no way I'm gonna lift!'"

De Ferran beat Andretti's Ford/Lola by a veritable country mile – 0.295 second or 2.331 mph – for the pole. Although Andretti was disappointed to lose the top spot, it hardly came as a surprise to him.

"The car was just OK," he said. "I was hoping to be a little bit quicker, but I had too much understeer. I said after I qualified that if anyone else hits [the setup] right, they would beat us – and I think Gil did."

Fittipaldi started in the second row alongside de Ferran's teammate, Helio Castroneves. Juan Montoya drove the quickest of the Toyota-powered machines, but he and his Target/Chip Ganassi stablemate, Jimmy Vasser, could manage no better than fifth and sixth places respectively.

Eric Mauk

NEVER was the old racing adage "To finish first, first you must finish" more true than in the season-ending event at California Speedway. On a day when most of the field seemingly had a chance of claiming the million-dollar prize, the majority of the chases ended in either a plume of chalk-white engine smoke or the jarring sound of carbon fiber being torn to pieces.

After being interrupted by rain and finishing almost 24 hours later than originally scheduled, a spectacular, attrition-filled Marlboro 500 presented by Toyota saw only six cars still running at the checkered flag. Christian Fittipaldi emerged from the carnage with a well-judged victory aboard Newman/Haas Racing's Big Kmart/Route 66 Ford Cosworth/Lola, while fellow Brazilian Gil de Ferran took third place to clinch the CART FedEx Championship Series title, also worth a million dollars, and win the coveted Vanderbilt Cup.

At the beginning of the weekend, a series-record five drivers remained in the championship reckoning. Each would have been a first-time winner. Amazingly, the title chase went down to the final few miles. De Ferran and Adrian Fernandez were separated by only five points when the weekend started, and the two principal protagonists fought the good fight until the bitter end.

Fernandez, however, struggled all day long with Patrick Racing's Tecate/Quaker State Ford/Reynard. Handling difficulties and a lack of power kept him from being a true threat to de Ferran, but the Ford ran well enough to finish fifth and force the latter to stay in the game. While all the other Honda contenders fell by the wayside as the race progressed, de Ferran took good care of his Marlboro Honda/Reynard and was overcome with emotion as he completed his cool-down lap after achieving one of his lifetime goals.

"I can hardly talk right now," said de Ferran, having remained in his car, crying uncontrollably, for several minutes before emerging to receive the plaudits of a joyous Marlboro Team Penske. "We always knew it was going to be a race of attrition. It's difficult to get to the end. That proved to be the case today, but Honda and Marlboro Team Penske both, they prepared that thing like you have no idea."

The dramatic season finale truly lived up to expectations, as no fewer than 12 different drivers took a turn in the lead – at least officially – with 57 changes recorded at the start/finish line. In fact, before eventual winner Fittipaldi led the last 29 laps of the race, the longest consecutive stretch that anyone had held the point was a mere 14 circuits.

Sunday's 33-lap, rain-abbreviated stint, which claimed the title hopes of Paul Tracy when the engine in his KOOL Honda/Reynard expired massively after 23 laps, featured some interesting back-and-forth racing at the front between Penske teammates de Ferran and Helio Castroneves. Their infighting caused some anxious moments when the two raced precariously side-by-side for a number of laps.

"That was the plan," declared Castroneves. "We decided we wanted to

FEDEX CHAMPIONSHIP SERIES • ROUND 20

get away from the field if we could. That's what we were doing. Gil and I talked about the first 33 laps and he didn't have any problems. I think it was a good show!"

Juan Montoya took up the running at Monday's resumption, but was passed right away at the lap 40 restart by Michael Andretti, who leapfrogged both the Colombian's Target Toyota/Lola and Dario Franchitti's KOOL Honda/Reynard. Montoya's teammate, Jimmy Vasser, leapt immediately ahead of de Ferran, while Kenny Bräck also vaulted into the picture with Team Rahal's Shell Ford/Reynard.

For Bräck, nothing less than a victory would do if he was to take the championship. Furthermore, he needed to gain the extra bonus point for leading most laps *and* rely on some kind of misfortune befalling the other contenders. The impressive Swedish rookie did all he could. He took the lead for the first time on lap 50, enjoyed a fierce drafting duel with Castroneves, and led a race-high 47 laps before being stranded by a turbocharger failure after 167 laps.

"That's the way it goes," commented Bräck with characteristic sangfroid. "Our strategy was very good. We had to lead the most laps, and we had a strong car today. We really wanted to win the race."

A host of other potential challengers also ran into difficulties. Franchitti went out early on Monday with a blown engine. Vasser led briefly and was running contentedly and conservatively when suddenly his gearbox let go.

Soon afterward, following a caution occasioned by a massive engine failure in Memo Gidley's DirecTV Toyota/Reynard, Tony Kanaan carried Mo Nunn Racing's Hollywood Mercedes/Reynard to the front, only to be rewarded like most of the others that were so bold. Mere moments after taking advantage of a huge draft to leap from fourth to second on the approach to Turn One, his engine failed in a big way. A vast cloud of smoke obscured the view of everyone behind, resulting in Oriol Servia's Telefonica Toyota/Reynard running into the back of Andretti's Big Kmart/Texaco Ford/Lola. Three more contenders were out.

Mauricio Gugelmin took over in front during the ensuing caution, only for his Nextel Mercedes/Reynard to encounter engine troubles shortly after the restart. PacWest Racing teammate Mark Blundell also ran well in his last ride for the Bruce McCaw-owned team before suffering a similar fate. Following an engine change prior to the Monday restart, Blundell made his way to the front, and drafted past Castroneves and Montoya to take the lead going into Turn One on lap 129. Half a mile later, the engine exploded violently on the entry to Turn Three, leaving the track blanketed in smoke again.

Coincidentally, Michel Jourdain Jr., in the only other Mercedes-powered car (Luiz Garcia Jr. had not been able to start the Arciero-Project Racing Group's Hollywood Reynard due to an oil leak on the grid), suffered a similar failure only moments after he had taken the lead on lap 202. Like Blundell, Jourdain never gained official

FEDEX CHAMPIONSHIP SERIES • ROUND 20

Above: Christian Fittipaldi *(left)*, here dicing with Patrick Carpentier, was in the right place at the right time to become the season's 11th different winner.

Far left: A respectable crowd braved uncertain weather conditions when the race was restarted on Monday morning

Center left: Team KOOL Green's Paul Tracy was hoping (in vain) that a green hair tint would assist his title aspirations.

left: Team co-owners Paul Newman and Carl Haas join Marlboro's Ina Broeman and podium finishers Roberto Moreno and Gil de Ferran as Christian Fittipaldi contemplates his biggest-ever pay check.

Photos: Robert Laberge/Allsport USA

FEDEX CHAMPIONSHIP SERIES • ROUND 20

credit for leading the race, having expired before the start/finish line.

As the explosive 500-miler headed toward its climax, Montoya and Castroneves appeared best equipped to chase the victory. But the fates kept picking off cars as if they were grapes on the vine.

On lap 219, Montoya's engine scattered parts across the expanse of Turn Two. Soon after the restart, Castroneves suffered a similar fate – except that the failure occurred at the entrance to Turn One, and the youngster promptly lost control of his Marlboro Honda/Reynard on the ensuing oil slick. After a heavy impact with the wall, Castroneves complained of various aches and pains, and was taken to Loma Linda Hospital, where, thankfully, his injuries were found not to be serious.

Alex Barron became the next to incur disappointment when the engine in Dale Coyne Racing's *Sports Today* Ford/Lola let go on lap 240, ending his hopes of victory for the second straight event.

"I was going for the million bucks," said Barron. "It's just too bad. I really thought we could get this race."

That would prove to be a popular rallying cry throughout the paddock.

The race was restarted with only five laps remaining, but the production had another act on the playbill. Fittipaldi led Roberto Moreno's Visteon Ford/Reynard when the green flag flew, but Alex Tagliani, running third in Jerry Forsythe's Player's Ford/Reynard, hadn't given up his hope of taking his first Champ Car victory. Three laps later, he joined so many others on the sidelines when yet another engine explosion sent the French-Canadian hard into the Turn Two wall. Tagliani, like Castroneves, was extracted gingerly from his mangled car and transported to the hospital for X-rays.

As the yellow lights blazed, Fittipaldi was able finally to relax and cruise to the checkered flag to score his second CART victory and his first on an oval. He was followed by Moreno, de Ferran, Casey Mears, who drove an impressive Champ Car debut aboard Team Rahal's WorldCom Ford/Reynard, and Fernandez. Tarso Marques was the only other finisher, three laps off the pace in the Panasonic Ford/Swift.

"These 500-mile races are all about finishing," noted Fittipaldi, who set a new CART record by becoming the season's 11th different race winner. "I knew it was going to come down to the last ten to 15 laps. Right at the very end when we went green, 'Bob' [Moreno] was right behind me. I was going as fast as I could, and I couldn't have gone another tenth of a mile an hour quicker."

Fittipaldi was a deserving victor. De Ferran, too, was a popular champion, and later was able to reflect upon his successful conclusion to a suspense-filled season.

"It's so tough to put this into words," said the new CART FedEx Series Champion. "Obviously, it's a very, very emotional day for me. I've dreamed all my life about winning a title like this. I always felt it was within my abilities to win one of these championships. To be here talking to you as the champion is very, very satisfying."

Jeremy Shaw/Eric Mauk

Torch song

FOR the second time in as many weeks, the race proved just a few laps too long for Dale Coyne Racing and promising driver Alex Barron. In Australia, the American had been running a solid second when the *Sports Today* Lola's Ford engine expired. In California, Barron was even more impressive – and even more unlucky, when you consider the million-dollar first prize.

Barron had come roaring back from a lap down, having experienced fuel-injection problems in the abbreviated Sunday start to the 500-mile race. By dint of speedy laps and cagey pit strategy, he was in a position to unlap himself from Helio Castroneves on lap 105. He showed an early hint of strength by running away without the benefit of a drafting partner, distancing himself from the lead pack. Barron then benefited from a free pass around to the tail of the lead lap when Shinji Nakano's blown engine brought out a full-course yellow on lap 113.

After getting back on the same page as the frontrunners, Barron gave as good as he got with the power brokers of the series, clawing his way past Adrian Fernandez, Gil de Ferran, Roberto Moreno, Alex Tagliani, Christian Fittipaldi, Juan Montoya and Max Papis to take the lead on lap 172. At the very least, he was looking like a potential podium finisher – perhaps even a winner – until his engine blew up on lap 238 *(above)*.

"I'd love to have had about ten extra laps the past two races," said Dale Coyne. "We probably had the fastest car on the track for the last half of the race. And we were in second place behind Christian when the engine broke – and second place is where you want to be in the closing laps."

The two late blow-ups cost Coyne a chance of earning his best CART finish as a car owner, eclipsing the third place scored by Roberto Moreno in the U.S. 500 at Michigan Speedway in 1996.

"Yes, pit-stop strategy got us up to the front in both races," admitted Coyne. "But I'll tell ya, Alex carried the torch from there."

Eric Mauk

Meet the newest member of the Mears Gang

IT took more than a decade, but to the delight of many, there was another member of the Mears family charging around an oval in California. Casey Mears parlayed a test session with Team Rahal into his Champ Car debut in the WorldCom-sponsored Ford/Reynard and made the most of it, rolling to a strong fourth-place finish on a day that saw most of his competitors fall by the wayside, including teammates Max Papis and Kenny Bräck.

Mears ran the race in much the same style as his famed uncle Rick and father Roger before him on the nearby Ontario Motor Speedway oval (and the Riverside road course), quietly keeping himself on the lead lap and in the hunt, before coming on at the end.

"I'm thrilled," said Mears *(left)* after earning the best-ever result for an Indy Lights graduate in his first Champ Car appearance. "I just took what everybody told me all weekend and just put it in play. They said, 'If the car doesn't feel right, don't push it too hard,' and we just stayed on the lead lap and did exactly what we wanted to do. Everything they said that I needed to do came true today."

Mears trod new ground by running in the Indy Lights race and the Champ Car event on the same weekend. And while most would consider the double to be a burden on a driver, Mears figured that it helped him shake the nerves of preparing for his FedEx Series debut.

"I think it was a good thing for me," said Mears. "While other guys were sitting in the transporters thinking about how they were going to run the race and wondering how it would go, I was out there racing. It was just, 'Oh, run this race, and then get out and run another one.'"

Although typically Mears-like in modesty (and candor), Casey was not shy in thinking he might have had a chance at a podium finish had the final three laps not been run under caution.

"The car was working real well and I think maybe I could've gotten around Gil [de Ferran]. But I made a mistake on that last restart – I got sideways in Turn Three, or I might have had a chance for a podium – but I'm a rookie, so I'm allowed those," reckoned Mears.

"I hope some owners were watching me today. I really want to drive these cars full-time."

Eric Mauk

FEDEX CHAMPIONSHIP SERIES • ROUND 20

FONTANA SNIPPETS

- Toyota Atlantic driver Andrew Bordin and Yoshimichi Inada, senior managing director at Pioneer Electronics, were **INJURED** when the Acura NSX pace car Bordin was driving hit the wall during pre-race activities. Bordin sustained a fracture and a dislocation of the fourth cervical vertebra, while Inada was unconscious briefly at the scene and was determined to have sustained a skull fracture. Both men were expected to make a complete recovery.

- Hans Jorg Fischer, president of the **EUROSPEEDWAY** at Lausitz, Germany, announced that tickets for the inaugural Champ Car race to be held at the new oval track in September, 2001, were selling at the rate of 1,000 per week. "The response has been great," said Fischer. "We estimate we will have an attendance of 60,000, and the race is a year away."

- Gil de Ferran's former Stewart Racing teammate and current McLaren-Mercedes Formula 1 star, **DAVID COULTHARD**, was on hand in the Penske pits moments after the checkered flag fell and said, "I think this is fantastic. Gil and I were teammates about ten years ago [in the British Formula Vauxhall/Lotus Championship], and we still go on holiday together from time to time. It's just fantastic, and I couldn't be more thrilled for him."

- Among several **ANNOUNCEMENTS** made during the Fontana weekend, Chip Ganassi confirmed that Brazilian Bruno Junqueira (below right), 23, and Frenchman Nicolas Minassian (below left), 27, who took the top two positions in the FIA Formula 3000 Championship, would replace Juan Montoya and Jimmy Vasser for the 2001 season.

- Christian Fittipaldi crushed the hopes of many female fans when he confirmed over the weekend that he would **MARRY** Brazilian Andrea Iversson. "Racing is major in my life, but there is a little more to it than that," said Fittipaldi. "I am getting married on the tenth of February."

- **FORD** clinched the 2000 CART Manufacturer's Championship (for the first time since 1986) with a one-two finish at California Speedway, courtesy of Christian Fittipaldi and Roberto Moreno.

- Tarso Marques claimed the Budweiser Hard Charger Award, for making the greatest **IMPROVEMENT** in track position from the beginning to the end of the race, while Adrian Fernandez moved ahead of Luiz Garcia Jr. to claim the season-long award, worth $50,000.

Robert Laberge/Allsport USA

FEDEX CHAMPIONSHIP SERIES • ROUND 20
MARLBORO 500 PRESENTED BY TOYOTA

CALIFORNIA SPEEDWAY, FONTANA, CALIFORNIA

OCTOBER 30, 250 laps of 2.029 miles – 507.250 miles

Place	Driver (Nat.)	No.	Team Sponsors Engine/Car	Tires	Q Speed	Q Time	Q Pos.	Laps	Time/Status	Ave. (mph)	Pts.
1	Christian Fittipaldi (BR)	11	Newman/Haas Big Kmart/Route 66 Ford Cosworth/Lola B2K/00	FS	239.073	30.553s	3	250	3h 38m 04.376s	139.563	20
2	Roberto Moreno (BR)	20	Patrick Racing Visteon Ford Cosworth/Reynard 2KI	FS	231.672	31.529s	19	250	3h 38m 04.570s	139.561	16
3	Gil de Ferran (BR)	2	Marlboro Team Penske Marlboro Honda/Reynard 2KI	FS	241.428	30.255s	1	250	3h 38m 04.902s	139.558	15
4	*Casey Mears (USA)	91	Team Rahal WorldCom Ford Cosworth/Reynard 2KI	FS	233.382	31.298s	15	250	3h 38m 05.097s	139.556	12
5	Adrian Fernandez (MEX)	40	Patrick Racing Tecate/Quaker State Ford Cosworth/Reynard 2KI	FS	233.659	31.261s	14	250	3h 38m 05.521s	139.551	10
6	*Alexandre Tagliani (CDN)	33	Forsythe Racing Player's/Indeck Ford Cosworth/Reynard 2KI	FS	235.633	30.999s	10	248	Accident		8
7	Tarso Marques (BR)	34	Dale Coyne Racing Panasonic Ford Cosworth/Swift 011.c	FS	226.037	32.315s	25	247	Running		6
8	Alex Barron (USA)	19	Dale Coyne Racing Sports Today Ford Cosworth/Lola B2K/00	FS	231.504	31.552s	20	239	Engine		5
9	Helio Castroneves (BR)	3	Marlboro Team Penske Marlboro Honda/Reynard 2KI	FS	239.011	30.561s	4	226	Accident		4
10	Juan Montoya (COL)	1	Target/Chip Ganassi Racing Toyota/Lola B2K/00	FS	237.688	30.731s	5	219	Engine		3
11	Michel Jourdain Jr. (MEX)	16	Bettenhausen Motorsports Herdez Mercedes/Lola B2K/00	FS	227.963	32.042s	23	203	Engine		2
12	Max Papis (I)	7	Team Rahal Miller Lite Ford Cosworth/Reynard 2KI	FS	234.521	31.146s	13	182	Engine		1
13	*Kenny Bräck (S)	8	Team Rahal Shell Ford Cosworth/Reynard 2KI	FS	236.297	30.912s	8	167	Turbo		1
14	Patrick Carpentier (CDN)	32	Forsythe Racing Player's/Indeck Ford Cosworth/Reynard 2KI	FS	234.959	31.086s	11	154	Gearbox		
15	Mark Blundell (GB)	18	PacWest Racing Motorola Mercedes/Reynard 2KI	FS	230.845	31.642s	21	129	Engine		
16	*Shinji Nakano (J)	5	Walker Racing Avex Group Honda/Reynard 2KI	FS	226.044	32.314s	24	113	Engine		
17	Mauricio Gugelmin (BR)	17	PacWest Racing Nextel Mercedes/Reynard 2KI	FS	230.365	31.708s	22	103	Engine		
18	Tony Kanaan (BR)	55	Mo Nunn Racing Hollywood Mercedes/Reynard 2KI	FS	234.861	31.101s	12	88	Engine		
19	Michael Andretti (USA)	6	Newman/Haas Big Kmart/Texaco Ford Cosworth/Lola B2K/00	FS	239.097	30.550s	2	88	Accident		
20	*Oriol Servia (E)	96	PPI Motorsports Telefonica Toyota/Reynard 2KI	FS	232.965	31.354s	16	88	Accident		
21	Memo Gidley (USA)	10	Della Penna Motorsports DirecTV Toyota/Reynard 2KI	FS	232.936	31.358s	17	78	Engine		
22	Jimmy Vasser (USA)	12	Target/Chip Ganassi Racing Toyota/Lola B2K/00	FS	237.217	30.792s	6	71	Gearbox		
23	Dario Franchitti (GB)	27	Team KOOL Green Honda/Reynard 2KI	FS	237.194	30.795s	7	45	Engine		
24	Paul Tracy (CDN)	26	Team KOOL Green Honda/Reynard 2KI	FS	236.213	30.923s	9	23	Engine		
25	Cristiano da Matta (BR)	97	PPI Motorsports Pioneer/WorldCom Toyota/Reynard 2KI	FS	231.952	31.491s	18	22	Accident		
NS	Luiz Garcia Jr. (BR)	25	Arciero-PRG Hollywood/Embratel-21 Mercedes/Reynard 2KI	FS	222.363	32.849s	26	–	Engine		

* denotes rookie driver

Caution flags: Laps 23-33, accident/da Matta; laps 34-39, red flag/restart; laps 79-85, tow/Gidley; laps 88-99, accident/Andretti, Carpentier & Servia; laps 115-123, tow/Nakano; laps 129-132, tow/Blundell; laps 182-194, tow/Papis; laps 218-224, tow/Montoya; laps 227-236, accident/Castroneves; laps 240-243, tow/Jourdain; laps 249-250, accident/Tagliani. **Total:** Eleven for 85 laps.

Lap leaders: Helio Castroneves, 1-2 (2 laps); Gil de Ferran, 3-6 (4 laps); Castroneves, 7-10 (4 laps); de Ferran, 11-21 (11 laps); Castroneves, 22-26 (5 laps); Juan Montoya, 27-40 (14 laps); Michael Andretti, 41-45 (5 laps); Jimmy Vasser, 46-49 (4 laps); Kenny Bräck, 50-57 (8 laps); Castroneves, 58-59 (2 laps); Bräck, 60-64 (5 laps); Castroneves, 65-66 (2 laps); Bräck, 67-68 (2 laps); Andretti, 69-71 (3 laps); Bräck, 72-64 (3 laps); Max Papis, 75 (1 lap); Montoya, 76-86 (11 laps); Papis, 87-90 (4 laps); Mauricio Gugelmin, 91-98 (8 laps); Roberto Moreno, 99-104 (6 laps); Castroneves, 105-108 (4 laps); Papis, 109-117 (9 laps); Bräck, 118-124 (7 laps); Papis, 125-126 (2 laps); Bräck, 127 (1 lap); Castroneves, 128 (1 lap); Bräck, 129-137 (8 laps); Christian Fittipaldi, 138-141 (4 laps); Bräck, 142-144 (3 laps); Castroneves, 145-146 (2 laps); Bräck, 147-149 (3 laps); Castroneves, 150 (1 lap); Bräck, 151-154 (4 laps); Fittipaldi, 155-156 (2 laps); Bräck, 157-158 (2 laps); Papis, 159 (1 lap); Castroneves, 160 (1 lap); Papis, 161-162 (2 laps); Montoya, 163 (1 lap); Papis, 164 (1 lap); Montoya, 165-167 (3 laps); Papis, 168-171 (4 laps); Alex Barron, 172 (1 lap); Moreno, 173-174 (2 laps); Papis, 175-176 (2 laps); Castroneves, 177 (1 lap); de Ferran, 178-185 (8 laps); Casey Mears, 186-195 (10 laps); Barron, 196 (1 lap); Montoya, 197-198 (2 laps); Castroneves, 199-200 (2 laps); Montoya, 201 (1 lap); Barron, 202-206 (5 laps); Castroneves, 207-217 (11 laps); Fittipaldi, 218 (1 lap); Castroneves, 219-221 (3 laps); Fittipaldi, 222-250 (29 laps). **Totals:** Bräck, 47 laps; Castroneves, 42 laps; Fittipaldi, 35 laps; Montoya, 33 laps; Papis, 26 laps; de Ferran, 23 laps; Mears, 10 laps; Gugelmin, 8 laps; Moreno, 8 laps; Barron, 7 laps; Andretti, 7 laps; Vasser, 4 laps.

Fastest race lap: Helio Castroneves, 31.414s, 232.521 mph on lap 17.

Final championship positions: 1 de Ferran, 168; **2** Fernandez, 158; **3** Moreno, 147; **4** Bräck, 135; **5** Tracy, 134; **6** Vasser, 131; **7** Castroneves, 129; **8** Andretti, 127; **9** Montoya, 126; **10** da Matta, 112; **11** Carpentier, 101; **12** Fittipaldi, 96; **13** Franchitti, 92; **14** Papis, 88; **15** Servia, 60; **16** Tagliani, 53; **17** Gugelmin, 39; **18** Herta, 26; **19** Kanaan, 24; **20** Gidley, 20; **21** Blundell & Jourdain, 18; **23** Nakano & Mears, 12; **25** Marques, 11; **26** Garcia & Barron, 6; **28** Fontana, 2; **29** Kurosawa, 1.

TO THE WIRE

by Eric Mauk

DAYTON INDY LIGHTS CHAMPIONSHIP REVIEW

DAYTON INDY LIGHTS CHAMPIONSHIP REVIEW

Left: Scott Dixon passed Casey Mears at Laguna Seca to score his fifth victory.
Robert Laberge/Allsport USA

Below: Mears exacted his revenge when he took an overdue first win at Houston.
Jon Ferrey/Allsport USA

FOR all of the outward optimism, Scott Dixon knew he was down to his last bullet in the shootout that would decide the Dayton Indy Lights Championship, and he was headed to a race track where he had lost a sure Rookie of the Year title during his last visit.

In 1999, Dixon had held a 19-point lead in the rookie chase heading to Fontana, but ended up second in the first-year standings after failing to score, while Jonny Kane rolled to the win. One year later, Dixon enjoyed an advantage that seemed to be equally insurmountable, leading the championship chase by 42 points with three races to run, only for crashes in successive events at Gateway and Houston to allow rivals Townsend Bell and Casey Mears to climb to within four and six points respectively. Now Dixon was headed for the two-mile oval where the 20-year-old New Zealander had been edged to the rookie title the year before.

This time, however, there would be no such heartache, as he swiped the lead from pole-sitter Felipe Giaffone after the first of the 50 laps and was led only briefly as he carried his PacWest Lights mount to the Bruce McCaw-owned team's first Lights championship.

"What a great feeling. This is definitely the biggest championship I've won in my career," declared Dixon. "This really was not the finish we wanted, based on having to fight it out in the final event, but I finally had some luck after two bad races."

Dixon appeared to have been in command after nine events, five of which were won by the Paul "Ziggy" Harcus-managed machine. The trophy engraver was busily checking to see if

Far left: Jason Bright ousted pole-sitting teammate Townsend Bell at the start in Portland and sped onward to victory.

Center left: Scott Dixon was a deserving champion after winning six of 12 races.
Photos: Donald Miralle/Allsport USA

Left: Barber Dodge Pro Series graduate Townsend Bell scored two wins for Dorricott Racing during a fine rookie year.
Jon Ferrey/Allsport USA

193

DAYTON INDY LIGHTS CHAMPIONSHIP REVIEW

Right: Jonny Kane took an accomplished victory in Detroit during an otherwise thoroughly disappointing season.

Below: Young Mexican Luis Diaz was fortune to walk away from a frightening crash within the final few yards of the season finale at Fontana.
Photos: Robert Laberge/Allsport USA

there were two "T"s in Scott at Gateway when youthful enthusiasm put the celebration on hold.

Needing simply to score in the tenth race of the season, Dixon engaged in a fierce battle at the front of the pack with Bell and lost the rear end of his car in Turn Three of the Gateway oval, crashing out of the event without scoring, while Bell went on to win and stay in the championship hunt.

"We came into the weekend and everyone was talking about how Dixon's got it all locked up," noted Bell. "We came in hoping to win the pole, lead the most laps and win the race, and we did that."

The series' penultimate race was more of the same, and although Dixon's misfortune was not of his doing, it was misfortune all the same. Running a more controlled race through the streets of Houston, the Kiwi was caught up in a four-car melee triggered by Kane's spin in Turn Seven, which collected four cars, including the luckless Dixon. Mears went on to claim his first Lights win from the pole, putting an element of drama into the finale that Dixon quickly squelched by leading 48 of the 50 laps around California Speedway.

Dixon's California win was his sixth of the year, so he had won half of the 12 events; but the road to the title was never as easy as the stats might suggest. He took advantage of a Kane misstep in the season opener at Long Beach, passing the Irishman with four laps to go to take the early-season lead. A wire-to-wire win at Milwaukee threatened to make it a runaway, but Team KOOL Green's Kane came back with a roll from the pole at Belle Isle.

Aussie rookie Jason Bright earned the first win of the season for Dorricott Racing at Portland, then took the series lead at a thrilling Michigan race, while Dixon and Mears sat a single point back. Bright would be unable to defend his tenuous grip on the lead in Chicago, however, as a crash in practice caused him to sit out the race as Dixon went on to win.

Bright's momentary lead marked the only time that the three-car Dorricott Racing team would hold the position in a series that it swept just a year before. The organization was every bit as strong as it was in 1999, with Mears, Bell and Bright all claiming their first series victories and rolling to a podium sweep at Gateway, but Dixon would prove to be too much to overcome. Bell would win the Rookie of the Year title and finish only nine points in arrears of Dixon, while Mears claimed third in the championship and went on to make a sensational Champ Car debut at Fontana. Bright finished second in the rookie chase, despite missing the Chicago event, as well as managing a strong one-off Champ Car appearance in his homeland.

Dixon benefited from a strong effort by PacWest teammate Tony Renna to aid his championship charge, including a third-place finish at Fontana that saw the American driver run second most of the day, keeping Bell and Mears off Dixon's tail in a race that was ruled by the draft. Renna, in his first full season with PacWest Lights, would claim three podium finishes and a trio of fourth places after clinching his seat with some inspired Champ Car test sessions in the offseason while subbing for Mark Blundell.

Team KOOL Green made a strong start to what would end up being the team's swan song, with Kane leading until a late restart in the first race of the year, then coming back to claim the team's only win of the season at Detroit. Jeff Simmons posted three podium finishes in his rookie campaign, all on road or street courses, but the team suffered inconsistency and more than its share of accidents, which took a toll on equipment and preparation. Simmons nearly missed the Mid-Ohio race after a crash in practice saw the Lou Schollum-led crew working all night to get the car ready, but the Barber Dodge Pro Series graduate would place seventh in the championship, while Kane would come home a disappointing tenth.

Turning 40 Never Felt So Good

Dayton Indy Lights President Roger Bailey (from left), series founder U.E. "Pat" Patrick, Adrian Fernandez and Dayton Motorsports Manager Joe Barbieri celebrate 40 FedEx Championship Series victories by Indy Lights graduates.

Another banner year for graduates of the Dayton Indy Lights Championship in the FedEx Championship Series helped CART's top-level development series reach more than one milestone in the 2000 season. Former Indy Lights standouts Paul Tracy, Adrian Fernandez, Helio Castroneves and Cristiano da Matta combined to win a record nine FedEx Championship races, the most victories ever recorded by series grads in a CART Champ Car season.

But the record setting didn't stop there. When Fernandez won his second race of the year in Australia, he posted the record 40th win for an Indy Lights graduate in the FedEx Championship Series. And it was only appropriate that the record 40th win was earned in the No. 40 Tecate/Quaker State Reynard Ford, owned by Indy Lights founder U.E. "Pat" Patrick.

Of course, turning the *Big Four-O* is something most of us don't long for, but it suits the Dayton Indy Lights Championship just fine.

Now we are just that much closer to 50.

2000 Dayton Indy Lights Champion Scott Dixon in the Invensys/Powerware/PacWest Lights Lola

For more information about the Dayton Indy Lights Championship, contact Roger Bailey at (248) 362-6200

DAYTON INDY LIGHTS CHAMPIONSHIP REVIEW

Right: Felipe Giaffone scored an overdue first win both for himself and 1991 champion Eric Bachelart's Conquest team.
Robert Laberge/Allsport USA

Below right: Scott Dixon was a dominant force in Bruce McCaw's PacWest Lights Lola.
Jon Ferrey/Allsport USA

Conquest Racing enjoyed a breakthrough year in 2000, as the team owned by 1991 Lights champion Eric Bachelart won its first-ever race. Felipe Giaffone won a drafting duel at Michigan, rolling from the pole to claim the team's first trip to Victory Lane. His day was aided by a late caution flag that kept the competition from taking a last-lap shot at him, but it did not diminish the joy of seeing the checkered flag.

"I was crying like a baby. It was so tense," said Bachelart. "Near the end I saw Felipe in front and thought it was impossible to win. Then came the yellow flag!"

The team's success was more than a one-off, as Giaffone also won poles at Fontana and Vancouver, while rookie Chris Menninga earned his first pole at Gateway in the second of the Conquest machines.

Mario Dominguez could not match his 1999 Homestead victory for Team Mexico Quaker Herdez, but was a factor in many events, finishing third in Milwaukee and fifth at Belle Isle. He was headed for a strong finish in the Long Beach opener when his car was clipped by Kane as the Irishman re-entered the track after his spin. Subsequently Dominguez fell back to tenth. Rookie teammate Luis Diaz earned a season-best sixth on the Chicago oval and went on to claim three other top-ten finishes.

Brian Stewart Racing finally coaxed some promise from Rodolfo Lavin Jr., who, in his fifth full season, at the tender age of 22, just missed finishing in the top ten in the points. Lavin was in his element on the ovals, posting his three best finishes on the circular tracks, including top-fives at Chicago and Fontana. Rookie teammate Todd Snyder also earned a fifth on the oval at Michigan, but would end up running only six events before his sponsor withdrew. The team also intended to run a limited program for French F3000 driver Soheil Ayari, although those plans collapsed after a disappointing 16th-place run in the Long Beach opener.

Chris Lucas took over the reins of the renamed Lucas Motorsports and ended the season on an upnote when Geoff Boss took a best of fourth at Houston. Surprisingly, that would be the team's only top-five result of the season. Andy Boss joined his brother again for a full-time run, and both finished among the top ten in three races, but neither could match Geoff's Toronto-winning form of 1999.

Rudy Junco Jr. carried the Mexpro Racing colors through a full season, earning three top-ten finishes, with eighth-place efforts at Chicago and Fontana heading the list. The team also ran a second car for veteran Derek Higgins, who also served as driver coach, in some late-season events. The Irishman went on to post team-high seventh-place runs at Mid-Ohio and Vancouver.

2000 DAYTON INDY LIGHTS CHAMPIONSHIP
Final point standings after 12 races:

Pos.	Driver (Nat.), Sponsor(s)-Team	Pts.
1	Scott Dixon (NZ), Invensys/Powerware-PacWest Lights	155
2	Townsend Bell (USA)*, DirecPC-Dorricott Racing	146
3	Casey Mears (USA), Sooner Trailer/WorldCom-Dorricott Racing	141
4	Felipe Giaffone (BR), Hollywood-Conquest Racing	118
5	Tony Renna (USA), Motorola-PacWest Lights	105
6	Jason Bright (AUS)*, Dorricott Racing	91
7	Jeff Simmons (USA)*, Team KOOL Green	88
8	Mario Dominguez (MEX), Herdez/Pegaso/Quaker State-Team Mexico Quaker Herdez	67
9	Chris Menninga (USA), Mi-Jack-Conquest Racing	61
10	Jonny Kane (IRL), Team KOOL Green	52
11	Rodolfo Lavin Jr. (MEX), Corona/Modelo/Sports YA.com-Brian Stewart Racing	48
12	Geoff Boss (USA), Cross Pens/Lacoste/ITIS-Lucas Motorsports	43
13	Luis Diaz (MEX), Quaker State/Herdez-Team Mexico Quaker Herdez	31
14	Rudy Junco Jr. (MEX)*, Preciobase.com-Mexpro Racing	26
15	Andy Boss (USA), Cross Pens/Lacoste/ITIS-Lucas Motorsports	19
16	Rolando Quintanilla (MEX)*, Telmex/Prodigy Internet-Conquest Racing	16
17	Todd Snyder (USA)*, Outpost.com-Brian Stewart Racing	15
18	Derek Higgins (IRL), Preciobase.com-Mexpro Racing	12
19	Cory Witherill (USA), WSA Health Care-Genoa, Indy Regency Racing	2

All drove Lola T97/20 chassis with GM V6 engines and Dayton tires.
* denotes rookie driver

Performance Chart

Driver	Wins	Poles	Fastest laps	Most laps led
Scott Dixon	6	–	5	4
Townsend Bell	2	2	1	2
Felipe Giaffone	1	3	–	2
Jonny Kane	1	2	2	2
Casey Mears	1	2	2	1
Jason Bright	1	1	1	1
Chris Menninga	–	1	–	–
Cory Witherill	–	–	1	–

Speeds of 190 mph.
A split second can change everything.

The same holds true for your business — when systems are down, business halts - lost communications, lost transactions, lost production, lost revenues. That's a risk you can't afford to take. And you don't have to with Invensys Power Systems, the global leader in end-to-end power solutions for IT, telecom and industrial applications.

Don't let downtime crash your business.

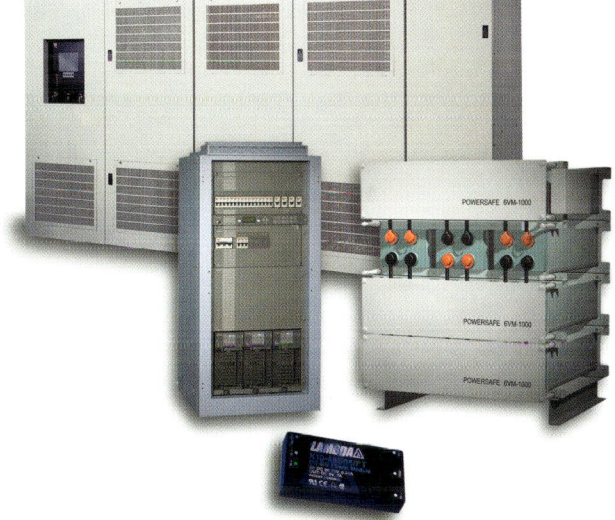

Invensys Power Systems is the proud sponsor of 2000 Dayton Indy Lights Champion Scott Dixon

www.invensys-power.com

invensys
Power Systems

PRINCIPAL PERFECT

TOYOTA ATLANTIC CHAMPIONSHIP REVIEW

by Jeremy Shaw

Opposite page: Martin Basso (46), Case Montgomery (14) and Buddy Rice (27) lead the Toyota Atlantic field at Gateway.
Robert Laberge/Allsport USA

Left: Daniel Wheldon, Rice and Basso celebrate on the podium at Elkhart Lake.
Jon Ferrey/Allsport USA

Below: Rice negotiates the Corkscrew at Laguna Seca en route to the series crown.
Robert Laberge/Allsport USA

TOYOTA ATLANTIC CHAMPIONSHIP REVIEW

WHEN Dede Rogers decided to step up from the U.S. F2000 National Championship and contest the CART Toyota Atlantic Championship with her DSTP (Don't Spend The Principal) Motorsports team, she had nothing but winning on her mind. Rogers had learned well. She had formed a fruitful partnership with fellow female car owners Peggy Haas and Jacky Doty (whose Lynx Racing organization had won a pair of Toyota Atlantic Championships in 1996 and '97, with Patrick Carpentier and Alex Barron respectively), and after a disappointing season in '99, she lured rising star Buddy Rice and Lynx's long-time engineer, Jim Griffith, to spearhead her own campaign in the more senior category.

The trio of Rice, Rogers and Griffith already had worked well together in F2000 and Toyota Atlantic, so it came as no surprise to see the new team running up front from the word go. In fact, Rice only narrowly failed to scoop a pair of victories in the season-opening double-header at Homestead, and before long had opened up a commanding lead in the points table. He romped to a clear victory at Long Beach and led at Milwaukee before tangling with season-long nemesis Daniel Wheldon.

Rice failed to finish the next race at Montreal, too, following a clash at the first corner with Wheldon's PPI Motorsports teammate, Andrew Bordin, but thereafter recorded seven consecutive podium finishes to wrap up the title in style with one race remaining. Rice underlined his dominance by leading 222 of the season's total of 471 laps (47 percent), and while he qualified on pole only twice, he was consistently fast and made precious few mistakes.

The 24-year-old native of Phoenix, Arizona, thoroughly impressed Chip Ganassi when he was invited to test a Champ Car in the fall, and although he seemed set to move into the European Formula 3000 Championship in 2001, he is sure to return to the Champ Car ranks 'ere long.

Wheldon, 22, from Buckinghamshire, England, was regularly the closest challenger to Rice, and for much of the season harbored hopes of snatching away the championship from his American rival. But the youngster's relative inexperience told on several occasions and he couldn't match Rice's consistency. Still, the '99 U.S. F2000 champion displayed immense promise and comfortably claimed Rookie of the Year honors.

Wheldon generally outshone his more experienced teammate, Bordin, who nevertheless equaled the Briton's tally of two wins and often seemed to be on the receiving end of misfortune. The laid-back Canadian showed his true ability by scoring a dominant win from the pole in the Houston finale to sneak ahead of Argentina's Martin Basso for third in the final standings.

For many, Basso was the revelation of the season. He impressed veteran driver-turned-team owner Mike Shank enormously during preseason tests and

TOYOTA ATLANTIC CHAMPIONSHIP REVIEW

Below: Daniel Wheldon excelled during his rookie season with PPI Motorsports.
Robert Laberge/Allsport USA

2000 CART TOYOTA ATLANTIC CHAMPIONSHIP
Final point standings after 12 races:

Pos.	Driver (Nat.), Sponsor(s)-Team	Pts.
1	Buddy Rice (USA), DSTP Motorsports	185
2	Daniel Wheldon (GB)*, Jayhard/BG Products-PPI Motorsports	159
3	Andrew Bordin (CDN), WorldCom-PPI Motorsports	133
4	Martin Basso (RA)*, 3b Engine Valves-Michael Shank Racing	129
5	Rocky Moran Jr. (USA), NTN Bearing Corp.-P-1 Racing	115
6	David Rutledge (CDN), Lynx Racing	93
7	Hoover Orsi (BR)*, u.s.print-Hylton Motorsports	76
8	Alex Gurney (USA)*, All American Racers	57
9	William Langhorne (USA), Miracle Whip/findthe.com-Active Motorsports	56
10	Mike Conte (USA), CHAMPS Karting-Lynx Racing	40
11	T.J. Bell (USA)*, Bell Trans-Michael Shank Racing	33
12	Case Montgomery (USA), N.W.Speedwerx/Intercat-World Speed Motorsports	26
13	Jean-Francois Veilleux (CDN), Cirque du Soleil-Shank, Speedwerx-World Speed	21
14	Bob Perona (USA)*, AT&T Broadband-Cobb Racing	18
15	Bruno St. Jacques (CDN)*, Atelier St-Jacques-Michael Shank Racing	14

All drove Swift 008.a chassis with Toyota 4A-GE motors and Yokohama tires.
* denotes rookie driver

Performance Chart

Driver	Wins	Poles	Fastest laps	Most laps led
Buddy Rice	5	2	6	7
Daniel Wheldon	2	4	1	1
Andrew Bordin	2	2	2	3
Martin Basso	1	1	–	–
David Rutledge	1	1	1	–
Case Montgomery	1	1	1	1
Alex Gurney	–	1	–	–

Fastest lap not given at Homestead, Round 1.

soon showed that his performances had been no flash in the pan. The graduate of the South American Formula 3 Championship scored a fine victory at Milwaukee, on his oval track debut, having taken full advantage of the clash between Rice and Wheldon. Basso claimed three more podium finishes, but erred at Houston when he hit the wall shortly after being passed by Rice.

Rocky Moran Jr. was the only driver to finish every one of the 12 races, providing ample testimony both to his own consistency – and ability – and the preparation of Bill Fickling and Robin Yount's P-1 Racing organization. Ultimate pace often proved elusive, however, and there's no doubt that P-1's budget fell well short of the other front-running teams.

David Rutledge, recruited to the Lynx Racing "scholarship" ride in place of the departed Rice, continued to make steady progress under the expert tutelage of Steve Cameron. The amiable 22-year-old Canadian's high point in his third Toyota Atlantic season was a spectacular victory in front of the Formula 1 crowd in Montreal, although he was fortunate to escape a penalty after "straight-lining" the infamous final chicane to snatch the win from Bordin.

Brazilian Hoover Orsi arrived in North America with excellent credentials after winning the hard-fought South American F3 Championship in 1999. He lived up to expectations by finishing third on his debut with Hylton Motorsports at Homestead, but his progress was stymied by the lack of a budget for testing.

Ditto Alex Gurney, who showed excellent form on occasion (notably at Cleveland where he qualified on pole) in the reborn All American Racers team managed by older brother Justin. Gurney, though, seemed like a magnet for mechanical misfortune and failed to finish five races.

Veteran Case Montgomery made a welcome return to action at Laguna Seca, then showed up the youngsters by taking a flag-to-flag victory at Gateway for Chuck West's World Speed Motorsports team. Others to demonstrate good form included William Langhorne, who, like Orsi, suffered from a lack of testing; French-Canadian Formula Ford grad Bruno St.-Jacques, who exhibited promise in four outings with Mike Shank's team; and Andy Lally, who rose from 16th to fifth at Houston for World Speed before being sidelined by electrical woes.